Music and Connectionism

edited by
Peter M. Todd
and D. Gareth Loy

Music and Connectionism

The MIT Press
Cambridge, Massachusetts
London, England

This book was set in Linotron Trump and Franklin Gothic by G&S Typesetters, Inc. and was printed and bound in the United States of America.

Library of Congress Cataloging-in-Publication Data

Music and connectionism / edited by Peter M. Todd and D. Gareth Loy.
p. cm.
"This book came out of . . . articles that first appeared in . . . two special issues of the Computer music journal"—Pref.
Includes bibliographical references.
ISBN 0-262-20081-3
1. Computer music—History and criticism. 2. Connectionism.
3. Psychoacoustics. I. Todd, Peter M. II. Loy, D. Gareth.
III. Computer music journal.
ML 1093.M86 1991
786.7'6—dc20 91-17833
CIP
MN

Contents

Preface

This book is about a new way of looking at human musical activity. As one of our highest expressions of thought and creativity, music has always been a difficult realm to capture, model, and study. The problems it poses have vexed a variety of scholars using traditional approaches from psychology and artificial intelligence. But the connectionist paradigm, now beginning to provide insights into many realms of human behavior, offers a new and unified viewpoint from which to investigate the subtleties of musical experience. Connectionist systems employ "brain-style" computation, capitalizing on the emergent power of a large collection of individually simple interconnected processors operating and cooperating in a parallel distributed fashion. Models of many aspects of musical behavior require the learning, constraint satisfaction, feature abstraction, and intelligent generalization properties that connectionist approaches embody, at the same time demanding further advancement of these techniques. The chapters in this volume, written by leading researchers from the realms of both music pyschology and neural networks, bring these two worlds together to address the challenges and opportunities of musical applications of network models.

The research presented in this volume includes advances both in our understanding of musical phenomena, encompassing perception, cognition, composition, and performance, and in our methods for network design and analysis. The musical domains covered range from the perception of pitch to the categorization of chords and tones, from the fingering of stringed instruments to the automatic composition of melodies and the aesthetic implications of such endeavors. The range of connectionist techniques included is similarly broad, not only comprising the traditional back-propagation networks, competitive feature maps, adaptive resonance theory, and advanced recurrent algorithms but also stretching to include expanding-context grammar construction and optimum-path discovery. These latter methods, although not always discussed in the context of connectionism, are still understandable as the interaction of simple connected processors and serve to illustrate the range of connectionist techniques that musical applications invite.

This project began as a pair of special issues of the *Computer Music Journal* focusing on neural networks and connectionism. We approached Curtis Roads, then editor of the *CMJ*, with the idea for a single issue on this topic, since we believed that this important new area of cognitive science and computer science could have great implications for the study of music as well. None of us had a clear idea of how far connectionism had yet penetrated the realms of music research, though, so we were prepared to slide an article or two on the topic unceremoniously into an otherwise full *CMJ* issue if that's all that was submitted. But the response to our call for papers was much more positive than that. In the end, working with current *CMJ* editor Stephen Pope, we decided the topic deserved two special issues, and even then we couldn't fit in everyone. While still in its infancy, the connectionist approach to musical applications was obviously capturing people's imaginations.

This book came out of the articles that first appeared in those two special issues of the *Computer Music Journal* at the end of 1989 (Fall and Winter, volumes 13(3) and 13(4)). We have kept these articles as they originally appeared, with the same titles and author affiliations; a list of current affiliations is provided at the end of the book. To cover the advances in research made since the original articles were written, we have also included the authors' new addenda for these chapters, discussing their more recent ideas and results. In addition, we are fortunate to be able to include a variety of new chapters by still more researchers in this field, which further extend the range of applications and methods from the original *CMJ* collection.

We have organized the book into four parts. Part I provides background material in the theory of neural networks and the place of connectionism in music research. More specifically, Dolson's chapter (which might more accurately be titled a tutorial on networks that learn musical tasks) covers the basic principles of back-propagation networks, one of the most commonly used neural network paradigms, and presents elementary ways of applying these learning pattern-processing systems to musical tasks from composition to signal processing. Loy then discusses the history of the use of automata in music research and creation, the advent of computers in this role as powerful musical automata, and where the emerging connectionist view will fit into this ongoing saga. These two chapters provide the intellectual and philosophical foundation for the rest of the book and should be read by those otherwise unfamiliar with the subject of this volume.

The second part covers the use of connectionist models in the simulation of musical perception and cognition, whereas the third part includes the application of connectionism to music composition and performance. The introductions to each of these parts give brief descriptions of the material covered in each chapter. The chapters in these parts present a variety of connectionist methods in a variety of contexts and can all be read independently. Furthermore, the authors do not always concur or present a unified world view but rather demonstrate the disagreement and diversity of opinion characteristic of a dynamic young field. The final part captures another element of this disagreement, presenting an exchange concerning the artistic place of connectionism in music that was prompted by the original *Computer Music Journal* articles. It concludes with a summary of other work in music and connectionism and future directions to be explored.

The intended audience for this book is as diverse as the collection of topics covered here. Both straddle the boundaries of several disciplines, including psychology, music theory, computer science, engineering, mathematics, and art. We hope that this book will find its way into a variety of fields and courses, including the psychology of music, where it will present a new approach to old questions; connectionist modeling, where it will provide a fertile domain within which to apply various methods; computer music, as a powerful and flexible tool in composition and signal processing; and cognitive science, as an example of the fruitful interaction of distinctive research paradigms and goals. Readers with backgrounds or at least interests in any of these areas should profit from the material presented here. Each chapter is intended to range from introductory discussions to details of implementation, to benefit newcomers, students, and active researchers. But besides spreading the insights and results of the authors to the appropriate corners of the globe, we also hope that this book will help communicate the excitement and opportunities of this new field and encourage others to join and take part.

As with any book, selecting a title was one of the more challenging tasks we faced in putting this project together. We knew that this book would be *about* music and connectionism, but we were encouraged to come up with a title that was more, if not obscure, then at least mysterious, to grab people's attention. Friends were ever-helpful sources of suggestions, from variations on *Bach-Propagation* to *Neural Noteworks,* and even, in reference to a sometime-mascot of the Stanford PDP Research Group, *Netman Sings the Blues,* which certainly had the requisite obscurity going for it. But in the end we opted for clarity and brevity; the title is the topic.

This book is very much a collaborative effort. It is not only about distributed cognition but also the result of such a process. In this case it took the form of a recurrent autoassociative network, with both of us as the two hidden units, hidden in our offices, receiving parallel inputs from the authors distributed over the globe, via connections of various strengths (from transatlantic packages to overnight e-mail), transforming their inputs into some reduced form and then sending them back to the authors for further processing in parallel, the whole cycle repeating until we all finally settled on an ultimate output, which you see before you. As with any network solution, we may not have succeeded completely in the attempt to satisfy mutliple constraints simultaneously, but we hope we have come close.

As a result of the collaboration involved in this book's production, there are many people to thank. The project would never have happened without the initial support of Curtis Roads for the original special issues of the *Computer Music Journal,* nor without the entrepreneurial spark from Stephen Pope, to whom we are indebted for devising and selling the notion of turning those issues into this book. Once Stephen created the spark, enthusiasm spread quickly. Terry Ehling, our editor at The MIT Press, has been invaluable in patiently guiding us through the shoals of first-time book publishing. Our colleagues in the fields of connectionism, psychology, and computer music have been continual sources of excitement and inspiration throughout our efforts, prompting us with eager queries of "when's the book coming out?" We wish particularly to single out David Rumelhart and Jamshed Bharucha for their support of this reasearch. In addition, Gareth Loy's work was supported in part by a major grant of encouragement and love from his wife and family, and Peter Todd's work was made possible through the generosity of family and friends. We are also very grateful to John Odam for his work in converting our ideas into art for the cover. But most of all we would like to thank the authors who have contributed to this volume, for their creative research and ideas, and for their patience through many rounds of editing, picky questions, and last-minute mailing emergencies. Their contributions have made this the valuable book it is.

I

Background

Mark Dolson
Center for Research in Language
University of California, San Diego
La Jolla, California 92093 USA

Machine Tongues XII: Neural Networks

Introduction

Most computer users have become so accustomed to the standard von Neumann approach to computing that they rarely question the fundamental assumptions implicit in the underlying architecture. Foremost among these is the idea that a computer basically consists of a powerful and sophisticated *central processing unit* (CPU) with lots of peripheral memory. This model—common to the vast majority of computers to date—has at least two important implications. First, it means that as successive generations of CPUs and memory become progressively faster, the communication between them becomes the major bottleneck. Second, it means that using the computer always comes down to instructing the CPU to perform some particular sequence of operations involving various portions of memory.

This latter point, in particular, has attracted much attention from computer scientists because it burdens the computer programmer with a great deal of unnecessary tedium. Instead of merely informing the computer as to *what* should constitute an acceptable solution to a problem, the programmer must painstakingly tell the computer *how* to obtain the solution (Balaban and Murray 1986). The continuing evolution of high-level languages (e.g., Lisp, Smalltalk, Prolog) can be seen as an ongoing attempt to transfer this undesirable complexity from the domain of the programmer to that of the computer itself. Thus, constraint languages such as TK!Solver allow the computer to arrive at solutions simply by evaluating user-specified constraints (Levitt 1984). Even here, the programmer must still inform the computer explicitly of each operative constraint.

Neural networks provide a very different approach to computing; they eliminate both the processor/memory dichotomy and the concept of a symbolic instruction set. Instead, they provide an essentially analog network of idealized "neurons" in which different patterns of excitation are observed as a function of the interconnections between neurons. Processing and memory are distributed uniformly throughout the network in a form ideally suited for implementation with extremely fast and highly parallel hardware, such as optical computing and analog VLSI.

Equally significant, neural networks often provide learning mechanisms so that the desired computation can be programmed simply by repeatedly exposing the network to examples of the desired behavior. The network merely adapts its interconnections until the resulting pattern of excitations is as close to the desired behavior as it can manage. Thus, neural networks have the potential to emulate complex (and perhaps human) behaviors that we programmers have no idea how to generate via explicit rules or instructions.

In some ways, this is actually a very old approach to computing, yet in other ways it is very new and exciting. In the pages that follow, I will attempt to provide both an introduction to this important new programming technique and some simple examples of its musical utility.

Neural Networks

Like computer music, the subject of neural networks is at present a highly interdisciplinary one. Mathematicians, physicists, electrical engineers, biologists, and cognitive scientists have all contributed to its evolution, and each has described it in different terms and in different journals. Thus, neural networks, artificial neural systems, connectionist models, parallel distributed processing models, and massively parallel systems all refer to essentially the same thing. Moreover, although neural networks are generally described in analog terms (and will someday be widely available as analog devices), almost all work to date has been performed via digital computer simulations. Even in

Computer Music Journal, Vol. 13, No. 3, Fall 1989,

Fig. 1. *A simple neural network.*

Fig. 2. A hard-limiter function (a), a logistic function (b).

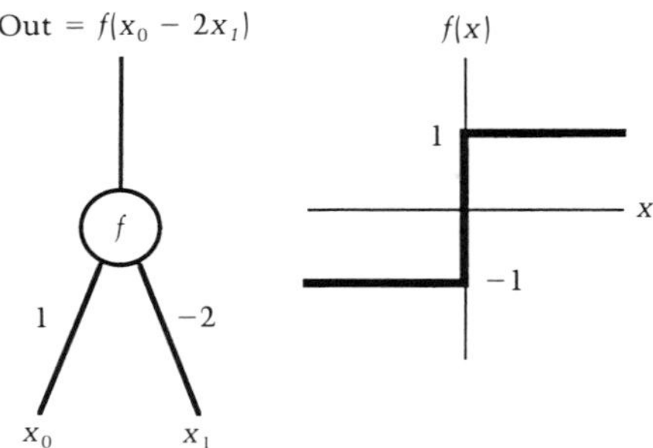

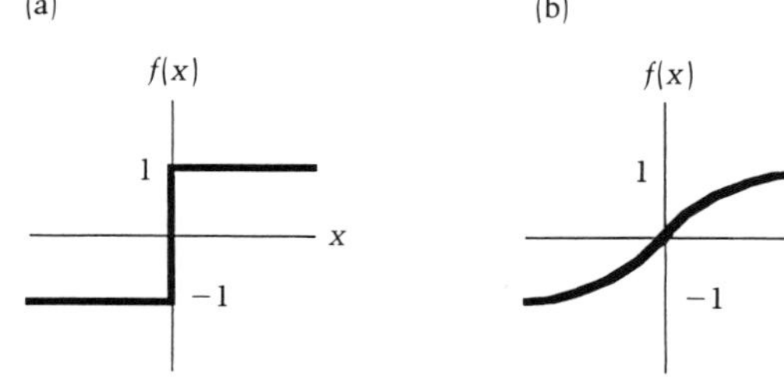

simulated form, however, neural networks can offer significant advantages over conventional approaches to computer programming.

A neural network is basically an interconnected set of simple computational elements, each of which is typically functionally identical. Each element or *unit* receives inputs from other units and produces a single output, which is some simple function of its inputs. The similarity of this structure to that of a biological neuron has led some authors to prefer the term "neuron" to that of "unit." Still others prefer the term "node." All three terms are essentially equivalent.

The reason that a neural network is capable of interesting computations is that each input to each unit has associated with it a unique weighting factor or *weight.* This weight can be thought of as a connection strength from one unit to another, indicating the amount of influence that the first unit has on the second. Weights can be positive or negative, so the influence may also be characterized as excitatory or inhibitory.

All we need to complete our simulated neural network is a precise rule for determining the output of a unit: add together all of the weighted inputs and let the output be some nonlinear function of the resulting sum. To state such a rule mathematically, we can let each of the N units in the network be identified with a unique number between 1 and N. The output x_i of the ith unit in the network is given by

$$x_i = f\left(\sum_{j=1}^{N} w_{ij}\, x_j \right),$$

where w_{ij} is the weight from the jth unit to the ith, and f is some nonlinear function.

As a simple example, we can consider the single-unit network in Fig. 1, in which the output is positive only if input x_1 is more than twice input x_2. Note that the nonlinearity of the function f is crucial in endowing the network with real computational (i.e., decision-making) power. The nonlinearity allows quantitative changes in the inputs to produce qualitative changes in the output (i.e., the output can switch from off to on instead of simply changing in direct proportion to the input). In practice, any number of choices for f are possible, but two of the most popular have proven to be the hard limiter of Fig. 2a, and the soft limiting *logistic function* of Fig. 2b.

Simple single-unit networks such as that in Fig. 1 were actually studied several decades ago (McCulloch and Pitts 1943; Hebb 1949; Rosenblatt 1959), but there were fundamental limitations to the kinds of problems to which they could be successfully applied. For example, no combination of weights will allow a single-unit network (known historically as a single-layer *perceptron*) to solve the exclusive-or problem (in which two inputs, x_1 and x_2, produce an output of -1.0 when both inputs are -1.0 or both are 1.0, and an output of 1.0 when one input is 1.0 while the other is -1.0). When these limitations and other potential difficulties were clearly identified (Minsky and Papert 1969), interest in neural networks greatly declined and research activity throughout the following decade focused instead more on artificial intelligence. In the early 1980s, however, more sophisticated

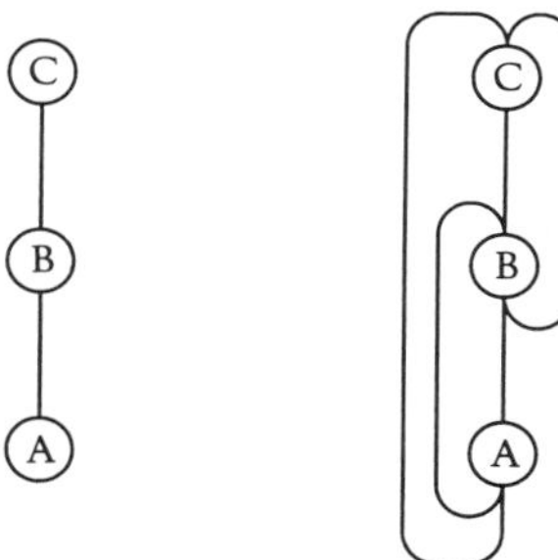

Fig. 3. A purely feed-forward network (a), a fully interconnected network (b).

neural networks (e.g., multilayer perceptrons) were devised that were not subject to the previous limitations, and interest in artificial neural systems was rekindled with vigor (Hopfield 1982; 1984; Hopfield and Tank 1986; Rumelhart et al. 1986; Sejnowski and Rosenberg 1986).

Today, there are more varieties and flavors of neural networks that can be enumerated here. However, several major subcategories can be identified. One of the most fundamental issues is whether the units in the network are fully interconnected, with the output of each unit serving as an input to every other unit, or whether the interconnection pattern is more limited. In particular, if the interconnections are limited to being exclusively *feed-forward,* as shown in Fig. 3a, then calculation of the output values from the given input values is very straightforward. In contrast, if there are feedback loops in the network, as seen in Fig. 3b, then the output of unit B depends on the output of unit A, which in turn depends upon the output of unit B, etc. It is possible for these outputs to oscillate indefinitely, but if the network is properly designed, it can be proven that the outputs will always converge to stable values (Hopfield 1982). Hence, both kinds of interconnection schemes are feasible in practice.

Another fundamental issue concerns the weights themselves. In some cases, the designer of the network can devise certain weights that will immediately cause the network to function as desired. There are many other cases, however, where the designer has no idea what weights will solve the problem at hand. In these situations, the designer can employ a *supervised learning algorithm*—an automated procedure for iteratively adjusting the weights on the basis of a set of training examples. When the outputs produced by the network are as close as necessary to the desired outputs, then the training phase is complete: the weights are fixed, and the network is ready to be used. It is the existence of such learning algorithms that makes neural networks so attractive for problems in which explicit rules are hard to formulate. (Unsupervised learning algorithms, in which desired outputs are not available for the training examples, are beyond the scope of this paper.)

In the remainder of this paper, I focus exclusively on feed-forward networks in which the units are organized into three layers and in which the nonlinear function f is smoothly varying. The first layer of units is called the *input* layer, because each unit in this layer receives an input from the external world and passes it directly to the next layer. This next layer is known as the *hidden* layer: its units receive excitation exclusively from the units in the input layer and send excitation exclusively to the units in the third layer. This third layer is called the *output* layer because the outputs of the units in this layer are also considered to be the outputs of the network as a whole. Actually, since the units of the input layer do not perform any interesting computation—each is simply set to whatever the corresponding external input value is—some researchers would say that the network really has only two layers. I shall continue to refer to three.

The motivation for restricting our attention to networks of this type is twofold: (1) there is a powerful learning algorithm for this class of networks, which can automatically determine the weights for each connection in feed-forward networks; and (2) three layers are sufficient to compute all the functions that interest us. Before examining the learning algorithm in detail, however, it may be helpful to consider a simple musical example.

Example: Evaluating Rhythms

Suppose that we want a piece of software that can emulate our own judgments (such as good versus bad) about simple rhythms. We may wish to use

Fig. 4. A three-layer, feed-forward network.

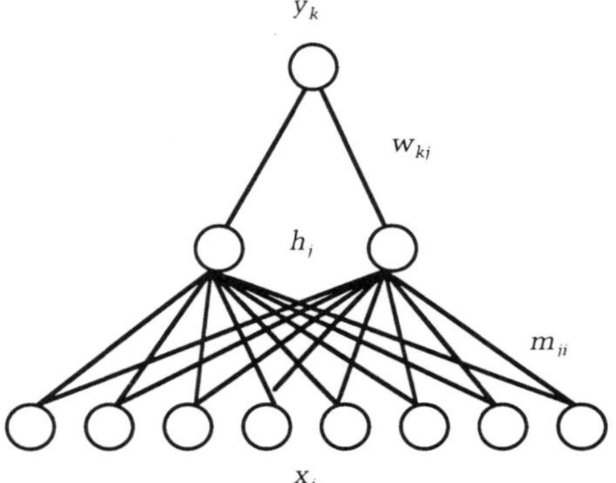

this software as a kind of filter in an automated composition application. Of course, if we could describe our preferences in terms of simple rules, then we could just write a program with a series of if-then statements to classify any rhythm as good or bad. But more often, we know *what* we like without really knowing exactly *why* we like it. In this case, a neural network approach is attractive. We can simply show the network examples of good and bad rhythms (telling it which are good and which are bad), and let it learn to mimic our judgments.

To make this example concrete, let us restrict ourselves to evaluating a single measure of 4/4 time with nothing more rapid than eighth notes. This means that there are eight time quanta per measure, each of which may have either an attack or a rest. Now for the purpose of our example, let us assume that there really is some underlying rule governing our preferences, but that we as listeners are unaware of its existence. Thus, let us suppose for the sake of this example that we are not aware that we like only those rhythms that have an attack on the first beat and that have either attacks on both the second and fourth beats or rests on both the second and fourth beats (i.e., the third and seventh time quanta). How can we formulate this problem in terms of a neural network?

First, we must decide upon an appropriate encoding for our input (the rhythm) and output (the judgment). There are many possibilities here, but the best ones are economical in their use of units and connections and map cleanly to the problem being solved. For example, since the rhythm is defined as consisting of eight time quanta, each of which can be an attack or a rest, it is natural to think of having eight input units, each of which can output a 1.0 or −1.0. Similarly, our judgment can be represented by a single output unit that should ouput a 1.0 for a good rhythm and a −1.0 for a bad one. Thus we will have eight units in the input layer and one unit in the output layer.

At present, there is no simple method of determining how many units we should have in the hidden layer. We may simply have to try various numbers and see how well the network performs in each case. In general, though, the fewer units used, the more efficient the computation will be, and the more general the result will be (for reasons that will become clear later). For the purposes of this example, let us agree to use exactly two hidden units. The resulting network is shown in Fig. 4. There are 8 input units, each connecting to 2 hidden units (for a total of 16 weights in all), and these 2 hidden units each connect to one output unit (2 more weights in all). In addition, there is a single extra input line to each hidden and output unit from an auxiliary bias unit that always ouputs a 1.0. Adjusting the weight on this bias input essentially varies the threshold that the other inputs must exceed in order for the unit's output to be positive.

In total, the network has 21 weights (16 input-to-hidden plus 2 hidden-to-output plus 3 bias weights). Now, we need to train the network: each of these values must be adjusted so that the network as a whole produces a positive output only when a good combination of attacks and rests is presented to the eight input units. We can do this by having the computer apply the automated learning algorithm known as *back propagation of error.*

Back Propagation

Back propagation is a very simple yet powerful learning algorithm for neural networks that contain only feed-forward connections between units (i.e., no loops are possible). The back-propagation procedure was developed independently by a number of different researchers, but it is most closely associated with Rumelhart, Hinton, and Williams (1986). More recently, Pineda (1988) has shown how this algorithm can be generalized to apply to non-feedforward networks as well.

To understand how back propagation works, consider the network of Fig. 4 and suppose that the weights have random values. Any pattern of input excitations (i.e., any set of values for the x_i) will produce an easily calculated pattern of output excitations (y_k). Presumably, though, we already have some examples of what the y_k should be for given sets of x_i. Thus, we can easily calculate an error for each output unit by taking the difference between its actual output and its desired output. We can compute a total error by adding up the squares of the individual errors, using squares so that positive and negative errors cannot cancel each other out and also to make the mathematical derivation simpler. Mathematically, our total error (designated as ε) is defined as

$$\varepsilon = \sum_k (y_k - \tau_k)^2,$$

where the τ_k represent the target values (i.e., the correct answers that we want the network to learn to produce itself), and the sum is taken over all values of k corresponding to output units.

Our desire is that the error ε be as small as possible. The only way that this can occur is to find a set of weights such that the network produces the target outputs directly from the given inputs. But what process (other than exhaustive search) can we possibly use to find this desired set of weights? It turns out that we can arrive at this optimal set of weights simply by making repeated minor adjustments to the random weights with which we begin. Each time that we present an input pattern to the network and measure the error ε, we then go through the network weight by weight, and we increase or decrease each weight just a little in such a way that ε will decrease. As long as our weight modifications consistently reduce ε, we will eventually arrive at a set of weights that result in very little error.

But how do we know exactly how much to increase or decrease each weight? The precise answer to this question requires some calculus and is therefore deferred until the Appendix. The general idea, though, is fairly intuitive. For output units, if a particular output excitation is less than the target value for that unit, then the unit basically needs better connections (i.e., larger weights) to those hidden units that are positively excited by the current input pattern. Likewise the output unit needs weaker connections (i.e., smaller weights) to those hidden units that are currently negatively excited.

The input-to-hidden weights are a little more difficult to evaluate because explicit target values for the hidden units are never available (only the output units have known target values). Nevertheless, the same general approach can be employed. We simply ask what proportion of the total output error each hidden unit is responsible for, and we strengthen and weaken connections from input units so as to decrease this responsibility. It is this backward tracing of error impact throughout the network that led to the label "back propagation of error" for this learning algorithm.

It is possible that this procedure will not result in an ε as low as desired. For one thing, there may not be any set of weights that is capable of producing the target outputs for the given inputs. Perhaps the network needs more hidden units, or perhaps the problem demands a different interconnection scheme.

A more insidious difficulty, though, arises when the network is capable of solving the problem, but when the back-propagation learning algorithm fails to find the best possible set of weights. This can happen whenever the situation depicted in Fig. 5 occurs. The graph of error as a function of weight values shows that there are two different sets of weights that result in a low error, but only one set (point B) that gives the lowest possible error. Once the learning algorithm discovers the set of weights represented by point A, though, it will be unable to reach point B. The learning algorithm only adjusts the weights a little at a time, and only in a direction that further decreases the error. Moving from point A to point B would result in an increased error at some intermediate set of weights, so it can never be done.

This is known as *local minima*, a potentially se-

Fig. 5. An error surface. (Note the two local minima.)

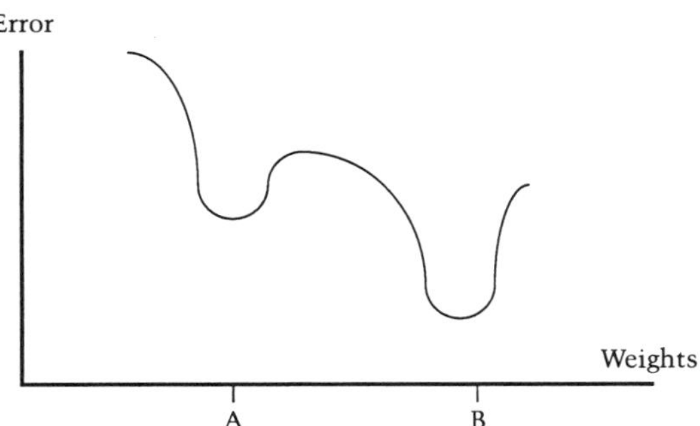

rious, though rarely fatal, problem. One reason for this may be that such local minima are easier to move away from when there are lots of weights to vary. Another possibility is that even if we do end up in a local minimum, it may have a sufficiently low ε that we are satisfied with it anyway. Or we may simply repeat the training procedure, starting with a different set of random weights in the hopes of avoiding the local minimum on our next try.

The Problem of Generalization

Now let us return to our musical example. The network has 8 binary inputs, so that the network could be exposed to 256 (2^8) possible input sets. But it would be unfortunate if the network needed to see all 256 possibilities during its training phase. We would like to be able to get away with training it on fewer examples, which would also take less time. The attraction of neural networks is not merely that they can learn from examples, but they can also learn from a limited subset of all possible examples. The solution they discover can remain valid even when they are presented with examples that they have not previously encountered.

How does this generalization beyond the training subset work? And how small a subset can be adequate? These questions are central to the use and understanding of neural networks. The previous section described a learning algorithm in which each weight in the network is iteratively and incrementally adjusted so that the network produces output values that are as close as possible to a set of target values. Thus the network essentially "discovers" patterns in the input-to-output mappings of the training examples, and these patterns are reflected in the particular set of weights that the network ultimately acquires. As far as the network is concerned, these patterns are purely statistical, but a human examining the network after the training phase is complete may be able to use the patterns to discover a set of underlying rules or a method that expresses the underlying problem.

The network is forced to discover such patterns whenever it does not have enough units and weights to respond to each training example independently. For instance, suppose that we try to train our network by showing it only two examples of good rhythms. Quite possibly, the learning algorithm will adjust the weights so that each hidden unit responds positively to exactly one of the rhythms.

This is not what we want, however, because a network that solves the problem in this fashion has failed to exploit any underlying relationships that might account for why some input patterns are to be judged as good while others are to be judged as bad. Thus, the network has no ability to generalize. Favorable input patterns that the network was not exposed to during training could now be judged as bad, because the network essentially took the easy way out during the training phase: it merely memorized the proper answers.

The question of how to ensure good generalization during training is currently an important research topic in neural networks. It is clear, though, that to have only a few hidden units and many training examples is a step in the right direction. Thus, in this case, we used 2 hidden units and trained the network on 40 patterns.

Table 1 shows the weights obtained for our network trained on 12 good input patterns and 28 bad ones. The network was first assigned a set of randomly chosen weights, and then the back-propagation learning algorithm was used to iteratively modify the initial weights until the squared error (averaged over all 40 training patterns) between the actual network output and the target output was less than .0002. This required about 20 adjustment cycles, where each weight adjustment

Table 1. Weight matrix. Row *i*, column *j* gives the weight from unit *j* to unit *i*. For example, unit O1 receives a −5.61 connection from unit H1.

	BIAS	*I1*	*I2*	*I3*	*I4*	*I5*	*I6*	*I7*	*I8*	*H1*	*H2*	*O1*
H1	−0.24	−5.35	0.01	5.65	1.55	1.30	−0.15	−5.57	−0.32	0.00	0.00	0.00
H2	−0.54	−3.50	−0.77	−6.65	−0.23	0.20	0.63	6.05	−0.57	0.00	0.00	0.00
O1	−5.13	0.00	0.00	0.00	0.00	0.00	0.00	0.00	0.00	−5.61	−5.65	0.00

was performed only after accumulating the error over all 40 training patterns. This was unusually rapid training, partly resulting from a fortuitous set of initial weight values.

How successfully was the network able to generalize from the 40 training examples? Testing with the full set of 256 patterns shows that the network produces the proper answer for every possible input (assuming that any output greater than 0.0 means good).

To gain additional insight, we can examine the weights themselves. As is common with neural networks, we will see that the network has discovered a solution that is rather different from the one that we might have invented ourselves.

The output unit is strongly predisposed to be off by the −5.1 connection to the bias unit. Because of the negative weights from the hidden units, it can turn on only when both hidden units have negative outputs themselves, so that

$$-5.6 \times unit_1 - 5.6 \times unit_2 > 5.1.$$

Both hidden units are only mildly biased off, but each is turned off more strongly by an attack on the downbeat (i.e., a 1.0 from the first input unit). However, in the case of the first hidden unit, an attack-rest combination on the second and fourth beats will overcome the negative input and will turn the unit on strongly. Conversely, the second unit will be turned on by a rest-attack combination on the same beats. Thus, the network does seem to have recognized the crucial significance of the first, second, and fourth beats in our example. It is worth noting, though, that starting the learning with a different set of random weights does not lead to the same solution. This is an indication that we are not always reaching the global minimum in our search for the smallest possible error.

The Problem of Time

Suppose now that we want a network to emulate our judgments about the presence or absence of objectionable rhythmic sequences in an entire musical piece. We could try to extend the approach of the sections above, but we would quickly encounter some serious difficulties. Presenting the entire piece as input at once would require an enormous number of input units and an enormous amount of computation, so we would probably try to input only a few measures at a time. There is no easy way to determine how long a segment to include, but it would have to be long enough to contain the longest rhythmic sequence that we might find objectionable. Moreover, the majority of objectionable sequences will surely be much shorter, and in these cases the extra input units will be a hindrance. Not only will they be a source of confusion, but the network will need to learn to recognize the shorter objectionable sequences in every possible shifted position within the larger context.

A more appealing approach is to present input to the network sequentially in the same way that we receive such input ourselves. But the purely feedforward network produces its output entirely on the basis of the present input. How can we explicitly build an awareness of time into the network?

A promising approach is to provide the network with some delayed feedback from one layer back to a preceding layer. For example, part of the input at time *t* can consist of the hidden or output unit

Fig. 6. Temporally recurrent network.

Fig. 7. Phase trajectory in response to rhythmic input (−1), 1, 1, 1, 1, 1 (a), response to rhythmic input (−1), −1, −1, −1, −1, −1 (b).

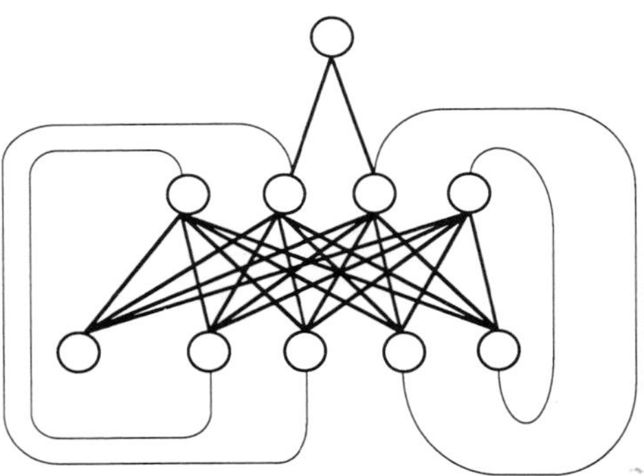

Table 2. Weight matrix. Row *i*, column *j* gives the weight from unit *j* to unit *i*. For example, unit O1 receives a 6.15 connection from unit H3. Similarly, unit H1 receives a 0.77 connection from the delayed H1 unit.

	BIAS	*I1*	*H1*	*H2*	*H3*	*H4*
H1	−1.67	1.34	0.77	2.97	1.28	−0.38
H2	0.88	2.67	2.12	−1.72	0.58	−1.64
H3	1.28	−2.39	−1.65	−2.62	3.66	1.68
H4	3.71	3.53	0.57	1.50	−1.22	4.25
O1	−4.00	0.00	0.00	0.00	6.15	6.15

Fig. 7

(a)

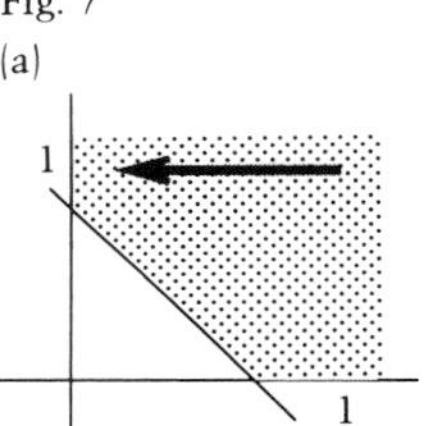

(b)

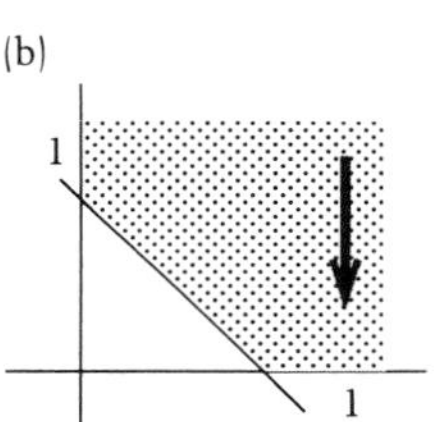

values at time $t - 1$. This allows the network to operate in the feed-forward mode at any particular instant, but it also allows it to develop a rudimentary memory by recycling information from the past. This information can be used by the network to construct a sequence of changing internal states. Strictly speaking, the back-propagation learning algorithm is no longer valid in this situation, but many investigators have obtained successful results by employing it anyway (Jordan 1986; Elman 1988). A rigorous extension to back propagation that deals correctly with this kind of delayed recurrence has recently been presented by Williams and Zipser (1988). This algorithm, known as "RTRL" (for Real-Time Recurrent Learning), is more computationally demanding than back propagation but it may also result in more efficient learning.

As an example, suppose that we object to any sequence of more than three consecutive rests or more than five consecutive attacks. Instead of using a purely feed-forward network, let us use the network of Fig. 6. At each step in time, there is a single external input (1.0 for an attack and −1.0 for a rest) and a single output (−1.0 if the input is objectionable—if it creates or extends a sequence of too many consecutive rests or attacks—and 1.0 otherwise). In addition, at each time step, each of the four hidden units receives input from all four of the delay units (which contain the values of the hidden units at the previous time step). For simplicity, the output unit only receives input from two of the four hidden units.

This network was successfully trained via the RTRL learning algorithm on a sequence of 96 inputs. The resulting weight values are listed in Table 2. With this kind of network, however, it is very difficult to make sense of the solution merely by inspecting the weights. As an alternative, we can borrow a technique from the field of dynamical systems analysis.

The output unit receives input only from the third and fourth hidden units. It turns on only when

$$6.1 \times unit_3 + 6.1 \times unit_4 > 4.0.$$

We can gain some insight into the network's solution by plotting the values of the third and fourth hidden units as a function of time. A convenient way to do this is to view the path traced out over time by plotting the values of these two units as pairs of x and y coordinates. This kind of plot is known as a *phase portrait*. It shows the internal state of a nonlinear dynamical system (in this case, our neural network) as a function of time.

For example, Fig. 7 shows several typical phase trajectories. The shaded area marks the region of

Table 3. Weight matrix. Row *i*, column *j* gives the weight from unit *j* to unit *i*. For example, unit O1 receives a −14.33 connection from unit H4. Similarly, unit H1 receives a 3.57 connection from the delayed H1 unit.

	BIAS	*I1*	*I2*	*I3*	*I4*	*I5*	*H1*	*H2*	*H3*	*H4*	*O1*
H1	−1.34	−0.34	1.00	−2.20	−1.12	2.07	3.57	−1.97	0.88	3.51	0.00
H2	1.66	−0.57	−0.47	1.91	−0.76	−1.24	−2.70	2.67	1.55	−0.98	0.00
H3	−1.70	−0.33	4.29	−2.39	−2.58	3.24	−1.44	−0.74	−2.14	3.45	0.00
H4	−1.02	−3.23	−3.24	3.54	2.98	5.27	3.29	−8.10	5.61	−4.30	0.00
O1	6.73	0.00	0.00	0.00	0.00	0.00	0.00	0.00	0.47	−14.33	0.00

the plane over which the output unit is turned on (i.e., where the threshold weights are achieved). As is clear from the weighting table as well as the phase trajectory, unit 3 moves the plot to the left and out of this region whenever too many consecutive attacks are input, as can be seen in Fig. 7a. Similarly, it is the responsibility of unit 4 in the network to move the plot down and out of this region whenever too many consecutive rests are detected, as in Fig. 7b. The other two hidden units have more complicated phase trajectories, but it appears that they serve essentially as counters.

Example: Computer-Assisted Composition

As a final, and slightly more ambitious, musical example, let us turn our attention to automated composition. Even more useful than a network that can evaluate rhythms would be one that could actually generate rhythms. During the training phase, we could simply expose our network to a number of rhythms that we like and then we could turn it loose to create innumerable variations. This kind of application of neural networks has actually been investigated in some detail by Todd (Todd 1988). For the purposes of this tutorial, though, we will take a slightly different approach.

Suppose that we like the four rhythmic sequences in Table 3. We could train the network of Fig. 6 to reproduce any one of these rhythms by simply training it to predict correctly whether the input immediately following the current one is an attack or a rest. Once the network learned to do this, we could run the network indefinitely by repeatedly using its most recent output as the next input. More precisely, we would use a cleaned up version of the most recent output in which anything greater than 0.0 would be input as a 1.0 and anything less than 0.0 would be input as a −1.0. This would ensure that the network would continue to receive inputs similar to the ones on which it was trained.

But how can we train the network to compose in any of four different rhythmic styles? One answer is simply to augment the single external input unit with four additional input units to serve as a set of labels. We activate only the auxiliary input furthest to the right when teaching the network the first rhythm, only the auxiliary input next furthest to the right when teaching the second rhythm, etc. This has the additional advantage that, once the network has learned to produce each rhythm alone, we can make it produce blends of several rhythms by activating several of the auxiliary inputs simultaneously. We can also fade from one rhythm to another, or whatever else we can imagine.

Table 4 lists the weights for a network that has successfully learned to generate the four rhythmic sequences via this approach (again, the learning was accomplished by means of the RTRL algorithm). The primary difference between this network and the type employed by Todd is that the feedback in our network is coming from the hidden units as opposed to the output units. An attraction of feeding back the outputs is that the normal back-propagation learning algorithm can be used, with the target values being fed back in place of the actual outputs. However, this approach does not appear to work well in all applications. In contrast,

Table 4. Four rhythmic sequences (1 = attack; −1 = rest)

#1:	1	−1	1	−1	1	−1	−1	−1
#2:	1	−1	1	−1	1	1	1	−1
#3:	1	1	−1	1	1	1	−1	−1
#4:	1	1	1	1	1	−1	1	−1

feeding back the hidden-unit values may allow the network far greater flexibility in building up useful, time-varying, internal representations. Learning the correct weights may be more difficult, however. This is currently an area of active research within the field.

Another interesting and as yet unexplored question is how this approach to automated composition compares to the transition, table-based approach using Markov chains as embodied in the works of Lejaren Hiller and more recently in the popular program *Jam Factory.* The transition table approach basically uses its training examples to calculate tables of probabilities specifying the likelihood of an attack or rest appearing next in any rhythmic sequence. There is a finite (and usually quite small) limit on the length of sequences that are accurately modeled, however. In contrast, the neural network is not constrained to a finite-duration memory; thus, in principle, it should be capable of extracting structure that cannot be captured by the transition table technique. Further experimentation is required to establish this empirically.

Future Directions

Neural networks provide an exciting alternative to conventional artificial intelligence and symbolic programming approaches to obtaining sophisticated automated behavior. For some problems, strong arguments can be made that the neural network is in fact the preferred approach (Abu-Mustafa and Psaltis 1987). For other problems, the jury is still out (Daedalus 1988). It is important to note that in many areas where neural networks appear promising, they have been tested only on severely scaled-down versions of the relevant problem. It remains to be seen whether larger neural networks can be trained as easily, or perhaps whether new techniques can be developed to facilitate their training.

Even with these caveats, it seems almost certain that neural networks will have a significant impact on computer music. At the very least (as the examples in this paper suggest), they have obvious application in computer-assisted composition. Moreover, as network sophistication continues to increase, and as simulation capabilities and computing power continue to grow, it seems likely that neural networks will have a substantial impact in the realm of timbre as well. I will cite two brief examples of this.

First, a great deal of research has been conducted over the years in an attempt to identify some set of specific features or dimensions of a musical signal that could serve as a basis for constructing and perceiving timbres. It is not difficult to imagine that a larger-scale version of the network in Fig. 6, perhaps with time-varying spectra as its input, could learn to activate different output nodes corresponding to different musical instrument identities. Thus, the network would essentially have learned to discriminate different timbres; yet it would have been told nothing about specific features, such as temporal envelope, brightness, etc. It would simply have learned to make associations in much the same way that we as listeners have learned to perform this task ourselves. Taken to its extreme, this observation suggests that timbre identification might be reliably performed without any deliberate decomposition of the signal into underlying features.

A second example can be found in the synthesis technique known as *waveshaping,* in which a simple periodic signal is employed as the argument of some nonlinear function (LeBrun 1979). With proper choice of the nonlinear function, any desired periodic waveform can be obtained as a result. Now, suppose that we have a purely feed-forward network such as that of Fig. 4, with only a single input and a single output unit, but with lots of hidden units. Our previous examples all used target values of 1.0 or −1.0, but this network can actually learn to approximate any continuous mapping from input to output (Lapedes and Farber 1988). Hence, it can easily learn to play the role of the nonlinear function required for waveshaping. The payoff, though, is the fact that the network can also learn to modify this function appropriately when it is provided with auxiliary inputs for loudness and pitch. Now, with a periodically varying input, the network will not only produce the desired periodic output waveform, but it will be able to vary this waveform appropriately in response to varying loudness and pitch inputs.

Further Reading

A very nice but limited (and somewhat technical) introduction to neural networks is the article by Lippman (1987). Another helpful introduction is contained in a series of articles in the magazine *AI Expert.* Less accessible but historically significant are the numerous papers by Hopfield and the famous NETtalk article by Sejnowski and Rosenberg (1986). It should also be noted that there is an important body of research in unsupervised learning techniques as well. Much of this work is described by Kohonen (1984) and in the many papers by Grossberg and his colleagues (1988).

Probably the most accessible, nonmathematical introduction to neural networks is the two-volume set edited by Rumelhart and McClelland (1986). Particularly helpful in this regard may be the more recent third volume by McClelland and Rumelhart (1988), which includes a floppy disk with excellent simulation programs for the IBM PC (or any Unix system). More graphically oriented simulators for the Macintosh are available from several different companies. Some hands-on simulation experience is almost essential for developing useful intuition in such a new area. The reader should be forewarned, however, that the compute ratio on even a VAX can become intolerably slow when training networks with more than, say, a thousand connections.

Acknowledgments

This paper might never have been written except for a series of stimulating discussions with Peter Todd and Gareth Loy in early 1987. It would most certainly never have been completed without the continuing encouragement and many helpful suggestions of Gareth Loy. I thank them both.

References

Abu-Mustafa, Y. S., and D. Psaltis. 1987. "Optical Neural Computers." *Scientific American* 256 (March): 88–95.

Balaban, M., and N. Murray. 1986. "Machine Tongues X: Prolog." *Computer Music Journal* 9(3): 7–12.

Daedalus. 1988. *Daedalus.* Special Winter, 1988 Neural Net Issue.

Elman, J. L. 1988. "Finding Structure in Time." Center for Research in Language, *Technical Report* 8801, University of California, San Diego.

Grossberg, S., ed. 1988. *The Adaptive Brain.* New York: Elsevier Science Publishing.

Hebb, D. O. 1949. *The Organization of Behavior.* New York: Wiley.

Hopfield, J. J. 1982. "Neural Networks and Physical Systems with Emergent Collective Computational Abilities." *Proceedings of the National Academy of Science* 79: 2554–2558.

Hopfield, J. J. 1984. "Neurons with Graded Responses Have Collective Computational Properties Like Those of Two-State Neurons." *Proceedings of the National Academy of Science* 81: 3088–3092.

Hopfield, J. J., and D. W. Tank. 1986. "Computing with Neural Circuits: a Model." *Science* 233: 625–633.

Jordan, M. I. 1986. "Serial Order: A Parallel Distributed Processing Approach." *Institute for Cognitive Science Report* 8604, University of California, San Diego.

Kohonen, T. 1984. *Self-Organization and Associative Memory.* Berlin: Springer-Verlag.

Lapedes, A., and R. Farber. 1988. "How Neural Nets Work." In D. Z. Anderson, ed. *Neural Information Processing Systems.* New York: American Institute of Physics.

LeBrun, M. 1979. "Digital Waveshaping Synthesis." *Journal of the Audio Engineering Society* 27(4): 250–266.

Levitt, D. A. 1984. "Machine Tongues X: Constraint Languages." *Computer Music Journal* 8(1): 9–21.

Lippman, R. P. 1987. "An Introduction to Computing with Neural Nets." *IEEE ASSP Magazine* 4(2): 4–22.

McClelland, J. L., and D. E. Rumelhart. 1988. *Explorations in Parallel Distributed Processing.* Cambridge, Massachusetts: MIT Press.

McClelland, J. L., D. E. Rumelhart, and the PDP Research

Group. 1986. *Parallel Distributed Processing: Explorations in the Microstructure of Cognition.* Vol. 3. Cambridge, Massachusetts: MIT Press.

McCulloch, W. S., and W. Pitts. 1943. "A Logical Calculus of the Ideas Immanent in Nervous Activity." *Bulletin of Mathematical Biophysics* 5:115–133.

Minsky, M., and S. Papert. 1969. *Perceptrons: An Introduction to Computational Geometry.* Cambridge, Massachusetts: MIT Press.

Pineda, F. J. 1988. "Generalization of Backpropagation to Recurrent and Higher Order Neural Networks." In D. Z. Anderson, ed. *Neural Information Processing Systems.* New York: American Institute of Physics.

Rosenblatt, R. 1959. *Principles of Neurodynamics.* New York: Spartan Books.

Rumelhart, D. E., G. E. Hinton, and R. J. Williams. 1986. "Learning Internal Representations by Error Propagation." In D. E. Rumelhart and J. L. McClelland, eds. *Parallel Distributed Processing: Explorations in the Microstructure of Cognition.* Cambridge, Massachusetts: MIT Press.

Rumelhart, D. E., J. L. McClelland, and the PDP Research Group, eds. 1986. *Parallel Distributed Processing: Explorations in the Microstructure of Cognition.* Vol. 1. Cambridge, Massachusetts: MIT Press.

Sejnowski, T., and C. R. Rosenberg. 1986. "NETtalk: A Parallel Network that Learns to Read Aloud." *Johns Hopkins University Technical Report JHU/EECS-86/01.*

Tank, D. W., and J. J. Hopfield. 1987. "Collective Computation in Neuronlike Circuits." *Scientific American* (December) 104–114.

Todd, P. M. 1988. "A Sequential Network Design for Musical Applications." *Proceedings of the 1988 Connectionist Models Summer School.* San Mateo, California: Morgan Kaufmann, Publishers.

Williams, R. J., and D. Zipser. 1988. "A Learning Algorithm for Continually Running Fully Recurrent Neural Networks." Paper submitted to *Neural Computation.*

Appendix

The mathematical derivation of back propagation is actually a familiar problem in introductory calculus. The crucial insight is to recognize that the error, being a simple function of the outputs, is also a function of all the weights in the network. The total sum squared error produced by the network over a set of training examples can be thought of as a surface in a multidimensional space, where each weight corresponds to a different axis. This is easiest to visualize if there are only two weights, because then there are only two axes, and the error surface is a familiar three-dimensional terrain above the two-axis plane. A good mathematical principle for quickly finding the lowest point (i.e., the minimum error) on this error surface is to move downhill in the steepest direction. In calculus, this is known as *gradient descent.*

Mathematically, the rule is that the change Δw_{rs} in the weight w_{rs} (where w_{rs} is meant to represent an arbitrary weight from a hidden unit to an output unit) is given by

$$\Delta w_{rs} = -\eta \frac{d\varepsilon}{dw_{rs}},$$

where η is a small number (so that the weight is only changed a little on any given learning trial). Similarly, we have (for an arbitrary weight from an input unit to a hidden unit)

$$\Delta m_{rs} = -\eta \frac{d\varepsilon}{dm_{rs}},$$

where m_{rs} is an arbitrary weight from an input unit to a hidden unit (see Fig. 4).

At this point, the problem is essentially solved. To obtain an explicit formula for how w_{rs} and m_{rs} should be changed, we need only substitute the above formulas for ε into the Δ equations and carry through the indicated differentiations (using the chain rule). The results are

$$\Delta w_{rs} = \eta(\tau_r - y_r)\, f'\,(\sum_j w_{rj}\, h_j)\, h_s,$$

$$\Delta m_{rs} = \eta \sum_k (\tau_k - y_k)\, f'\,(\sum_j w_{kj}\, h_j)\, w_{kr}\, f'\,(\sum_i m_{ri}\, x_i)\, x_s,$$

where $f'(\alpha)$ indicates the derivative of $f(\alpha)$ with respect to α and h_j is the output of the jth hidden unit. If we use the logistic function of Fig. 2b, then it can be shown that

$$f'(\alpha) = \frac{1}{2}(1 + f(\alpha))(1 - f(\alpha)),$$

and the above Δ equations become

$$\Delta w_{rs} = \frac{1}{2} \eta \, (\tau_r - y_r)(1 + y_r)(1 - y_r) \, h_s,$$

$$\Delta m_{rs} = \frac{1}{2} \eta \sum_k \, (\tau_k - y_k)(1 + y_k)(1 - y_k) \, w_{kr} \, (1 + h_r)(1 - h_r) \, x_s.$$

Upon reflection, these equations actually lend themselves to fairly simple interpretations. For example, in the case of Δw_{rs}, we have the following rule: If h_s is positive and y_r is less than the target value, then increase w_{rs} to allow h_s more influence. Similarly, if y_r is greater than the target, then decrease w_{rs} to decrease the effect of h_s. If h_s is negative, do the opposite. This same reasoning can also be applied to Δm_{rs} with the error $(\tau_r - y_r)$ replaced by the average error

$$\sum_k \, (\tau_k - y_k)(1 + y_k)(1 - y_k) \, w_{kr}.$$

Thus, the mathematics essentially tells us in detail how to make the adjustments that we recognize intuitively as reasonable.

Note: In practice, pure gradient descent is often intolerably slow to reach a minimum. One common acceleration technique, employed in all simulations reported herein, is to add a momentum term to the weight-change equation so that the actual change is the calculated Δw plus some fraction of the previous weight change (Rumelhart, McClelland, and PDP Research Group 1986, p. 330). This has the added benefit of helping to avoid local minima, because the adjustment of weights no longer corresponds to a strictly decreasing error.

Final note: To derive the RTRL algorithm, let the output of each unit at time t only become available to other units at time $t + 1$. For example, in Fig. 6 this means

$$h_j(t) = f(m_{j1} \, x_1(t - 1) + \sum_i m_{ji} \, h_i(t - 1)).$$

The derivative can now be calculated as above, but the result will contain terms of the form

$$\frac{dh_i(t - 1)}{dm_{rs}}.$$

These terms can all be calculated recurrently as time evolves from $t = 0$.

Addendum

The intended message of the foregoing chapter can be stated succinctly as follows: whenever you want to synthesize a behavior for which you can more easily provide examples than algorithmic prescriptions, think about training a neural network to do the job for you. To illustrate this approach, some extremely simple musical applications in the realm of rhythm were introduced. In this brief addendum, I wish to speculate about the applicability of feed-forward neural networks to the more ambitious task of synthesizing actual musical sounds.

Synthesizing Musical Sounds

The ability to synthesize "any sound imaginable" has been one of the most enduring and alluring attractions of computer music. A more restrictive (and, to many, a more desirable) version of this sonic freedom, however, continues to elude us: the ability to synthesize "the sound of any imaginable instrument." The difference in these two freedoms lies in the "naturalness" and the "principled variation and control" of the sounds emanating from nonelectronic musical instruments. We have succeeded to an extent in imbuing electronic sounds with these acoustic qualities, but our success has been largely limited to those cases in which we have deliberately emulated the sounds of existing acoustic instruments. Currently several important challenges remain: (1) to make these emulations evermore efficient (both computationally and in use of memory), (2) to make these emulations more responsive to naturalistic control (e.g., a continuous variation corresponding directly to bowing or air pressure), and (3) to devise convincing simulations of as-yet-uninvented acoustic instruments (e.g., to make new sounds that vary with pitch and loudness such that they are always heard as the output of a single acoustic source). To date, three approaches to sound synthesis have shown promise in this regard.

One obvious way to obtain naturalistic electronic sounds is to concatenate recorded snippets of actual instrument sounds. This approach, the so-called sampling technique used in many popular electronic synthesizers, has proved quite successful, but at the expense of large amounts of data storage, limited responsiveness to continuously varying control signals, and limited extensibility to novel instruments.

At the other extreme from this approach is the synthesis of electronic sounds based on computer-instantiated physical models of acoustic instruments (Wawrzynek 1989). This approach has great promise in meeting all three of the challenges cited, but it is still in its infancy, and its continued development will demand considerable mathematical and physical sophistication.

An interesting middle ground between these two extremes is that of model-based analysis-synthesis (Moorer 1985). The success of this approach depends upon the choice of an appropriate underlying model for sound synthesis and upon the analysis of recorded sounds to determine the time-varying parameters of that model which will cause it to resynthesize the original recorded sound. For example, in *additive synthesis* the model is a sum of sine waves, and the analysis determines the time-varying amplitudes and frequencies for each of the sine waves so that their summed result will be the original sound. Conversely, in *subtractive synthesis* the model is a filter excited by a periodic impulse-train; the analysis determines the periodicity of the impulse-train and the frequency-response of the filter.

Both the additive and subtractive models can be used to efficiently synthesize high-fidelity approximations to natural instrument tones, but neither is very appropriate for synthesizing an arbitrary musical passage. The reason for this is that the models themselves have no way of acquiring or utilizing information about the ways that real instrument tones naturally vary as a function of changing pitch or loudness. The models are completely static; they merely reproduce the instantaneous spectrum specified by the analysis data. They have no mechanism for capturing the underlying dynamics of the physical system producing the sound.

In contrast, a neural network model of musical sound production might well be capable of accessing this deeper level of sonic structure. One can imagine a kind of pie-in-the-sky neural network with inputs specifying what instrument is currently being emulated and what (continuously varying) pitch and loudness are currently desired and with a single output unit emitting the synthesized waveform as a succession of sample values. The network would be trained on a variety of actual musical performances, and it would then be asked to serve essentially as a general-purpose musical instrument. If the network were successful in capturing the underlying dynamical relationships characterizing each acoustic instrument, it might then do a good job of responding to novel control parameters. Conceivably, it might even be capable of interpolating between the timbres that it was trained on and perhaps extrapolating to new ones.

In the following paragraphs I will briefly address some of the issues that are likely to arise in actually attempting to design and train neural networks of this type.

A Neural Network Approach

A good rule of thumb in designing neural networks for challenging applications is to build as much knowledge as possible into the network. The better the network's internal structure can be matched to the problem at hand, the more likely the network will be able to function effectively. In the present case, two rather different approaches immediately suggest themselves.

On the one hand, we might try to develop a network whose output would literally be, as suggested above, the time-domain waveform on a sample-by-sample basis. Several researchers have recently demonstrated that feed-forward neural networks can be effectively trained to predict the next sample of a chaotic time series when the network is given some immediately preceding samples as input (Lapedes and Farber 1987; Wiegend et al. 1990). In principle, this prediction could be extended further and further into the future by making each predicted sample an input for a subsequent prediction task. In practice, though, predictions of this type, whether applied to chaotic or nonchaotic signals, usually diverge fairly quickly from the correct waveform, because errors tend to amplify with each successive application of the network. A more promising architecture for producing a time-domain output might be a temporally recurrent feed-forward network. For example, networks of this type have been successfully trained via the RTRL technique (described in the preceding chapter) to produce a sinusoidally oscillating output (Williams and Zipser 1990).

Still, a network of this type has only a very short-term memory. It will encode enough context information to produce successfully a periodic output, but it will probably make no distinction between the attack portion of a note and the decay portion. Yet it would be called upon to produce very different outputs for these two conditions. One way to overcome this limitation might be to explicitly provide more long-term context information (e.g., attack versus decay) in the form of additional inputs to the network. Another approach would be to employ a hierarchical structure in which the short-term-delay network is embedded in a network with longer-term memory based on longer delays (c.f. Todd 1990, and his addendum in this volume).

An even more intriguing possibility is to provide the network with a wired-in recursive delay of exactly one pitch period. For example, we could feed back output values not from the previous clock tick but from the previous pitch period (many clock ticks earlier). By varying the length of delay in this feedback loop, we might expect to vary the pitch correspondingly. The resulting architecture would bear some interesting similarities to simplified physical instrument models (c.f. McIntyre et al. 1983).

Yet another serious problem remains, however. If the training data consists of recordings of real instruments, it will inevitably contain many instances in which different waveforms are associated with the same set of inputs to the network (and without any reliable relationship to the temporal context). There are two reasons for this. First, many real instrument timbres contain a significant noise component (e.g., bowing noise, breath noise, finger and keyboard noise, etc.). The network will have no hope of learning to synthesize these essentially random variations in the waveform; hence we will have to stipulate at the outset that the network will be responsible only for the deterministic portion of the sound. An approach that may prove helpful in this regard is to extract the noise component beforehand and process it independently (c.f. Serra and Smith 1990).

Even without the noise, though, there is still likely to be significant multiplicity in the target waveforms. Two notes with identical pitch and loudness contours may nevertheless differ substantially on a cycle-to-cycle basis due to various instrument-dependent differences in performance. This variability may be very important in lending a "lifelike" character to the sound, but it presents yet another challenge for our neural network approach. When a neural network is asked to learn a one-to-many mapping, it has no way of knowing which of the various "correct" outputs is appropriate in a particular instance. Instead, it generally responds by learning a single average response that minimizes the resulting error. To circumvent this problem, we might supplement the inputs with additional random numbers that would allow the network to distinguish between otherwise identical inputs and then memorize the correct responses. It is likely, though, that a good deal more research may be required to address this issue fully.

On the other hand, we could reject the purely time-domain approach at the outset and pursue a very different path. This second approach is basically a hybrid in which the already well-established model (e.g., the additive or subtractive model) is used to produce the actual time-domain waveform, and a neural network is employed to learn the dynamics of the variations in the model's parameters over the course of a performance. For example, we could employ a temporally recurrent neural network whose inputs are the same as those above but whose outputs are now a set of parameters as opposed to an actual waveform.

This hybrid approach is attractive for three reasons. First, the variability discussed in the preceding paragraphs will typically be far more dramatic in the waveform itself than in the model parameters, so the problems of one-to-many mappings for the networks will be greatly reduced. Second, the time scale that the network will need to contend with will be far less severe: a new output will be required every 10 milliseconds as opposed to every .02 milliseconds. Lastly, this approach is attractive because it employs each structure only for what it does best. The standard synthesis models are good at producing waveforms from parametric descriptions of the spectrum. Temporally recurrent, feedforward networks are good at extracting underlying patterns of variation. It is exciting to imagine that these two powerful techniques may someday be successfully combined.

Summary

The above descriptions are of course extremely sketchy. They will necessarily remain so until actual simulations with real musical data are undertaken. The important message, though, is that the networks themselves will have to be designed with considerable ingenuity. In particular, various forms of modularity and hierarchy may need to be built in at the start. If such an approach is successful, however, the rewards will more than compensate for the effort involved.

Acknowledgments

I wish to thank Peter Todd for his constant encouragement and for his insightful comments on a draft version of this manuscript.

References

Lapedes, A., and R. Farber. 1987. "Nonlinear Signal Processing Using Neural Networks: Prediction and System Modeling." *Technical Report LA-UR-87-2662.* Los Alamos National Laboratory.

McIntyre, M.E., R.T. Schumacher, and J. Woodhouse. 1983. "On the Oscillations of Musical Instruments." *Journal of the Acoustical Society of America* 74:5.

Moorer, J.A. 1985. "Signal Processing Aspects of Computer Music: A Survey." In J. Strawn, ed. *Digital Audio Signal Processing.* Los Altos, California: William Kaufmann, Inc.

Sera, X., and J.O. Smith. 1990. "A Sound Decomposition System Based on a Deterministic Plus Residual

Model." *Journal of the Acoustical Society of America* 87:s97 (abstract).
Todd, P.M. 1990. "Hierarchical Sequential Networks for Music Composition." *Journal of the Acoustical Society of America* 87:s18 (abstract).
Todd, P.M. This volume. Addendum to "A Connectionist Approach to Algorithmic Composition."
Wawrzynek, J. 1989. "VLSI Models for Sound Synthesis." In M. Matthews and J.R. Pierce, eds. *Current Directions in Computer Music Research*. Cambridge, Massachusetts: MIT Press.
Weigend, A., B. Huberman, and D.E. Rumelhart. 1990. "Predicting the Future: A Connectionist Approach." *Technical Report PDP-90-01*. Stanford: Stanford University, PDP Research Group, Department of Psychology.
Williams, R.J., and D. Zipser. 1989. "A Learning Algorithm for Continually Running Fully Recurrent Neural Networks." *Neural Computation* 1:270–280.

D. Gareth Loy
509 Barbara Ave.
Solana Beach, CA 92075
dgl@sdcarl.ucsd.edu

Connectionism and Musiconomy

Introduction

The use of formal systems to generate and model music is surprisingly recent. Most examples are within the last forty years, nearly all are within this century. The use of computers to model music—composing, performing, listening—is more recent still, dating from the 1950s. And although the perceptron has been around in one form or another since the early days of the cyberneticists in the middle of this century, neural network techniques have not been applied to music until well after the renaissance of connectionism in the early 1980s.

There are exceptions, of course. The earliest exception I know to my first assertion is a simple composition system by the learned Benedictine and famous music theoretician Guido of Arezzo (or d'Arezzo) in 1026, nearly a thousand years ago. He described a table-driven method for generating cantus firmus melodies directly from a liturgical text in a quasi-automatic fashion (Guido 1955).

The exception to my second assertion came from Ada Lovelace. She was among the first to propose what is now common practice among modern composers when she said of Charles Babbage's analytical engine that its "operating mechanism might act upon other things besides number, were objects found whose mutual fundamental relations could be expressed by those of the abstract science of operations. . . . Supposing, for instance, that the fundamental relations of pitched sound in the signs of harmony and of musical composition were susceptible of such expression and adaptations, the engine might compose elaborate and scientific pieces of music of any degree of complexity or extent" (quoted in Moore 1990). Although Babbage's machine never achieved this proposal, its descendents certainly did (Loy 1989).

The exception to my third assertion about connectionist techniques and music is a possibly apocryphal story I was told once concerning a cyberneticist in the early 1960s who applied a reinforcing electrical current to a jar containing a viscous metallic suspension whenever his radio played a particular song or kind of music. The jar also received a strong acoustical signal from the radio's loudspeaker, forming standing waves in the fluid. The story goes that the liquid goo trained itself to recognize his taste in music (Moore 1989).

It is the purpose of this paper to characterize and to provide some context for the interest music researchers find in connectionist theory. I will present first an informal survey of some of the traditional interests and problems of music research in the computer music community, then I will describe the influence of connectionist theories that work today.

But before going on, the reader deserves an explanation for the invented term "musiconomy." It should be taken as a lighthearted verbal pun. In casting about for a term that successfully characterizes the kind of music research discussed in this paper and how it differs from, for instance, traditional musicology and such other topics as the psychology of music, I noted that Webster's Dictionary describes a *nomy* as a " . . . sum of knowledge regarding a (specified) field," and a *logy* as a "doctrine." For instance, compare astronomy and astrology. Then it occurred to me that there was a terminological hole that I could fill as follows: If astronomy followed from astrology, what follows from musicology?

Compositional Analysis and Synthesis

When musicians speak of the form of a musical work, we traditionally mean its *structural form*—that is, its analytic deep structure and the syntactic rules relating to it; we tend not to mean the methods governing its actual fabrication and composition process—what we might call *procedural form.* It is well known that composer J. S. Bach, for instance, usually incorporated certain structural elements in his counterpoint and fugues. Because many of these elements have been deduced, we can make detailed structural models of his works.

The roots of the structural analysis of common-practice music come from such Renaissance theorists as Zarlino (1558), baroque theorists such as Fux (1725), and the baroque composers Marpurg, Rameau, and others. These men developed compositional rule systems that captured the most regular aspects of the music of their times—such as voice leading, harmonic resolution, counterpoint, and the structure of fugues—in enough detail to reveal the main elements of compositional structure. Fux, in his treatise *Gradus ad Parnassum* (1725), developed a didactic rule set for species counterpoint (a graduated system for teaching the rules of counterpoint) that has been taught for centuries.

As I will describe below, however, even modern versions of these music theories are not complete: they are a necessary, but not a sufficient, guide for a composer who wants to learn to write music in a well-known style such as J.S.Bach's. In practice, besides performing structural analysis of the target style, such a composer must "absorb" the target style by spending many hours with the corpus of works created in that style and additional hours doing approximation trials with pencil and eraser. When interrogated about knowledge thus acquired, such a trained composer can usually list off the already known rules of the style and show how he or she navigated within their limits, but when it comes to questions of taste (such as why one note was chosen over another where no objective rule seems to apply), the composer will probably revert to feeling-toned language such as "it seemed like the choice Bach would have made."

Because traditional musical structural analysis is not complete, it cannot be the basis of a truly formal music theory. Synthesis of compositions cannot proceed on the basis of traditional analytic practice alone, because such analysis requires further conscious or unconscious processes in the mind of a composer for completion of the composition. The consciously articulated rules of even the best-understood musical styles have not shown themselves to be sufficient to capture satisfactorily the underlying compositional process.

Furthermore, it is not well understood—except at a preconscious level in the mind of a suitably trained composer—how to absorb the essence of another composer's style, such that the knowledge acquired can be used to synthesize original compositions within the target style. Though it is a frequent enough occurrence (most composers begin their training by emulating the styles of others), no analysis of this process that meets the criterion of an algorithmically definite and effective procedure has yet come to my attention. Instead, research has tended to focus on related problems in the same vicinity, such as the more robust approaches to structural analysis of Schenker (1906), an early pioneer of hierarchical structural analysis, and Lerdahl and Jackendoff (1983), and on attempts to use deterministic and statistical techniques to simulate (but not necessarily to emulate) the procedural knowledge of composing. Some pioneering work has focused directly on the question of how humans perform this compositional learning task (such as Laske 1973), but progress has been slow, awaiting a suitably powerful understanding of learning, such as the one emerging from connectionism now.

So we are left with the questions: From where does a composer's procedural knowledge derive? How can we access it? How can we model it? It is possible that a more rigorous structural analysis can succeed in becoming a complete formal theory incorporating procedural knowledge, or not? Important evidence about these questions can be had by surveying the different formal systems that composers have used through history. If we can understand the relationship between a composer and the formal composition methods described in the literature, it might give us a feeling for the possibility of a complete formal theory of composition.

Using Automata to Create Original Works

At least since the time of Guido of Arezzo, there has been an attraction to the notion of automatic music generation and the use of structuring devices to constrain the space of possible choices. Guido proposed his method of composing cantus firmus melodies based on the vowels appearing in a selected text for two reasons. First, he thought it was appropriate that the music should be derivative of the sacred Latin mass text he was setting, and making the choice of pitch a function of the vowels in the text was a valid way to accomplish this. Second, he thought his method was a good way for beginning composers to get started, since it unburdened them from some of the combinatorial weight of the space of all possible cantus firmus melodies. Guido's system is very rare in that it actually stipulates a procedural method. All composers have used structural systems, such as isorhythm, rondo form, sonata form, etc., to frame compositions (Kirchmeyer 1963). But these are structural systems, not procedural ones like Guido's. Italian opera composors were known to consult tables of musical figures to help facilitate the act of composition, but this is of little help in deducing procedural rules, since we don't know what criteria they used to choose what they took from their tables.

All formal systems, whether they are procedural or structural, are mechanisms of externalization of at least some of the composer's decision-making processes onto an automaton of some sort. The forms of musical composition, such as canon, fugue, rondo, sonata, cantata, etc., and the various dance forms, such as sarabande and gigue, also serve as a framework for compositional elaboration, much the way the frame of a building supports the decorative facade. They frame, but only incidentally do they facilitate the composer's task. Formal generative techniques, on the other hand, can actively facilitate the production of compositions, either by amplifying the composer's intentions or by relieving the composer of the necessity of making decisions for some parameters of the compositional process. Formal generative systems can also provide a means to model arbitrary compositional processes, either for research or composition.

Concurrently with the development of probability theory during the Enlightenment, some uses of chance techniques to generate compositions arose. Around 1719 in Prague, Vogt suggested casting bent nails on the ground to generate the rise and fall of melodic lines (Kirchmeyer 1963). This technique, along with the idea books of the Italian opera composers, were mostly to prime the pump, so to speak, of a composer's imagination. They did not act as a substitute for the composer's decision-making process.

A few years later, the composer and theorist Kirnberger developed a musical game he called *musikalische wurfelspiel* or "dice mice." This was a means whereby anyone, equipped only with a single die and a set of musical tables, could compose proper minuettes and polonaises (Potter 1971). It became a vogue, and examples survive from the hands of no less than Wolfgang Mozart, C.P.E. Bach, and Joseph Haydn, among others, who evidently enjoyed the construction of such musical puzzles. Though it was easy to use these tables to generate music, it took a very gifted composer to construct the tables in the first place. Here, though, for the first time is a truly formal method of generating compositions without requiring any unconscious procedural knowledge on the part of the user of this technique. It goes even farther than Guido's method, which still relied on the composer to choose among several possible alternatives.

Arnold Schoenberg's twelve-tone system of composition, developed in the early decades of this century, can also be used to stipulate the note-by-note fabrication of a musical work, though it was not usually used that way in practice (Perle and Lansky 1981). The method is derived from combinatorics and has two parts. During the first *precompositional* phase, the composer makes decisions about the ordering of musical materials, such as the laying out of the twelve chromatic pitches into a *row.* Through the use of transpositions of the row, and the use of inversion and retrograde transformations, the composer develops a set of prototypical materials, "outside" of time. This precompositional material then supplies the composer with a deterministic sequence of pitches that are to be appended to the work being composed in time order. The composer is still free to place the resulting series of pitches into whatever context seems to be called for, such as rhythm, timbre, duration, articulation, etc., so again this is not a completely specified method.

Composers just before and after World War II extended Schoenberg's deterministic techniques to all other parameters of composition, resulting in a style called serialism. During the precompositional phase in serialism, various series are chosen and assigned to the set of all controlled musical parameters. The actual compositional process is concerned with controlling the interactions of the predetermined serial orderings (Perle and Lansky 1981). Anton Webern, a disciple of Schoenberg, was an early proponent of this technique. After World War II, composers such as Herbert Eimert observed that these techniques, formerly only applied to instrumental music, could be extended to the very specification of acoustical waveforms via analog electronic apparatus. This signaled the advent of electronic music.

Compositional Synthesis by Analysis

In the 1930s, Joseph Schillinger proposed the then-radical notion that theories of art should not simply be observation-based tools of art historians and musicologists but should be so rigorously analytical that they are also useful in the production of art (Schillinger 1948). He attempted to create such theories for the visual arts and music based on a quasi-mathematical foundation. He complained about art theory in general, saying,

> It is time to admit that esthetic theories have failed in the analysis as well as the synthesis of art. These have been unsuccessful both in interpreting the nature of art and in evolving a reliable method of composision. . . . Theories a posteriori are very characteristic forms of art theories in general. Offering nothing in the analysis of the creative processes of art, such theories expose their futility in the contention that a genius is above theories, and that his creativity is free and does not conform to any laws or principles. This is the mythological period of esthetics. There is less and less room for mystery and divinity so far as the manipulation of material elements is concerned. (p.10)

So Schillinger would undoubtedly answer in the affirmative to our query whether a more rigorous structural analysis could succeed in becoming a complete formal theory incorporating procedural knowledge.

Though his two-volume tome *The Schillinger System of Musical Composition* (Schillinger 1978) has been largely ignored, many composers and music researchers have heeded the above message. Most if not all recent music theories, such as Lerdahl and Jackendoff (1983), have as a criterion of their success that they are generative as well as analytical. In the traditional realm of computer music, Laske (1973), for instance, has proposed a comprehensive system for analysis, composition, and performance, called OBSERVER, using artificial intelligence techniques. The system, though never finished, was to have served as a platform for synthesis by analysis of compositions. Other such systems are described below.

Composing with Computers

The formalization of the musical process did not come to the forefront in music until computers became available to composers and music researchers in the mid-1950s. Computing not only facilitated the formalization of musical composition, it required it: only with rigorously formal languages can one program computers.

Computer-Mediated Composition

The early work in computer composition consisted of developing artificial procedural systems, mostly without attempting to relate them to any model of human processes. We may call this work computer-mediated composition. The speed and power of a computer for quickly exploring the consequences of different compositional strategies was exhilirating to those with the inclination and the necessary access to such tools.

Composer Iannis Xenakis, for instance, wrote programs to generate musical compositions using stochastic techniques (Xenakis 1971). He enthused, "With the aid of electronic computers the composer becomes a sort of pilot: he presses the buttons, introduces coordinates, and supervises the controls of a cosmic vessel sailing in the space of sound, across sonic constellations and galaxies that he could formerly glimpse only as a distant dream." Xenakis took some very interesting theoretical work by Gabor (1947) on a proof of identity between Fourier spectral and quantum representations of sound and mixed this with stochastic techniques and elements of symbolic logic. Like Schoenberg, Xenakis thought of his system as a theory of composition, but given its degree of complexity, it is not surprising that the assistance of a computer was essential to a practical realization of his ideas.

Many other artificial compositional processes have been proposed and implemented. Gill (1963) wrote computer programs to generate music using the artificial intelligence technique of backtracking. Mathews and Rosler (1968) described a model of composing based on mathematical function composition. They focused on deterministic algorithms that were not ordinarily associated with music for the generation and combination of musical functions of time. They achieved interesting effects through the application of regular and irregular quantizing functions applied to functions representing melodies. For instance, imagine painting a musical staff on a window looking out over the New York skyline and copying down as notes the heights of the buildings from left to right to create a melody. (Latin American composer Hector Villa-Lobos actually did this in the 1940s.) In this case, the skyline is the function representing the melody, and the staff is a quantizing function, used to find the closest approximation to the note representing the height of a building. Mathews and Rosler developed a theory about such representations and manipulations and wrote computer programs for manipulating them, including some that operated in real time.

Many computer languages, programs, and systems have been written for representing the compositional process (Loy 1989). They all generally include mechanisms for textual or graphical descriptions of music, common practice notation, iconic or symbolic representations of musical objects, and procedural or declarative manipulations of musical data. Virtually all standard programming languages have been used, in addition to the many invented specifically for music. Invented languages generally attempt also to incorporate a notion of time, parallelism, and special musical data structures, such as pitches and dynamics. Besides composition-generating systems, there are so-called compositional editors, such as the one developed by Buxton et al. (1978, 1979), that attempt to assist the composer in the hand-generation and modification scores.

Gottfried M. Koenig (1970a, 1970b) combined computer-mediated and computer-generated composition with the development of his Project I and Project II programs. They are, in some respects, experiments in how to share the compositional process between man and machine. Project I takes minimal input from the composer and uses serial and stochastic procedures to create a text-based representation of a musical work, leaving out such parameters as durations, orchestration, and assignment of attack points to instruments. The composer must then complete the structure in the process of orchestrating it. Project II, on the other hand, requires detailed specifications of the operations the program is to perform. The program produces a textual output that can be directly converted into an orchestrated score.

Computer-Generated Composition

The approaches discussed above use the computer as a composer's assistant, sometimes intelligent—an amanuensis—and sometimes not. Another approach is to ask the question of whether (Myhill 1952) and how (Hiller and Isaacson 1959) the compositional process might be modeled as a computation. The former question is properly in the domain of philosophy. The latter is more a computer science question: the goal is not the generation of compositions so much as the design of machines to carry out this task. The question, How does a human compose? is properly a cognitive science question. Models using this approach would not only have to compose music but also would have to account for the available knowledge about how composers actually carry out the task of composing.

Influenced strongly by cybernetics and information theory, Lejaren Hiller and Leonard Isaacson conducted some experiments in the computability of the compositional process (Hiller and Isaacson 1959).They thought of composition as the problem of using musical rules to select acceptable musical sequences out of the space of all possible combinations of musical sequences. They developed a computer model of the process of composing common-practice music using stochastic and Markov-chain techniques.

Briefly, Hiller and Isaacson's process worked like this. Taking an available musical rule set, such as the rules of chorale harmonization, they found ways to represent the musical rules as a set of computer subprograms. Then they used these subroutines to compose a new piece of music. Beginning with a note at random to start a new composition, they would then choose another candidate note at random to follow it. The current composition (so far just the first note) and the candidate note are then evaluated by all the subroutines implementing the collection of compositional rules. If the subroutines do not find any violation of the rules, the note is appended to the current composition, but if there are violations, a new candidate note is chosen and the evaluation process repeats until a candidate is found that satisfies all the rules. This note is then appended to the current composition. This process continues until eventually a composition of suitable length is achieved. I have described a simple first-order generate-and-test process. If two notes of the existing piece are used to determine the acceptabiality of a candidate note, it is a second-order process. The higher the order of a process, the more difficult it is to find an acceptable candidate note, and more candidate notes must be evaluated on the average to find acceptable extensions of the composition.

Hiller is generally credited as being the first to use computers to compose music. He did numerous experiments with various styles, and published the results in the form of a string quartet, called the *Illiac Suite* (Hiller and Isaacson 1959). The *Illiac Suite* included sections in several styles, beginning with a chorale and ending in free atonality.

Apart from the fact that it obeys certain compositional rules, Hiller and Isaacson's system does not describe the method of the typical human composer: composers usually do not employ a generate-and-test methodology. If this technique is accompanied by a probabilistic analysis of a corpus of musical works, however, the result is a system that can mimic an arbitrary musical style. In this version of the method, probability distribution functions are generated at various orders (i.e., numbers of notes as context) that describe the probabilities of all note transitions in all musical contexts in the corpus. These probability distribution functions are then substituted for the rule subroutines in Hiller and Isaacson's original method. The functions are used to specify, on a *statistical* rather than a *prescriptive rule* basis, the likelihood of a note being acceptable within a particular musical context, given a particular corpus of examples as guide. This method is now a type of *Markov-chain process,* commonly used in the generation of sequences that have the same probabilistic structure as some set of examples. (In standard Markov-chain usage, the computed probability distribution is itself used to choose the next element of a sequence, rather than being used to test an originally random candidate.) Low-order Markov-chain analysis captures the local structure of the corpus; higher-order analysis captures more and more global structure.

To compose on the basis of a set of probability distribution functions, one chooses a particular order as the criterion for the choice of new notes. The higher the order, the closer the music will be to the target style. But the process breaks down at high orders without a very large corpus of materials, as it becomes progressively more difficult to find candidate notes to satisfy contexts that become more and more rare. Also, at higher orders, one begins to hear significant chunks of the original material. Furthermore, as Lewis points out in his chapter (Lewis, this volume), the probabilistic method is not economical, as it requires the specification of the probabilities of all undesirable as well as all desirable structures within the corpus. A prescriptive, rule-based system would only need to represent the desirable structures. One way around this problem is described by Kohonen and colleagues in their chapter of this book (Kohonen et al., this volume). Their method allows an analysis procedure to vary the order (or depth) of analysis according to the requirements of the corpus of musical examples. Thus only the effective context need be stored to guide the composition-generating phase. Many other possibilities exist as well.

Prescriptive Rule-Based Composition

Since the advent of computers, it has been a widespread fantasy of generations of music undergraduates studying species counterpoint to extend Fux's nearly formal rule set into a computable method for generating species counterpoint—a rule-based expert composing system. Then all a student need do is feed a program the cantus firmus given out by the professor (often a plain chant from a Medieval liturgical work or another simple melody) and let the program grind out a counterpoint. A similar fantasy concerns the rules of chorale harmonization used by Bach—another subject often inflicted on music undergraduates.

Unfortunately for the students, it turns out that it is a lot less trouble and much more effective simply to learn to compose counterpoint and harmonize chorales than to try to write programs to generate them. Fux's rules, though thorough, are far from a closed formal description of species counterpoint. In fact, though the style has been studied for centuries, no completely formal description exists, even though composers can be trained to write in that style easily enough.

Many composers and computer scientists have tried, with varying degrees of success, to finish the job Hiller began for chorale harmonization and species counterpoint. One example of a very decent job of solving the species counterpoint problem was done by Schottstaedt (1984). (Among the charming features of his effort is the fact that the publication is autodocumented program code: the single text contains both a very good explanation of the design and operation of the algorithm and the code itself.) Whereas Hiller's work was a pioneering proof of concept, Schottstaedt set out to implement a full expert system for composing counterpoint.

What Schottstaedt found when he was done implementing Fux's rules was that there were many remaining ambiguities. There were places where rules conflicted. Elsewhere the rules seemed incomplete. As a consequence, the results did not sound as well formed as compositions created by trained humans. He struggled on until he had nailed down many more rules, supplied a means of reconciling conflicting constraints, and fine-tuned the weights of the various rules. The rules that he had to add, numbering over one hundred, rivaled the number of rules he got from Fux. Still the program could not be said to write wonderful species counterpoint. It seemed to perform about as well as a typical freshman composition student. So one can say Schottstaedt succeeded in creating an expert system for composing undergraduate counterpoint exercises. It is, of course, still a far cry from an undergraduate cannon etude to a major work of counterpoint, such as the *Missa prolationum* of Johannes Ockeghem, every movement of which is constructed as a double mensuration canon making use of various intervals and various combinations of key signatures.

Other modern examples of emulating historical styles using prescriptive rules include VIVACE, a melody-harmonizing program by Thomas (1985). Ebcioglu (1984) describes a very elaborate system using traditional artificial intelligence techniques to solve chorale harmonization in the style of Bach. All of these methods are essentially rule evaluators driven either by a preconstructed melody or with a random sequence. Other systems based on prescriptive rules include Roads (1979), who described a composition system based on generative grammars.

These systems represent some success in the formalization of the composition process, to be sure. It must be kept in mind, however, that what they have succeeded with are the most elemental aspects of compositional structure: common-practice harmonization and melody formation, that is, the most well-known and regular aspects of the most well-known and regular of Western musical styles. There is clearly and admittedly a considerable distance to go before more advanced issues can be addressed that deal with the less well understood and less regular elements of musical practice, and it is not at all clear that the techniques used so far are capable of scaling up to these larger problems. The likely reason for this is that prescriptive, rule-based systems do not handle ambiguity gracefully and are difficult to operate meaningfully in parallel. And yet, structural ambiguity is very common in most forms of music, due in part to the inherent parallelism (as for instance, between the melodic, harmonic, rhythmic, and timbral dimensions) of music.

Analysis, Performance, and Listening

Other areas of music research, such as analysis, listening, and performance, have also been intensely studied. Although musical analysis typically means the visual inspection of scores, we obviously analyze music also during listening. Sensors on musical instruments can also be used to give further details about the exact actions of a performer.

In fact, musical performance analysis has been greatly facilitated by the advent of musical instruments that can be monitored by computers, either by acoustic capture (such as a flute with contact microphone attched to an analog to digital converter) or directly via switches (as with MIDI keyboards). Prior to this, musical performance could be studied only semiquantitatively. As a result, the subject of performance interpretation has only recently started to have an empirical basis. There is clearly more to a musical performance than simply realizing the notes written by the composer. It is difficult to study the difference between the performance and the score without being able to capture and analyze actual performances. The same kinds of problems crop up for performance, analysis, and listening as for composition: What are the rules, structural and procedural? How does a person with no prior experience learn to appreciate different kinds of music?

Sundberg and Friberg (1986) describe a Lisp programming environment for modeling rules of musical performance. Clynes (1984) proposed some interesting heuristics for capturing performance nuance that rely on some of the dynamical aspects of the physical mechanisms associated with performance. He developed this to the point of claiming to have captured some of the invariant characteristics in the performance of certain classical European composers. Rodet et al. (1984) developed a vocal synthesis technique called CHANT and a control system for it called FORMES, which is essentially a customized Lisp environment for modeling the voice and vocal performance. They achieved very realistic imitations of soprano bel canto, among many other simulations, with this system.

Another problem is score tracking, which includes passive listening (e.g., by an audience) or active listening (e.g., by other performing musicians). Regarding active listening, Dannenberg and Bloch (1985) used a dynamical programming technique borrowed from voice recognition to track tempo fluctuations of live performers in real time and thereby also to track the temporal location of the musician in a score during performance. An accompaniment could then be generated that would follow the performer. Vercoe and Puckette (1985) developed a variant on this technique incorporating a weighting scheme that, through rehearsal, would allow the accompaniment to track the performer more reliably. This system would seem to have a learning algorithm in it to the extent that the accompanist can come to expect certain deformations of the tempo curve at predictable locations in the score. However, there is no generalization in this system, only memorization. When the synthetic accompanist observes a ritard during a particular cadence in a piece it is rehearsing, it does not come to anticipate a ritard in similar circumstances elsewhere. So while it displays a learning characteristic, it does not provide a means to determine where the rules of performance practice come from in the first place, an understanding that would foster proper generalization.

Another topic related to performance tracking is how to parse music, first in the sense of taking dictation, second in the sense of reducing what is heard into stylistic or structural descriptions. Moorer (1975) described a system that (with certain restrictions) would reduce the acoustical performance of two-part music to traditional notation. Winograd (1968) developed an elaborate program called EXPLAIN to analyze key relationships. It would automatically parse chordal progressions to extract the underlying key scheme. Winograd was inspired by Chomsky's work with generative grammars. Tenney and Polansky (1980) developed a program for phrase analysis of single melodic lines based on principles derived from Gestalt psychology. Melodies were reduced to essential structure by principles believed to be operative in the listener's mind. Most historical music theory has been based on analysis of motives and phrases of the printed score taken out of time and without reference to the cognitive frame of reference of the listener. Tenney and Polansky's work was notable for asserting the listener's temporal perspective as the point of reference. Cope (1990) describes a pattern-matching approach to the simulation of musical style. He has written a large Lisp environment, which he calls Experiments in Musical Intelligence, for modeling musical styles and composing music within those styles. Related research involves score capture from performance (Chafe, Mont-Reynaud, and Rush 1982), and score editing (Byrd 1984).

A major emphasis within the field of computer music that I have not mentioned so far is sound synthesis and processing. This subfield primarily resorts to digital signal-processing theory more than to cognitive models of music, so I have not spent much time discussing it. The work of Rodet et al. (1984) cited previously is an exception to this. The CHANT vocal synthesis model is tightly coupled to a powerful Lisp environment called FORMES that provides hierarchical structure for representing successive levels of control required to model the singing voice.

The Problem of Formal Specification of Music

The efforts described above to model music using rule-based techniques face the difficulty of satisfactorily handing the numerous informal aspects of music. As I will discuss shortly, music has numerous informal aspects, but to model them on a computer requires that they be formalized. But the formalization of these musical domains requires some reductive process to be applied, which has the effect of trivializing the reduced musical process. This limits the usefulness of reduced formal models either to toy musical problems or to trivializations of complex musical problems. Let me demonstrate why this is important.

It is generally the case that composers are more interested in establishing a formal device as a point of departure than as an end in itself. Taking an example from Bach again, consider his rules of harmonic resolution and motivic sequencing. In the episode of a fugue, for example, he might sequence a fixed motive of four notes through a strictly determined set of transpositions based on the circle of fifths. At first glance it seems that this simple process could be formalized easily and applied to generate automatically part of a fugal episode by rule. Such automatic techniques were actually used by some lesser baroque composers.

But simply putting note after note was not a main goal of the better baroque composer; it was rather the attempt to keep the listener off balance and hence mentally engaged in the unfolding composition. To this end, composers such as Bach might, after sequencing a motive through two and a half transpositions, prematurely break off the sequencing. This was accomplished, for example, by shifting the compositional focus from sequencing (a horizontal musical dimension) to harmonic resolution (a vertical dimension). After two sequences of a motive the listener has a sense of expectation; after two and a half, a confirmation; then the listener is tempted to stop paying attention, thinking that the remainder of the phrase will probably just continue the pattern. To break off at precisely this point with a cadence is to deceive this expectation and re-engage the listener's attention. This is in line with the theory that music is organized by the interweaving of expectation and surprise, developed by Meyer (1956); his ideas were strongly influenced by the original work of Shannon and Weaver in information theory.

Thus the tension between one dimension of formal structure in a composition (e.g., a motivic plan) is played off against another (a harmonic plan) to achieve the higher aim of sustaining attention to the larger musical gesture. The position of the composer in this process is therefore really in the cracks between categories of formal description. Describing the compositional process within the framework of a strictly formal representation will necessarily miss this dimension of the composer's art. And yet a computable approach is perforce necessarily strictly formal. This is the dilemma shared by all computer models of music.

It is interesting to observe the strengths and weaknesses of the various kinds of models and to observe what is easy and what is difficult for them to represent in music. Although rule-based systems are better than probabilistic ones in that they can describe both large- and small-scale structure with equal facility, it is difficult for rule-based systems to reconcile multiple parallel contexts simultaneously. Conversely, probablistic systems are good for handling surface structure but are less useful at higher orders for broader structure. One can accommodate multiple simultaneous hierarchies using rule-based systems by such techniques as method combination in object-oriented programming languages. Process models of music representation can be augmented by daemon processes operating in the background that step in to provide a means of rule transition where necessary. Backtracking and other forms of intelligent search can be used to find appropriate solutions to multidimensional rule-based problems. It is even possible for these techniques to incorporate a model of learning.

For instance, Daniel Scheidt's MC system (Scheidt 1985) generates new compositions based on an analysis of a corpus of examples. It builds a knowledge base of compositional style by analyzing examples during a training phase, generating a rule base to guide a subsequent compositional process. Scheidt describes his work as

> the design and implementation of a software package capable of generating original music compositions. The system's compositional model is based on feedback-driven parallel processes which cooperatively interact toward the creation of coherent musical structures. The feedback mechanism is based on an analysis/synthesis paradigm in which domain-specific algorithms are applied to distinct musical components. The system allows the user/composer to supply initial musical information which is used by the generative processes as the basis of a composition. The compositional model provided can be extended through the addition of new analysis/synthesis routines and processes in order to meet the goals of a wide range of compositional approaches. (p. i)

Scheidt's system addresses the fact that music, and therefore composition, is a highly parallel activity and provides a way to model this activity through parallel processes. Though there is an explicit model of learning in his method, the learning system is "domain specific," requiring the addition of specialized new routines to cover new situations, which is the weakness of this and related approaches. Although such modern modeling techniques seem to require less drastic reduction of the problem space to fit it into a formal model, it is still the case that these techniques require a de facto hypothesis for how music should be understood before the model can be used. Neither MC nor any system described so far answers the question of where the knowledge of composing comes from in the first place.

Some Observations

What strikes me most about the work described so far is not just that the output of these systems is primitive when compared to the mature works of the composers being modeled, though this is significant. Even more remarkable is the disparity between the ease with which an average undergraduate can learn to analyze and compose in an evolved style (a process lasting an academic year, perhaps) and the high degree of difficulty of finding suitably objective knowledge to represent composing, so that a computer can do as well (a process that has not yet been shown to halt).

Weaknesses of Traditional Techniques

It seems that traditional techniques for modeling intelligence do not fare well when applied to deep humanistic problems such as music. This concern parallels the one expressed generally in the field of connectionism (e.g., Rumelhart and McClelland 1986), which observes the failure of traditional artificial intelligence techniques to lead to satisfying solutions to deep problems in human cognition.

Probablistic systems only adapt distribution functions to a corpus of examples without discovering or acting upon any deep-level correlations in that corpus. Rule-based systems, such as MC, do not spontaneously generalize knowledge from their input but only analyze according to the domain-specific rules supplied, which must still be developed heuristically. Learning with generalization is not addressed by either approach. Attempting to derive complete rule sets from inspection of scores has not yielded much insight into procedural aspects of composition. Perhaps the deeply unconscious nature of many procedural aspects of composition make them unavailable to introspection. Perhaps this explains why it took 900 years for the idea of formal generative methods to come to be taken seriously, in our century. It is possible to absorb unconsciously a particular style; but it is not clear that the rules of that style can then be made wholly conscious, and therefore formalizable, and therefore computable.

Musical modeling of historical styles has been frustrated in its search for complete rule sets for basic common-practice music. Species counterpoint and Bach-style chorale harmonization are simple styles that have been stable for about 300 years. The music of some late romantic composers stresses even the most capable modern music analysis systems to their breaking points. Students of even more recent composers, such as Boulez, Berio, Ligetti, and Stockhausen, will testify how much more difficult this music is to analyze even than the late romantic styles. Imagine the task of formalizing a rule set that captures the compositional practice of Stravinsky to the same degree as we have succeeded with Bach (and we haven't progressed very far with him).

Is Composing a Rule-Solving Problem?

As I discussed previously, Hiller and many others have modeled music composition as using prescriptive rules to discover valid musical sequences out of the total space of all musical sequences, much like a chess-playing computer program might attempt to find optimal strategies to beat an opponent by considering the space of all valid chess games. For this purpose, a more-or-less complete specification of the rules of composition is necessary in order to determine the valid sequences.

Let's conjecture for a moment that it is possible by some means to achieve a complete rule set for some artistic style; what then? Would it produce Art? I submit that art is not merely about following rules, though rules are its foundation. It is said of Renaissance composer Josquin des Pres, for instance, that he seemed to command the notes, not vice versa; he did not compose merely by finding correct solutions to the rules of counterpoint (Grout 1980). The rules were only a vehicle for his artistry, just as the rules of rhyming couplets were a vehicle for the poetry of Shakespeare. Simply satisfying the rules is only the beginning of art, not its goal. So the notion of an art form as a kind of rule-solving problem must be discarded; however, we must make sure we do not slip into the kind of thinking that Schillinger so correctly attacked: that the composer is Genius, and that Genius is above rules. What other approaches are there? Let us look again at the function of music in culture.

It would seem that the problem of emulating existing styles grows even larger when we must consider that a musical style does not exist in a vacuum but is based on the consensual experience of a whole culture, taking into account its past and its concurrent reality. It is precisely this cultural context, however, that provides the artist with the necessary hooks into the minds of his or her listeners. Expectation is the foundation of music; without it the listener hears only noise. In order for a listener to appreciate music of a particular culture, he or she must have an understanding of the rules of that music. But whereas awareness of the consensual rules is necessary, it is not sufficient. Were it sufficient, art would consist entirely of saying things people already understand. It is additionally necessary for the artist to play off different levels of structure by the means of expectancy violation, for at least two reasons. First, expectancy violation (that is, violation of what Bharucha and Todd, this volume, call "schematic expectancy") is necessary to keep the listener's attention engaged. Second, expectancy violation can, in the hands of a great artist, result in the communication of new ideas that reward our attention.

Therefore, it is not likely that musical styles can be isolated successfully by simple heuristics and introspection, nor can they be readily modeled as a rule-solving problem. More powerful theories and techniques are necessary, ones that can model expectation and surprise and that can generalize from their experiences to novel arrangements.

Connectionism and Music

It is easier to describe the static relationships between various elements of a composition (structural form), than it is to describe the actions (let alone the thought process) of a composer in producing such a structure. Part of the difficulty is simply the number of musical dimensions that must be simultaneously reconciled. Another part is that a good composer will continually combine material and ideas in novel ways in order to sustain attention to the composition in time to communicate better with listeners. The challenge to rule-based models of music is to allow the rules to interact with each other in novel situations. Since expectation and frustration in novel situations play such a key role in musical understanding, this is a critical and difficult problem. But Bharucha and Todd show in their chapter (Bharucha and Todd, this volume) that is is possible for a network to be trained to understand and anticipate common musical practices, and yet to learn to expect the exceptions to the norm that are embodied in actual compositions. That is, a connectionist network model can simultaneously memorize and generalize, these being two key elements in learning. Perhaps connectionism can show the way to techniques that do not have the liabilities of strictly formal systems.

Music Cognition

There are many deeply unconscious aspects of the processes of composing and performing and listening, as of all complex learned skills. Although the claim can be made that it should be possible to create artificial expert composers by raising the rules of the art form to consciousness—ferreting out the underlying rules through experiment and introspection—this has yet to be demonstrated. The traditional solution to understanding the compositional mind is to learn to be a composer oneself. But as the testimonies of composers and theorists over the centuries attest, this is not much help: diversity in undertanding of their craft is the only discernable consistency.

What becomes of a student's understanding of music theory after music theory classes are over? One would think that here, if anywhere, is the preeminent occasion for taking precognitive musical knowledge and raising it to consciousness. But the common experience is that the knowledge acquired originally in childhood by memorization and its attendant intuitive abstraction may be said to be sharpened and validated by formal training, though it is certainly not replaced by it. The fact that even mature theories of music are informal is strong evidence that the performer, the listener, and the composer do not operate principally as rule-based problem solvers.

Instead, imagine that strong association networks are formed in the musical mind such that, given a partial input (as during a performance), the pattern-completion mechanisms that are a natural consequence of the neuronal structure of the listener's mind consider the possible completions of that input against the expectancies of the current style. Through pattern-completion structures inherent in the brain, the listener anticipates the possible outcomes. The composer, understanding this predictive mechanism, manipulates these expectancies to his or her artistic aim.

The neuronal nature of the brain also helps explain how we manage to keep up with the number of simultaneous dimensions necessary to appreciate music. The brain is a massively parallel processing sytem. The conventional wisdom is that developing an expertise in music consists of acquiring a rule set, which then receives progressively more rules with experience. If the brain followed music by evaluating rule systems (which must to a certain extent be a sequential process), then the more experienced a musician became, the more constraints he or she would be required to resolve for each note heard, a process which would eventually exceed the capacity of the brain to follow a musical thought in real time. And since the constraints that we do know about in music mix levels in imprecise ways, there would neccessarily be an explosion of rules to cover all realistic cases. But it is a common experience that musical judgment for many tasks, such as improvisatory harmonization, actually becomes quicker, even as the musician gains experience, as more and more rules are learned. This could not be the case if human musical cognition required any substantial sequential arbitration among competing rule systems.

Musical Knowledge through Self-Organization

Besides providing an interesting model of human musical cognition network techniques can also help us further the work in the formalization of music by analysis of examples. Network techniques may be able to help discover musical rules in a way that will make them available to a formalization process. Insofar as one could subject a suitably capable network to the same constraints as a human composer learning the craft, it should be possible, theoretically, for the network to acquire automatically the same knowledge, but with the difference that the network should be much more amenable to fundtional decomposition than the human. Such a grand experiment may never be conducted, but other experiments are taking place on a more modest scale now, as the other chapters of this book demonstrate. In this approch, connectionism would be seen as continuing to derive procedural knowledge about composition from automatic analysis of existing works, like some of the traditional techniques already discussed. But it would be doing so with a minimum of prespecified knowledge and bias and with tools that can resolve and generalize about multidimensional correlations.

As Gjerdingen shows in his chapter (Gjerdingen, this volume), neural networks have a demonstrated ability to passively acquire musical knowledge simply from the principles of self-organizing systems, such as those developed by Stephen Grossberg (1982). Bharucha and Todd (this volume) have furthermore demonstrated that we need only postulate general principles of self-organization in order to model the otherwise seemingly contradictory practices of memorization and abstraction.

Conclusions

Theories can fail for a variety of reasons. A good sign that a theory is in danger is when one observes an explosion of rules when trying to explain a problem within the bounds of the theory. Copernicus observed the weakness of the theory that attempted to describe the orbits of planets by an infinite summation of epicycles. Newton formulated a mathematics of elliptical orbits based on gravitational attraction, and the epicyles, and the theories that created them, vanished. Connectionist techniques are able to avoid the combinatoric explosion problem associated with rule-based techniques of musical knowledge. They can also provide many other useful features as side effects, such as spontaneous generalization, pattern completion, and graceful degradation. Thus the theories of connectionism may be able to eliminate what we might call musical epicycles introduced by conventional models of musical knowledge.

Connectionism is a very pragmatic theory, in that it takes as its model something basic and incontrovertable, namely, the neuronal basis of the brain. Clearly it is still a research domain in its infancy. Current network architectures show a relatively poor ratio of generalizations to training examples needed when compared to humans. Work to date has focused on relatively straightforward aspects of music: finding the beat, the pitch, the key signature, and simple attributes of the form of the work. A criticism has been laid to connectionism that it may not scale any better than traditional artificial intelligence techniques as the problems to which it is applied grow more complex (Papert 1988). And for problems of any size, as Scarborough, Miller, and Jones (this volume) describe in their chapter, it is often difficult to investigate and interpret the results of a network, either to improve its performance or even to undertand it at all. Undoubtedly the search for more advanced network architectures will be focused on these problems.

Still, the inherent advantages of the connectionist approach are compelling, because one need only postulate general principles of self-organization with little or no domain-specific knowledge in order to begin modeling arbitrary musical processes. Thus we can proceed with an objectivity heretofore difficult to obtain.

Epilogue: A Further Artistic Question

Up to now, I have described automata as unreflective tools of composers or researchers. I have used such verbs as *produce* and *generate* to describe compositions made by automata, and the verb *create* for human compositions.

But is there really a categorical difference between compositions created by humans and those produced by automata? Could there be an automaton that could pass a Turing test for music? Alan Turing proposed a test for determining whether a system had artificial intelligence: A subject sitting at a terminal is asked to determine whether he or she is communicating with another human in the next room or with a computer. The subject can ask any questions. If subjects consistently guess that the responding entity is a human, but it is in fact a computer, a reasonable person would be forced to consider that the machine had intelligence. A musical Turing test might be easier for a computer to pass someday, since music is a very abstract artistic medium. But even if a system passed a musical Turing test, that would prove no more than that a reasonable facsimile of human musical functioning could be constructed using computational means. It would say nothing about several other questions, taken up next.

There are really at least three questions here: First, can musical automata be constructed that exhibit human behavior to a sufficient degree as to exhibit intelligence? This would be the computer scientist's test. Second, can musical automata be constructed that successfully model our understanding of human musical cognition? This would be the cognitive psychologist's test. Third, can human musical cognition be represented computationally at all? This would be the philosopher's question. Whether computers can successfully approximate human musical cognition says next to nothing about the theoretical prospects of characterizing musical cognition via computations. Peter Kugel (1990) expressed this point when he said, "The argument that computing machines can simulate all information processing that [humans] can do well enough to 'fool' people is no better founded than a parallel claim that $\sqrt{2}$ must be a rational number because we can produce a rational approximation so close to its real value that it would fool anyone." (p.13)

It is beyond the scope of this chapter to address these questions any more than I have. Even without considering the intelligence level of compositional automata, however, there are still other important points to be made.

When using composing automata under current practices, a composer is essentially operating at a metalevel where he or she creates a process, possibly guides it during its execution, possibly selects or rejects the results, and integrates the results into the compositional fabric. In this case it may be fair to say that the results of an automaton are part of a creation and it deserves some of the credit (the letters by Laske, Todd, and Loy at the end of this volume address this issue of the place of connectionist techniques in the creative process of composition). But what of, for instance, Hiller's *Illiac Suite* experiments, where all he did was to select different runs of his automaton with neither guidance nor editing? What of a chance-based composition of composer John Cage, where the notes are selected by the throw of coins? How much credit does an automaton deserve?

In Cage's example, the automaton is not a computation but is a choice made by Nature, observed meaningfully by the composer. Cage's answer might be to say that the chance aspects of his work are a result of (capital C) Creation: where no human agent makes the selections, Cage would attribute the choices ultimately to Creation, considered as an oracle (Cage 1961). Cage's musical philosophy is precisely to turn over the role of composer to the cosmos, to give it all the credit. Although this is a fine sentiment, it is generally less easy to penetrate the meaning in Creation's choices than in those of a human. One needs a predictive theory to interpret them, and as the supplicants at Delphi (such as Oedipus) demonstrated, this is hard to do. One can simply appreciate them, however, as one does a mountain or sunset.

Finally, consider the difference between compositional automata and human composers in the light of what is communicated through music. The generic meaning of composition is the combining of elements in patterns, similar to the composing of mathematical functions. Clearly, by this definition, automata can compose. But where those patterns are the result of some stochastic or deterministic process, we would tend to say that the patterns were generated, or produced, because the meaning of the pattern is a function of the process used to produce it: analyze the music it produces and what you get is the reverse-engineered automaton. On the other hand, when those patterns are the result of the considered activity of a human mind, we tend to say that the patterns were created, because the meaning of the patterns is related to the considerations of their creator. Observing the patterns, we recover those considerations and derive satisfaction from the insights thus shared. The considerations need not be intellectual but can touch on any aspect of experience.

The above points suggest that it is a reflexive quality based on meaning that distinguishes a creative act from a generative one. The meaning communicated by a formal system is, essentially, itself. The meaning communicated in a creative act lies beyond the created product itself. Its meaning is the tying together of previously unrelated ideas and experiences in the mind of the listener and connecting them to ideas and experiences in the mind of the composer that led to the creation.

So we come back to the question posed at the beginning of this section again: Can automata—in particular, artificial neural networks—create in the sense developed above? The simplest answer is: Yes, if they have something to say beyond simply expressing their own formal structure; otherwise no. Unfortunately, this simple statement doesn't go very far, especially in the case of artificial neural networks, which can be modeled as having "experiences" and "ideas." However, the reflexive aspects of current artificial neural systems are still dominant: networks "create" because they are designed to do so. To model creativity itself, creativity would have to be an emergent property. Otherwise, it is simply the vicarious expression of some other's creativity designed into the system (see also Lewis, this volume, for another perspective on this question).

These comments only focus on the philosophical level of machine models of human artistic expression. As I mentioned before, there are numerous other perspectives from which to view music and composition, for example, from the point of view of computer science, psychology, musicology, etc., each of which comes with its own set of questions. From these varied viewpoints, as the chapters in this volume demonstrate, computer-based—and especially connectionist—models of musical behavior may be very successful indeed.

References

Bharucha, J. J. and P. M. Todd. This volume. "Modeling the Perception of Tonal Structure with Neural Nets."

Buxton, B., W. Reeves, R. Baecker, and L. Mezei. 1978. "The Use of Hierarchy and Instance in a Data Structure for Computer Music." *Computer Music Journal* 2(4): 10–20.

Buxton, B., R. Sniderman, W. Reeves, S. Patel, and R. Baecker. 1979. "The Evolution of the SSSP Score-editing Tools." *Computer Music Journal* 3(4): 14–25.

Byrd, D. 1984. "Music Notation by Computer." Ph.D. diss., Indiana University Department of Computer Science.

Cage, J. 1961. *Silence.* Cambridge, Massachusetts: MIT Press.

Chafe, C., B. Mont-Reynaud, and L. Rush. 1982. "Toward an Intelligent Editor of Digital Audio: Recognition of Musical Constructs." *Computer Music Journal* 6(1): 30–41.

Clynes, M. 1984. "Secrets of Life in Music." *Proceedings of the International Computer Music Conference.* San Francisco: Computer Music Association, pp. 225–232.

Cope, D. 1990. "Pattern Matching as an Engine for the Computer Simulation of Musical Style." *Proceedings of the International Computer Music Conference.* San Francisco: Computer Music Association, pp. 288–291.

Dannenberg, R., and G. Bloch. 1985. "Realtime Computer Accompaniment of Keyboard Performances." *Proceedings of the International Computer Music Conference.* San Francisco: Computer Music Association, pp. 279–290.

Ebcioglu, K. 1984. "An Expert System for Schenkerian Synthesis of Chorales in the Style of J. S. Bach." *Proceedings of the International Computer Music Conference.* San Francisco: Computer Music Association, pp. 135–142.

Fux, J. J. 1725. *Gradus ad Parnassum.* Reprinted in 1943 as *Steps to Parnassus.* New York: W.W. Norton.

Gabor, D. 1947. "Acoustical Quanta and the Theory of Hearing." *Nature* 159:591–594.

Gill, S. 1963. "A Technique for the Composition of Music in a Computer." *The Computer Journal* 6:129–133.

Gjerdingen, R. O. This volume. "Using Connectionist Models to Explore Complex Musical Patterns."

Grossberg, S. 1982. *Studies of Mind and Brain: Neural Principles of Learning, Perception, Development, Cognition, and Motor control.* Boston: Reidel/Kluwer.

Grout, D. J. 1980. *A History of Western Music.* New York: W.W. Norton.

Guido of Arezzo. 1026. "Guidonis Aretini Micrologus." In J. Smits van Waesberghe, ed. *Corpus Scriptorum de Musica IV.* Rome: American Institute of Musicology. Printed in 1955.

Hiller, L., and L. Isaacson. 1959. *Experimental Music.* New York: McGraw-Hill.

Kirchmeyer, H. 1963. "On the Historical Constitution of a Rationalistic Music." *Die Reihe* 8:11–24.

Koenig, G. M. 1970a. "Project One." *Electronic Music Reports* 2. Utrecht: Institute of Sonology.

Koenig, G. M. 1970b. "Project Two." *Electronic Music Reports* 3. Utrecht: Institute of Sonology.

Kohonen, T., P. Laine, K. Tiits, and K. Torkkola. This volume. "A Nonheuristic Automatic Composing Method."

Kugel, P. 1990. "Myhill's Thesis: There's More than Computing in Musical Thinking." *Computer Music Journal* 14(3):13–25.

Laske, O. 1973. "Towards a Musical Intelligence System: OBSERVER." *Numus-West* 1(4):11ff.

Lerdahl, F., and R. Jackendoff. 1983. *A Generative Theory of Tonal Music.* Cambridge, Massachusetts: MIT Press.

Lewis, J. P. This volume. "Creation By Refinement and the Problem of Algorithmic Music Composition."

Loy, G. 1989. "Composing With Computers—A Survey of Some Compositional Formalisms and Music Programming Languages." In M.V. Matthews and J.R. Pierce, eds. *Current Directions in Computer Music Research.* Cambridge, Massachusetts: MIT Press, pp. 291–396.

Mathews, M. V., and L. Rosler. 1968. "Graphical Language for the Scores of Computer-generated Sounds." *Perspectives of New Music* 6:92–118.

Meyer, L. 1956. *Emotion and Meaning in Music.* Chicago: Chicago University Press.

Moore, F. R. 1989. Private communication.

Moore, F. R. 1990. *Elements of Computer Music.* Englewood Cliffs, N.J.: Prentice-Hall.

Moorer, J. A. 1972. "Music and Computer Composition." *Communications of the ACM* 15.

Moorer, J. A. 1975. "On the Segmentation and Analysis of Continuous Musical Sound by Digital Computer." Ph.D. diss., Stanford University Department of Computer Science.

Myhill, J. 1952, "Some Philosophical Implications of Mathematical Logic: Three Classes of Ideas." *Review of Metaphysics* 6(2):165–198.

Papert, S. 1988. "One AI or Many?" *Daedalus* 118(1): 1–14.

Perle, G., and P. Lansky. 1981. *Serial Composition and Atonality.* Los Angeles: University of California Press.

Potter, G. M. 1971. "The Role of Chance in Contemporary Music." Ph.D. diss., Indiana University Department of Music. Available through University Microfilms.

Roads, C. 1979. "Grammars as Representations of Music." *Computer Music Journal* 3(1):48–55.

Rodet, X., Y. Potard, and J.-B. Barrière. 1984. "The CHANT Project: From the Synthesis of the Singing Voice to Synthesis in General." *Computer Music Journal* 8(3): 15–31.

Rumelhart, D. E., and J. L. McClelland, eds. 1986. *Parallel Distributed Processing: Explorations in the Microstructure of Cognition.* Cambridge, Massachusetts: MIT Press.

Scarborough, D. L., B. O. Miller, and J. A. Jones. This volume. "Connectionist Models for Tonal Analysis."

Scheidt, D. J. 1985. "A Prototype Implementation of a Generative Mechanism for Music Composition." M.S. Thesis. Kingston, Ontario, Canada: Queen's University Department of Computer and Information Science.

Schenker, H. 1906. *Newe Musikalische Theorien und Phantasien.* Universal Editions. Published between 1906 and 1935 in two volumes.

Schillinger, J. 1948. *The Mathematical Basis of the Arts.*

New York: The Philosophical Library.
Schillinger, J. 1978. *The Schillinger System of Musical Composition.* New York: Da Capo Press.
Schottstaedt, B. 1984. "Automatic Species Counterpoint." *Technical Report STAN-M-19.* Stanford: Stanford University, Center for Computer Research in Music and Acoustics.
Sundberg, J., and A. Friberg. 1986. "A Lisp Environment for Creating and Applying Rules for Musical Performance." *Proceedings of the International Computer Music Conference.* San Francisco: Computer Music Association, pp. 1–4.
Tenney, J., and L. Polansky. 1980. "Temporal Gestalt Perception in Music." *Journal of Music Theory* 24(2): 205–241.
Thomas, M. T. 1985. "VIVACE: A Rule-based AI System for Composition." *Proceedings of the International Computer Music Conference.* San Francisco: Computer Music Association, pp. 267–274.
Vercoe, B., and M. Puckette. 1985. "Synthetic Rehearsal: Training the Synthetic Performer." *Proceedings of the International Computer Music Conference.* San Francisco: Computer Music Association, pp. 275–278.
Winograd, T. 1968. "Linguistics and the Computer Analysis of Tonal Harmony." *Journal of Music Theory* 12:2–49.
Xenakis, I. 1971. *Formalized Music.* Bloomington: Indiana University Press.
Zarlino, G. 1558. *Instiutioni Harmoniche.* Republished in 1968 as *The Art of Counterpoint.* New York: W. W. Norton.

II

Perception and Cognition

Introduction

Connectionist models are finding increasing use in many domains within psychology and cognitive science. Their ability to learn and store information, satisfy multiple constraints simultaneously, categorize stimuli, abstract features, create new representations, complete patterns, and generalize to novel inputs in ways akin to human and animal behavior makes these systems particularly attractive for modeling a variety of phenomena. Music perception and cognition require this same set of abilities, and so it is not surprising that connectionist models are well suited to capturing aspects of musical behavior as well. The models presented in the chapters in this part cover the low levels of pitch perception to the formation of high-order musical concepts, from identifying a particular instrument being played to understanding a distorted rhythm. Widely varying techniques, from standard back-propagation architectures to special duration-adjusting networks, are used to study these behaviors. But taken together, this variety serves to demonstrate the power of subsymbolic, self-organizing, parallel distributed processing systems for increasing our understanding of music perception and cognition.

One of the most natural ways of thinking about what connectionist systems do is as processing patterns: classifying and categorizing them, modifying them, and associating them with other patterns. Much of what goes on in human musical behavior can be thought about in these same ways, as the chapters in this part demonstrate. Low-level perceptual processes are particularly suited to this network-modeling approach, as Sano and Jenkins show in their model of pitch perception. Starting with proposed inputs from the cochlear nerves in response to a complex tone, their network proceeds through levels of just-noticeable-difference frequency discrimination, competitive semitone computation, pitch determination via harmonic unification, and normalized pitch-class and octave determination. These final distributed patterns are then cleaned up and classified as a particular single pitch-class and octave by a back-propagation network trained for this task. Jenkins' addendum extends this work to inputs of multiple tones, allowing more complex classifications of intervals and chords.

Scarborough, Miller, and Jones present a network model that begins with the pitch-class units that Sano and Jenkins conclude with, and uses these as time-decaying inputs to determine first chords and then keys that occur in a piece of music. This tonality determination is extended by a network structure for mapping pitch inputs to normalized scale degrees depending on the determined key; such normalization is necessary to account for people's ability to recognize melodies when transposed to a different key. Their addendum presents the advantages of this simple linear network model of tonal induction, including its correspondence to recent experimental data, as well as some of the disadvantages caused by simplifying assumptions.

In the next chapter, Laden and Keefe compare different ways of representing pitch in connectionist systems. They use a chord classification task to judge the merits of each method, training a network to classify inputs in each pitch representation as either major, minor, or diminished triad chords. A cognitively inspired representation, using only the pitch classes present in each input chord, is compared to two psychoacoustically based schemes, one using the harmonics of each pitch in the chord, and the other using the subharmonics of each pitch, according to Terhardt's theory of musical perception. The authors find that the psychoacoustically based representations lead to better performance at chord classification and furthermore allow generalization to inverted and incomplete chord inputs. In their addendum, Laden and Keefe extend their model by using the harmonic-complex input representation in network models for pitch-class and pitch-height extraction. These networks can generalize across input harmonic spectra from different musical instruments and can process multiple input tones simultaneously to some extent. The outputs of these low-level networks can then be used to drive a higher-level chord classification network, so that both pitches and chord types can be extracted from the same network inputs.

Bharucha's goal is to develop a model of human music perception that can account for the data from psychological and neurological research in this area, while satisfying the structural and functional constraints also known to hold in the human case. He begins by outlining the aspects of such a system, which can reasonably be modeled with a learning paradigm that uses a teacher, and which must use unsupervised learning or hardwiring. He proceeds to discuss the psychophysical, cognitive, and neurological research results that bear on the representation of pitch appropriate for connectionist models of human music perception and then compares a variety of proposed network representations—including those used by other authors throughout this book—in light of these considerations. No single one of these pitch representations suffices to cover the known data alone, he shows, and so the model of pitch, chord, and key perception and memory that Bharucha next proposes relies on a combination of spectral representations, pitch-height representations, pitch-class representations, and invariant pitch-class representations to meet the empirical requirements. Finally, Bharucha shows how the perception portion of this model, called MUSACT, can develop appropriate chord and key units through a process of unsupervised competitive self-organization, again in keeping with the psychological constraints on learning described earlier in his chapter. The memory portion of this model, which accounts for expectancy creation and violation in music perception, is described in the chaper by Bharucha and Todd.

The self-organization of the perceptual structures of tonality is further explored by Leman in his chapter on the development of tonal semantics. Leman first discusses the mental structures of tonal perception that have been proposed by psychologists and neuroscientists. One of these structures, the mental map, is particularly appealing for certain aspects of tonality. Leman presents a connectionist method of modeling such structures, the Kohonen Feature Map algorithm, which takes high-dimensional representations of input data and reduces them to a two-dimensional map through a process of competitive excitement and inhibition. This map organizes itself so that similar inputs are clustered to spatially nearby points. When applied to input data corresponding to musical chords represented according to Terhardt's subharmonic spectra (as used by Laden and Keefe), the algorithm produces maps that display important psychological structures such as the circle of fifths. The course of the maps' self-organization over time can yield hypotheses about infant development of tonal structures and about the neurological structures we might look for in the brain. Leman also describes how the ongoing behavior of a feature map responding to chords could lead to the emergence of higher-level concepts of musical patterns and keys.

The influences of context on musical perception are addressed by Bharucha and Todd in their chapter, which focuses in particular on tonal implication and expectation. The authors first review psychological research showing that tonal expectancy—judgments about what pitch or chord should follow after the presentation of context pitches or chords—must be acquired through learning. As a result, neural networks are the most appropriate psychological paradigm for modeling tonal expectancy, because of their parsimonious ability to account for its acquisition. Bharucha and Todd distinguish two types of tonal expectancy: schematic expectancies, culturally based structures which indicate events typically following familiar contexts; and veridical expectancies, instance-based structures indicating the particular event that follows a particular known context. Schematic expectancies can be modeled with auto-associative networks, hierarchical self-organizing networks, or sequential networks. Veridical expectancies can be captured by a sequential network that includes sequence-distinguishing inputs. But Bharucha and Todd further reveal that such a sequential network, if trained on a variety of individual musical sequences, can also induce schematic expectancies that can be revealed through a process called cascaded activation. Thus their model accounts for the passive construction of culturally based schematic expectancies solely through learning the veridical expectancies corresponding to particular musical sequences from the culture.

Gjerdingen presents another self-organizing connectionist method, Grossberg's adaptive resonance theory (ART), as a means of modeling the development of more complex musical concepts. Like the

Kohonen Feature Map, ART uses a layer of input (feature) units that are competitively categorized by a layer (or more) of higher-level (concept) units. ART models add top-down feedback from the concept layer(s) to the feature layer, however, so that new inputs are processed in the context of previously learned and processed patterns. Gjerdingen's particular system uses this setup to learn musically valid categorizations of complex patterns appearing in passages of Mozart, based on a set of time-decaying input features that include melodic and bass scale degrees, contours and inflections, and inner voices.Though relatively simple in structure, the ART network is nonetheless able to derive categories corresponding to various cadences and voice-leading combinations. By adding further higher-level categorization layers at the top of this model, and enhancing the input representation at the bottom, still more complex musical concepts—corresponding to larger structures in the music—can be learned and detected, as Gjerdingen describes in his addendum.

Finally, Desain and Honing depart from the realm of pitch and tonality perception to consider the perception of musical time. In particular, they propose a connectionist approach for quantizing durations in a musical passage. Their method uses simple local interactions among neighboring durations, attempting to create integer ratios between them. As a result, this method proves to be much more robust than competing techniques, which are increasingly complex and knowledge intensive. The connectionist time quantizer is useful as a model of human performance, exhibiting graceful degradation in the face of more and more complex rhythms and categorizing variations in duration sequences in a way comparable to human listeners. But such quantization is also useful in applied settings such as the automatic transcription of music scores from performances. Desain and Honing include a set of Lisp routines to implement their system and present a variety of diagnostic tools and mathematical analyses in their addendum to aid further in investigating its behavior, providing a valuable example of the efforts necessary to understand the often complex workings of all of these connectionist systems.

Hajime Sano
741 Mar Vista Ave.
Pasadena, California 91104 USA
sano@vlsi.jpl.nasa.gov

B. Keith Jenkins
Department of Electrical Engineering
University of Southern California
Los Angeles, California 90089-0272 USA
jenkins@brand.usc.edu

A Neural Network Model for Pitch Perception

Introduction

In this paper we will examine the human ear—and cochlear mechanics in particular—in order to better understand the signals sent to the brain. We will also discuss some theories of pitch perception. We propose a neural network model to examine the sensitivity discrepancy in general and pitch perception in particular, with emphasis on the neural representation of pitch perception. The resulting model concentrates on the preprocessing of the auditory stimulus, reducing it to a simple pattern classification problem.

Western music defines an octave as an interval that represents a frequency ratio of 2 : 1. The most commonly used scale is the dodecaphonic (twelve-tone), well-tempered scale. It divides the octave into 12 evenly spaced halftones, 6 percent ($\sqrt[12]{2}$) apart in frequency.

Frequency detection is performed by an array of sensory hairs in the cochlea in the ear. The characteristic frequency of these hairs depends on their location along the cochlea and increases monotonically along the array. Each hair behaves as a bandpass filter with a bandwidth of approximately 10 percent of the characteristic frequency. The human auditory system is sensitive to as little as .3 percent to 1.5 percent changes at certain frequencies (Evans 1982). This sensitivity discrepancy between the human auditory system and its components may be explained by neural processing performed by the brain on the output from the cochlea.

Computer Music Journal, Vol. 13, No. 3, Fall 1989,

The Human Ear

The human ear may be divided into the outer ear, the middle ear, and the inner ear, as shown in Fig. 1. The outer ear consists of the pinna and external auditory meatus (canal). It provides a 10–20 dB boost in the speech frequencies (2–5 kHz) and aids in directional location of the stimulus. The middle ear consists primarily of the tympanic membrane (eardrum), malleus (hammer), incus (anvil), and stapes (stirrup). Their primary function is impedance matching of air to inner ear fluid. An estimated 60 percent of the energy is transmitted through the middle ear, compared to only 3 percent if direct coupling were used (Evans 1982).

The inner ear, which contains very hard bone, consists of a series of passages, fluid, and the cochlea. The cochlea is a snail-shaped spiral wrapped around the cochlear nerve trunk. It has three longitudinally oriented channels within: the scala vestibuli, the scala tympani, and the scala media, as shown in Fig. 2. The scala vestibuli lies in front, starts at the oval window, and accepts the acoustic input. The scala tympani lies behind, terminates at the round window, and releases intracochlear pressure. The middle channel, the scala media (cochlear duct), contains the organ of Corti. The organ of Corti—the acoustic sensory epithelium—contains sensory hairs that are connected to the cochlear nerve fibers. There is a single row of inner hairs that impart frequency information, and three to five rows of outer hairs that serve as an *automatic gain control* (AGC).

Cochlear Mechanics

Air pressure variations are focused by the outer ear. The middle ear serves as an impedance matcher,

Fig. 1. The human ear (Evans 1982).

Fig. 2. Schematic functional diagram of middle ear and uncoiled cochlea. (Evans 1982).

Fig. 1

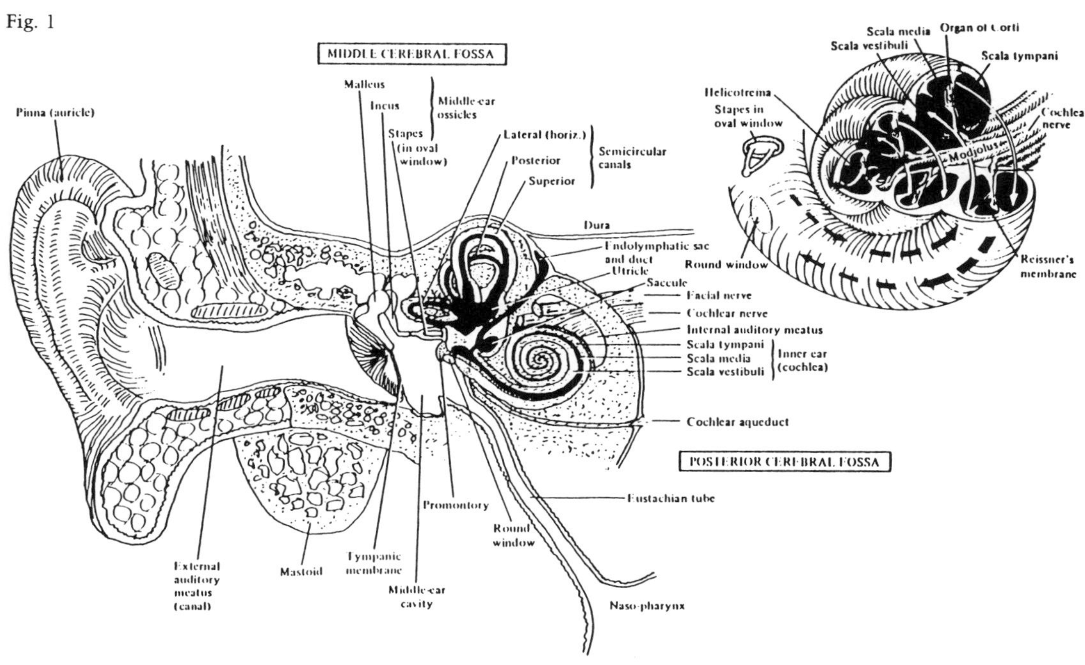

Fig. 2

Fig. 3. The fundamental frequency of C3 (125 Hz) and seven of its harmonics in common music notation. The seven harmonics (and their closest notes) are: C4 (250 Hz), G4 (375 Hz), C5 (500 Hz), E5 (625 Hz), G5 (750 Hz), B♭5 (875 Hz), C6 (1000 Hz). (de Boer 1974).

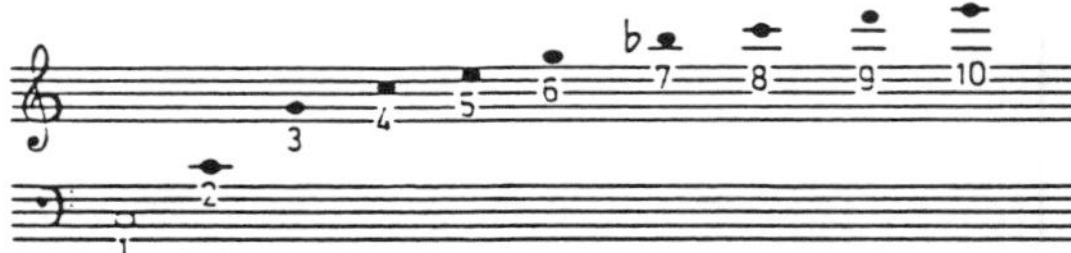

transmitting these pressure variations to the cochlea, where they are then propagated as waves travelling along the scala media. The waves travel from the base to the tip (basal to apical ends). They grow in amplitude to a peak and then collapse. The point of collapse depends on the stimulus frequency—high frequencies at the basal end, low frequencies at the tip (helicotrema). The inner hair cells are triggered by these waves.

The outer hair cells act as an AGC on the waves, greatly increasing the sensitivity of the range of intensity. The inner hairs and afferent nerve fibers act as a cascade of low-order, linear, bandpass filters. These filters have a Q value of approximately 10 for frequencies greater than 500 Hz, where

$$Q = \frac{\text{characteristic frequency}}{\text{bandwidth}}.$$

Each filter then is only sensitive to a bandwidth that is 10 percent of its characteristic frequency. In contrast, the *just noticeable difference* (JND) versus frequency curve for humans is .3 percent for intermediate frequencies (500 : 2 kHz), and 1.5 percent at 10 kHz. Musical halftone intervals are 6 percent, and quarter-tone intervals are 3 percent. The brain obviously processes the low-grade information received from the ear to greatly increase its spectral resolution.

Pitch Perception Theories

There are two theories of how pitch discrimination works. The *place model* states that the frequency of stimulus dictates which inner hair cells along the array get activated, with high frequencies stimulating the basal end and low frequencies stimulating the helicotrema end. The *periodicity model* states that neural discharges are proportional to the frequency of stimulus. Little is known about the actual mechanism of the periodicity model.

Any musical instrument (except a sine wave oscillator) produces complex waveforms for a given note consisting of the fundamental frequencies and weighted sums of harmonics. In extreme cases like the oboe, there is very little fundamental signal present.

In the analytical mode of pitch perception, each component is heard individually. The more familiar synthetic mode allows the listener to hear all components as a unified pitch, even in the absence of the fundamental and some of the harmonics, as seen in Fig. 3 (de Boer 1974; Evans 1982). The apparent fundamental is called virtual or residue pitch, and the characteristic sound generated by that particular spectrum of frequencies is the timbre.

The Neural Net Model

This neural net model is based on the following four assumptions: (1) we use the place model for frequency discrimination; (2) we use the synthetic mode of pitch perception; (3) our stimulus levels are reasonable, such that the linear bandpass filters are not saturated causing leakage into adjoining filters; and (4) the input will be single complex tones. The model is not meant to handle multiple note inputs. The network model will identify both pitch and octave of the complex tone. No timbral qualities will be identified.

Detailed modeling is based on the portion of the frequency spectrum where the JND versus frequency curve is linear, between 500–2000 Hz, and extended to the whole range of human hearing (approximately 30–8000 Hz), as demonstrated in Figs. 4 and 5 (Evans 1982). Since the interval 500–2000 Hz covers two octaves, and human hearing spans approximately eight octaves, a factor of four increase in complexity is assumed whenever the model is extended to the full range.

Three stages of preprocessing are utilized to reduce the level of information used as input to a back propagation network. The first stage has three layers, the first of which models the output of the cochlea via the nerve fibers. These are reduced by nonoverlapping fan-in to the second layer, the JND

Fig. 4. Isophon curves plotted as a function of sound pressure level. Frequency ranges covered by piano, voice laryngeal vibration fundamentals and resonances, vowels, and consonants are shown below the frequency scale. (Evans 1982).

Fig. 5. Relative discrimination limen (JND) versus frequency. (Evans 1982).

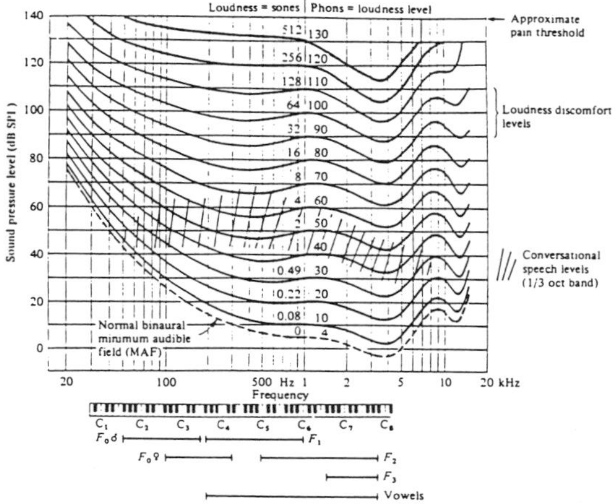

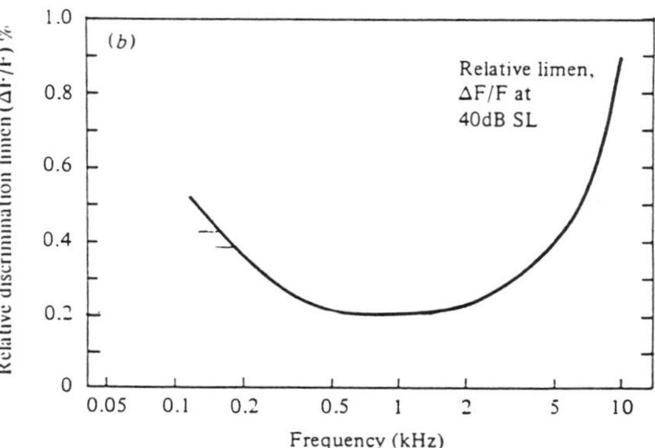

buckets (or neurons), as in Fig. 6a. An overlapping fan-in reduces these JND buckets to semitone buckets—the third layer—for the well-tempered, twelve-tone scale, as illustrated in Fig. 6b. This step is culturally dependent. The semitone buckets employ an on-center, off-adjacent, competitive learning scheme to determine that only one of several adjacent notes in a harmonic is associated with the stimulus input, as in Fig. 6c.

There are 28,000 fibers that carry cochlea output to the brain (Lazzaro 1988). Human hearing range is about eight octaves. Assuming that the fibers carry frequency information logarithmically, and since the range from 500–2000 Hz spans two octaves, it is assumed that 7000 fibers are dedicated to this frequency range. This assumption is made for the simplicity of this model, and may or may not be biologically accurate. The spacing for the nerve fibers, called x here, is computed assuming logarithmic spacing as follows:

$$500 \text{ Hz} * x^{7000} = 2000 \text{ Hz}$$

so that

$$x = \sqrt[7000]{4} \approx 1.0002.$$

This can be interpreted as saying that the characteristic frequency of two adjacent nerve fibers differs by a multiplicative factor of 1.0002, or .02 percent. The fibers are modeled as binary exciters, as is the first layer of neurons. When a fiber is excited, the corresponding first layer neuron is also excited. In this two-octave frequency range, the JND versus frequency curve is approximately constant at .3 percent (Evans 1982, p. 318). This .3 percent JND curve is employed over the whole range of human hearing for the simplicity of the model. Biologically, the JND curve increases towards the limits of the hearing range as shown in Fig. 5 (Evans 1982). Computing the number of JND buckets, n

$$500 \text{ Hz} * (1.003)^n = 2000 \text{ Hz},$$

$$1.003^n = 4,$$

$$n = \frac{\log 4}{\log 1.003} \approx 463.$$

We see that there are 463 JND buckets in this frequency range. The JND bucket neurons are also binary, but are excited by consensus. With a threshold of 7.5, if more than half of the inputs are excited, the JND bucket neuron will be too. There are 24 semitone buckets, with a 6 percent frequency spacing between semitones:

$$2 \text{ octaves} = 24 \text{ semitones},$$

$$500 \text{ Hz} * x^{24} = 2000 \text{ Hz},$$

$$x^{24} = 4,$$

$$x = \sqrt[24]{4} \approx 1.06.$$

Fig. 6. Preprocessing stage 1, layers 1 and 2—nonoverlapping fan-in from cochlea nerve fibers to JND buckets (a). Preprocessing stage 1, layers 2 and 3—overlapping fan-in from JND buckets to semitone buckets. Nonoverlapping portion is indicated by darker shading (b). Preprocessing stage 1, layer 3—on-center, off-adjacent competitive interconnections for determining harmonic associated with input (c).

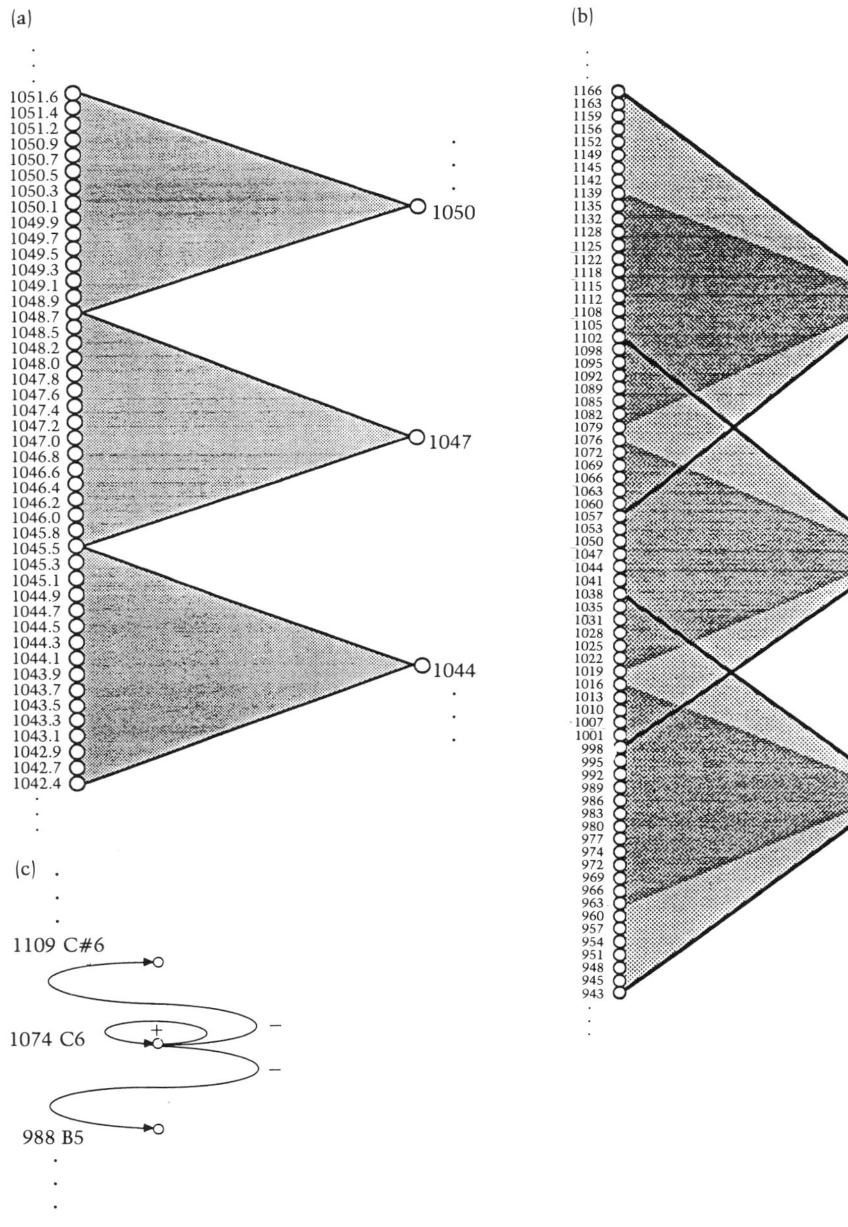

Table 1. Number and spacing of buckets (neurons) in each layer of first preprocessing stage within the constant JND frequency range (500–2000 Hz)

layer	*1: nerve fibers*	*2: JND buckets*	*3: semitone buckets*
number	7000	463	24
spacing (Δ%)	.02	.3	6

The semitone bucket neurons are additive, so that each one counts how many excitatory inputs it has. The "scores" of each neuron are then used in the competitive interconnections to determine which is the most likely harmonic of the input stimulus. Table 1 summarizes the number of buckets, or neurons, in each layer of the first preprocessing stage.

There is a 15:1, nonoverlap fan-in between the 7000 nerve fibers and 463 JND buckets of the first two layers. This fan-in quantizes the excited nerve fibers to the smallest level of frequency sensitivity in human hearing, as was presented in Fig. 6a. From 463 JND buckets to 24 semitone buckets is a 19:1 reduction. Since each cochlea inner hair is a linear bandpass filter with a Q of 10 percent for frequencies above 500 Hz (Evans 1982), there is a considerable amount of imprecision in response to stimulus. For example, a single sinusoidal signal with a frequency of 1047 Hz (C6) causes hair cells from 998–1102 Hz to respond.

$$x \pm 5\% = 1047 \text{ Hz},$$

$$1.05\ x_1 = 1047 \text{ Hz},\ .95\ x_2 = 1047 \text{ Hz},$$

$$x_1 = 998 \text{ Hz},\ x_2 = 1102 \text{ Hz}.$$

With the 19:1, nonoverlapping fan-in between the second and third layers, 1047 Hz would fan in from 1019–1076 Hz. Increasing the fan-in region to 998–1102 Hz introduces a nonlinearity into the system and helps smooth the transition region between semitones. This results in about a 40 percent overlap at each end of the fan-in. In Fig. 6b, the darkly shaded area represents the 19:1 nonoverlapping fan-in region. The overlapping fan-in region is bounded by the bold lines and is the union of the darkly and lightly shaded regions.

The third layer of the first stage—the semitone buckets—has some competitive interconnections (on-center, off-adjacent) built in between adjacent semitone buckets to ensure that only one of several adjacent semitone buckets is the winner (as shown in Fig 6c). It is especially important in cases where the stimulus tone falls in the transition areas between notes. Table 2 shows some first iteration scores at the semitone buckets for single, simple input stimulus in the neighborhood of 1047 Hz (C6).

The second preprocessing stage performs the synthetic mode pitch unification. Each of the 96 buckets in the eight octaves of human hearing range are tied together with their upper harmonics. Figure 7 shows pitch unification for C3 (125 Hz) and its three lowest harmonics from Fig. 3. These 96 halftones are generally perceived as repeating 12-note octaves. The majority of chordal emotional affect is related to the relative positions of notes within an octave, not to which octaves they are in. In stage three (illustrated in Fig. 8) the 96 absolute notes are mapped to a normalized 12-note octave, and the octave height is stored separately, thereby stratifying the tone and octave information.

The 96 class halftone set has now been reduced to a 12 class set (tone within an octave) and an 8 class set (octave). The tonal data is then fed into a 12 class separating, autoassociative, fully connected back propagation neural network, as can be seen in Fig. 9. Initially, the system will require supervised training to set up the twelve bucket octave, but in time, it should be able to perform unsupervised training to learn to discriminate the twelve notes in a musical scale. Similarly, the octave information may be fed into an eight class back propagation network. Figure 10 shows a block diagram of the entire system.

Comments and Further Questions

Will the network handle multiple inputs? That depends on the relationship of the multiple notes. If they are arranged so that their components are close in frequency, probably not. It would be interesting to study how many multiple stimuli the human auditory system can process and differentiate.

Fig. 7. Preprocessing stage 2—pitch unification requires tying together a note with its upper harmonics.

Fig. 8. Preprocessing stage 3—stratification of tone and octave information.

Fig. 9. A 12 class separating, autoassociative, fully connected back propagation neural network.

Fig. 10. Block diagram of the entire pitch perception neural network.

Table 2. Input stimulus and corresponding output scores at first iteration (Asterisk (*) denotes winning semitone bucket neuron.)

Input (Hz)	*Responding JND bucket neurons (Hz)*	*1177 Hz (D6)*	*1109 Hz (C♯6)*	*1047 Hz (C6)*	*988 Hz (B5)*
1031	982–1085	0	10	29*	19
1047	998–1102	0	15	34*	14
1076	1025–1133	0	24	25*	6
1112	1059–1171	9	34*	14	0

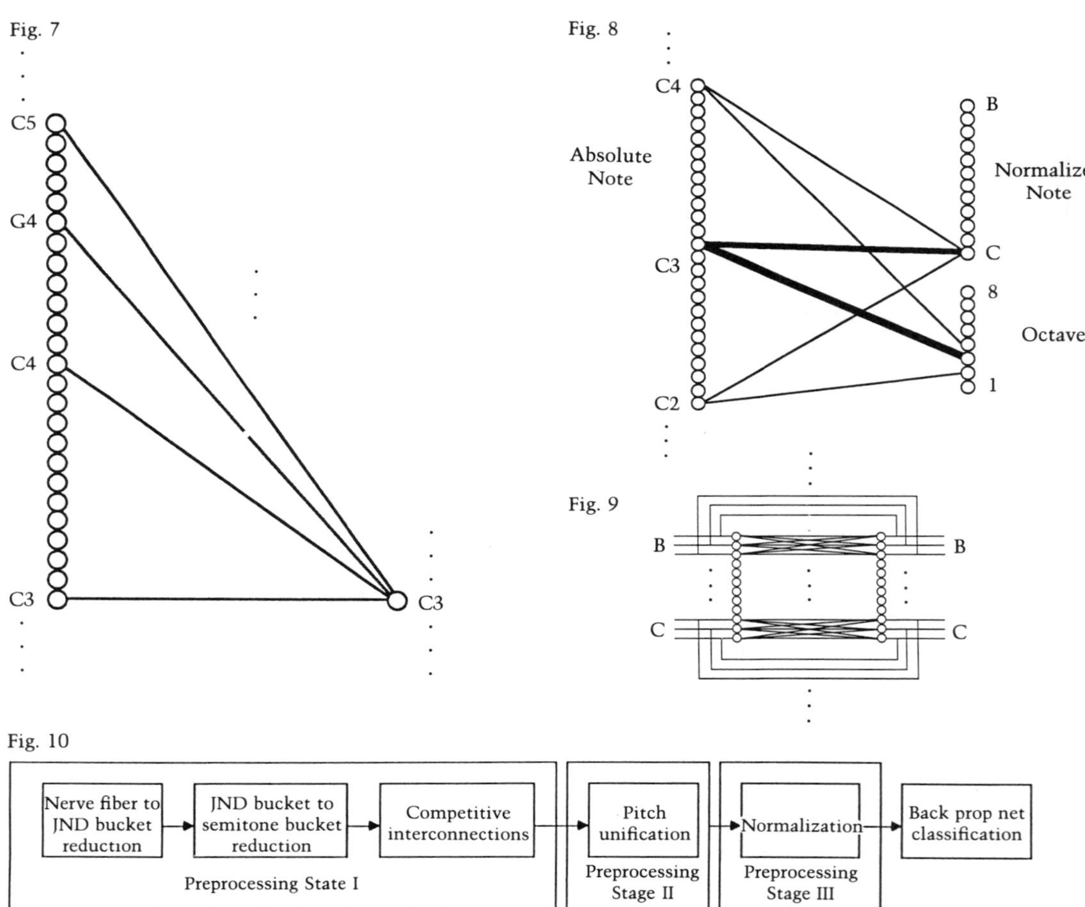

Modeling the emotional effect of chords would most likely require several pitch perception networks tied together feeding into a chord classification, heteroassociative neural network.

The accuracy of the system is probably affected a great deal by the sensitivity of the linear filters. Studies have shown that people and animals show great variation in the affective bandwidth of the cochlear nerve fibers (Evans 1982). Some people and animals are more sensitive than others. If pitch perception is related to hardware characteristics, it would explain why it seems to be hereditary in nature. It is interesting to note that those with cochlear damage have wider bandpass filters and experience broader psychophysical tuning curves, increase spread of masking, and have difficulty understanding speech, especially in the presence of background noise.

As with modeling other natural phenomena, the most difficult part was determining the representation of the problem. Once that was solved, it was relatively straightforward to select a pattern matching and classifying neural network. While not entirely biologically accurate, this paper attempts to present a neural network model for pitch perception. It would be interesting to hook up such a pitch perception neural network to an artificial cochlea, such as the analog electronic cochlea (called the Silicon Cochlea) developed by Carver Mead's group at the California Institute of Technology (Lyon and Mead 1988), and observe its performance.

Acknowledgments

Figures 1, 2, 4, and 5 are courtesy of Cambridge University Press, copyright 1982, and E. F. Evans. Figure 3 is courtesy of Springer-Verlag, copyright 1974, and E. de Boer. Special thanks to Rob Nickells for his assistance, suggestions, proof reading, and encouragement. His experience was invaluable in the preparation of this paper.

References

de Boer, E. 1974. "On the Residue and Auditory Pitch Perception." In W. C. Keidel, ed. *Handbook of Sensory Physiology—Auditory System, Volume 3—Clinical and Special Topics.* Berlin: Springer-Verlag, pp. 489–490.

Evans, E. F. 1982. "Basic Physics and Psychophysics of Sound, Functional Anatomy of the Auditory System, Functions of the Auditory System." In H. B. Barlow and J. D. Mollon, eds. *The Senses.* Cambridge, United Kingdom: Cambridge University Press, pp. 239–332.

Lazzaro, J. 1988. California Institute of Technology, Carver Mead Research Group, personal correspondence. March.

Lyon, R. F., and C. A. Mead. 1988. "An Analog Electronic Cochlea." *IEEE Transactions on Acoustics Speech and Signal Processing.*

Wever, E. G. 1974. "The Evolution of Vertebrate Hearing." In W. C. Keidel, ed. *Handbook of Sensory Physiology—Auditory System, Volume 1—Anatomy, Physiology (Ear).* Berlin: Springer-Verlag, pp. 450–452.

Appendix

Comparing the ears of animals along the vertebrate scale reveals some interesting facts. Lizards have from 50–1,600 hair cells; snakes and turtles have hundreds; crocodiles 11,000–13,000; birds from a few thousand to 12,000; man approximately 15,000; and dolphins 16,000–17,000. Cochlear nerve fibers increase also: lizards have 450; man 30,500; and dolphins 65,000–95,000.

As the number of hair cells increase, the length of the cochlea also increases. Mammal cochlea sizes range from one and one-half turns in the hedgehog to four in the guinea pig. Man's cochlea has almost three turns.

The larger cochlea tend to be accompanied by functional improvements. Its range is extended into the higher frequencies. Pitch discrimination is achieved by place of action in higher mammals. Lower vertebrates use rates of firing that are synchronous with the stimulating sound waves to determine frequency. This periodicity mechanism places a limitation of 200–300 firings per second.

The inner hair cells account for most of the 30,000–50,000 impulse-carrying (afferent) fibers in the cochlear nerve (95 percent in cats, 85 to 90 percent in guinea pigs). It is believed that each fiber innervates only one inner hair. The more numerous outer hair cells are innervated by only a fraction of the afferent cochlear nerve fibers (Wever 1974).

Addendum

B. Keith Jenkins

Extension to Multiple Tone Inputs

The pitch perception network is restricted to inputs of single complex tones by assumption. Here we describe an extension of the pitch perception network that permits multiple complex tones to be input simultaneously. This additional capability opens up possibilities of functionality added at (or after) the final stage of the network; examples include recognition of, and response to, intervals and chords.

In the following, additions and modifications to the perception network that permit simultaneous inputs are described. The changes include (1) the introduction of lateral connections to the output layer of preprocessing stage 2 (pitch unification), (2) the additional input of unstratified tones (output of the pitch unification stage) to the classification network, and (3) a change in the structure and function of the final classification network. In addition, to ensure correct input tone identification, one restriction is imposed on the inputs: all tones being input at one time must differ from each other by at least 1 1/2 semitones (thus, an interval of a second is more than sufficient separation).

Preprocessing stage 1 receives input signals from the cochlea nerve fibers and passes them through the layer of just noticeable difference (JND) bucket neurons and then on to the semitone bucket neurons as before. This stage functions correctly without modification for multiple tone inputs. When multiple complex tones are input, each resulting simple tone (a single fundamental or harmonic of a complex tone) excites essentially one semitone bucket neuron. As we mentioned, since each cochlea inner hair acts as a low-Q bandpass filter, approximately 33 JND neurons are excited for a given simple tone input (see Fig. 6 and Table 2). A single such simple tone will still excite just one semitone bucket due to the competitive lateral interconnections within the semitone neuron layer (layer 3 of preprocessing stage 1).

If two simple tones are each spaced midway between two adjacent semitone buckets, this can, often erroneously, lead to a single semitone being excited. For example, simple tones centered at 1079 Hz and 1019 Hz will in fact cause the 1047 Hz (C6) semitone neuron to fire and will suppress the adjacent two semitone neurons (C#6 and B5). This anomaly can be avoided by requiring the input tones to be spaced 1 1/2 semitones or more, which is the reason for our newly added restriction. We will also assume hereafter that the lateral connections in this semitone bucket layer have weights that permit the output response of a given semitone neuron to be analog in value and (in the absence of excitation of the neighboring neurons) to be an increasing function of the strength of the corresponding input tone. This will permit each output of the pitch unification stage to be correlated in strength with the relative power or loudness of the corresponding input tone.

The pitch unification stage (preprocessing stage 2, Fig. 7) retains its connections from the first layer of neurons to the second (output) layer of neurons. To permit reasonable pitch unification of multiple complex tones simultaneously, lateral connections are added to the output layer of neurons (Fig. 11). These new connections use the output of each neuron to inhibit the neurons that correspond to its harmonics. The magnitude of each such weight decreases with increasing distance from the fundamental to the harmonic. Thus, if a complex tone of C3 is excited at the output, then the output units corresponding to its harmonics (C4, G4, C5, etc.) are inhibited, each by a decreasing proportion of the signal strength of the complex tone C3. This has the effect of subtracting the relative strengths of the first, second, third, etc. harmonics from the C4, G4, C5, etc. outputs, respectively. Note that if a complex tone of G4 is also present on the input simultaneously, the activation of the G4 output layer neuron is now approximately proportional to the signal strength of the G4 complex tone alone. Thus, the output of this second preprocessing stage is a set of excitations, one for each complex tone at the input of the network.

The values of the synaptic weights on the lateral connections in stage 2 are fixed in time and can be set approximately equal to the expected ratio of the

Fig. 11. Lateral connections within the output layer of the pitch unification stage (layer 2 of preprocessing stage 2). All connections are inhibitory and have weights that decrease in magnitude as the connection length (or equivalently the harmonic order) increases. Every neuron unit is connected to its harmonics in the same manner.

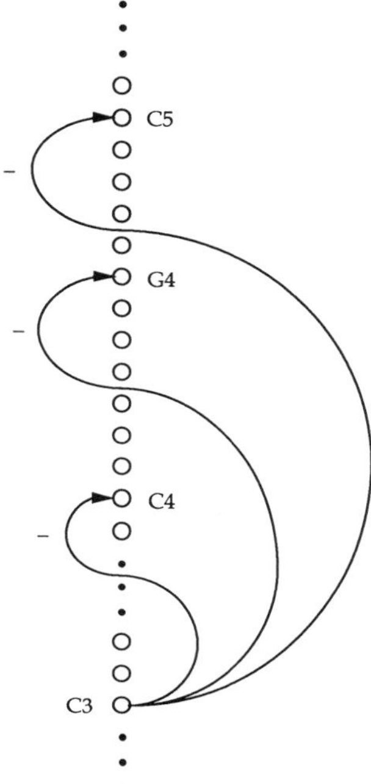

strength of each harmonic to its fundamental. These ratios can be determined from an ensemble average over all (or a representative set of) musical instruments. Each weight can be set equal to the expected (mean) value of the corresponding harmonic, normalized by the strength of the fundamental. Since the relative strength of each harmonic varies depending on the timbre of the original input complex tone, this does not provide for exact subtraction of each harmonic. It is anticipated that approximate subtraction will be sufficient, however, because it is unlikely that perfect unification of multiple complex tones will be critical in the proper function of subsequent processing and understanding stages. The amount of subtraction error that is acceptable is determined by the particular function of the subsequent processing and understanding stages.

It is interesting to note a few consequences of this modification to the pitch unification stage. First, a strong input of C3 with a weak simple tone (pure sine wave) input of C4 to the network could be interpreted as a single complex tone input of C3. This model could incorporate the results of studies of how humans interpret such an input. Second, for the case of single complex tone inputs, the addition of inhibitory connections to the pitch unification stage cleans up its output; in general only one output neuron of the pitch unification will be (substantially) on at a time. This consequence in turn has a positive effect on the final classification stage. In the original pitch perception network, the final classification stage had two functions. Note that the output of the previous normalization stage (stage 3), for a single complex tone input, was in general not one unambiguous normalized tone and octave but rather a distributed pattern of activation. Thus, a requisite function of the classification stage in the original net is to convert this activation pattern to a desired representation, such as two activated neurons, one to represent pitch, and one to represent octave. The second and optional purpose of the classification stage is to incorporate any additional functionality, such as higher-level recognition/understanding tasks. Since the revised pitch unification stage produces only one strong output unit activation for each input complex tone, the representation-conversion/cleaning-up process is no longer needed in the classification network. This frees up this back-propagation network to be used solely for the higher-level recognition/understanding functions. Finally, in the case of a complex tone that has very little fundamental signal in it (as in the oboe example given earlier), this modified pitch unification stage still functions as expected and should excite the correct complex tone neuron (corresponding to the semitone pitch of the fundamental).

Without changing the topological structure of the pitch unification stage, we can rearrange the locations of the output neurons for convenience of interpretation. If we arrange the output neurons into a matrix, with each row representing a different normalized pitch class and each column representing a different octave, then the output is very easy to interpret even with no further processing

Fig. 12. Arrangement of output neurons of the pitch unification layer (preprocessing stage 2) in a matrix for convenience of interpretation (a). Sums over rows and columns to obtain stratified tone and octave information (b).

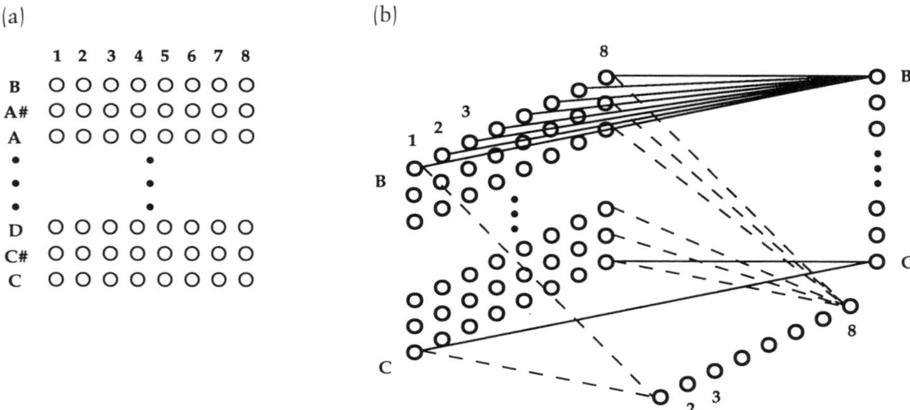

(Fig. 12a). In addition, the pitch and octave information can now be stratified by simply summing over all neurons in a row to obtain pitch information and by summing over all neurons in a column to obtain octave information (Fig.12b). Both the stratified signals and the unstratified signals (from the entire matrix) are sent to the final stage, the classification net. Fig. 13 shows a block diagram of the entire pitch perception net, in its revised form for multiple complex tone inputs.

The final stage of Fig. 13, the classification net, can now be used for higher-level tasks. Its input is the set of recognized complex tones that are present at the network input. The classification net structure depends to some degree on the application, that is, the desired functionality to be imposed. For most envisioned applications, it is likely to be a multilayer feed-forward net. For example, consider the case of recognizing intervals and chords. The first stage of this net would recognize intervals. This stage would contain a group of "second-interval" neurons, with each getting inputs from two neurons in the pitch unification output stage that are separated by an interval of a second. There would be a "major second" neuron for each possible two-semitone interval. Similarly, there would be groups of *minor third* neurons, *major third* neurons, etc. Major second neuron outputs could be combined in subsequent layers to activate a single neuron that recognizes the occurrence of any two-semitone interval; the same could be done for the other intervals. Then, in further stages of this net, these generalized intervals could be combined in a similar fashion to represent chords. In some cases it may be beneficial to use a back-propagation-type learning algorithm to train the net to learn the desired functionality or recognition task (see the chapter by Laden and Keefe, this volume, for further details of this approach to chord and interval processing).

In conclusion, we see that the pitch perception network, as originally described, was close to providing for multiple inputs. The primary limitation of the original net is its output representation. Stratifying the tone and octave information as described in the original version of preprocessing stage 3 (Fig.8) provides no loss of information in the single complex tone case but does remove information in most multiple complex tone cases. For example, if B and E are active, and if octaves 3 and 4 are active, this could mean B3 and E4 were input, or B4 and E3, or even B4, B3, and E3. By stratifying this information differently, as shown in Fig. 12, multiple-tone cases can be handled properly.

Interesting possible extensions of this work include studying the use of the classification net for interval and chord representation and recognition, as well as possible variants of the pitch perception network that incorporate effects of absolute versus relative pitch perception. Some people have the ability to judge absolute pitch ("perfect pitch");

Fig. 13. Block diagram of the entire pitch perception neural network, including capability for recognizing multiple complex tones. The classification stage can potentially be used for additional functionality such as representation and recognition of intervals and chords.

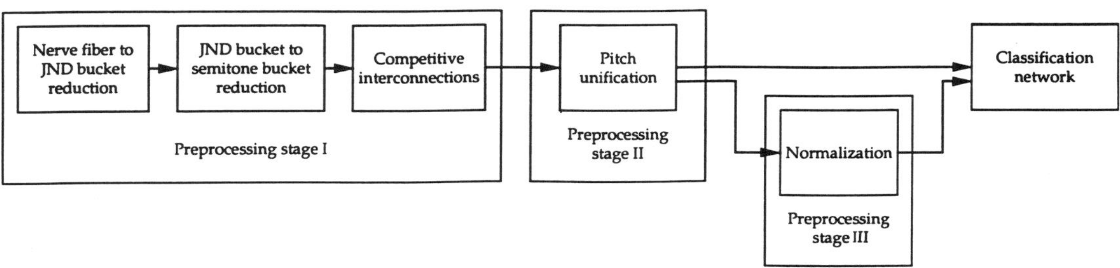

others never achieve this ability, even after much musical training, only performing accurately when judging pitch relative to some reference tone. The current pitch perception network is designed only to detect absolute pitch, but enhancements to allow the investigation of relative pitch phenomena would be a valuable future goal.

Reference

Laden, B., and D. H. Keefe. This volume. "The Representation of Pitch in a Neural Net Model of Chord Classification."

Don L. Scarborough, Ben O. Miller, and Jacqueline A. Jones
Department of Psychology
Brooklyn College of the City University of New York
Brooklyn, New York 11210 USA
BITNET:DOSBC@CUNYVM

Connectionist Models for Tonal Analysis

Introduction

When people listen to music from the Western tonal tradition, their sense of the music depends on perceiving the tonal structure. A piece is written in a particular key (though it may change), and the choice of key specifies a subset of 7 of the 12 notes of the chromatic scale as the primary elements of the composition. A key defines a schema for the individual notes of the scale and for chords within the key. Some notes and chords of a key are considered to be consonant and stable, while others are considered to be dissonant and unstable. Besides the tonic, several of the other six notes of the scale play especially prominent roles. For instance, the third and fifth notes of the scale, along with the tonic, define the tonic or root chord, which is considered to be the most stable chord within the key. Thus, a key defines a complex set of interrelationships among a subset of the notes of a chromatic scale.

This tonal structure plays a central role in a listener's perception in that individual pitch events and chords are heard within the framework or context provided by the tonal structure (Krumhansl 1979; Dowling and Harwood 1986). Furthermore, the organization of an entire piece is tied to this tonal structure, and the sense of harmonic development, progression, and resolution within this framework is a central aspect of the expressive quality of music. It is not clear, however, how listeners infer the key of a piece. A performer does not begin a piece by playing the appropriate scale or the tonic chord to define the tonal context. Rather, listeners must induce the key of the piece from the individual notes and chords as they are heard.

Computer Music Journal, Vol. 13, No. 3, Fall 1989,

Induction of Tonality

Simon (1968) developed a computer program, called LISTENER, which attempted to identify tonality and phrasing from a single melodic line. Simon noted that the frequency with which various notes occurred provided a clue to the tonality. The LISTENER program therefore simply counted how often each note of the chromatic scale occurred. The program then counted how often the notes that formed the tonic chord (e.g., C-E-G in C major) of each key occurred. The chord with the highest note count established the tonality. In three of four test cases (Beethoven, Mozart, and Schumann) this algorithm correctly identified the key of the piece. In a fourth case (Brahms), the program's choice of key (A minor) disagreed with the key signature (E minor). However, a large portion of the Brahms's piece modulates to A minor, although it begins and ends in E minor.

LISTENER produces a single tonality judgment for a piece, an approach that has problems with modulations because it sums the note count over the entire piece. Another problem is that it is insensitive to the order in which notes occur. Deutsch (1984) and Bharucha (1984a; 1984b) point out that the order of a note sequence can influence the perceived tonality. This seems plausible from considerations of voice leading (Piston 1948), whereby an unstable note resolves by moving to a stable note. Thus, with the ascending sequence, D♯-E-F♯-G-B-C there is a tendency to hear D♯ as resolving to E, F♯ to G and B to C, yielding the notes E-G-C of the first inversion of the C-major tonic triad. In descending order, people hear the triad D♯-F♯-B and the tonality as either B major or E minor (Deutsch 1984).

A later effort to develop a computer program for musical analysis (Jones, Miller, and Scarborough 1988; Scarborough, Jones, and Miller 1988) based on Lerdahl and Jackendoff's generative theory of tonal

Fig. 1. Linear network for tonal induction.

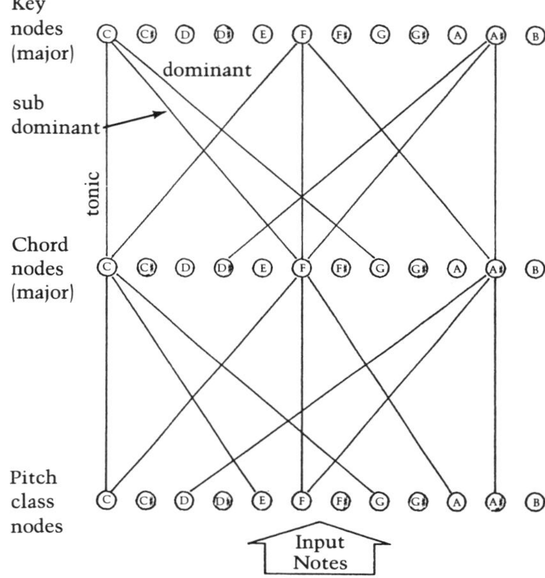

music (1983) builds on Simon's approach. Jones, Miller, and Scarborough (1988) implemented a version of Simon's algorithm in terms of a simple connectionist network (Rumelhart and McClelland 1986). A network of interconnections was used as a simple method for counting notes and weighing the evidence for one key versus another. In this network, the input layer consists of pitch-class nodes that represent the notes of the chromatic scale independent of octave. These pitch-class nodes are connected to a layer of chord nodes, each of which receives input from just three pitch nodes. Finally, sets of three chord nodes—representing the tonic, subdominant, and dominant chords of a particular key— are connected to key nodes.

In the model, the occurrence of one or more notes in the music activates the corresponding pitch nodes. Activation then flows from the pitch nodes to each chord node that includes the active pitches. Finally, activation flows from the chord nodes to any key nodes for which those nodes are the tonic, subdominant, or dominant chords. At any point in the piece, the most active key node defines the perceived key.

The degree to which the activity at one node influences other nodes is determined by the weight between the nodes. This weight reflects the strength of the connection between nodes, which in turn reflects how much one node influences or depends on another node. A schematic diagram of the network for major keys is shown in Fig. 1. The diagram shows, for example, that at the key node level, the key node for C major is activated by a C chord (tonic), an F chord (subdominant) and a G chord (dominant). Other key nodes would be activated by the chords representing the tonic, subdominant, and dominant for those keys. A complete network contains additional nodes for minor chords and keys.

This network algorithm differs from Simon's in several respects. First, the amount of activation provided by an input note is proportional to the note's duration: i.e., a half-note has more influence than a quarter-note. Second, once a note stops, the activation of the corresponding pitch node does not stop immediately but rather decays with time. Similarly, the activations of chord and key nodes also decay with time. This decay of activation means that the activity of the network is influenced most by recent notes, but the overall pattern of activity represents a weighted sum over all notes that have occurred. The tonality at any point in a piece is taken to be specified by the most active of the key nodes at that point. The ratio of this key node's activity to the sum of the activities of all the key nodes provides a measure of the certainty associated with the choice of that key node as the tonality.

In general, this network does a better job than Simon's counting algorithm because more of the input is considered. The duration of a note, for instance, contributes to the activation of a node, and this reflects the fact that tonally important notes are often sustained. In addition, it can respond to modulations and is sensitive to note order because of the decay parameters. The performance of the network, however, depends critically on the weight and decay parameters. Thus, an important issue is how the best set of parameters can be selected. This is fairly easy in the case of this simple network because it is linear: the output at time *t* is simply a weighted sum of the inputs up to that time, where the weights include a decay parameter. For example, for a two-note sequence, if $o_i(2)$ is the output of key node unit i at time 2, then:

$$o_i(2) = \sum_j w_{ij} \cdot o_j(2) + \beta \sum_j w_{ij} \cdot o_j(1)$$
$$= \sum_j w_{ij} \cdot (o_j(2) + \beta o_j(1)),$$

where w_{ij} is the strength of the connection or weight from chord node unit j to key node unit i, and β is the decay parameter. The output, o_j, of a chord node unit depends, in turn, on the sum of the inputs it receives from the pitch node layer, but this is also just a linear weighted sum of the same form. Because this network is linear, the middle chord layer adds no computational power in the determination of the key but exists only to represent chord perception. The output produced by the composition of two matrices of the same shape can be duplicated by a single matrix. Jordan (1986) provides a good discussion of basic linear algebra.

In principle, we can estimate the best weights by training the network using the Widrow-Hoff delta rule (Rumelhart, Hinton, and Williams 1986). However, this requires knowing what the network output should be at any given point in a piece, data that does not currently exist except at an intuitive level. What is needed is systematic data on perceived tonality to be able to provide good parameter estimates. Instead, parameters were picked largely based on intuitive guesses. Pitch node activation decays quickly, chord nodes more slowly, and key nodes slowest of all. In terms of the input evidence for a particular chord, the root is weighted most heavily, and the third and fifth somewhat less. For a key node, a tonic chord provides the strongest evidence, with the dominant and subdominant counting less. Other chords of a key could easily be included but were assigned zero weights in testing the algorithm. With these parameters, the network can identify the tonality of many pieces.

As an extreme example, it correctly guesses the key of *Auld Lang Syne* on the first note. The piece is in the key of F, and the first note is C, the fifth degree of the scale, an important note that occurs in both the tonic and dominant chords of the key of F. The particular choice of weights made F the most plausible key, a hypothesis that later gained confirmation. In most other cases, it takes only a few notes before the network can correctly identify the key.

The network can handle monophonic and polyphonic music and modulations. Because of the decay parameters, this network is also sensitive to note order and makes the tonal judgments described by Deutsch (1984) for ascending and descending sequences. In terms of many of the connectionist models appearing today (e.g., Grossberg 1980; 1988), this model is crude and simple. Nonetheless, the network does a more than creditable job in identifying the tonality of simple pieces of music. It is not clear how well this network simulates human performance because we know very little about how people identify tonality.

Bharucha (1987a; 1987b; 1988) has also proposed a connectionist network to solve the tonality induction problem. His network is similar in topology to the linear network described above, though it differs at the computational level. Bharucha uses *phasic* interactions so that a node responds only to changes in other nodes to which it is connected. Also, his network has both bottom-up and top-down connections. That is, while pitch nodes can activate chord nodes, which in turn can activate key nodes in a bottom-up sequence, a key node can prime chord nodes, which in turn can prime pitch nodes in a top-down fashion. A consequence of this architecture is that there are interactions between bottom-up and top-down effects, and it takes the network several simulation cycles to settle into a stable activation state in response to an input. Because of the top-down activation in his model, Bharucha can readily account for some chord priming effects on chord perception that he has found (Bharucha and Stoeckig 1987). Bharucha reports that his network exhibits many reasonable properties with respect to simulating tonal induction, although the simulation results have not been reported in detail. Bharucha has also proposed ways in which such a network might be tied into a larger model of music processing (Bharucha 1987b; 1988).

An even earlier network model was proposed by Deutsch (1969), which at first glance has several

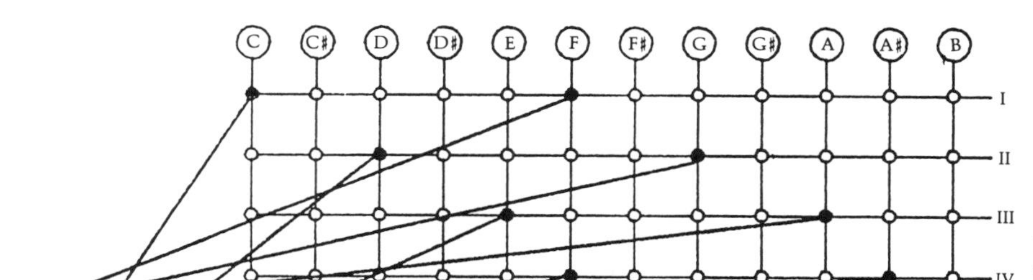

Fig. 2. Network to map pitch nodes into scale degrees based on key identification.

similarities to the linear network model described above. For example, her chord analyzers are similar to the chord node array in the linear model. There are two main differences between her network and the linear network, however. First, her chord analyzers respond only to simultaneously sounded notes rather than note sequences, which the linear network does by integrating information over time. (The structure of the Deutsch network was designed to account for several other aspects of chord and interval perception and transposition.) Second, the Deutsch network has no provision for extracting the tonality of music.

A Network for Tonal Schemata

A problem with the network approaches described so far is that they fail to deal with some aspects of human music perception. For example, the networks do not explain how we recognize a familiar piece despite transposition. Another problem is that the networks do not explain how the definition of a key then provides a schema for the interpretation of the notes with respect to the key. The tonal induction networks described above provide a good basis for an extended network to address these problems, however. Bharucha (1988) has suggested a scheme similar to the one described below.

To place any note within a tonal schema, we need to identify that note with respect to its position within the scale defined by a particular key. If we use the network in Fig. 1 to identify the key of a piece, we can then use this information to add an additional layer to the network that will map individual notes onto scale degrees. The idea is that the key node that is most active will control the mapping of the notes. That is, if the key node for C major is most active, then a pitch of C should be mapped to the first degree of the scale, while if the F key node is most active, then C should be mapped to the fifth degree. The simple cross-bar switching matrix shown in Fig. 2 can do this.

In Fig. 2, the pitch-class nodes are shown along the top. Each of these pitch nodes feeds into this network (in parallel with their input into the tonality network in Fig. 1) and has a connection with each of seven output units representing the seven degrees of a scale. Which one of the seven connections is active is determined by key nodes that selectively gate these connections. For example, the C-major key node would gate the input from C to the first scale degree, from D to the second degree, and so on, while an F-major key node would gate D to the sixth degree. Only two of a complete set of key nodes are shown in Fig. 2.

This gating can be accomplished in several ways. One way is to use sigma-pi connections (Rumelhart and McClelland 1986) between the key nodes and the pitch nodes shown in Fig. 2. A second approach is to have an output threshold for each degree node so that an output is produced only if the sum of the input to it from the key and pitch nodes is large enough. For either of these two approaches to work well, it is necessary to have only one key node active at a time. For the simple linear tonality network described earlier, however, the output of a key node is proportional to the strength of the evidence for that key. Singling out one key node and disabling the others can be accomplished by letting the output of key nodes be a non-linear sigmoidal function of the input, and by adding inhibitory connections between key nodes. With these changes and with appropriate choice of parameters, we can get a "winner-take-all" (Grossberg 1988) output from the strongest key node.

Another approach to the gating problem is to have a processing unit at each of the intersections shown in Fig. 2 that receives input from the key node and the pitch node. Each such unit, in addition to sending an excitatory output to the appropriate degree node, has inhibitory weights to all other units in the same column (satisfying the constraint that a given pitch node can only be mapped to a single degree). Each unit also has inhibitory weights to all other units in the same row (satisfying the constraint that a single degree node can receive input from only one pitch node). Again, with a nonlinear, sigmoidal output function, we can achieve a clear mapping from the input pitch nodes to the degree nodes even if several key nodes show some activation.

Figure 2 illustrates only two major key nodes, although this scheme permits mapping the pitch nodes into any mode with seven degrees. For example, by adding a set of minor key nodes, the pitch nodes can be mapped to the degree nodes in the appropriate way for minor scales.

Tonal Pitch Space

Tonality involves more than a set of pitches that constitute a scale. A theory of tonal perception should account for the perceptual structure of tonal pitch space such as the perceived proximity of pitches, chords, and keys (Lerdahl 1988). At first glance, the networks described above seem to require additional mechanisms to address such issues, although this may not be necessary. If we think of the nodes in a network as components of a vector, then the state of all the nodes at any moment defines a state vector for the network. A state vector can be thought of as defining a point in a multidimensional space, where each node of the network represents a dimension of the space. From this perspective, if we choose an appropriate network model, pitches, chords, or keys that are perceptually proximal should be represented by nearby points in the vector space.

We can compare state vectors representing two different states of the system (corresponding to, say, different chords) by calculating the inner product of the vectors (Jordan 1986). If the two states are similar, the inner product (which is related to the correlation coefficient) will be large, while vectors representing dissimilar states will tend to have smaller inner products. For example, suppose we compare the state of the system in response to the pitch C in the key of C major, with the response of the system to the pitch G in C major. Many of the nodes of the network will be in a similar state of activation for the two notes. That is, the same key node will be active, the same C-E-G chord node will be activated by the two notes, and the same diatonic set of pitch-class nodes that occur in C major will have been activated by notes prior to the C and the G to a similar degree. The state of the network will differ in terms of the activation of the specific pitch nodes for C and G and of the diatonic degree nodes (I versus V) represented in Fig. 2. The two notes will also tend to activate overlapping but not identical sets of chord nodes: e.g., F-A-C for C versus G-B-D for G.

In contrast, the state vector for the note C in the key of C major will show a larger difference from the state vector for the note G if the key is F major, for example, because the set of active pitch nodes (i.e., B versus B♭), chord nodes and key nodes will differ, and the mapping of pitch-class nodes to diatonic degree nodes will differ. The closeness of C to G within the network as defined by the state vectors thus depends on the tonal context, as is also true for human listeners (Krumhansl 1979). It seems, then, that the state vector for the network taken as a whole may provide an appropriate representation of tonal relationships.

Learnability

The tonal structure of music is culturally determined (Dowling and Harwood 1986). Thus another test of the network approach is to ask how such a network could be learned. In fact, much of the network structure may be acquirable through a competitive learning mechanism (Grossberg 1987). Such a learning mechanism could develop chord nodes that corresponded to the regular simultaneous occurrence of note patterns in the input. We can also bypass the chord nodes with a linear network, as noted earlier, and let the key nodes be directly activated from pitch nodes. This means that learning the pitch collections that correspond to various keys can parallel learning chord configurations.

On the other hand, the network described in Fig. 2 above presents a more serious challenge for learning because it is a multilevel, nonlinear architecture that depends upon having a key node level of representation. In this case, a simple competitive learning algorithm is inadequate, and more complicated learning algorithms are required (Grossberg 1987).

Conclusion

Connectionist approaches offer a promising and seemingly natural way to deal with the problem of tonality identification, though currently we do not know how well the networks described here simulate human performance. Another question is whether these networks can account for the rich perceptual structure of tonal pitch space, such as the proximity relations of individual notes, chords and keys (Lerdahl 1988). A further issue hinges on the fact that tonal relations are culturally determined (Dowling and Harwood 1986). This raises the question of how such networks could be learned (Grossberg 1987).

Acknowledgments

This work was sponsored in part by a PSC-CUNY Research Award to Jacqueline A. Jones.

References

Bharucha, J. J. 1984a. "Anchoring Effects in Music: The Resolution of Dissonance." *Cognitive Psychology* 16(4):485–518.

Bharucha, J. J. 1984b. "Event Hierarchies, Tonal Hierarchies, and Assimilation: a Reply to Deutsch and Dowling." *Journal of Experimental Psychology* 113(3):421–425.

Bharucha, J. J. 1987a. "MUSACT: A Connectionist Model of Musical Harmony." *Proceedings of the Ninth Annual Conference of the Cognitive Science Society.* Hillsdale, New Jersey: Lawrence Erlbaum Associations, pp. 508–517.

Bharucha, J. J.1987b. "Music Cognition and Perceptual Facilitation: A Connectionist Framework." *Music Perception* 5(1):1–30.

Bharucha, J. J. 1988. "Neural Net Modeling of Music." *Proceedings of First Workshop on Artificial Intelligence and Music.* Menlo Park, California: American Association for Artificial Intelligence, pp. 173–182.

Bharucha, J. J., and K. Stoeckig. 1987. "Priming of Chords: Spreading Activation or Overlapping Frequency Spectra?" *Perception and Psychophysics* 41(6):519–524.

Deutsch, D. 1969. "Music Recognition." *Psychological Review* 76(3):300–307.

Deutsch, D. 1984. "Two Issues Concerning Tonal Hierarchies: Comment on Castellano, Bharucha, and Krumhansl." *Journal of Experimental Psychology* 113(3):413–416.

Dowling, W. J., and D. L. Harwood. 1986. *Music Cognition.* Orlando, Florida: Academic Press.

Grossberg, S. 1980. "How Does the Brain Build a Cognitive Code?" *Psychological Review* 87(1):1–51.

Grossberg, S. 1987. "Competitive Learning: From Interactive Activation to Adaptive Resonance." *Cognitive Science* 11(1):23–63.

Grossberg, S. 1988. "Nonlinear Neural Networks: Principles, Mechanisms, and Architectures." *Neural Networks* 1(1):17–61.

Jones, J. A., B. O. Miller, and D. L. Scarborough. 1988. "A Rule-based Expert System for Music Perception." *Behavior Research Methods, Instruments and Computers* 20(2):255–262.

Jordan, M. I. 1986. "An Introduction to Linear Algebra in Parallel Distributed Processing." In D. Rumelhart and J. McClelland, eds. *Parallel Distributed Processing: Explorations in the Microstructure of Cognition,* vol. 1. Cambridge, Massachusetts: MIT Press, pp. 365–422.

Krumhansl, C. L. 1979. "The Psychological Representation of Musical Pitch in a Tonal Context." *Cognitive Psychology* 11(3):346–374.

Lerdahl, F. 1988. "Tonal Pitch Space." *Music Perception* 5(3):315–350.

Lerdahl, F., and R. Jackendoff. 1983. *A Generative Theory of Tonal Music.* Cambridge, Massachusetts: MIT Press.

Piston, W. 1948. *Harmony.* Revised ed. New York: Norton.

Rumelhart, D., and J. McClelland. 1986. *Parallel Distributed Processing: Explorations in the Microstructure of Cognition,* vol. 1. Cambridge, Massachusetts: MIT Press.

Rumelhart, D. E., G. Hinton, and R. Williams. 1986. "Learning Internal Representations by Error Propagation." In D. Rumelhart and J. McClelland, eds. *Parallel Distributed Processing: Explorations in the Microstructure of Cognition,* vol. 1. Cambridge, Massachusetts: MIT Press, pp. 151–193.

Scarborough, D., J. Jones, and B. Miller. 1988. "An Expert System for Music Perception." *Proceedings of the First Workshop on Artificial Intelligence and Music.* American Association for Artificial Intelligence. Menlo Park, California: pp. 9–19.

Simon, H. A. 1968. "Perception du Pattern Musical par AUDITEUR." *Sciences de l'art,* Tome V-2:28–34.

Addendum

We have been using the simple linear network for tonal induction (see fig. 1) as a component of a larger program to simulate music perception (Jones, Miller, and Scarborough 1988; Scarborough, Jones, and Miller 1988). In the course of this work, we have gained a greater appreciation of the advantages and disadvantages of this approach to tonal induction.

Advantages of the Simple Linear Tonal Induction Network

One advantage of this simple network is that it is easy to understand. A second advantage is that it is quite successful at identifying the tonality of a musical segment. A third advantage is that it is consistent with some psychological results on tonal perception.

Krumhansl and Kessler (1982) studied tonal perception by asking subjects to rate how well a particular probe tone fit into a tonal context. The tonal context was established in various ways, such as by playing a scale or playing a chord or a cadence. In general, subjects tended to rate most highly a probe tone corresponding to the first degree of the key represented by the context. The fifth degree of the key was rated next highest. At the other extreme, nondiatonic notes from the chromatic scale were rated low. Krumhansl (1990a, 1990b) noted that if the most highly rated notes of a key were also the notes that occurred most frequently in music of that key, then the profiles of the ratings for each of the 12 chromatic pitch classes for various context keys could be used to predict the key of a piece. That is, we can take the profile of ratings for each of the 24 major and minor keys and compare them with the distribution of pitches that occur during some portion of a piece, weighing each note by its duration. The rating profile that produces the best match to the pitch distribution is hypothesized to be the key of the piece. For example, if a piece is in C-major, then we would expect the C pitch class to occur most often, because this note received the highest rating for this key. Krumhansl (1990b) applied this algorithm to the preludes in major keys from Bach's *Well-tempered Clavier.* Based only on the first four notes (including all voices), she found that the algorithm identified the correct key for 92 percent of the preludes (44 out of 48).

We can interpret Krumhansl's goodness-of-fit probe tone ratings as specifying the relative strengths of the weights in a network, with key nodes receiving connections from input pitch nodes, each weighted according to the pitch ratings for that key. Then Krumhansl's algorithm is a one-step equivalent to our simple three-layer linear network. That is, our network first computes a weighted sum of the notes (in pitch classes) that occur for the chords of each key. This evidence for each chord is then combined in the properly weighted way to produce a number that represents evidence for each key. But because the network is linear, we can eliminate the chord level and assign weights to each pitch class representing how much evidence it provides for each of the key nodes directly. The result is that each of the key nodes weights each of the 12 chromatic pitch classes according to the importance of each pitch class for its particular key. The weight set for a key node can be regarded as functionally equivalent to Krumhansl's profiles.

Starting with the weights for chords and for notes within chords that we have been using, we calculated the equivalent pitch-to-key vector for a network that has only pitch-class nodes and key nodes, and no chord nodes. The correlation between this weight vector and Krumhansl's ratings was 0.88. Thus, the linear network model will show similar performance to Krumhansl's rating profile comparison algorithm. For comparison, we tested the network on all the preludes (both major and minor keys, all voices) from Book 1 of Bach's *Well-tempered Clavier.* Our network correctly identified the key signature for all 24 preludes. In 18 of the 24 cases, the correct key was hypothesized on the first musical event (note or chord), and, on average, for all 24 preludes, 1.5 events were required for correct identification of the key, compared to Krumhansl's (1990b) 96 percent success (23 of 24 preludes) after four notes for the Book 1 preludes.

A final advantage for this simple network approach is that, apparently, weights can be learned directly based on the note frequencies for each key. Krumhansl (1990a, 1990b) computed the correlation between her ratings and the frequency with which different notes occurred in a particular key. She found correlations as high as 0.97 between note frequencies in various samples and her ratings. Thus, it seems that the note frequencies themselves contain the relevant information about the key. Given this hypothesis, a competitive learning model such as described by Kohonen (1982) would be able to learn the association between keys and note weights.

Disadvantages of the Simple Linear Tonality Induction Network

Despite the success of the simple linear network model, there are a number of issues and questions that must be considered in evaluating the network. One problem is that the network is linear. Though this is not a problem from, say, an AI perspective, it may be a problem if we want to model human perceptual mechanisms. Clearly, neurons are not linear elements. We might assume, however, that the linear network model captures human perceptual processing at a higher level of abstraction than the level of individual neurons.

Another issue is that our simple linear network model assigns equal epistemological status to pitch-class nodes, chord nodes, and key nodes. That is, each type of node represents a type of knowledge we assume the human listener to have. Intuitively, however, it is questionable that these different levels of representation have equivalent perceptual status, particularly in different contexts. Sometimes a listener may be particularly aware of individual notes, while at other times the harmonic texture may be more salient. In addition, our chord nodes treat all chord inversions as equivalent. Different inversions have different perceptual consequences for human listeners, however, and also may have different effects on tonality perception.

The simple linear network model is supported by its correspondence with Krumhansl's rating data. On the other hand, Butler (1989, 1990) has argued that Krumhansl's ratings reflect more (and possibly less) than just how representative a note is of a particular key. He has argued that the judgments that subjects make may be affected by other factors, such as by how recently a probe note occurred in the context. To the extent that Butler is right, the correspondence between the linear network model and Krumhansl's rating data becomes less persuasive.

Butler (1989, 1990) has also argued that the perception of specific intervals such as a tritone or a minor second plays a central role in tonality perception. Although the linear network model implicitly includes intervals (e.g., fifths, thirds), it does not include the intervals Butler thinks are most important. It is not clear how much importance should be attached to Butler's argument. He has shown that people can make accurate tonal judgments based on such intervals. On the other hand, Krumhansl's work as well as the success of our linear model makes it seem likely that people can perceive tonality based on the frequency of note occurrence, too. Another point of view would be to suppose that both intervals and note distributions play a role in tonal perception. This would suggest that we could improve the linear network model by adding other nodes for specific intervals in addition to the chord nodes. Because the network is linear, however, all that ultimately counts is the particular pitch classes that occur and how they are weighted as they feed into key nodes, whether via chord nodes or interval nodes.

Another problem is that the linear network model acknowledges the existence of time only by the inclusion of decay parameters, but it seems likely that time plays a more central role in tonality perception. First, the order in which tones occur is probably important, as Deutsch (1984) noted and as Butler's work indicates. Thus, an interval of an ascending minor second is likely to be interpreted as movement to the first degree of the key, whereas a descending minor second tends to be interpreted as movement from the 4th to the 3rd degree. In addition, meter may be important. The effect of a note or chord on tonal perception is probably influenced by whether it occurs on a metrically strong or weak beat. The linear network model has no way to incorporate such effects. Even if meter does affect tonal judgments, however, these interactions need not occur at an initial stage of tonal perception but might occur later in processing, such as in the time span and prolongational reduction stages of Lerdahl and Jackendoff's (1983) theory.

The simple linear network model is based on the concept of pitch classes. Laden and Keefe (this volume) note that this pitch-class concept is an example of the cognitive assumption that the mind codes experiences in an abstract symbolic code. In fact, this assumption was made in most of the work in AI until the recent resurgence of connectionism; however, this assumption may be wrong.

The problem of pitch perception is a difficult one. For example, the phenomenon of the missing fundamental indicates that people may hear a pitch that does not correspond to a physically present frequency. Terhardt's work (e.g., Terhardt, Stoll, and Seewann 1982) suggests that this phenomenon may arise because listeners have learned an association between the harmonic partials and the fundamental. That is, the missing fundamental is perceptually restored via its associations with the partials. Further, work on the perception of voice leading suggests that perception involves an analysis of the partials (Allik et al. 1989; Tanguiane 1988). This could mean that the simple linear network, with its reliance on the notion of pitch class, may use too abstract a level of representation and that tonality perception could be affected by the occurrence of partials. As an alternative, we could retain the linear model but assume that pitch is coded by a more complicated state vector that includes the partials. That is, the components of the input vector would correspond to the components of the Fourier spectrum. Pitch class would be implicitly represented by the correlation between vectors representing notes separated by octave intervals but would not be uniquely (symbolically) represented.

Summary

The linear network model is remarkably successful in predicting the tonality of a piece of music. Furthermore, it is consistent with Krumhansl's work on tonal judgments. However, a number of other issues, ranging from the perceptual and representational status of pitch classes to the effects of time on tonality perception, raise a variety of interesting questions for further exploration.

References

Allik, J., E. Dzhafarov, A. Houtsma, J. Ross, and N. Versfeld. 1989. "Pitch Motion With Random Chord Sequences." *Perception and Psychophysics* 46:513–527.

Butler, D. 1989. "Describing the Perception of Tonality in Music: A Critique of the Tonal Hierarchy Theory and a Proposal for a Theory of Intervallic Rivalry." *Music Perception* 6:219–242.

Butler, D. 1990. "Response to Carol Krumhansl." *Music Perception* 7:323–338.

Jones, J. A., B. O. Biller, and D. L. Scarborough. 1988. "A Rule-based Expert System for Music Perception." *Behavior Research Methods, Instruments and Computers* 20(2): 255–262.

Kohonen, T. 1982. "Self-Organized Formation of Topologically Correct Feature Maps." *Biological Cybernetics* 43:59–69.

Krumhansl, C. L. 1990a. "Tonal Hierarchies and Rare Intervals in Music Cognition." *Music Perception* 7:309–324.

Krumhansl, C. L. 1990b. *Cognitive Foundations of Musical Pitch.* New York: Oxford University Press.

Krumhansl, C. L., and E. J. Kessler. 1982. "Tracing the Dynamic Changes in Perceived Tonal Organization in a Spatial Representation of Musical Keys." *Psychological Review* 89:334–368.

Laden, B., and D. H. Keefe. This Volume. "The Representation of Pitch in a Neural Net Model of Chord Classification."

Scarborough, D., J. Jones, and B. Miller. 1988. "An Expert System for Music Perception." *Proceedings of the First Workshop on Artificial Intelligence and Music.* Menlo Park, California: AAAI Press, pp. 9–19.

Tanguiane, A. S. 1988. "An Algorithm for Recognition of Chords." *Proceedings of the 14th International Computer Music Conference.* Cologne, Germany: Feedback Studio Verlag.

Terhardt, E., G. Stoll, and M. Seewann. 1982. "Algorithm for Extraction of Pitch and Pitch Salience from Complex Tonal Signals." *Journal of the Acoustical Society of America* 71:679–688.

Bernice Laden and Douglas H. Keefe
Systematic Musicology Program
School of Music DN-10
University of Washington
Seattle, Washington 98195 USA

The Representation of Pitch in a Neural Net Model of Chord Classification

A fundamental concern in the construction of neural nets for musical applications is the representation of input to the system. The way in which input is ultimately represented is determined by several factors: (1) the theoretical viewpoint of the researcher, (2) the primary use of the net, and (3) available computational resources. Psychoacousticians may be interested in representations that capture aspects of the peripheral processing of musical signals by the basilar membrane as well as with central mechanisms. "Cognitivists" may be more concerned with representations at the abstract level of concepts, such as musical key. Researchers who want to use neural nets for musical signal processing may be interested in both low- and high-level representations in order to enable analysis of recorded musical sound and the subsequent conversion into the high-level abstraction of a musical score.

This article explores alternative representations of musical pitch and demonstrates the feasibility of these representations through the application of a neural net to a musical task—that of classifying chords as major, minor, or diminished triads. Representation is discussed from two perspectives: psychoacoustical and cognitive.

Because musical psychoacoustics and music cognition focus on different levels of representation, the musical tasks employed by each discipline typically differ. The psychoacoustician may vary the physical parameters (e.g., frequency) of a musical tone in order to observe whether or not the listener's featural representation of the tone (e.g., loudness or pitch) shifts. In contrast, the cognitivist tends to hold constant psychoacoustic factors that correlate with the featural representations of pitch, loudness, or timbre, while manipulating higher-level musical constructs, such as rhythm or scale. In a music cognition task, a listener may rate how well various musical tones fit into a melody. Rating tasks allow inferences to be made about the mental representation of abstract concepts, such as musical key.

Computer Music Journal, Vol. 13, No. 4, Winter 1989,

Cognitive and psychoacoustic models are complementary. Representational levels can be arranged hierarchically so that acoustic features give rise to musical concepts. In this hierarchy, processing can proceed in both bottom-up or top-down directions. The representation of the output from the psychoacoustic level may differ from the acoustical properties of the input and from the symbolic representation utilized in cognitive processes. This motivates the investigation of subsymbolic representations that figure prominently in theories of musical psychoacoustics as input representations to cognitive processes.

The Chord Classification Task

Musical Perspectives

From the standpoint of the music researcher interested in applying the concepts and tools of artificial neural nets to music, a variety of musical tasks might profitably be chosen. Bharucha (1987), for example, has used neural nets to model the cognitive representation of musical harmony and has applied the net to a number of tasks, such as musical chord rating judgments and short-term memory for chord sequences. We have chosen to focus on representations of musical pitch in a chord classification task as an area of inquiry extending across the domains of psychoacoustics and music cognition.

Fig. 1. Sample nets illustrate the difference between fully connected and adjacent layer architectures. The fully connected architecture has forward connections to all units in all upper layers. The adjacent layer architecture has forward connections to units in the adjacent upper layer only.

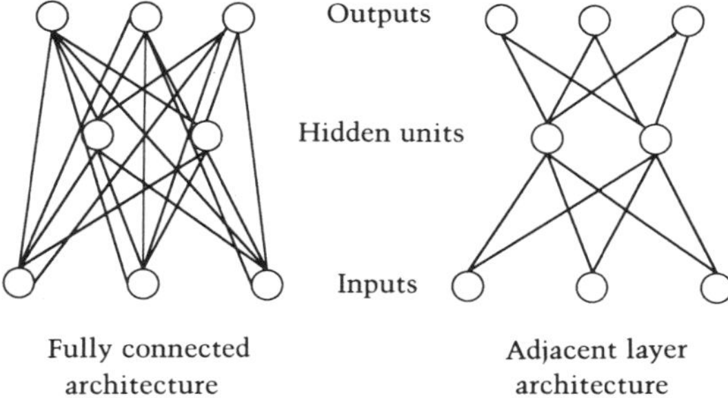

Chord classification is relatively easy for a musician. A listener hears a chord and decides whether it is a major, minor, or diminished triad. Thus a neural net model of chord classification must take some representation of the pitches in a chord as input, and produce as output one of three chord types. Chords are restricted to root position triads in all the learning models discussed in this article.

The Pitts-McCulloch Model

Attempts to construct neural net models of musical chord classification go back to Pitts and McCulloch (1947), the founders of theoretical neurocomputing. They were interested in how the brain might extract invariants from auditory and visual signals, and they discussed how the perception of musical chords might be extracted independently of absolute frequency information. The tonotopic organization of the auditory cortex was fairly well established in 1947, and equal intervals on the frequency axis were assumed, quite plausibly, to map into equal cortical distances. Given this tonotopic structure, Pitts and McCulloch reasoned that if a given neural pattern of excitation along the cortical strip were translated by an arbitrary cortical distance, the intervallic structure of the neurally represented musical stimulus would remain invariant. If the stimulus were a musical chord, the intervallic structure of the chord would remain invariant under this transformation, while the pitch class of all spectral components would be transposed by the same intervallic step size.

In the Pitts-McCulloch model, the net itself performed this translation by generating multiple copies of the excitation pattern on the cortical strip, each pattern translated a given distance. The ensemble of cortical strips were subsequently averaged. However, there is no neurophysiological evidence for this hypothesized copy-and-translate operation. Our approach is consistent with current practice in that a learning phase of training the neural net is first carried out. The connection strengths between processing elements are adjusted for input patterns that differ only in that the excitation is translated along the tonotopically organized frequency axis, equivalent to a piano keyboard representation. Instead of ensemble averaging, the adjustment in connection strengths is carried out for each instance of the musical chord used as input during the learning phase. What we have in common with the Pitts-McCulloch approach is that a net can classify a musical chord by averaging across different presentations of the same chord translated upwards and downwards by a range of intervallic steps.

Neural Net Architectures

General Features

Regardless of the pitch representation used, the neural nets discussed here have some features in common. The architectures for the chord classification models fall into one of two categories: fully connected or adjacent layer. In a fully connected architecture, each unit has forward connections to all units in all upper layers. This is in contrast to an adjacent layer net in which each unit has forward connections to all units in the adjacent upper layer only. The differences between the two architectures are illustrated in Fig. 1.

The nets have three layers: an input layer, a hidden layer, and an output layer. The number of input units varies depending upon the specific representation of pitch. Input takes the form of non-negative numbers. A value of 0.0 means the unit is inactive. Active input units take on a value of 1.0 unless there are multiple inputs to the same unit. In the case of multiple inputs, values are added. For example, two inputs to the same unit result in a value of 2.0.

Hidden units allow neural nets to associate pattern-response pairs that have a nonlinear relationship. Choosing the number of hidden units is a key decision in constructing the net architecture, yet no explicit rules exist to guide an optimal—or even a workable—choice. In general, small numbers of hidden units have the potential to exhibit signs of concept formation. In some of our models the number of hidden units are kept to a minimum in order to explore this notion of concept formation. In others the number of hidden units are increased to facilitate convergence to a solution.

Nets use a three unit output coding scheme. The activation pattern across the output units indicates whether a chord is a major, minor, or diminished triad. Output units have a tolerance of 0.1, meaning that a value ± 0.1 of a target value is considered a correct response.

Learning

Error propagation (Rumelhart, Hinton, and Williams 1986) is used as the learning algorithm for all nets. This method has attracted our attention for musical applications due to its recent success in solving a variety of pattern recognition problems in other domains. The error propagation technique uses an initial learning phase in which weights between units are changed by minimizing the error between the output of the net and the desired response of the net. After the learning phase is completed, the performance of the net using novel inputs may be assessed.

During a training epoch the net is exposed to each member of the training set. Our training set consists of 36 chords, i.e. 12 major, 12 minor, and 12 diminished triads. After each chord is presented to the net, the output value is compared to the desired value, and weights for all net connections are updated so as to reduce the difference between the two (the error). In the chord classification net, weights are updated 36 times during each epoch, once per chord in the training set.

Error propagation does not guarantee a net will learn to solve a particular problem. In some cases even if a solution exists in theory, the error propagation technique will not derive a set of weights that will lead to a satisfactory solution. When this occurs, the net is said to be trapped in a local minimum of the state space of the error function. The tendency for a net to be trapped in local minima may be reduced by modifying parameters that determine how much the net connections are changed (Dolson 1989). One parameter is referred to as the momentum (α) and another as the learning rate (η). The momentum determines to what extent previously computed weight changes will affect the direction of the current weight change, and it takes on values between 0 and 1. Franzini (1988) suggests the use of a small momentum value, i.e., 0.2 for the first 40 training epochs, followed by a larger value, i.e. 0.9. This reduces the tendency for local minima and decreases training time measured in number of epochs. We used these suggested values in many of the nets. In several of the earlier nets, however, a single momentum value was used for all epochs.

The learning rate in standard models is a positive constant close to 1.0, which scales weight changes so that the larger the learning rate, the larger the weight change. Although a large learning rate runs the risk of missing the global minimum, a small learning rate slows the learning process. Rumelhart, Hinton, and Williams (1986) reported that a large learning rate used in conjunction with a large momentum rate (i.e., 0.9) gave satisfactory results. In most cases we selected a learning rate between 0.6 and 0.9.

The Pitch-Class Approach for Representing Musical Pitch

We initially chose the simplest possible representations of tonal signals for the inputs to the neural net that would lead to interesting musical results. For tonal materials, this is the pitch class of the musical tones, expressed as dodecaphonic note names for convenience. Examination of the music

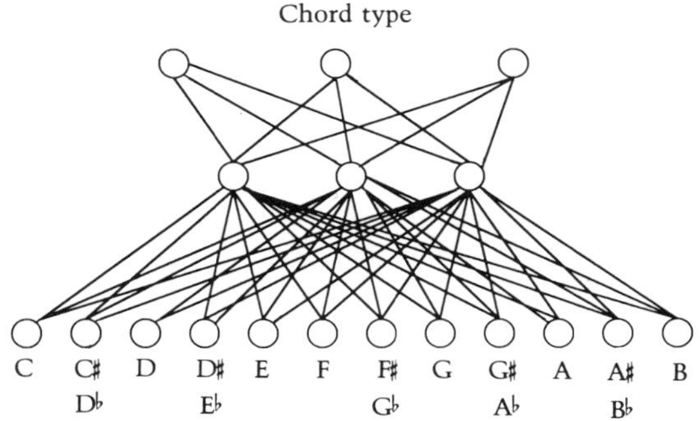

Fig. 2. An adjacent layer net which uses a pitch class representation. The net has 12 input units, 3 hidden units, and 3 output units.

cognition literature (e.g., Krumhansl 1979; Bharucha and Stoeckig 1986; Bharucha 1987) shows that nearly all cognition studies have assumed this form of representation for musical pitch.

We refer to nets using the cognitive approach to pitch representation as pitch class nets. A triad is specified as three pitches. Each pitch represents a pitch class (0–11 in the modulo 12 system) that can be mapped onto the repetition rate of a musical tone. This model assumes preliminary analysis of the auditory stimulus at a peripheral level into an octave-equivalent pitch class representation.

The real power of a neural net is its ability to compute solutions for distributed representations. In most cases, the solutions for these complex cases are not obvious. The pitch class representation of pitch is a local rather than a distributed one. In this case a possible solution for the chord classification problem is apparent without the use of a learning algorithm. A net containing 36 hidden units, one representing each of the possible major, minor, and diminished triads, could be constructed so as to map chords to chord types. Thus our interest in using a pitch class representation was not to find this obvious solution, but to find a solution which used a minimum number of hidden units. We hypothesized that three hidden units would be adequate and that the hidden units would form concepts of the intervals found in triads: i.e., major third, minor third, perfect fifth, and diminished fifth.

Each pitch-class net used 12 input units to represent the 12 pitches of the chromatic scale and 3 output units to represent chord type. The number of hidden units and the values of the learning parameters are summarized in Table 1 for each of the eight pitch class nets discussed.

Net 1 had an adjacent layer architecture as shown in Fig. 2 and three hidden units. It identified 25 percent of the chords after more than 11,000 learning epochs. When a fully connected architecture was used in conjunction with three hidden units in Net 2, 72 percent of the chords were identified after 2,800 learning epochs.

Although a 72 percent correct identification indicates a degree of success, we wanted to see whether increasing the number of hidden units would improve net performance. A fully connected net with six hidden units (Net 3) identified 61 percent of the chords after 3,300 learning epochs. A fully connected net with eight hidden units (Net 4) identi-

Table 1. Comparison of pitch class nets

Net Number	*Hidden Units*	*Architecture*	*eta*	*alpha*	*Output Encoding*	*Percent Correct*	*Epochs*
1	3	Adjacent	0.6	0.6	Simple	25	11000
2	3	Fully	0.5	0.5	Simple	72	2800
3	6	Fully	0.6	0.7	Simple	61	3300
4	8	Fully	0.6	0.7	Simple	50	3200
5	9	Adjacent	0.6	0.6	Simple	25	2800
6	3	Adjacent	0.6	0.6	Interval	44	10000
7	25	Adjacent	0.8	0.8	Interval	94	3100
8	25	Adjacent	0.9	0.2/0.9	Interval	58	5000

fied 50 percent of the chords after 3,200 epochs. Adjacent layer nets, with their less powerful architecture, did not perform as well as the fully connected nets. This is evident from the 25 percent identification rate of Net 1 discussed above. In addition, Net 5, using nine hidden units, identified 25 percent of the chords after 2,800 learning epochs. We next assessed whether net performance could be improved in the adjacent layer nets by changing the way the output was coded.

Initially a simple output coding scheme was used, in which the first output unit designated a major chord, the second output unit a minor chord, and the third output unit a diminished chord. If a chord were major, the desired response of the net was that the first output unit be near a value of 1.0 and the other two output units be near a value of 0.0. An alternative three-output coding scheme was explored that reflected the interval structure of the chord category. The first output unit represented the interval between the root and the third of the chord (1.0 for a minor third, 0.0 otherwise). The second output unit represented the interval between the third and the fifth of the chord (1.0 for a minor third, 0.0 otherwise). The third output unit indicated the interval between the root and the fifth of the chord (1.0 for a perfect fifth, 0.0 otherwise). Thus, when a chord was major, the desired response of the net was (0 1 1). When a chord was minor the response was (1 0 1), and when a chord was diminished it was (1 1 0).

When an adjacent layer net with three hidden units (Net 6) was trained using this interval-based coding scheme, it learned to identify 44 percent of the chords within 10,000 epochs. The only difference between this net and Net 1 was the output coding scheme, yet Net 6 performed 19 percent better. As a result, we adopted this output coding in all subsequent nets. Not only does this coding scheme seem to lead to better identification, but this approach eliminates the need to rely upon hidden units to form concepts of the intervals comprising each chord. This opens the possibility of using the output of this net as the input to another net that processes intervals.

These initial attempts made it apparent that nets with relatively few hidden units (i.e., 3–9) could not be trained as easily as we had anticipated. In addition, the new output coding made it unnecessary to pursue forcing the hidden units to form concepts of intervals, because these concepts were encoded in the output. For these reasons a larger net with 25 hidden units was constructed. We also chose to use exclusively the adjacent layer architecture. Although this architecture is less powerful than the fully connected architecture, there are fewer connections to be learned, hence reduced training time. Since all input must be channeled through the hidden units, this allows the behavior of the hidden layer to be observed.

Nets 7 and 8 were trained with 25 hidden units. The learning rate and momentum of Net 7 were set to a value of 0.8, while Net 8 used a learning rate of 0.9 and a momentum value set according to Franzini's guidelines (Franzini 1988) mentioned earlier. Each net was started with a different set of randomly chosen initial weights. Within 3,100 epochs, Net 7 correctly identified 34 out of 36 chords, or 94 percent. Net 8 identified 58 percent of the chords after 5,000 epochs. Net 8 was trapped in a local minimum.

It appears that the addition of more hidden units was the primary reason why one of the 25 hidden unit nets learned well and the nets with fewer hidden units were not as successful. However, the fact that one of the large nets encountered a local minimum and the other net did not learn to classify all 36 chords points to the sensitivity of the net to the starting state and learning parameters. Rather than running more cases on this architecture to systematically study this problem, we turned our attention towards alternative pitch representations.

Psychoacoustical Approaches to Pitch Representation

The pitch class representation excludes any possible role of the pattern recognition mechanisms considered in modern pitch perception theories. Since pitch perception theories also postulate central processing mechanisms, they describe additional cognitive structures that could conceivably play a role in music cognition studies. We have employed representations of tonal signals that include a subset of the most salient features of the Goldstein (1973) and Terhardt (1974) theories of pitch perception of complex sound. We assume that the continuous psychophysical pitch scale has been projected into the twelve pitch class categories of the chromatic scale and that the same quantification is carried out for the harmonics of the Goldstein model and the subharmonics of the Terhardt model (see below). Two psychoacoustically based representations result. One is referred to as the harmonic complex representation and the other as the subharmonic complex representation.

Harmonic Complex Representation

In the nineteenth century, von Helmholtz (1954) hypothesized that the auditory system performed a frequency analysis of the incoming musical sound. The tonotopic organization of the auditory system from the periphery to the cortex is convincing evidence that frequency selectivity is a primary auditory function. Even before von Helmholtz, psychoacoustical theories of pitch perception attempted to reconcile the contrasting cues of frequency and temporal coding (de Boer 1976). In current terminology, the place theory of pitch perception assumes that the auditory system extracts the spectral level and frequency of each well-separated sinusoidal partial in a complex tone from the position of its localized excitation maximum in tonotopically organized processing centers in the auditory periphery. The temporal theories of pitch, on the other hand, rely on the temporal response of a single tuned neural unit and the dissimilarity in the temporal responses of pairs of neural units tuned to the same, or possibly different, frequencies.

For a complex of harmonically related partials, listeners are able to distinguish the first five to seven harmonics, and the conventional interpretation of these results is that the human ear can individually resolve partials that are separated in frequency by more than a critical bandwidth (Rasch and Plomp 1982). In their original form, the Goldstein and Terhardt theories are place theories, since they operate on spectral cues alone.

The Goldstein model (Gerson and Goldstein 1978; Goldstein et al. 1978) assumes a peripheral auditory analysis that extracts the frequency of each well-separated partial, subject to an internal random error. A central processor computes an optimal match between a harmonic series and the distribution of frequencies. The match indicates the most likely fundamental frequency of the complex tone.

Another reason for investigating harmonic complex representations has nothing directly to do with psychoacoustics. The singing voice, wind instruments, and bowed string instruments produce harmonic spectra, and plucked or struck strings instruments produce nearly harmonic spectra. Even those percussion instruments that communicate pitch information robustly have spectra with clusters of nearly harmonically related partials in combination with inharmonic partials. Artificial nets constructed to extract musically meaningful patterns from such acoustical signals might as well build the knowledge of harmonicity into their input representations. In the absence of such structure in the input layer, a neural net for music processing will have to learn the regularities of the harmonic series for itself.

The musical significance of current psychoacoustical theories of complex pitch perception includes the notion that listeners attempt a best fit of a spectral pattern to even strongly inharmonic sounds such as bells. Such theories include not only the harmonic template pattern recognition mechanism of Goldstein, but also the subharmonic pattern recognition mechanism of Terhardt.

Subharmonic Complex Representation

Terhardt (1974) proposed a central, cognitive mechanism that is responsible for a listener's ability to hear a complex of sinusoids as a single, fused musical pitch. In this model, each separable component of a complex tone generates eight subharmonics. The matrix of generated subharmonics from each separable component are compared, and the frequency of the most commonly generated subharmonic determines the perceived pitch. In this original model, Terhardt suggested that the subharmonic matrix mechanism might be learned through exposure to periodic sounds. At first glance, the Terhardt subharmonic pitch model might seem less intuitive than the Goldstein model, even though both models account equally well for the perceived pitch of musically salient tones. However, Houtgast (1976) has shown that under certain conditions listeners can discriminate a subharmonic pitch of a sinusoidal tone whose frequency is much higher.

Terhardt (1982) has considered the perception of musical chords from different perspectives: the partials that the auditory system can extract from the spectra of each of the tones in the chord; the perceived pitch of each of the tones in the chord; and the fundamental note or root, described by the eighteenth century music theorist Rameau. For example, the subharmonics of each of the tones in a C major (or minor) chord in root position include the pitch class C, which lies two octaves below the chord root. This indicated to Rameau that the C major chord implies a tonal center of C. The presence of the coincident subharmonic at the Rameau fundamental is signaled by the strength of the virtual pitch cue at that frequency in the Terhardt model. Terhardt's model has generated predictions for the fundamental bass of major and minor chords played in all inversions using recorded tones played on a piano. In root position, the major and minor chords generate virtual pitch cues that strongly reinforce the tonal center of the root. In the inversions, the virtual pitch cues lend ambiguity to the tonal center, particularly for minor chords. For the A minor chord for example, the pitch classes D, C, and F occur as virtual pitch cues, in addition to A and E. This psychoacoustical method of viewing musical chords may assist in the extraction of tonal information in conjunction with other cognitivist-structural systems of tonal processing.

Learning with Psychoacoustically Based Pitch Representations

A representation of pitch based upon the Goldstein model must capture the notion of a harmonic complex. A musical tone needs to be specified as a

Fig. 3. Harmonics are illustrated as the pitch class labels whose intervallic structure approaches the harmonic series of the fundamental (i.e., the first pitch in each row). Overlapping harmonics are indicated by the outlined font.

Overlapping harmonics (first five harmonics)

Major	C3	C4	G4	C5	E5
	E3	E4	B4	E5	G#5
	G3	G4	D5	G5	B5
Minor	C3	C4	G4	C5	E5
	E♭3	E♭4	B♭4	E♭5	G5
	G3	G4	D5	G5	B5
Diminished	C3	C4	G4	C5	E5
	E♭3	E♭4	B♭4	E♭5	G5
	G♭3	G♭4	D♭5	G♭5	B♭5

number of pitch classes that approximate the harmonic partials of the tone rather than as a single pitch class representing the repetition rate as was the case in the pitch class representation. For this neural net we chose to limit the representation to five partials per tone. Thus we specified each chord tone by the five pitch classes whose frequencies are nearest those of the first five harmonics. This approximates the frequency analysis ability of the human auditory system and keeps the neural net architecture to a manageably small size. Also we wished to avoid the seventh harmonic, whose frequency ratio does not fit well within the chromatic scale categories.

A triad activates 15 of the net's input units (3 chord tones × 5 partials). The input unit representing each partial is given a value of 1.0. In cases where partials of two chord tones overlap, the input to the corresponding unit is doubled, thus receiving a value of 2.0. Major and minor chords each have a characteristic pattern of overlap between their partials (shown in Fig. 3), while diminished chords have no overlap between their first five partials.

Forty-seven input units are required to accommodate a harmonic complex representation. The harmonic complex representation for a C major chord

Fig. 4

Harmonic complex representation

The input units corresponding to these pitch classes would be activated for a C major chord.

C3 C4 G4 C5 E5 E3 E4 B4 E5 G♯5 G3 G4 D5 G5 B5

Fundamental pitches of chord

Fig. 4. The harmonic complex representation requires 47 inputs—nearly four octaves. Filled-in circles indicate an activated input unit. Overlapping harmonics are indicated by multiple filled-in circles.

is illustrated in Fig. 4. We opted to use 25 hidden units in this net because of our experience with the pitch class nets. After a learning phase of 1,622 epochs, the net correctly classified all 36 chords. In terms of number of epochs, the harmonic complex representation is superior to the pitch class representation. The pitch class net with 25 hidden units required 3,100 training epochs in order to learn to classify 94 percent of the chords correctly. This is roughly twice the number of training epochs needed by the harmonic complex net to achieve perfect classification. We conclude that the overlap pattern between partials has facilitated learning in this net.

A neural net with a subharmonic pitch representation was constructed as well. The first six subharmonics of each chord tone were specified in terms of the pitch class notation with values assigned in a manner analogous to the harmonic complex. With the subharmonic pitch representation, chord types can be distinguished by their coincident subharmonics in Fig. 5. Input units corresponding to each subharmonic generated by a chord are activated. If subharmonics from two chord tones overlap, the corresponding input unit is given a value of 2.0. If three subharmonics overlap, the input unit takes on a value of 3.0. The net has 50 input units, 25 hidden units, and 3 interval-based output units. The subharmonic complex representation for a C major chord is illustrated in Fig. 6. The net successfully classified 35 of the 36 chords, or 97 percent, after 5,000 learning epochs. The error was made classifying a minor chord.

The harmonic and subharmonic nets each encode information pertinent to the chord classification

Fig. 5

Overlapping subharmonics (first six subharmonics)

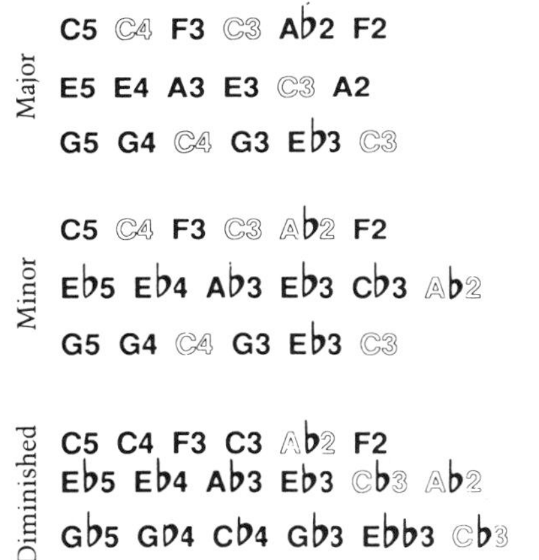

Fig. 5. Subharmonics are illustrated as the pitch class label whose intervallic structure approaches the subharmonic series of the fundamental (i.e., the first pitch class in each row). Overlapping subharmonics are indicated by the outlined font.

problem in the distribution of their coincident harmonics in the input layer, and no significant difference was observed in their performance for the limited number of cases we examined. Leaving aside psychoacoustics per se, these nets are better able to learn the mapping of input pitch representation to chord type because the template-based pitch representations have more structure than the simple pitch-class nets. The pitch class nets employ patterns of input activation that are quite sparse, while the template-based nets distribute activation across more input units.

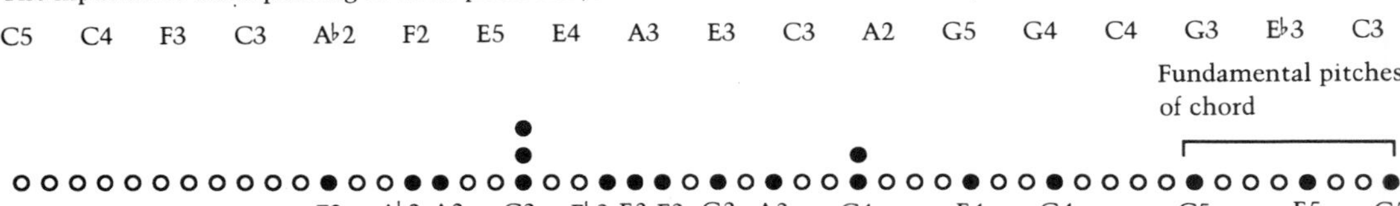

Fig. 6. The subharmonic representation requires 50 input units—a little more than four octaves. Filled-in circles indicate an activated input unit. Overlapping subharmonics are indicated by multiple filled-in circles.

Musical Pattern Generalization

One of the attractive features of neural nets is that they have the potential to respond in meaningful ways to novel input or partial patterns once they have been trained upon a set of exemplars. The ability of a chord classification net to generalize can be tested by examining its response to incomplete patterns, chord inversions, and input obtained from a steady-state power spectrum.

Incomplete Harmonic Template Patterns

Human listeners can extract pitch and classify chords in the absence of complete harmonic template patterns. Even though each of the first five harmonics almost always lies within its own auditory critical band (Rasch and Plomp 1982), some of the harmonics may be absent or may not be individually resolvable in real musical tones due to the effects of masking. However, there is essentially no detrimental effect on the human listener's ability to detect pitch or classify chords. The phenomenon of the missing fundamental demonstrates that even the fundamental of a complex tone does not need to be present in order for it to be perceived as the pitch of the complex tone.

Harmonic complexes were represented in the learning phase of the neural net by the first five harmonics of each chord tone. Upon completing the learning phase, we tested the harmonic complex net to observe how well it would respond to incomplete chord patterns in which one or more partials of each chord tone were absent. Harmonics were sequentially subtracted from the representation, so that incomplete patterns contained from one to four out of the five partials for each of the three chord tones. The results are listed in Table 2. The net performed best when the incomplete pattern was missing only the first partial or fundamental of each chord tone. In this instance, 69 percent of the patterns were correctly classified. Interestingly, when the reverse situation occurred (i.e., only the fifth partial was missing), the net did not perform as well, with only 50 percent correct. Thus the net was better able to generalize from a combination of the upper partials than from a combination of the lower partials. This sensitivity of the pattern recognizer is as anticipated, since it is the presence or absence of coincidence of the fifth harmonic of the root with the fourth harmonic of the major third that is decisive in classifying the major chord.

The net performed poorest when the first four partials of each chord tone were missing from the pattern, leaving only the fifth partials. Only 25 percent of the patterns were classified correctly. When the pattern included only the first partial of each chord tone, i.e. a "pseudo-sine tone" signal, the net performed slightly better, with a score of 31 percent correct. These results indicate the net was able to generalize from the harmonic complex representation, since the random baseline performance is 12.5 percent correct. Performance might be improved by including in the training set a subset of exemplars in which from one to four partials were randomly deleted.

Table 2. Chord classification performance for incomplete harmonic template

Harmonics Present (1–5)	*Percent Correct*
1,2,3,4	50
1,2,3	31
1,2	33
1	31
5,4,3,2	69
5,4,3	50
5,4	31
5	25

Identification of Chord Inversions

In the learning phase, the harmonic and subharmonic neural nets used chords in the root position as inputs. We have explored the extent to which both the harmonic and subharmonic nets can identify chords in their first and second inversions. For example, the first inversion of the C major chord is E, G, C, and the second inversion is G, C, E. The results, expressed as percent correct identification, are shown in Table 3. Second inversion chords were identified more often (39 percent) than first inversion chords (29 percent). Regardless of representation or inversion, major chords were correctly identified 40 percent of the time, diminished chords 37 percent, and minor chords 24 percent. The highest percentage of chord identification (50 percent) occurred for second inversion minor and diminished chords in which the subharmonic representation was used.

Although the input patterns for chord inversions differ from the root position patterns, there are enough similarities to allow the net to make some correct classifications. In order to improve performance, the nets could be trained on chords in all inversions.

Simulation of Power Spectrum Input Representation

The auditory system extracts from steady-state tones the spectral amplitude and frequency of each

Table 3. Classification performance for chord inversions

Representation Type	*Chord Inversion*	*Percent Correct*			
		Total	*Major*	*Minor*	*Diminished*
Harmonic	First	26	36	20	20
	Second	39	40	36	40
Subharmonic	First	32	36	20	40
	Second	39	50	18	50

sufficiently distinct partial. The partials of periodic tones are harmonically related, and the resulting spectral envelope is an important contributor to timbre, instrument identification, and the ability to distinguish separate instruments in an ensemble (particularly when vibrato is present). When three tones are sounded simultaneously to produce a triad, the spectral overlap between harmonics is similar to that employed in our harmonic, template-based neural net. Significant differences also exist that we must deal with first. Slight mistunings, such as are found in equal temperament, produce varying degrees of roughness (i.e., time-domain amplitude modulation), and roughness cues translate into variations in the consonance/dissonance scale. Bharucha and Stoeckig (1987) have reported that such psychoacoustical factors account for some of the major/minor chord discrimination data obtained with human subjects and demonstrate that psychoacoustical cues can be more salient than structural cues derived by tonality relationships. In the context of the neural net models described here, the power spectrum inputs are quantified into distinct pitch classes. No attempt has been made to include tempered tunings and their consequent influence in consonance/dissonance judgments. Such a tuning microstructure would serve to increase the complexity of the intermediate representation and may be needed in modeling other cognitive processes in music.

With this cautionary note, we have assessed the ability of the harmonic, template-based neural net to identify musical chords as the input values are modified to simulate variations in power spectra.

Table 4. Classification performance for power spectrum input

Spectral Envelope Slope	*Normalized Input?*	*Percent Correct*			
		Total	*Major*	*Minor*	*Diminished*
−6 dB/octave	No	47	75	25	42
	Yes	67	83	67	50
−12 dB/octave	No	33	58	25	17
	Yes	36	67	18	50
+6 dB/octave	No	67	83	67	50
	Yes	56	42	67	58

The original net learned with inputs having only the discrete values of 0.0, 1.0, or 2.0, the latter in the case of coincident harmonics. Since human listeners can successfully identify chord type while the power spectra of the individual tones are varied, such as when different trios of instruments play the same chord, it is of interest to assess the net's performance in a similar situation. We are essentially viewing the net not from the perspective of pitch perception, but rather as a net that classifies musical chords from a power spectrum input representation. The perceptual act of grouping harmonics together for each of the three tones is not addressed in this model.

We varied the net input values, referred to as *power spectral amplitudes,* by varying the frequency roll-off (spectral slope) of the spectral envelope. Variation of spectral slope is a single-parameter modification of the input pattern with clear musical significance. Research in musical timbre has identified functions of spectral envelope important for timbre perception (Rasch and Plomp 1982). Room-averaged spectral envelopes of Western orchestral instruments have systematic structure, and many can be approximated by a filter shape that rolls off at −18 dB/octave (Benade and Kouzoupis 1985; Benade 1986). Each input value was assumed proportional to the spectral amplitude of the corresponding harmonic. Each spectrum is specified by its low-pass filter slope, and the performance of each input is given in Table 4. Not surprisingly, the net performance declined from 57 percent to 35 percent correct as the level of the upper harmonics diminished from −6 to −12 dB/octave. This behavior is consistent with the net response to incomplete patterns, in which the presence of the fifth harmonic was critical. We had initially intended to test the −18 dB/octave spectral envelope characteristic of a variety of orchestral instruments. However, the poor performance on the −12 dB/octave envelope inputs made it obvious that the learning phase must use patterns that are more characteristic of the spectral envelopes to be encountered in the testing phase. Such behavior is well known in speech processing systems that customarily use a +6 dB per octave preemphasis filter to boost the upper spectral components important for speech perception. In pitch perception, the dominance region from 500–2000 Hz also implies the presence of an effective boost in the upper harmonics of the power spectrum with regard to pitch salience (Rasch and Plomp 1982).

Grossberg (1976) has emphasized the need to normalize net activations, and this idea can be partially implemented in the net architecture by artificially normalizing the inputs to the same total value used during the learning phase. This corresponds to normalizing spectral power. In present terminology, the total input spectral power utilized during the learning phase was 15, the product of three tones each composed of five partials all with values of one. For example, in the absence of normalization for an input pattern whose spectral envelope slope was −6 dB/octave, the input value for the nth partial ($n = 1, \ldots 5$) of each tone was $1/\sqrt{n}$. Hence, the total power was less than 15. During normalization, a constant was added to each input so that the total input power remained equal to 15.

Averaged across all spectral envelopes and all chords, the net correctly classified 49 percent of the patterns with unnormalized power spectra and 53 percent of the patterns with normalized power spectra. The net performance for the −6 and −12 dB/octave normalized spectral envelope patterns was improved relative to the unnormalized inputs, but was degraded for the +6 dB/octave case. This latter decrease in performance was controlled by the reduction in the major chord classification performance from 83 percent to 42 percent. As a general rule, increasing the spectral level of the partials during the testing phase improved net performance. When the spectral envelope slope was negative, normalization boosted all partials and performance improved. When the spectral envelope was positive, normalization attenuated all partials and overall performance diminished. As a function of chord type, the major chord classification performance followed the same trends as the average classification performance. Exceptions to the general rule are found for one of the three spectral input conditions in both the minor and diminished chord classification performance. In comparing the performance for unnormalized versus normalized inputs, the minor chord classification performance increased from 25 percent to 67 percent, respectively, for the −6 dB/octave slope, but decreased from 25 percent to 18 percent for the −12 dB/octave slope. The diminished chord classification performance followed the general rule when the spectral envelope slope was negative, but was in the opposite direction of the general rule when the slope was positive.

It is mildly disconcerting that net performance is sensitive to the average level of the inputs during the testing phase relative to those in the learning phase. One of the difficulties of error propagation is that of selecting a training set for learning that is sufficiently diverse that it can respond appropriately to the range of novel stimuli to which it is exposed after learning (Grossberg 1987). Since no attempt was made to train the net over the diversity found in musical instrument power spectra, it is not surprising that this error occurred. Due to the restriction of our training set to patterns whose activations were either 0 or 1, we chose to encode the input activation as a linear function of spectral amplitude. In the context of a training set in which spectral amplitudes were varied, it would be preferable to use a logarithmic encoding scheme (i.e., in decibels) in order to encode greater dynamic range for a comparable number of bits.

Discussion

A reasonable approach to building neural nets for music perception and cognition is to include as much information as is available and computationally practical from musical acoustics, physiology, and psychoacoustics into the net architecture. This approach guided our use of the harmonic and subharmonic complex representations. However, some recent research in experimental psychology (Bharucha and Stoeckig 1987) has offered evidence which would appear to opt for the simplest representation.

In a study on chord classification using a priming task, Bharucha and Stoeckig (1987) attempted to isolate acoustic from cognitive factors. Previously Bharucha and Stoeckig (1986) had found that listeners classified chords faster when the target chord was primed by a harmonically related chord, rather than by a harmonically unrelated chord. The purpose of their 1987 study was to investigate whether the priming effect could be attributed to overlapping partials, or whether it was indicative of a more cognitive form of representation. They used stimuli that either contained the first four harmonics, or the first, second, and fourth harmonics. The latter combination of octave-related harmonics produces nonoverlapping frequency spectra when tones are sounded simultaneously to form a triadic chord. In addition to controlling the spectra of the chords, they selected prime and target chords that did not share any fundamental tones. They hypothesized that if priming effects still occurred when partials did not overlap, then priming was due to a cognitive structure. Such a conclusion would support the use of a simple pitch class representation in our neural nets rather than the richer harmonic or subharmonic complex representations. Why then should we opt for a complex representation of pitch in a neural net?

First of all, mean reaction times in Bharucha and Stoeckig's (1987) experiment were approximately 100 msec (~12 percent) slower for chords stripped of overlapping harmonics. The slower performance seems to implicate the decrease in harmonic information as a factor in chord classification. If one considers chords stripped of overlapping partials as incomplete patterns, then an increase in the amount of time needed to classify a chord would be expected. Presumably activation by incomplete patterns takes longer to reach asymptote than activation caused by complete patterns. This needs further exploration with a larger number of subjects.

Secondly, current pitch perception theories argue that a sine wave stimulus invokes a pattern recognizer that, for present purposes, may be either the harmonic or the subharmonic template recognizer. This being the case, it is reasonable to posit a cognitive overlap of frequency spectra between the harmonic or subharmonic templates evoked by simultaneously sounded tones, even if the acoustical spectra of these tones are nonoverlapping. This mechanism can be invoked as an alternative explanation of Bharucha and Stoeckig's data.

Listeners have two pitch extraction modes—an analytic mode and a synthetic mode. Synthetic mode allows listeners to perceive a complex of sinusoids as a single pitch. Analytic mode allows listeners to hear out individually resolvable partials in a complex tone. In order to demonstrate that overlapping partials have nothing to do with chord priming effects, Bharucha and Stoeckig would need to assure that listeners are operating in analytic pitch processing mode. In order to accomplish this, the factors that contribute to a listener's processing mode need to be isolated first.

The issue of cognitive versus psychoacoustical causes of chord priming seems moot considering the parallel processes in the brain and the interaction of top-down and bottom-up processing. Hence, complex representations of pitch in a neural net are attractive representations for exploring the interaction of psychoacoustical and cognitive processes in music.

Future Directions

Neural nets show promise as models of the human auditory system. The initial conversion of the continuous acoustic signal to a pulse train of neural spikes has been modeled by a parallel filter bank whose bandwidths and filter shapes are reminiscent of the auditory critical bands. Each of the filter bank outputs is half-wave rectified and low-pass filtered to represent the short-time, averaged neural transduction process. More ambitious attempts are underway in the work of Lyon and Mead (1988), who are attempting to implement computational models of the auditory system that include automatic gain control using an active mechanism and lateral inhibition. Neural nets that employ a time-varying representation of the input acoustical signal may be capable of learning a wide variety of perceptual and cognitive tasks without the explicit guidance of higher-level, symbolic processing.

Computational models that implement complex pitch perception exist for the Goldstein model (Duifhuis, Willems, and Sluyter 1982), as well as for the Terhardt model (Hermes 1988). Our results suggest the possibility that both the Goldstein and Terhardt theories could be fully implemented as neural net models. If successful, such models would be useful in tasks other than pitch estimation, since the nets could be combined in a modular fashion with other music (and speech) perception neural nets.

Musicians are efficient, real-time signal processors. A skilled listener can process raw acoustical information into high-level abstractions. For example, many musicians can quite effortlessly hear a simple melody and notate it on staff paper. The ease of performing this type of cognitive task results from years of training in which the musician has learned to associate a label with a particular auditory pattern. A neural net that could model the melody transcription task may need to incorporate psychoacoustical as well as cognitive representations. A modular approach to constructing such a net may be necessary. A psychoacoustically based net could map the incoming signal into a higher-level representation, which is used as input to a cognitively based net for higher level analysis.

Conclusions

We have examined the issue of the representation of musical pitch in a neural net designed to classify musical chords. The type of representation can influence the ability of a net to learn a task and the number of epochs needed to train the net. Nets using the pitch class representation successfully completed the learning phase when the number of hidden units was sufficiently large. More work is needed to identify the factors limiting the performance of the pitch class nets. The harmonic complex and subharmonic complex representations led to nets that were successful in terms of correct chord classifications.

Leaving aside learning performance issues, we favor psychoacoustically based pitch representations. The pitch class representation is motivated by musical notational practice and symbolic representations that figure in cognitive studies. In contrast, the complex pitch representations are motivated by the spectral structure of musical sound, the physiological structure of neural activation patterns in the auditory system, and the pattern recognition mechanisms of complex pitch perception theories. The complex pitch representations have advantages in that they encode information concerning chord inversions and spectral content. This information is lost in the octave-equivalent representation of pitch in the pitch class net. With only 12 inputs, root position, first inversion, and second inversion chords are identically represented, whereas psychoacoustically based pitch representations distinguish between inversions. Furthermore, because only the fundamental pitch of a chord tone is represented in the pitch class net, spectral features are absent. There appears no virtue, and possibly some harm, in eliminating this information from the presentation of the net input. These more complex representations and the distributed connectivity using hidden units were successful in processing novel inputs including incomplete harmonic template patterns, chord inversions, and simulated power spectrum input. In each case, the net performance exceeded chance levels. The merger of psychoacoustical and cognitive approaches in a neural net paradigm may offer a way to model a musician's cognitive processes from ear to brain.

Acknowledgments

This research was partially supported by the National Institute of Health, and the University of Washington Graduate School Research Fund. The authors would like to thank Pierre Divenyi and anonymous reviewers for comments given on an earlier draft.

References

Benade, A. H. 1986. "Generic Spectrum Envelope Functions for Orchestral Wind Instruments." *Journal of the Acoustical Society of America* 79:93.

Benade, A. H., and S. N. Kouzoupis. 1985. "Spectral Envelopes of Orchestral Instruments." *Journal of the Acoustical Society of America* 78:75–76.

Bharucha, J. J. 1987. "MUSACT: A Connectionist Model of Musical Harmony." *Proceedings of the Ninth Annual Meeting of the Cognitive Science Society.* Hillsdale, N.J.: Erlbaum Press, pp. 508–517.

Bharucha, J. J., and K. Stoeckig. 1986. "Reaction Time and Musical Expectancy: Priming of Chords." *Journal of Experimental Psychology: Human Perception and Performance* 12:403–410.

Bharucha, J. J., and K. Stoeckig. 1987. "Priming of Chords: Spreading Activation or Overlapping Frequency Spectra?" *Perception and Psychophysics* 41(6):519–524.

de Boer, E. 1976. "On the 'Residue' and Auditory Pitch Perception." In W. D. Keidel and W. D. Neff, eds. *Handbook of Sensory Physiology. (Volume V, Auditory System, Part 3, Clinical and Special Topics).* Berlin: Springer-Verlag.

Dolson, Mark. 1989. "Machine Tongues XII: Neural Networks." *Computer Music Journal* 13(3):14–28.

Duifhuis, H., L. F. Willems, and R. J. Sluyter. 1982. "Measurement of Pitch in Speech: An Implementation of Goldstein's Theory of Pitch Perception." *Journal of the Acoustical Society of America* 71(6):1568–1580.

Franzini, M. A. 1988. "Learning to Recognize Spoken Words: A Study in Connectionist Speech Recognition." In D. Touretzky, G. Hinton, and T. Sejnowski, eds. *Proceedings of the 1988 Connectionist Models Summer School.* San Mateo: Morgan Kaufmann, pp. 407–416.

Gerson, A., and J. L. Goldstein. 1978. "Evidence for a General Template in Central Optimal Processing for the Pitch of Complex Tones." *Journal of the Acoustical Society of America* 63:498–510.

Goldstein, J. L. 1973. "An Optimum Processor Theory for the Central Formation of the Pitch of Complex Tones." *Journal of the Acoustical Society of America* 54:1496–1516.

Goldstein, J. L., et al. 1978. "Verification of the Optimal Probabilistic Basis of Aural Processing of Pitch of Complex Tones." *Journal of the Acoustical Society of America* 63:486–497.

Grossberg, S. 1976. "Adaptive Pattern Classification and Universal Recoding: I. Parallel Development and Coding of Neural Feature Detectors." *Biological Cybernetics* 23:121–134.

Grossberg, S. 1987. "Competitive Learning: From Interactive Activation to Adaptive Resonance." *Cognitive Science* 11:23–63.

Hermes, D. J. 1988. "Measurement of Pitch by Subharmonic Summation." *Journal of the Acoustical Society of America* 83:257–264.

Houtgast, T. 1976. "Subharmonic Pitches of a Pure Tone at Low S/N Ratio." *Journal of the Acoustical Society of America* 60(2):405–409.

Krumhansl, C. L. 1979. "The Psychological Representation of Musical Pitch in a Tonal Context." *Cognitive Psychology* 11:346–374.

Lyon, R. F., and C. Mead. 1988. "Analog Electronic Cochlea." *IEEE Transactions on Acoustics, Speech, and Signal Processing* 36(7):1119–1134.

Pitts, W., and W. S. McCulloch. 1947. "How We Know Universals: The Perception of Auditory and Visual Forms." *Bull. Math. Biophysics* 9:127–147.

Rasch, R. A., and R. Plomp. 1982. "The Perception of Musical Tones." In D. Deustch, ed. *The Psychology of Music.* Orlando: Academic Press.

Rumelhart, D. E., G. E. Hinton, and R. J. Williams. 1986. "Learning Internal Representations by Error Propagation." In D. E. Rumelhart and J. L. McClelland, eds. *Parallel Distributed Processing: Explorations in the Microstructure of Cognition.* Vol. 1. Foundations. Cambridge, Massachusetts: MIT Press, pp. 318–362.

Terhardt, E. 1974. "Pitch, Consonance, and Harmony." *Journal of the Acoustical Society of America* 55:1061–1069.

Terhardt, E. 1982. "Pitch of Complex Signals According to Virtual-Pitch Theory: Tests, Examples, and Predictions." *Journal of the Acoustical Society of America* 71:671–678.

von Helmholtz, H. 1954. *On the Sensations of Tone.* New York: Dover Books.

Addendum

Music is composed of tones that group together to form melodies and chords. Although chords proliferate in music, "well-behaved" triads are usually the exception, when compared with the number of nontriadic chords and individual notes that occur. Thus, the triadic chord classification networks discussed up to this point have limited applicability. This motivated us to construct networks that can instead identify either tone chroma (i.e., pitch class) or pitch (i.e., both pitch class and pitch height). Such networks would be useful not only as melody transcribers but as models of complex pitch perception. We thought this approach might also offer another solution to the chord classification problem by coupling two networks. That is, the chord classification network with pitch-class inputs could be piggy-backed on top of a pitch classifier network, so that both pitch and chord type could be extracted in turn from the same input values.

The harmonic and subharmonic complex representations used in the chord classification networks were fairly comparable in their performance. We decided to opt solely for the harmonic complex representation for the chroma and pitch classification networks because it reflects information that can be extracted from the spectra of musical tones. The drawback with the harmonic complex representation as it was used for the chord classification network is that input was limited to discrete values. Values indicated the presence of a partial in a complex tone, but not its amplitude level. The inadequacies of this approach became apparent when the network was tested with simulated power spectrum input (see table 4). To remedy this situation, subsequent work has adopted a logarithmic encoding scheme that captures the level of partials in a complex tone. Continuous values that represent normalized level are used as input to a network.

Two networks are discussed in this addendum. One computes the tone chroma of a harmonic complex that has five partials. The other network computes the pitch of a harmonic complex with five partials. Both networks are similar in that they use the same number of input units (64). Each unit has a one-semitone bandwidth, thus units represent log frequency. These 64 input units are sufficient to represent complex tones over a range of three octaves, since the tone's harmonics span a great octave range.

Both networks were trained and tested with the same pattern sets. Training sets consisted of 36 complex tone patterns from a pool of 144 patterns as follows. The initial 144-pattern pool was based upon previously published steady-state spectra from four instruments—clarinet, violin, trumpet, and pipe organ (Douglas 1976). The single published spectrum for each instrument represented one specific musical tone and was used as a template to build 36 patterns that spanned a three-octave range. The training set was then constructed by randomly selecting one of the four instrument spectra for each of the 36 pitches over three octaves. For example, a complex tone pattern with its first partial at C3 might have the spectrum of the clarinet, the complex tone with its first partial at C#3 might have the spectrum of the pipe organ, and so on up through B5. It was hoped that the network would learn to tolerate variations in the input values so it could generalize to other spectra.

Tone Chroma Classification Network

The tone chroma classification network had 30 hidden units and 12 output units—one output unit for each of the 12 tone chroma. After supervised learning, the network correctly classified all 36 input patterns in the training set. Various sets of patterns were used to test the network's ability to process novel patterns. The first test set consisted of the steady-state spectra the network did not train on, that is, the 108 test patterns not chosen from the initial pool of 144. The results are shown in Table 5, in the row labelled "Test Set." The performance (precent correct) was computed by scoring the output unit with the highest value as the network's response. Results for two output criteria, 0.1 and 0.5, are reported. At the 0.5 level an output unit activation of at least 0.5 was required for the output to be considered a response, while at the 0.1 level an output unit needed an activation of at least 0.1 to be considered a response.

Table 5. Tone chroma classification performance using harmonic complex input patterns consisting of normalized levels. Numbers in parentheses indicate the total number of patterns included in each set. Percent correct for two levels of performance (0.1 and 0.5) is shown.

	Percent Correct	
	0.1 Criteria	*0.5 Criteria*
Training Set (36)		100
Test Set (108)	98	98
Sine (36)	64	22
Missing Fundamental (144)	84	64
Real (19)	100	84

It is helpful to examine both levels of output criteria to surmise what contributes to the network's behavior. Test patterns elicit low activation values because of the differences between the training patterns and the test patterns. Notice in Table 5 that 98 percent of the test patterns (i.e., 106) activated the correct units at values of at least 0.5. Values close to 0.5 usually occurred in response to the clarinet spectrum. Because the clarinet spectrum has low input levels in the even harmonics, this response could indicate that in certain regions the network was using information about the even harmonics to compute its results.

The network was next tested on its ability to process two types of incomplete patterns—sine tone patterns (i.e., patterns with only the first partial present) and complex tone patterns with a missing fundamental. The results are depicted in Table 5. Note that output units were generally activated at a low level (i.e., less than 0.5) by the sine tone patterns. The network was better at identifying the tone chroma of missing fundamental patterns than sine tone patterns, suggesting that upper partials are more important to network performance than the first partial, as was found in the case of chord generalization in Table 2.

The steady-state spectrum of a musical instrument varies over its frequency range. However, the network was trained on steady-state spectra that were all copied and transposed from one specific tone on a musical instrument. Thus, the next test set explored the network's response to patterns that reflect variations encountered in real-world musical signals. Twelve clarinet tones were digitized starting at concert G3 and ascending chromatically. Spectra were computed and levels normalized. This same procedure was used on three classical guitar tones (B3, G3, and E4), two piano tones (G3 and E4), and two alto recorder tones (F4 and F#5). Normalized levels were used as input to the network. The results are shown in Table 5, in the row labeled "Real." In general, the network was able to tolerate variances in level across instruments and frequencies. Sixteen of the 19 patterns (84 percent) elicited correct responses using the 0.5 criteria, whereas all the patterns were correctly identified using the 0.1 criteria. Two of the guitar spectra and one clarinet spectrum activated the correct output units at a level below 0.5.

Although the network was trained to compute the tone chroma of a single tone, the harmonic complex representation has the capacity to process two or more simultaneous tone patterns. Dyad and triad patterns were used to assess this capacity. A total of 258 dyad patterns and 196 triad patterns were constructed by combining spectral patterns randomly chosen from the initial pool of 144 patterns. A dyad could consist of a combination of any two of the four basic instrument spectra. For example, one dyad pattern might include a clarinet paired with a violin. Another pattern might pair a trumpet with a violin. It is also possible to pair an instrument with itself. A similar approach was used in the construction of triads. Dyads included intervals of a minor second through major seventh, across two octaves. Triads included root position, first inversion, and second inversion major, minor, and diminished chords across two octaves. The results are reported in Table 6.

Unlike the network response to single tone complexes, the output for the dyad and triad patterns exhibited some spurious activity. Sometimes four output units were clearly activated when only three should be. The data in Table 6 is displayed in a signal detection format to reflect this activity. The

Table 6. Behavior of output nodes in response to simultaneous input patterns of either dyads or triads, for the tone chroma classification network. Results are reported in signal detection format. Values indicate percent correct at the 0.1 performance criterion.

a. Dyads (258 patterns)

	On	Off
On	93	3
Off	7	97

Percent correct using Highest 2-Win criteria: 92

b. Triads (196 patterns)

	On	Off
On	81	5
Off	19	95

Percent correct using Highest 3-Win criteria: 79

value in the On-On cell indicates the percentage of correct "on" responses, whereas the value in the Off-Off cell indicates the percentage of correct "off" responses (i.e., no output when a unit was supposed to be silent). The value in the On-Off cell indicates the percentage of output units that responded when they should have remained silent (i.e., false alarms). Finally, the Off-On cell indicates the percentage of output units that did not respond when they should have (i.e., misses). Units were judged to be on if their output was greater than or equal to 0.1. As Table 6a indicates, the network performed quite well in identifying the tone chroma of dyads, but it still occasionally made both false alarms and misses.

Another way to characterize network performance is to examine the percentage of time the two most highly activated output units were actually the correct response, that is, using a "Highest 2-Win Criteria." This was 92 percent, 1 percent less than the On-On cell in Table 6a. The 1 percent difference is an indicator of how many times "falsely alarmed" units (On-Off behavior) exceeded correctly responding units. In this case, the difference translates to six times.

The network did not perform as well on triads as it did on dyads, as can be seen in Table 6b. The output units corresponding to the tones in the triad were on 81 percent of the time, whereas 95 percent of the time output units that were supposed to be off were off. Misses were at 19 percent whereas false alarms were 5 percent. When a "Highest 3-Win" criteria was applied, the network correctly identified the tone chroma of triads 79 percent of the time.

The fact that the network could classify even 79 percent of the triads' tone chroma suggests that coupling networks may lead to improved performance on certain tasks, such as chord identification. The tone chroma output of this network exactly matches the input used by the chord classification network with the pitch-class representation. Thus, the output of the tone chroma classifier could be used as input to the chord classification network. Coupled in this manner, performance on chord inversions should be superior to the performance of the harmonic complex network, which was 40 percent or below (see Table 3) when classifying chord inversions.

Pitch Classification Network

Pitch classification is a more difficult task than classifying tone chroma because it requires both tone chroma and pitch-height identification. This is reflected in the additional number of output units in the pitch classification network. Twelve output units are needed for each octave in the network's range, rather than just the 12 total in the chroma-classification network. Our network had a range of three octaves, from C3 through B5, so it had 36 output units. In all other respects it was similar to the tone chroma classification network.

At first glance it may seem that pitch identification is a simple mapping of the fundamental frequency to its corresponding output unit; however, the presence of harmonics in the input causes interference, which makes this simple response impossible. If the network is to learn the task, it must associate the *pattern* of harmonics with the fundamental frequency. This neural network implementation is similar to Goldstein's theory (1973) of pitch perception in that pattern matching using a harmonic template is central to the model.

Table 7. Pitch classification performance using harmonic complex input patterns consisting of normalized levels. Numbers in parentheses indiate the total number of patterns included in each set. Percent correct for two levels of performance (0.1 and 0.5) is shown.

	Percent Correct	
	0.1 Criteria	*0.5 Criteria*
Training Set (36)	97	97
Test Set (108)	97	96
Sine (36)	33	3
Missing Fundamental (144)	82	50
Real (19)	95	89

Table 8. Behavior of output nodes in response to simultaneous input patterns of either dyads or triads, for the pitch classification network. Results are reported in signal detection format. Values indicate percent correct at the 0.1 performance criteria.

a. Dyads (264 patterns)

	On	Off
On	85	1
Off	15	99

Percent correct using Highest 2-Win criteria: 84

b. Triads (196 patterns)

	On	Off
On	74	2
Off	26	98

Percent correct using Highest 3-Win criteria: 72

The same 36 steady-state spectra used to train the tone chroma classification network were used to train the pitch extraction network. In this case, however, the network only learned 35 of the 36 patterns (97 percent). It did not learn to identify the A#3 complex tone pattern. The failure to learn A#3 indicates the network found a local, rather than a global, minimum during the training phase. It is possible that either a different starting state or a different hidden unit configuration could lead to a network in which all 36 patterns were learned; however, we did not find such a solution.

The ability of the network to process novel input was explored with the same test sets used to examine the previous network. This included the 108 novel patterns from the initial 144 pattern pool, as well as 36 sine tone patterns, 144 missing fundamental patterns, and the 19 patterns based upon the measured spectra of the clarinet, guitar, alto recorder, and piano. The results are reported in Table 7.

Although the network was able to generalize to novel spectra, it did not perform quite as well as the tone chroma classification network. This is due to the A#3 pattern the network did not learn in the training phase. These results are shown in Table 7 in the row labeled "Test Set." The network identified all the test patterns at the 0.1 criteria or better except in the three cases in which the test patterns had a pitch of A#3.

The first partial, as seen by the results for the sine tone patterns listed in Table 7, contributes less to performance of this network than in the tone chroma network. In this case, the sine patterns only yield 33 percent performance at the 0.1 level, compared to 64 percent for tone chroma. As with the tone chroma network, though, the first partial activated most of the output units at a level below 0.5. The network performed better on the missing fundamental patterns than on the sine tone patterns, again suggesting that a combination of the upper partials contributes more to the network's performance than the first partial does. When given the 19 "real" patterns, the network failed to respond to the one—the A#3 pattern it had failed to learn in the training set. Of the 18 patterns it correctly identified, however, only one pattern, G3 on the clarinet, had activation below the .05 level.

The network was next tested with 264 dyads and 196 triads and exhibited an ability to identify the pitches in simultaneous input patterns, although the performance was poorer than the tone chroma network. These results are listed in Table 8. Some of the errors were due to octave misidentification. For example the network might identify the D3 pattern as D4 instead. As with the tone chroma network, the "Highest Win" criteria lags behind the percentge of output units correctly turned on by 1 or 2 percent. In several cases, activation at the erroneous octave caused the correct output unit to lose under the "Highest 2-Win" or "Highest 3-Win" criteria.

Summary

A harmonic complex representation that accepts normalized level as input can be used to model perceptual phenomena such as the pitch perception of a complex tone. This representation reflects the steady-state spectra of real musical instruments and could conceivably be used in a signal-processing capacity to map acoustical information to tone chroma, pitch, or chord type. A neural network approach might possibly be further applied to tougher problems, such as timbre identification.

The harmonic complex representation is versatile enough to allow a variety of novel patterns, including dyads and triads, to be processed by a network. Networks were fairly successful at identifying the components of simultaneous patterns despite the fact that training sets were rather modest and included only single complex-tone patterns.

Although the input units of the networks discussed here have a semitone bandwidth, networks that have a finer resolution may be of use when it is desirable to capture the notion of out-of-tuneness. Initial efforts in this area have been reported recently (Laden 1990).

Acknowledgments

Access to the San Diego Supercomputer Center was provided through NorthWest Net at the University of Washington. The authors would like to thank Pamela Goad for assistance in performing and digitizing the musical instrument tones used in the testing phase.

References

Douglas, A. 1976. *Electronic Music Production.* Blue Ridge Summit, Pennsylvania: TAB Books.

Laden, B. 1990. "Representation of Pitch Input to Neural Network Models of Music Perception." *Journal of Acoustical Society of America* 87:s18.

Jamshed J. Bharucha
Psychology Department
Dartmouth College
Hanover, New Hampshire 03755 U.S.A.
bharucha@dartmouth.edu

Pitch, Harmony, and Neural Nets: A Psychological Perspective

Two divergent but overlapping goals characterize work on neural net models of music. One is the attempt to understand and develop intelligent musical systems. Networks proposed in pursuit of this goal may be called artificial networks (or models thereof). This is an important goal of research in computer music. The other goal is the attempt to understand a given intelligent musical system: the human brain. Networks proposed in pursuit of this goal may be called human networks (or models thereof). This is the primary goal of research on the psychology and neuroscience of music. Since the brain is only one of presumably many possible intelligent systems, there are necessarily more constraints on models of human networks.

The pursuit of artificial networks follows the machine design methodology of engineering. One begins with a task (such as extracting pitch from an acoustic instrument signal), and then asks the question, How can a machine be designed to carry out this task? The test of the ensuing model's adequacy is whether it carries out the stated task. Alternative models based on very different approaches could in principle carry out the same task. A comparison of alternative models would typically be based on such criteria as how efficient they are and how well they scale up.

The pursuit of human networks follows the hypothesis-testing methodology of basic empirical science. The question here is, How (either physically or functionally) does the brain carry out this task? The test of the ensuing model's accuracy is not only whether it carries out the stated task but whether it also carries out other tasks that are known to be performed by the same system and whether it satisfies all known constraints on the structure and function of the system. Although the additional constraints would result in fewer possible models than for artificial networks, there will nevertheless be alternative models. A comparison of alternative models would be based on the testable predictions that they make and the outcomes of experiments designed to test these predictions.

For example, a neural net that extracts pitch from a frequency fails as a model of human networks if it cannot account for the corpus of laboratory data on shifts of residue pitch (Patterson 1973; Schouten, Ritsma, and Cardoza 1962). A neural net that learns melodies fails as a model of human networks if it cannot account for key-distance effects associated with transposition in the short term (Cuddy, Cohen, and Miller 1979). A neural net that extracts chords fails as a model of human networks if it cannot account for the corpus of data on the perceived relationships between chords (Bharucha and Krumhansl 1983; Bharucha and Stoeckig 1986, 1987; Krumhansl, Bharucha, and Castellano 1982).

This chapter has two goals. The first is to focus attention on some issues pertinent to the development of models of human networks for music perception. The second is to sketch aspects of a particular model. The chapter will begin with a discussion of some issues concerning the choice of algorithm. It will then launch into a brief review of psychological accounts of pitch, followed by a critique of the psychological adequacy of pitch representations adopted in extant models. The remainder of the chapter will summarize continuing work on a model that originated as a spreading activation network for harmony (Bharucha and Stoeckig 1986) and evolved into a constraint satisfaction network called MUSACT (Bharucha 1987a). MUSACT extracts chords from tones and keys from chords. It accounts for the effect of tonal contexts on the perception of tones and chords, and the establishment of keys. The focus in this chapter will be on how MUSACT learns its connectivity, and on how networks that process pitch prior to MUSACT might learn their connectivity. A network for achieving invariance under transposition is also summarized

(Bharucha 1988). This invariance mechanism feeds a sequential memory that is described in another chapter (Bharucha and Todd, this volume).

Supervised Learning Algorithms and Expectancy Violation

The choice of a neural net algorithm (supervised or unsupervised) depends at least as much on the goal (artificial versus human networks) as on the task to be modeled. Supervised learning (e.g., the back-propagation algorithm of Rumelhart, Hinton, and Williams 1986) requires that the output of the network in response to a given input be compared to a target or desired output. The difference is the error signal, which the algorithm seeks to minimize. The pursuit of human networks limits the use of supervised learning algorithms to tasks in which target vectors are clearly available to the system under natural conditions.

Consider a central problem in speech, that of learning to extract discrete phonemes from a speech signal. If the goal is to build an artificial network that can perform this task, one might consider a back-propagation network that learns to identify the phoneme given the speech signal. This option is available because one can supply the network with the target phonemes for each input signal (e.g., Landauer and Kamm 1987). If the goal is to model how humans learn, however, this option is not available. Humans don't have any way of knowing what the target phoneme is except by extracting it from the speech signal, which is of course what we want to learn in the first place.

A similar example in music concerns the ability to extract chords from complex spectra. Laden and Keefe (this volume) invoke back propagation to learn this. The network receives a spectrum as input and the correct chord as the target and thereby learns to identify the chord given the spectrum. A music student who receives feedback from a teacher while learning to classify chords as major or minor would indeed have the necessary target. One can demonstrate in a psychological laboratory, however, that Western subjects with no musical training, who are unable to name chords, are nevertheless able to make judgments about chords and their relationships; these judgments are extraordinarily sophisticated and consistent with the explicit descriptions of music theorists (Bharucha 1987b; Bharucha and Stoeckig 1986). This implicit or tacit knowledge of chords must have been obtained through passive perceptual exposure without feedback; supervised learning is thus inappropriate here.

When the use of supervised learning is unsupported by the learning conditions that would exist for a human, it is necessary to search for unsupervised, self-organizing networks (such as those proposed by Fukushima 1975; Grossberg 1976; Kohonen 1984; Rumelhart and Zipser 1985; von der Malsburg 1973). These networks are compelling psychologically because they do not require target vectors in order to learn. They are compelling neuroscientifically because they involve a learning mechanism about which there is a consensus, namely, Hebbian learning (Hebb 1949). These algorithms have been employed to model the learning of melodic patterns (Gjerdingen, this volume) and to model the acquisition of the MUSACT structure for harmony, as described below.

Are supervised learning algorithms therefore of limited value for modeling human networks? Gjerdingen (this volume) argues in the affirmative, stating that "for higher-level tasks, the notion of an explicit teacher becomes problematical." Gjerdingen's blanket rejection of supervised learning is flawed, however, because it ignores tasks for which target vectors are available and necessary—tasks that depend upon registering an error signal.

Learning musical sequences is a task for which error signals are both available and necessary. They are available because each event is the target to be compared with the expectation generated prior to that event. They are necessary because the error signal plays an important role in the aesthetic or emotional response to music. It is widely held that expectancy violation is an important aspect of the aesthetics of music (Meyer 1956). In the sequential model discussed by Bharucha and Todd (this volume), the error signal that drives learning is precisely the information that would lead to expectancy violation. Thus both learning and the experience of expectancy violation are driven by the same process.

This would suggest that Gjerdingen's model, billed as unsupervised, either fails to account for expectancy violation or doesn't utilize this information for learning. But Gjerdingen is clearly concerned with expectancy violation, and closer examination reveals that, contrary to its billing, the model does indeed rely on this information for learning. The model registers the disparity between what it expects and what actually occurs, the latter being a target in supervised learning. If there is a disparity, "the network's orienting subsystem will automatically react to the mismatch." The model is thus inescapably supervised, and the same error signal that drives the learning also explains expectancy violation.

Psychological Background for Modeling Pitch and Harmony

Psychophysics

The modern scientific study of pitch perception has been conducted primarily by psychologists and neuroscientists. In psychology, most of the work prior to the 1970s was in psychoacoustics, a branch of psychophysics. Psychophysics is the study of how dimensions that characterize the physical world are transformed into dimensions that characterize perception. For example, frequency is a physical dimension whose psychological correlate is pitch. The mapping from frequency to pitch, as employed in music, is logarithmic.

Perhaps the most valuable contribution of psychophysics to our understanding of pitch perception in music is research on the extraction of pitch from complex spectra. The pitch of a complex wave with a harmonic spectrum is generally perceived to be identical to the pitch of a sine wave of the same frequency as the fundamental frequency of the complex wave, whether or not the complex wave contains energy at the fundamental. Helmholtz (1885/1954) explained this "missing fundamental" phenomenon as a distortion product introduced by the auditory system. This view is incorrect because a pitch is perceived at the missing fundamental even when the region of the fundamental is masked with noise (Licklider 1954). Furthermore, the pitch is not necessarily perceived at the frequency of a distortion product (deBoer 1956; Schouten, Ritsma, and Cardoza 1962). It was subsequently thought that perceived pitch (often called the *residue* or *virtual* pitch) is computed from the shape of the waveform resulting from adding the components (deBoer 1956). This theory fails because residue pitch is not sensitive to the relative phases of the components, whereas the shape of the waveform is (Patterson 1973). The perceived pitch thus seems to be the result of a pattern recognition system that performs a best fit of the component frequencies to harmonic spectra that have been learned (Goldstein 1973; Terhardt, Stoll, and Seewann 1982). Because this is a pattern recognition process and because learning seems to be involved, neural nets are ideally suited to modeling pitch extraction.

Aside from pitch extraction, much of the psychophysical study of pitch has dealt with identification, discrimination, and magnitude estimation of pure tones (Green 1976). Although a wealth of knowledge has been gleaned from studies of the pitch of pure tones, the implications for understanding music are limited and can be misleading. For example, scales based on measures of JND (just noticeable differences) between pitches, or on the subjective estimation of magnitudes (the *mel* scale of Stevens and Volkmann 1940), are unable to account for one of the most salient constraints on the perceptual scaling of pitch, namely, the similarity of pitches that are separated by octaves.

Cognitive Psychology

The central limitation of psychoacoustic studies of pitch was that pitch was construed as one dimensional. Cognitive psychologists refer to this dimension as *pitch height.* Pitch height is the dimension of pitch that is described by up and down. As one pitch is raised relative to another, the striking similarity between the two that is noticed at octave intervals requires another dimension of pitch that is described by up and down. As one pitch is raised relative to another, the striking similarity between the two that is noticed at octave intervals requires another dimension in the psychological scaling of pitch (Deutsch 1973; Shepard 1964). When the pitch-height continuum is collapsed across octaves, the relative position of a tone within any given octave is referred to as its *chroma*. It is the chroma dimension that is captured by the octave equivalent letter names, or *pitch classes* (e.g. C, C#, etc.), used in Western music. Other dimensions of psychological pitch space are imposed by the consonance and dissonance of other intervals, such as perfect fifths (Shepard 1982). In the context of a piece of music, pitch classes reveal affinities that define additional dimensions. For example, the three tones of the tonic triad are perceived to be closely related in the context of a piece of Western tonal music (Krumhansl 1979), and diatonic tones are more easily confused with each other than with nondiatonic tones (Dowing 1978; Krumhansl 1979). Analogous effects occur in experiments with the music of other cultures. For example, tones that belong to a *raga* (one of the traditional melodic patterns or modes in Indian music) are perceived to be closely related in the context of a piece of North Indian music (Castellano, Bharucha, and Krumhansl 1984). Cognitive psychologists thus consider pitch to be a multidimensional attribute (Krumhansl 1990).

Cognitive psychologists have also been concerned with the mental processes that compute these pitch relationships. Many of these processes operate automatically (i.e., without conscious awareness) and are not limited to listeners who have had formal musical training. The processes that are of primary interest to this author are those that occur in the minds of people with little or no formal musical training. For example, Western listeners have an elaborate representation of tonal relationships in harmony, even if they have had no formal musical training. This can be shown in a priming task, in which the speed and accuracy with which a musical event is processed can be measured as a function of the preceding musical context. For example, when a major chord is musically related to the prior context, it is processed more quickly and more accurately, and is heard as more consonant, than when it is musically unrelated to the prior context (Bharucha and Stoeckig 1986, 1987). The speed and accuracy of judgments varies monotonically with the distance, around the circle of fifths, of the chord from the prior context (Bharucha 1987b).

Subjects ranging from those with no formal training to professional composers show similar effects. The only apparent prerequisite to exhibiting these data is having grown up in Western society, in which the music that is most pervasive, and impossible to avoid, is overwhelmingly based on triads in tonic, dominant, and subdominant relationships.

Learning

Which aspects of pitch are innately specified and which are learned? Are they universal or culture relative? Although these questions are relevant if one is modeling human networks, they should be asked with care. A mechanism can be innately specified but can fail to develop if the necessary environmental conditions are not present. Conversely, a perceptual phenomenon can be universal simply because the environmental constraints are universal. In this latter case, there may or may not be learning (see Bharucha and Olney 1989).

Harmonic spectra are found universally, because of the physical properties of the human voice and other naturally occurring periodic signals. If complex tones whose pitches are an octave apart are universally judged to be similar, this could be accounted for on the basis of the presence of octave harmonics in natural periodic signals. Octave equivalence would thus be neither innate nor learned but would simply presuppose an auditory mechanism, such as the *place mechanism* in the ear, that registers spectral similarity.

Whereas some relationships can be found in a comparison of the spectra themselves, others can be found in the array of pitches that are extracted from spectra. Parncutt (1989) argues that the perceived relationships in Western harmony can be accounted for in this fashion, eliminating the need for higher level processes, innate or learned, that mediate our perception of harmony. According to this view, the complex spectrum of a musical chord induces a number of pitches, called *virtual* pitches, as described by Terhardt's pitch extraction model (Terhardt, Stoll, and Seewann 1982). The more pitches there are in common between two chords, the more closely related will the chords be perceived. Thus, although Terhardt's pitch extraction mechanism itself involves learning based on exposure to speech, the relationships that define harmony are driven (in a bottom-up or date-driven fashion) by the structure of harmonic spectra via the extracted virtual pitches, and no additional circuitry specific to harmony is necessary.

Although Parncutt's theory may be sufficient to account for important aspects of harmony, including the origins of Western harmony, it is not sufficient to account for all of the available data. His theory predicts that chords that share tones will be more closely related than chords that don't. Yet the circle-of-fifths relationship between chords violates pitch commonality. The circle of fifths is a spatial arrangement of chords that depicts their proximity in Western tonal music. (The circle of fifths for major chords, expressed in enharmonic equivalents, is as follows: C,G,D,A,E,B,F♯,C♯,G♯,D♯,A♯,F,C). C and D major are closer along the circle of fifths than are C and A major, yet C and D have no tones in common, but C and A have one tone in common. Thus, the commonality of pitches cannot explain the circle of fifths, and the circle of fifths is not just a theoretical construct but emerges from the responses of subjects in psychological experiments.

It is clear, then, that the perceived structure of pitch as it occurs in Western harmony is not driven by characteristics of harmonic spectra alone or by characteristics of the pitch extraction process. Additional evidence comes from an experiment in which spectral components that are shared by related chords are removed. Even without spectral overlap, chords are processed more quickly and more accurately and are perceived as more consonant when preceded by chords that are closely related along the circle of fifths than when preceded by chords that are distant along the circle of fifths (Bharucha and Stoeckig 1987). Relationships such as those described by the circle of fifths thus must have been learned. Since most people do not receive rule-based instruction in the theory of harmony, this learning must occur from passive exposure, presumably over a long period of time.

The view advanced in this chapter is that most of the dimensions of pitch are learned through extended passive exposure. Some aspects of learning are driven by patterns that are universally pervasive (such as octaves in the harmonic spectra of speech) and are thus likely to be manifested universally. Other aspects of learning are driven by patterns that are pervasive only within a culture (such as major and minor chords) and are thus likely to be culture relative. In either case, since the human brain is an extraordinary learning machine, patterns that are pervasive in the environment are likely to be learned inadvertently. This learning can yield emergent phenomena that themselves cannot be accounted for by environmental patterns alone. Neural nets have particular promise as models of this form of learning. The circle of fifths can be shown to emerge from a neural net that learns the typical clustering of tones to form chords and the typical clustering of chords to form keys.

Neuroscience

At least two classes of neuroscientific data are relevant to the development of neural net models of music perception. The first concerns the tuning characteristics of neurons, and the second concerns the anatomical dissociation of musical functions.

In a neural net model, learning consists of changing the weights of links between neural units. This is tantamount to changing the response characteristics or tuning of neural units. In support of this, Weinberger and Diamond (1988) report a response plasticity of neurons in the auditory cortex following associative learning.

Self-organizing algorithms (e.g., Fukushima 1975; Grossberg 1976; Kohonen 1984; Rumelhart and Zipser 1985; von der Malsburg 1973) predict that, as a result of weight changes, certain neurons will become tuned to complex patterns that represent the clustering of simple features. Beyond some preliminary suggestions of the existence of neurons that respond to pitch contour (Weinberger and McKenna 1988), little is known about whether or not neurons with complex tuning characteristics exist in the auditory system and, if so, what these tuning characteristics are.

Neurons in the early stages of auditory processing have innately specified tuning characteristics. Because of the place coding of the cochlea, a neuron that receives excitation from the basilar membrane is tuned to a particular frequency (its *characteristic* frequency). Adjacent neurons have slightly different characteristic frequencies, with overlapping receptive fields. Collectively, these neurons constitute a tonotopic representation of the audible frequency range, scaled logarithmically (see Sano and Jenkins, this volume).

A tonotopic mapping of log frequency is also found in the auditory cortex (Lauter et al. 1985), albeit with less clarity. The presence of a tonotopic mapping throughout the auditory system and the absence of robust evidence of the existence of more abstract tuning characteristics should not preclude the postulation of abstract representational units in neural net models. Indeed, neural net models can play a valuable role in making predictions for the neuroscientific study of response selectivity, provided the models are of human and not artificial networks. Thus, the MUSACT model described in this chapter predicts the formation of units tuned to tone clusters that are typically encountered, such as chords.

One reason why little other than the tonotopic mapping is known is that neuroscientific studies have typically employed pure tones, thus limiting the discovery of neurons with more complex response characteristics. This predicament was noted by Deutsch (1969) and is not much different today. Commenting on Goldberg and Lavine's (1968) bewilderment at the "surprisingly large number of unresponsive units" (p. 331) in the auditory system, Deutsch (1969) states that this "would hardly be surprising, since animals in their natural environment are much more concerned with auditory pattern recognition than with pure tones" (p.304).

Neuroscientific studies have also provided information about the dissociation of musical functions. Perhaps the greatest consensus concerns the hemispheric dissociation between temporal and atemporal processes, for which the left and right hemispheres, respectively, are dominant. Consequently, in the model sketched in this chapter, an atemporal structure, MUSACT, is dissociated from a temporal memory for sequences.

Another example of a dissociation comes from the study of a stroke patient, named M. S., who lost all of his primary auditory cortex and much of his nonprimary areas as well (Tramo, Bharucha, and Musiek 1990). M. S. was unable to detect spectral changes (in musical chords) that would be simple for normal subjects. Yet he showed evidence of chord priming as described above. These results suggest that tacit knowledge of the relationships between chords is at least partially dissociable from the mechanism that permits fine-grained comparisons of spectra.

The Representation and Organization of Musical Pitch in Neural Nets

How should pitch be represented? What constraints can be brought to bear on this decision? In this section we shall consider the representation of pitch as it funcitons in the perception and encoding of pitch sequences and pitch clusters in music.

The first modern proposal of a neural net model for musical pitch that was motivated by a discussion of a wide range of constraints was due to Deutsch (1969). Although this model is modest by today's standards, it anticipates some central architectural characteristics of contemporary models, including the use of representations for spectra, pitch class, intervals and chords. Deutsch offers a discussion of the merits of different representations. A discussion of selected representations can be found in other chapters (Laden and Keefe, this volume; Sano and Jenkins, this volume; and Todd, this volume). Since several important points have not been touched on in these chapters, the present chapter will attempt to do so, with the perspective of including as many known constraints as possible on the selection of representations.

Spectral Representation

A spectral representation is one that most resembles the acoustic signal in the frequency domain. The existence of tonotopic representations throughout the auditory system, including the cortex, might suggest that the perception and encoding of pitch in music is accomplished directly with spectral representations. Laden and Keefe (this volume), for example, suggest that a spectral representation obviates more abstract representational units such as pitch class. They note that spectral representations "are motivated by the spectral structure of musical sound, the physiological structure of neural activation patterns in the auditory system, and the pattern recognition mechanisms of complex pitch perception theories."

Although there can be no doubt that spectral representations are necessary and do in fact exist, what's at issue is whether they are sufficient for the representation of pitch, particularly as it functions in music. Laden and Keefe argue that a "musical tone needs to be specified as a number of pitch classes that approximate the harmonic partials of the tone rather than as a single pitch." This view obscures the distinction between frequency and pitch and is at odds with what we know from psychophysics. It is difficult even to articulate the known phenomena on pitch perception without assuming two kinds of representations, one for frequency spectra and one for pitch, such that the former begets the latter.

Since a spectral representation encodes a tone as its spectrum, no distinction is made between the many frequency components and the singular pitch that is typically heard. A complex periodic waveform is heard as a singular pitch (the synthetic mode of pitch perception, which is the norm) and not as many pitches, with one for each harmonic (the analytic mode of pitch perception, which requires training). A melody played on an instrument or sung is heard as a sequence of unitary pitches, not as a sequence of pitch clusters.

Furthermore, from one spectral event to the next, a pitch may be heard as rising, falling, or staying the same. Two tones, x and y, can be constructed such that x has a higher pitch than y even though the center frequency of x is lower, or even though all frequencies in x are lower. Laden and Keefe would argue that although x has lower acoustic components, the spectrum is filled out via a pattern completion process, hence the psychological representation of the spectrum is richer than the physical one. Although it is plausible that spectral pattern completion occurs and accounts for important psychoacoustic phenomena, it is most unlikely that filled-out spectra alone can account for the perception of pitch. What aspect of the filled-out spectra of x and y account for x being heard as higher than y? Perhaps one could compare the (actual or filled-in) fundamental frequencies to determine which is higher. But the spectral representation by itself gives no special status to the fundamental frequency, hence it is not equal to this task. There must be a subsequent stage of processing in which the pitch (usually at the actual or filled-in fundamental) is extracted and represented as unitary. Sano and Jenkins (this volume) postulate just such a mapping from a spectral representation to a unitary pitch representation, although they do not provide a mechanism by which it is learned. In any case, the spectral representation alone is not a representation of pitch at all but rather an elaborated representation of the signal, from which pitch is extracted.

Pitch-Height Representation

If pitch height is extracted from a spectral representation, perhaps this is a level of representation sufficient for representing pitch as it functions in music. In network models, this representation can consist of an array of units, each of which responds selectively to a particular pitch, such that collectively they span the audible pitch range.

There can be little doubt that we have a pitch-height representation, since the up/down dimension of pitch is perhaps the most salient. Although most people have poor long-term memory for pitch height (i.e., most people do not have *absolute pitch*), we do indeed have the ability to remember pitch height over the short term. If two tones are played in succession, a judgment of whether the second tone is higher or lower in pitch requires that the first tone be represented in memory long enough to make the comparison.

Although a pitch-height representation may be necessary in models of human musical cognition, it is not sufficient, for at least three reasons. First, it ignores octave equivalence. Often some of the units in a pitch-height representation are labeled with a pitch-class name followed by the octave number (e.g., C3, C♯3, . . . , B3, C4 . . .). This scheme captures octave equivalence only in the labeling, not in the representation. Second, a pitch-height representation entails the ability to remember absolute pitch levels over the long term (this may be called long-term absolute pitch). In other words, if the only pitch representation we have is pitch height, the original pitch-height levels of a tune will be remembered if the tune is remembered at all. But most people show little evidence of this. The third reason why a pitch-height representation is not sufficient (related but not identical to the second reason) is that it ignores *invariance under transposition,* that is, the ability to recognize a sequence transposed to any reference pitch.

The infinite number of pitches in the pitch-height continuum is usually broken up for representational purposes into a finite number of pitch-ranges or bins. For instance, a pitch-height representation could have a unit for every JND of pitch in the audible range. Pitch height representations that are much sparser than this have often been postulated as well. An example of this is a representation with only the twelve chromatic categories in each octave (e.g., C3, C♯3, . . . , B3, C4 . . .). Such a representation may be called a *categorical pitch-height* representation. Todd (this volume) has used such a representation as the input to a network that learns musical sequences and then composes new ones. Sano and Jenkins (this volume) assume that there are units only at the semitone foci and that actual pitch deviations from the category foci are assimilated to the categories.

Categorical pitch-height representations have little psychological basis, since pitch-height categories are not anchored at absolute points along the audible frequency continuum. Without a physical reference such as a tuning fork, there is little agreement (across individuals or across occasions for an individual) about the location of the pitch A4, the traditional Western tuning reference of 440 Hz. This contrasts with the situation in vision. Although color categories have fuzzy boundaries, the three main color categories (red, green, blue) are anchored at absolute focal points along the visual wavelength continuum, and there is universal agreement about these foci, even in cultures (such as the Dani) that do not have names for these categories (Heider 1972).

Interval Representation

In an interval representation (discussed by Todd, this volume, as a pitch-interval representation), a pitch sequence is represented in terms of the successive intervals between tones. Each interval defines the pitch distance from one tone to the next, in semitone or log frequency units. A sequence of n tones would thus be represented by $n-1$ intervals (and possibly the starting pitch).

This representation is compelling until one considers further constraints. Although some might contend that we hear intervals, few would deny that we hear individual tones. If two tones are played in succession, separated by a brief period of silence, one's perceptual impression is of hearing two events separated in time, the events beginning at the onsets of the tones. Strong contrary evidence would be required in order to maintain that the memory representation of the sequence is fundamentally different from the perceptual representation, such that only the relationships between the perceptually salient events, and not the perceptually salient events themselves, are encoded in memory.

An interval representation requires that at least the first two tones of a sequence be heard before recognition is possible. This is surely false. A piece can be recognized by its very first event if the combination of tonal, temporal, and timbral cues is sufficiently unique. Since timbre is the property of the acoustic event itself, and not a property of the interval between two acoustic events, the acoustic events must necessarily be enclоded. In other words, it would be bizarre if timbre were indexed by the acoustic event but pitch by the relationship between acoustic events.

An interval representation doesn't account for tonal confusability. If a brief diatonic melody is followed by a (transposed) melody that is either the same melody or has one tone changed (while preserving the contour), listeners are more likely to judge the second melody to be the same as the first if the changed tone is also diatonic than if it is nondiatonic (Dowling 1978). In other words, changes that preserve diatonicity are more difficult to detect than changes that disrupt it. An interval representation alone would not make this prediction, because transitions from diatonic tones to nondiatonic tones traverse intervals that are also found between diatonic tones. That is, the intervals between all possible pairs of tones from the major diatonic scale encompass *all* possible intervals (e.g., me-fa is one semitone, do-re is two semitones, and so on). There are no new intervals introduced by including nondiatonic tones. Thus the interval traversed by a nondiatonic change will, taken alone, provide no information about a violation of diatonicity, unless the scale degree is also encoded as a reference. But if scale degree is to be represented, there's no need for the interval. (If one defines intervals not in terms of number of semitones but in terms of the theory-laden nomenclature, in which, for example, an augmented second is different from a minor third, even though both traverse three semitones, then indeed new intervals will be introduced by nondiatonic tones; however, a representation defined over these theory-laden categories presupposes considerable processing prior to the representation in question.)

An interval representation predicts that a single mistake will cause the key to transpose suddenly, making recovery difficult (Todd, this volume). After playing a wrong note, a performer is likely to recover by playing the next note correctly. An interval representation predicts that in this case the listener hears two errors, the first incorrect interval followed by the performer's compensatory interval. If the performer fails to compensate and skillfully transposes from then on, the listener ought to hear this as a less erroneous performance than the compensatory one, because only one interval error is made. This seems unlikely.

Pitch-Class Representation

In a pitch-class representation, pitch height is collapsed across octaves, but absolute pitch levels within an octave are preserved. This satisfies octave equivalence but is still not sufficient, because it entails long term absolute pitch and fails to account for invariance under transposition, for the same reasons given earlier for pitch height. Furthermore, a pitch-class representation that is restricted to the twelve chromatic categories (a *categorical pitch-class representation*) suffers from the same difficulties as the categorical pitch-height representation.

Although not sufficient, a pitch-class representation is necessary, since transpositional invariance is not uniform in the short term. If a tonal sequence is quickly followed by a transposition to another key, recognition is better for transpositions to related keys than to unrelated keys (Cuddy, Cohen, and Miller 1979). Here relatedness is defined in terms of distance along the circle of fifths, which can be computed in terms of the pitch classes in the keys of the two sequences. Since the perception of the transposed sequence is thus influenced by the relatedness between the pitch-class levels of the two sequences, information about the pitch-class levels of the first sequence must still be available when the second sequence is heard. In the model presented in this chapter, a pitch-class representation resonates over a short period of time and computes a pitch-class representation of keys or tonal centers, thereby producing such key-distance effects. Another representation, an invariant pitch-class representation, supports the encoding of sequences into a sequential memory.

Invariant Pitch-Class Representation

An invariant pitch-class representation is necessary for the long-term encoding of pitch sequences, in order to account for invariance under transposition. In such a representation, all sequences are normalized into a common set of invariant pitch categories by coding them with reference to a sequence-specific origin. In the case of music with a tonal center, the tonal center would serve as the origin. The invariant pitch categories for the twelve chromatic pitch classes of Western tonal music utilizing equal-tempered tuning would be encoded in a network model by units tuned to twelve equally spaced points, {0,1,2,3,4,5,6,7,8,9,10,11}, along a continuum spanning an octave. (A gating mechanism that will transform a sequence into an invariant pitch-class representation of this type is shown in Fig. 10.) The sequential memory reported by Bharucha and Todd (this volume) for long encoding of sequences presupposes such an invariant pitch-class representation.

A representation that is denser than the twelve chromatic categories would be able to accomodate other tunings as well. The pitch class representation in Fig. 9, the gating mechanism in Fig. 10, and the sequential memory of Bharucha and Todd (this volume) should be assumed to utilize arrays that are denser than those shown in the figures for convenience.

Some invariant pitch-class representations (e.g., Gjerdingen, this volume) consist of only the diatonic categories (do, re, me, fa, sol, la, ti), with additional units to specify sharp or flat. Aside from the psychological implausibility of units for sharp or flat, such a representation presupposes a mechanism for assigning diatonic categories, is specific to only one kind of scale (e.g., major), and is too sparse to accommodate tuning differences.

Fig. 1. An overview of the model (an expansion of an overview from Bharucha 1987a). Layers a–e *represent the extraction of pitch from signals and the organization of pitch in the form of a learned musical schema of chords and keys. Layers* c–e *comprise the MUSACT network shown in Fig. 9. The gating mechanism,* f, *is shown in Fig. 10; it uses the tonal center to gate absolute pitch class into a pitch invariant format,* g, *for encoding into a sequential memory,* h.

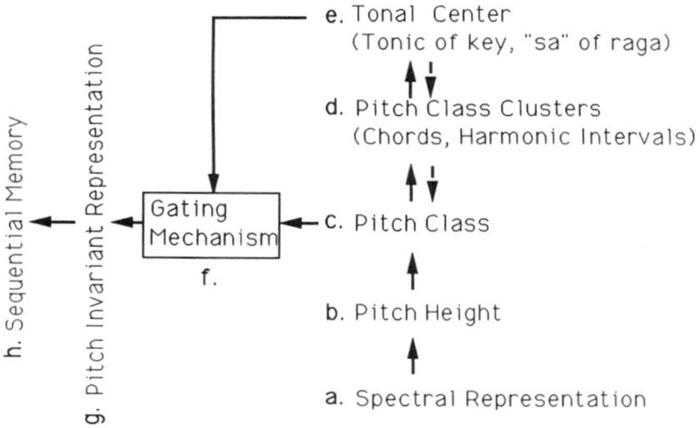

A Model

An overview of a model of pitch organization and memory is sketched in Fig.1. Items *a* through *e* represent hypothetical layers of neuronal units that accomplish the extraction and organization of pitch. Pitch height, *b*, is extracted from a spectral representation, *a*. Layers *d* and *e* represent the organization of pitch in the form of a learned musical schema of chords and keys, defined over pitch classes in layer *c*. A gating mechanism, *f*, converts pitch class into an invariant pitch-class format, *g*, that feeds into a sequential memory, *h*. Separating the sequential memory, *h*, from the network that encodes tonal relations, *c* through *e*, is mandated by the known neurological dissociation between these two functions, as described earlier.

The model presupposes spectral, pitch-height, pitch-class, and invariant pitch-class representations. The known psychological constraints on pitch perception in music can be accounted for by attending to different representations to varying degrees or by allocating one's attention in different ways within a representation. For example, the synthetic mode of pitch perception, which is the norm, involves attending only to the most highly activated units in the pitch-height representation. The analytic mode of pitch perception, which enables one to hear multiple pitches within a complex tone but takes practice, involves attending to pitch-height units with low levels of activation.

Portions of this overview are reported elsewhere and will only be summarized here (for layers *c* through *e*, referred to as MUSACT, see Bharucha 1987a, 1987b; for the gating mechanism, *f*, see Bharucha 1988; and for the sequential memory, *h*, see Bharucha and Todd, this volume). The remainder of this

Fig. 2. Each unit in layer c is connected to each unit in layer d. Layer c is an array of pitch class units that is dense (i.e., not restricted to chromatic steps) and tonotopically repeating (i.e., each pitch class is represented by many units, each within a one-octave tonotopic strip). Layer d is an array of units that are initially agnostic because of random weights from layer c. Layer d is organized into clusters. (Reprinted from Bharucha, in press. Copyright by The Macmillan Press.)

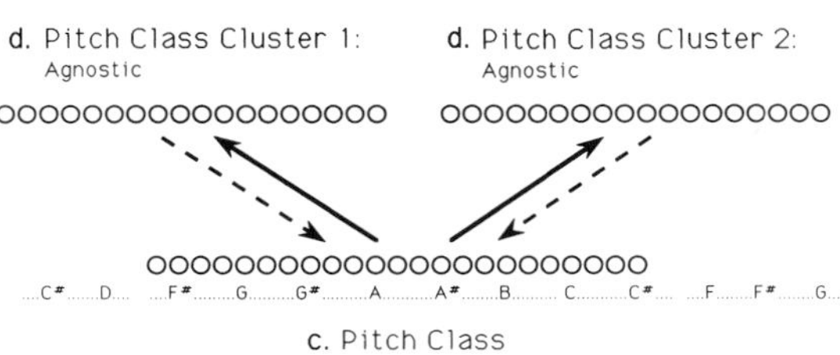

Fig. 3. An arbitrarily selected major chord, F♯ major, is presented, and turns on the pitch class units for F♯, A♯, and C♯. The units in the next layer are activated to varying degrees, and the winner happens to emerge in cluster 2. (Reprinted from Bharucha, in press. Copyright by The Macmillan Press.)

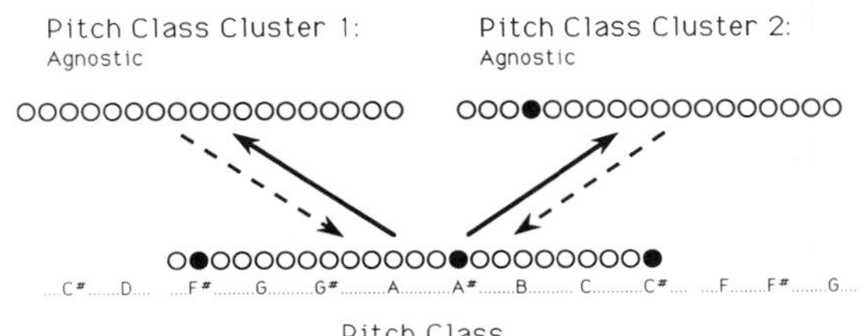

chapter will focus on how the mapping from *c* to *d* is learned, giving rise to the connectivity that is assumed in the MUSACT model.

The Formation of Chord and Key Units through Self-Organization

In Fig.2, units in the bottom layer, *c*, are tuned to overlapping bands along the pitch-class continuum. This layer is dense (i.e., not restricted to chromatic categories) and tonotopically repeating (i.e., each pitch class is represented by many units, each within a one-octave tonotopic strip). Units in the top layer, *d*, are in clusters. Each cluster is tonotopically mapped but initially without an absolute pitch reference. Units in this layer are initially agnostic (not tuned to recognize any particular group of pitches) because of random weights from the pitch class units.

Now, let us imagine that an arbitrarily selected major chord, F♯ major, is presented and turns on the pitch-class units for F♯, A♯, and C♯ in layer *c* as shown in Fig. 3. The units in the next layer, *d*, are activated to varying degrees, and the winner happens to emerge in cluster 2. Note that any unit in any cluster could have been the winner, because the starting weights were set at random. But one unit must necessarily win, because the starting weights are real numbers that represent a continuum of possible synaptic strengths; hence the probability that two units will have exactly the same activation is infinitesimally small.

Fig. 4 depicts how the weights are changed. Weights to the winner are changed in a manner that is essentially Hebbian learning. Links that fed the winner (i.e., that provided positive input) are strengthened (solid lines); links to the winner that did not feed it are weakened (dashed lines). The winning unit in cluster 2 is on its way to being transformed from an agnostic unit to a unit that responds selectively to an F♯ major triad.

This learning procedure is based on the competitive learning algorithm of Rumelhart and Zipser (1985), which incorporates features from earlier algorithms by von der Malsburg (1973) and Grossberg (1976). Each cluster in Fig. 4 represents a unit in Rumelhart and Zipser's algorithm. What's new about the application of this algorithm to pitch is the tonotopically mapped clusters and the manner in which learning is yoked tonotopically as indicated below.

Parallel links are yoked within a cluster for purposes of weight change (Fig. 5). Thus, the unit in cluster 2 to the right of F♯ unit becomes tuned to a major chord slightly sharper than F♯. The yoking of weight changes on parallel links in cluster 2 results in a dense and tonotopically repeating cluster of units in that cluster that respond selectively to major chords (Fig. 6). A chord type (in this case, major) heard at one absolute pitch level will thus be recognized at any absolute pitch level by the same cluster.

If an arbitrarily selected chord of another type, F♯– minor (a flattened F♯ minor), is presented, the random winner is likely to be in an undeveloped cluster, say, cluster 1 (Fig. 7). Cluster 1 is then transformed by the same yoked weight-change mechanism from agnostic units to a dense and tonotopically repeating cluster of units that respond selectively to minor chords (Fig. 8). An analysis of the circumstances uner which new chord types become

Fig. 4. Weights to the winner are changed according to a modified version of competitive learning (Rumelhart and Zipser 1985). Links that fed the winner are strengthened (solid lines); links to the winner that did not feed it are weakened (dashed lines). The winning unit in cluster 2 is on its way to being transformed from an agnostic unit to a unit that responds selectively to an F♯-major triad. (Reprinted from Bharucha, in press. Copyright by The Macmillan Press.)

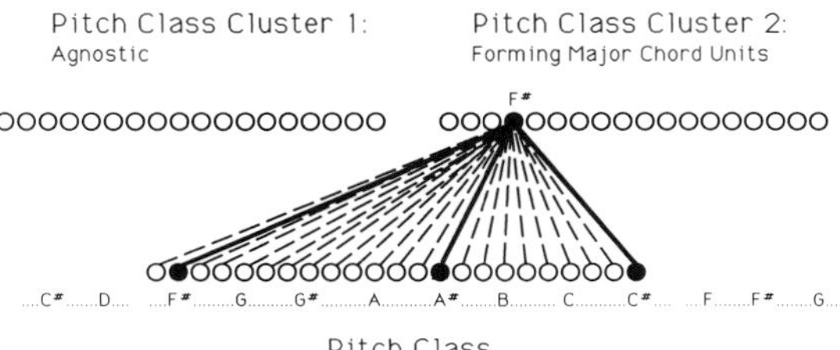

Fig. 5. Parallel links are yoked within a cluster for purposes of weight change. Thus, the unit in cluster 2 to the right of the F♯ becomes tuned to a major chord slightly sharper than F♯. (Reprinted from Bharucha, in press. Copyright by The Macmillan Press.)

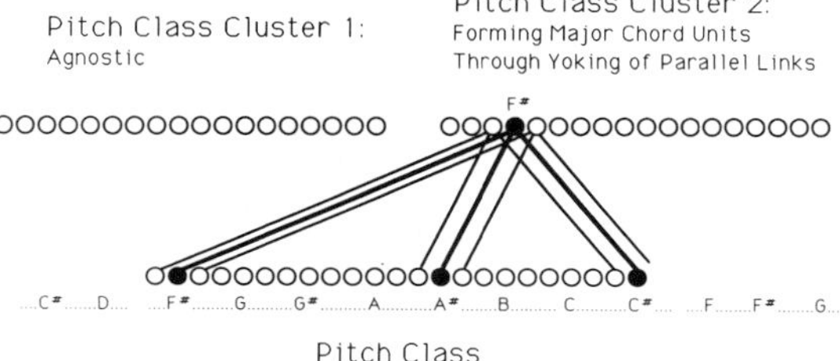

represented by new clusters rather than being assimilated by existing clusters is beyond the scope of this summary chapter. Interested readers are directed to Grossberg (1976) and Rumelhart and Zipser (1985) for formal discussions of this issue.

A similar mechanism will yield units at level *e* (see Fig. 1) that are specialized for typical chord groupings, provided activation at the chord units decays slowly. Thus, chords that are typically heard within the same piece of music become organized around a single unit at level *e*. These are therefore key units. Once again, they are tonotopically repeating.

MUSACT

The final network resulting from the learning in layers *c* through *e* consists of units representing pitch classes, chords, and keys (see Fig. 9, taken from Bharucha 1987a). In Fig. 9, only the chromatic units are shown, for convenience. All layers should be assumed to be denser than these categories. Furthermore, the arrangement of chords according to the circle of fifths is for convenience only. It should be clear from the learning procedure described above that the physical layout is actually tonotopic but can be depicted in any layout provided the links are preserved.

Input to the network is a sequence of events, each event being a simultaneous cluster of tones. Input is received by the spectral units and sent up through the layers. A unit may be activated from the bottom up or from the top down. A chord unit, for example, is activated either by the explicit sounding of some or all of its component pitch classes or by indirect influences, via its parent keys, from related chords. When only some of the chord's component tones are sounded, the context may help disambiguate the chord by top-down activation from parent key units. Indirect activation of chord units permits smooth excursions (such as secondary dominants and modulations) from the focus of activation. A key unit is similarly activated by some or all of its daughter chords or by indirect influences, via its daughter chords, from related keys.

After an event is heard, activation spreads through the network, via the weighted links, reverberating back to units that were previously activated. In this model, activation is phasic, meaning that units respond only to changes in the activation of neighboring units. Phasic activation is used because of the salience of event onsets in music. Phasic units are commonly found in the nervous system. On each cycle, units are synchronously updated on the basis of activation levels, from the previous cycle, of neighboring units. Phasic activation eventually dissipates until the network settles into a state of equilibrium. Settling will occur provided the weights are small relative to the fan-in or fan-out of the unit connections.

The pattern of activation of key units represents the degree to which keys are established. Tonal music will tend to build up activation in one region of the network, such that one key unit is most highly activated, with activation tapering off with increasing distance along the circle of fifths. Note that the circle of fifths is exhibited as a truly emergent prop-

Fig. 6. The yoking of weight changes on parallel links in cluster 2 results in a dense and tonotopically repeating cluster of units that respond selectively to major chords. A chord type learned at one absolute pitch level will be recognized by the same cluster at any absolute pitch level. (Reprinted from Bharucha, in press. Copyright by The Macmillan Press.)

Fig. 7. If an arbitrarily selected chord of another type, F♯ – minor (a flattened F♯ minor), is presented, the random winner is likely to be in an undeveloped cluster, say, cluster 1. (Reprinted from Bharucha, in press. Copyright by The Macmillan Press.)

Fig. 8. Cluster 1 is transformed from agnostic units to a dense and tonotopically repeating cluster of units that respond selectively to minor chords. (Reprinted from Bharucha, in press. Copyright by The Macmillan Press.)

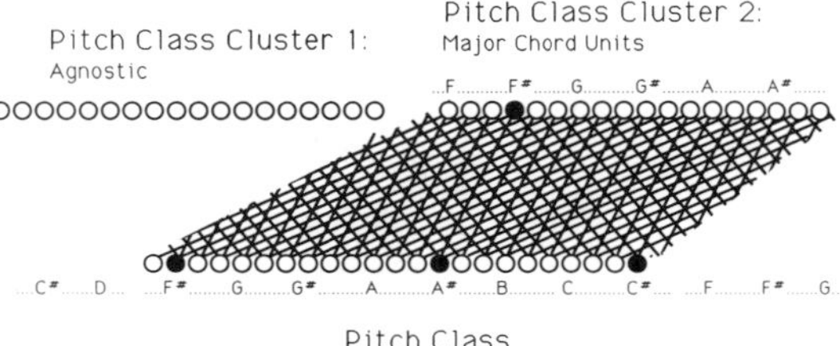

Fig. 7

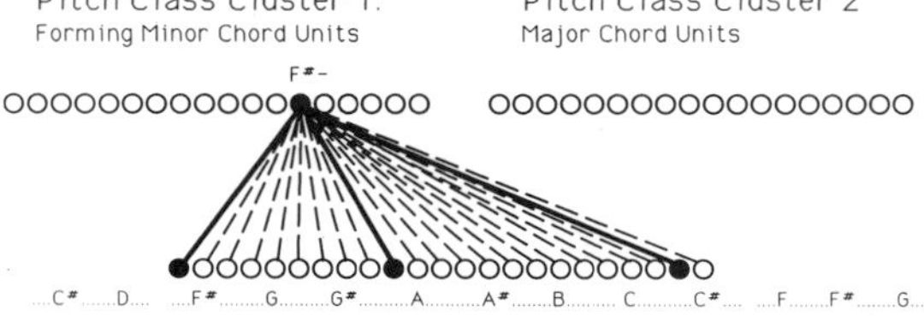

Fig. 8

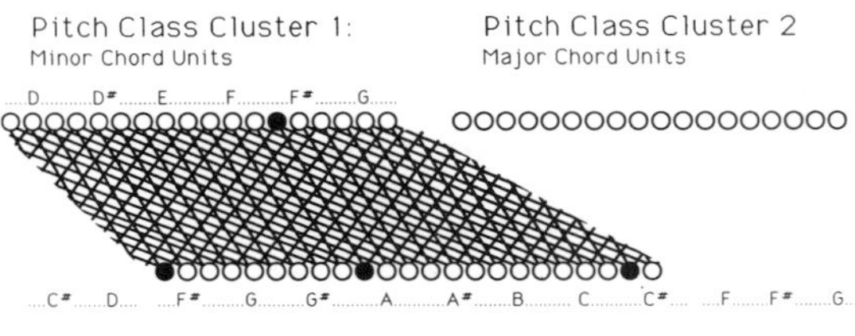

erty of the network, since the network has learned only the local (temporal) clustering of pitch classes to form chords and the clustering of chords to form keys. The circle of fifths emerges as a consequence of the joint satisfaction of all constraints in the network.

Atonal music will typically induce a less focused pattern, and polytonal music might result in multiple, though not very strong, foci. The model thus allows for gradations of key, and for multiple keys, consistent with evidence from experiments (Krumhansl 1990; Krumhansl and Schmuckler 1986).

A chord is implied or schematically expected to the extent that its unit is activated. The activation of a chord unit also biases judgments about the chord's consonance. This mechanism would explain the finding that the internal consonance of a chord increases when it is schematically expected (Bharucha and Stoeckig 1986, 1987). The model also predicts the pattern of rating and memory judgments obtained in experiments measuring perceived chord relationships (Bharucha and Krumhansl 1983; Krumhansl, Bharucha, and Castellano 1982; see Bharucha 1987a, 1987b, for details of experiment simulations).

In response to a major chord, the network will activate the diatonic tones (of the major scale whose tonic is the root of the chord) more than the nondiatonic tones. It is important to note that these effects are emergent properties of the network—effects that arise out of the joint action of local connectivity based on the clustering of tones and the clustering of chords as they are typically heard. Nothing about the diatonic set was explicitly wired into the network.

Gating Mechanism and Sequential Memory

Fig. 10 shows a gating mechanism that takes pitch-class information from MUSACT and transforms it into an invariant pitch-class representation (Bharucha 1988). Units labeled "pi" multiply activation received from pitch-class units and tonal center (key) units. This gates the pitch classes into an invariant pitch-class format in which the tonic is always "0," so that all tonal sequences have the same tonic or origin.

Musical sequences are then stored in terms of this invariant pitch-class format. Versions of the sequential memory, which is a Jordan (1986) net that learns sequences by back propagation, are presented in the chapters by Todd (this volume) and by Bharucha and Todd (this volume). An invariant pitch-class representation as input to the sequential memory will permit invariance under transposition in long-term memory.

When MUSACT and the sequential memory op-

Fig. 9. MUSACT: The network resulting from a learned clustering of pitch classes into chords and a clustering of chords into keys. Music activates the pitch-class units, and activation reverberates through the network until it settles into a state of equilibrium. The pattern of activation at equilibrium represents the array of chord and key implications, and influences the perception and recognition of events that follow. (From Bharucha 1987a. Copyright by the Cognitive Science Society.)

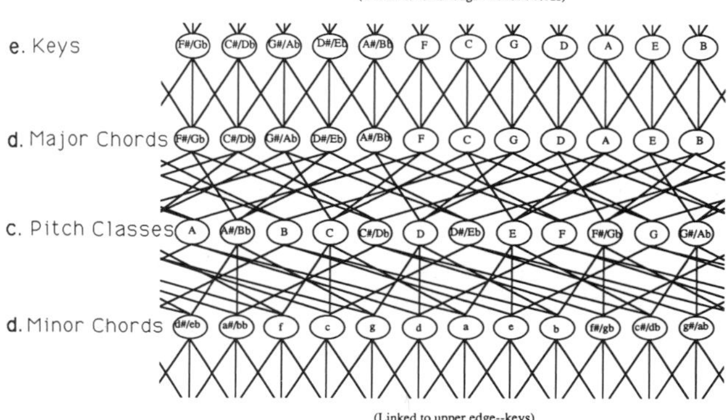

Fig. 10. A gating mechanism (from Bharucha 1988). Units labeled π multiply activation received from pitch-class units and tonal center (key) units. This gates the pitch classes into a pitch invariant format in which the tonic is always 0. Sequential memories are then stored in terms of this pitch invariant format, permitting invariance under transposition. (Versions of the sequential memory are presented in the chapters by Todd and by Bharucha and Todd, this volume.)

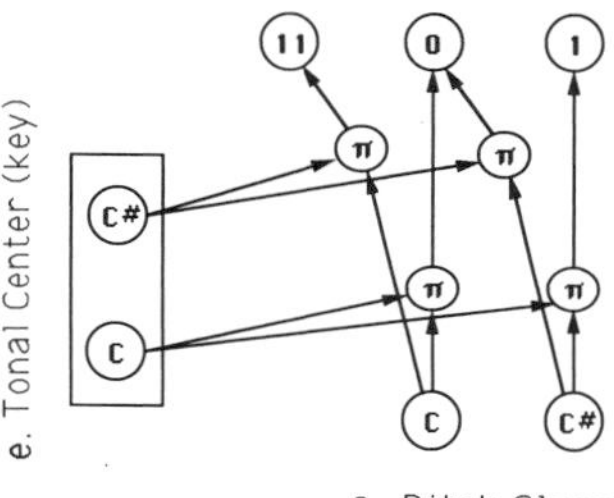

erate in tandem, they predict key-distance effects in the transposition of sequences in the short term. If a sequence of chords is transposed immediately, before activation has had a chance to decay completely, the perceived similarity of the two sequences increases with the proximity (around the circle of fifths) of their keys. This is because as each chord in the second sequence is heard, both the sequential memory and MUSACT are checked to see if this chord was expected. The closer the key of the two sequences, the greater the activation of the units in MUSACT that are checked, therefore the greater the degree of expectation will be. The interaction of these two networks is currently being explored.

Conclusion

The development of neural net models of human networks requires attention to a range of empirical and theoretical constraints. In order to account for known constraints on the perception of pitch as it functions in harmony, two networks have been postulated. One (described in the chapter by Bharucha and Todd, this volume) learns musical sequences in an invariant pitch-class format, employing the back-propagation algorithm. The other, summarized in this chapter, learns relationships between pitch classes, chord, and keys, employing a self-organizing algorithm. These networks are linked by a gating mechanism. Together, they account for invariance under transpostion, modulated by key-distance effects in the short-term, while accomplishing their primary tasks of serving as a memory for sequences and a schema for tonal relationships.

Acknowledgments

This work was supported by a grant from the National Science Foundation (BNS-8910778). Portions of this paper have been excerpted from papers published in the proceedings of three conferences as follows: The Ninth Annual Meeting of the Cognitive Science Society (1987, Erlbaum Press); Music, Language, Speech, and Brain (Stockholm 1990, proceedings forthcoming, Macmillan Press); and Music and the Cognitive Sciences II (Cambridge 1990, proceedings forthcoming in *Contemporary Music Review*). The author thanks Peter Todd for valuable comments.

References

Bharucha, J. J. 1987a. "MUSACT: A Connectionist Model of Musical Harmony." *Proceedings of the Ninth Annual Conference of the Cognitive Science Society.* Hillsdale, N.J.: Erlbaum Associates, pp. 508–517.

Bharucha, J. J. 1987b. "Music Cognition and Perceptual Facilitation: A Connectionist Framework." *Music Perception* 5:1–30.

Bharucha J. J. 1988, "Neural Net Modeling of Music." *Proceedings of the First Workshop on Artificial Intelligence and Music.* St. Paul, Minnesota: American Association of Artificial Intelligence.

Bharucha, J. J. In press. "Cognitive and Brain Mechanisms in Perceptual Learning." *Proceedings of the International Wenner-Gren Symposium on Music, Language, Speech and Brain.* New York: Macmillan Press.

Bharucha, J. J. and C. L. Krumhansl. 1983. "The Representation of Harmonic Structure in Music: Hierarchies of Stability as a Function of Context." *Cognition* 13:63–102.

Bharucha, J. J. and K. L. Olney. 1989. "Tonal Cognition, Artificial Intelligence and Neural Nets." *Contemporary Music Review* 4:341–356.

Bharucha, J. J. and K. Stoeckig. 1986. "Reaction Time and Musical Expectancy: Priming of Chords." *Journal of Experimental Psychology: Human Perception and Performance* 12:403–410.

Bharucha, J. J. and K. Stoeckig. 1987. "Priming of Chords: Spreading Activation or Overlapping Frequency Spectra?" *Perception and Psychophysics* 41:519–524.

Bharucha, J. J. and P. M. Todd. This volume. "Modeling the Perception of Tonal Structure with Neural Nets."

Castellano, M. A., J. J. Bharucha, and C. L. Krumhansl. 1984. "Tonal Hierarchies in the Music of North India." *Journal of Experimental Psychology: General* 113: 394–412.

Cuddy, L. L., A. J. Cohen, and J. Miller. 1979. "Melody Recognition: The Experimental Application of Musical Rules." *Canadian Journal of Psychology* 33:148–157.

de Boer, E. 1956. "On The Residue in Hearing." Ph.D. diss., University of Amsterdam.

Deutsch, D. 1969. "Music Recognition." *Psychological Review* 76:300–307.

Deutsch, D. 1973. "Octave Generalization of Specific Interference Effects in Memory for Tonal Pitch." *Perception and Psychophysics* 13:271–275.

Dowling, W. J. 1978. "Scale and Contour: Two Components of a Theory of Memory for Melodies." *Psychological Review* 85:341–354.

Fukushima, K. 1975. "Cognitron: A Self-organizing Multilayered Neural Network." *Biological Cybernetics* 20:121–136.

Gjerdingen, R. O. This volume. "Using Connectionist Models to Explore Complex Musical Patterns."

Goldberg, J. M., and R. A. Lavine. 1968. "Nervous System: Afferent Mechanisms." *Annual Review of Physiology* 30:319–358.

Goldstein, J. L. 1973. "An Optimum Processor Theory for the Central Formation of The Pitch of Complex Tones." *Journal of the Acoustical Society of America* 54:1496-1516.

Green, D. M. 1976. *Hearing.* Hillsdale, N.J.: Erlbaum Associates.

Grossberg, S. 1976. "Adaptive Pattern Classification and Universal Recoding: Part I. Parallel Development and Coding of Neural Feature Detectors." *Biological Cybernetics* 23:121–134.

Hebb, D. O. 1949. *The Organization of Behavior.* New York: John Wiley & Sons.

Heider, E. 1972. "Universals of Color Naming and Memory." *Journal of Experimental Psychology* 93:10–20.

Helmholtz, H. 1954. *On the Sensation of Tone.* New York: Dover. Originally published 1885.

Jordan, M. 1986. "Attractor Dynamics and Parallelism in a Connectionist Sequential Machine." *Proceedings of the Eighth Annual Conference of The Cognitive Science Society.* Hillsdale, N.J.: Erlbaum Associates, pp. 531–546.

Kohonen, T. 1984. *Self-organization and Associative Memory.* Berlin: Springer-Verlag.

Krumhansl, C. L. 1979. "The Psychological Representation of Musical Pitch in a Tonal Context." *Cognitive Psychology* 11:346–374.

Krumhansl, C. L. 1990. *Cognitive Foundations of Musical Pitch.* Oxford: Oxford University Press.

Krumhansl, C. L., J. J. Bharucha, and M. A. Castellano. 1982. "Key Distance Effects on Perceived Harmonic Structure in Music." *Perception and Psychophysics* 32:96–108.

Krumhansl, C. L., and M. A. Schmuckler. 1986. "The Petroushka Chord: A Perceptual Investigation." *Music Perception* 4:153–184.

Laden, B. and D. H. Keefe. This volume. "The Representation of Pitch in a Neural Net Model of Chord Classification."

Landauer, T. K. and C. A. Kamm. 1987. "Teaching a Minimally Structured Back-propagation Network to Recognize Speech Sounds. *Proceedings of the Ninth Annual Conference of the Cognitive Science Society.* Hillsdale, N.J.: Erlbaum Assoicates, pp. 531–536.

Lauter, J. L., P. Hersovitch, C. Formby, and M. R. Raichle. 1985. "Tonotopic Organization in the Human Auditory Cortex Revealed by Positron Emission Tomography." *Hearing Research* 20:199–205.

Licklider, J. C. R. 1954. "Periodicity Pitch and Place Pitch." *Journal of the Acoustical Society of America* 26:945(A).

Meyer, L. 1956. *Emotion and Meaning in Music.* Chicago: University of Chicago Press.

Parncutt, R. 1989. *Harmony: A Psychoacoustic Approach.* Berlin: Springer-Verlag.

Patterson, R. D. 1973. "The Effects of Relative Phase and the Number of Components on Residue Pitch." *Journal of the Acoustical Society of America* 53:1565–1572.

Rumelhart, D. E., G. E. Hinton, and R. J. Williams, 1986. "Learning Internal Representations by Error Propagation." In D. E. Rumelhart and J. L. McClelland, eds. *Parallel Distributed Processing: Exploration in the Microstructure of Cognition.* Vol. 1. Cambridge, Massachusetts: MIT Press.

Rumelhart, D. E., and D. Zipser. 1985. "Feature Discovery by Competitive Learning." *Cognitive Science* 9:75–112.

Sano, H., and B. K. Jenkins. This volume. "A Neural Network Model for Pitch Perception."

Schmuckler, M. A. 1988. *Expectation in Music: Additivity of Melodic and Harmonic Processes.* Ph.D. diss., Cornell University.

Schouten, J. F., R. J. Ritsma, and B. L. Cardoza. 1962. "Pitch of the Residue." *Journal of the Acoustical Society of America* 34:1418–1424.

Shepard, R. N. 1964. "Circularity in Judgments of Relative Pitch." *Journal of the Acoustical Society of America* 36:2346-2353.

Shepard, R. N. 1982. "Geometric Approximations to the Structure of Musical Pitch." *Psychological Review* 89:305–333.

Stevens, S. S., and J. Volkmann. 1940. "The Relation of Pitch to Frequency." *American Journal of Psychology* 53:329–353.

Terhardt, E., G. Stoll, and M. Seewann. 1982. "Pitch of Complex Tonal Signals According to Virtual Pitch Theory: Tests, Examples, and Predictions." *Journal of Acoustical Society of America* 71:671–678.

Tramo, M. J., J. J. Bharucha, and F. E. Musiek. 1990. "Music Perception and Cognition Following Bilateral Lesions of Auditory Cortex." *Journal of Cognitive Neuroscience* 2:195–212.

Todd, P. M. This volume. "A Connectionist Approach to Algorithmic Composition."

von der Malsberg, C. 1973, "Self-organizing of Orientation Sensitive Cells in the Striate Cortex." *Kybernetik* 14:85–100.

Weinberger, N. M., and D. M. Diamond. 1988. "Dynamic Modulation of the Auditory System by Associative Learning." In G. M. Edelman, W. E. Gall, and W. M. Cowan. *Auditory Function: Neurobiological Bases of Hearing.* New York: John Wiley & Sons.

Weinberger, N. M., and T. M. McKenna. 1988. "Sensitivity of Single Neurons in Auditory Cortex to Contour: Toward a Neurophysiology of Music Perception." *Music Perception* 5:355–390.

Marc Leman
University of Ghent
Institute for Psychoacoustics and Electronic Music
Blandijnberg 2 B-9000 GHENT Belgium
musico@bgerug51.bitnet

The Ontogenesis of Tonal Semantics: Results of a Computer Study

Introduction

One of the fascinating properties of tones is the fact that they stand in a particular relationship to each other. A given tone sounds higher or lower, brighter or less bright, consonant or dissonant, with respect to another tone. Of particular interest is the fact that tones have some function within a tonal context. These functions are not inherent to the tones themselves but are in a sense created by the context in which they appear.

A system of relations and meanings between tones within a context is called a *tonal semantics.* The tonal system of classical European music (1600–1850) is often associated with a particular tonal semantics. but this is certainly not the only one conceivable. Other cultures have developed tonal contexts that imply other relationships between tones. And recent investigation by Mathews et al. (1988) suggest ways of exploring still other types of tonal semantics with computer methods.

An analysis of tonal semantics reveals two fundamental aspects: a sensory aspect and a cultural aspect. The sensory aspect is related to the acoustical properties of the stimulus and the sensory properties of the ear, whereas the cognitive aspect captures what is added by the cultural character of the music and by learning processes of the listener with respect to this character.

The question of what aspects actually set the tonal context has a long history. Helmholtz (1863) explained the roughness of tones (their dissonance) as the result of an interference of waves in the ear. More recent research (Plomp 1976; Kameoka and Kuriyagawa 1969) has revealed that this is in particular true for those waves that fall in the frequency bands of the ear where integration occurs (the so-called critical bands).

Helmholtz, however, was accused at the time of having restricted the phenomenon of consonance to only sensory aspects of the ear (see, for example, Terhardt 1984). Indeed, much of the German music research (*Systematische Musikwissenschaft*) after Helmholtz can be seen as an attempt to explain tonal semantics from a cognitive viewpoint rather than from the sensoric point of view.

The expression *Musik macht den Ton* ("Music makes the tone") captures very well the paradigm adopted during this period. Basically it means that tonal properties are actually dominated by the musical context in which they appear. In addition to the Gestalt-theoretic conception that underlies this expression, it has been pointed out by Wellek (1963) that aspects of genetical (developmental) psychology are involved as well. He says, "In diesem Leitsatz ist nicht bloss der Grundsatz der Ganzheitpsychology ausgesprochen sondern auch der einer genetischen Psychologie: von dem Aufbau einer musikalischen Kultur haengt es ab, was jeweils der Ton, in ihrem Rahmen und also an einem gegebenen Punkte der menschlischen Entwicklung un Geschichte, ist und bedeutet. Den Ton im musikalischen Sinne als Ton erleben, heisst die ganze Musik in ihm setzen," (p. 81). ("This phrase expresses not only the fundamental principle of the Gestalt psychology but also that of developmental psychology: the meaning and nature of a tone depends on the construction of a musical culture, and in this context also on a given point of human development and history. Experiencing a tone in musical sense means to put the whole music in it.")

At the end of the nineteenth century it was hypothesized that tonal semantics could be accounted for by three levels of constraints: (1) sound acoustics, (2) processes of sensory perception and Gestaltformation, and (3) the cultural environment. Due to recent developments in psychology, neurobiology, and computer science, we now have more powerful means to test this hypothesis in a more scientific way. The results reported in this paper should be thought of as a first attempt to construct a computer-based model of these three levels.

Fig. 1. Tone profile of similarity (goodness-of-fit) ratings for tones given a C-major cadence as context.

In this paper we describe a model for the study of the ontogenesis of tonality functions (see also Lehman 1990). The aim is not to give a systematic exploration of the three levels mentioned but rather to pursue some initial pathways that could form the basis for further study. An epistemological and methodological approach is adopted, which differs from most of the current research in tonality modeling.

Tonality as a Cognitive Phenomenon

Recent research in psychology has revealed that it is possible to account for tonal semantics from a quantitative point of view. Data obtained by similarity rating studies concerning tonal functioning have been analyzed by multidimensional scaling and hierarchical clustering methods (e.g., Krumhansl and Kessler 1982). Often these quantitative results have been qualitatively interpreted and related to the listener's musical knowledge representation and cognitive information processing. In particular, spatially organized configurations or hierarchical trees have been said to relate to an abstract internal representation of the structural and cognitive regularities underlying tonality.

Krumhansl (1983), for example, makes a distinction between three different domains of tonality organization: single tones, chords, and keys. On the basis of her experimental work, she concludes that there is evidence for an articulated knowledge system embodying the interrelations between tones and between chords as they are used in tonal music: "This knowledge system has both within-level and between-level features. A common within-level organizational principle was found for single tones and chords: a tonality-specific hierarchy with particular elements dominating over others. Certain elements are most central in each of these domains, with other elements more distantly related both to the central core and to each other. In addition, within-level structure in each of the three domains (tones, chords, and keys) was found to be intimately tied to structure in other domains. These between-level associations are, thus, generative of structure within each domain, and in them reside the

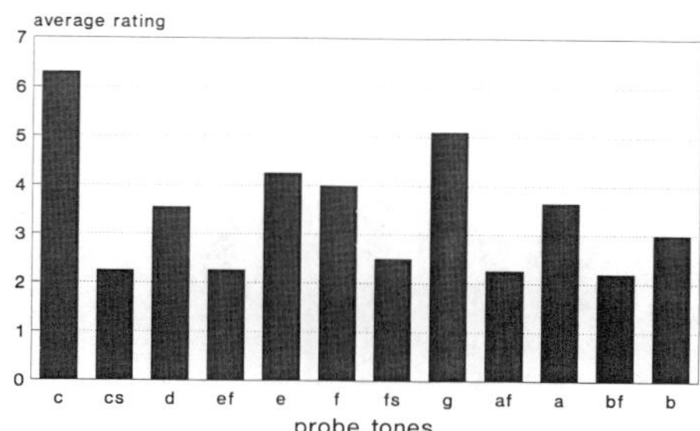

connections between melodic and harmonic organization and between the musical elements actually sounded and a system of interrelated key regions," (p. 59).

One of the experimental measures Krumhansl uses to explore the relationships between tones, chords, and keys is the *tone profile* (Krumhansl and Kessler 1982). The tone profile is the average rating that subjects give when they are asked to judge the similarity (goodness-of-fit) of a given tone from the chromatic scale to a tonal context set by some cadence in a particular key. Fig. 1, for example, shows the profile for the tones of the C-major key. These tones are labeled c, cs (c-sharp), d, ef (e-flat), etc. High values represent high-similarity (good-fit) ratings.

In order to reduce the influence of pitch height and focus the attention of the subject instead on the relevant aspects of pitch chroma in obtaining these tone profiles, octave component (Shepard) tones were used. The spectrum of these tones is built up of harmonics at the octaves, stressing those components that fall in the region between 500 Hz and 1 kHz and gradually decreasing energy at the higher and lower ends (the spectral envelope thus often having the shape of a bell).

Fig. 2 shows another experimental measure, the average rating of major triads (numbered as I, I-s (I-sharp), II, III-f (III-flat), etc.) in the basic set of harmonies. Here, the same probe technique is adopted, but major triads of the chromatic scale are used instead of individual tones. The figure is based on

Fig. 2. Triad profile dissimilarity (poorness-of-fit) ratings for major triad chords given a C-major cadence as context.

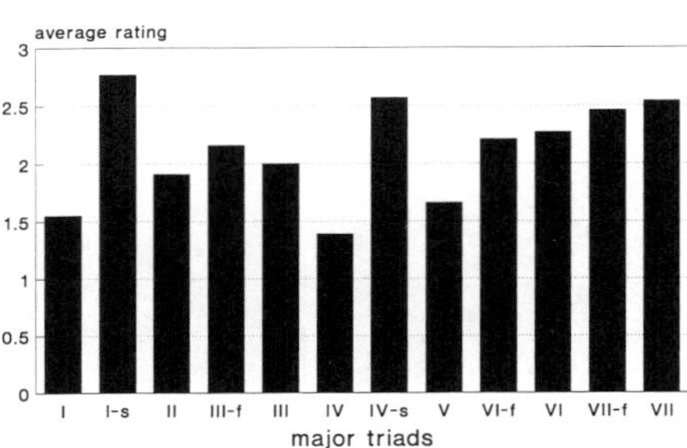

Fig. 3. A spatial configuration of interkey distances obtained by applying multidimensional scaling to intercorrelations of rating profiles of the type shown in Fig. 1.

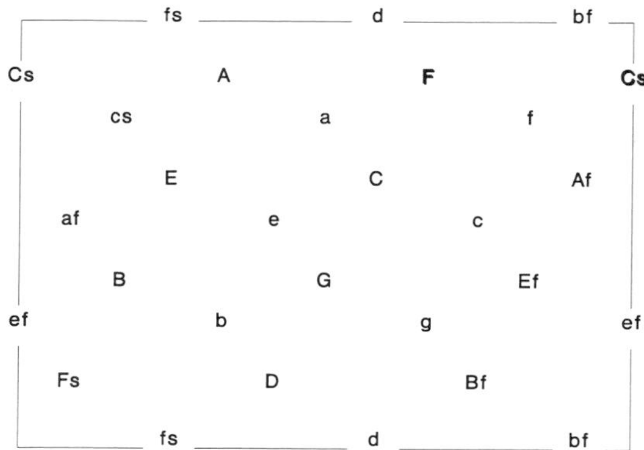

data provided by Bruhn (1988, p.162) and is presented differently from the previous figure: in this case the values represent *dissimilarity* (poorness-of-fit) ratings. So, given a context set by some cadence in the key of C major, the C-major triad (I), F-major triad (IV) and G-major triad (V) are found to fit very well, whereas other major triads, such as C♯ (I-s) and F♯ (IV-s) are found to be very dissimilar to, and fit poorly with, the C-major context.

As a final example of proposed musical knowledge structures obtained from experimental data, Fig. 3 provides the spatial configuration of interkey distances obtained from intercorrelating the rating profiles shown in Fig. 1 and applying multidimensional scaling (cf. Krumhansl and Kessler 1982). For more details of this kind of psychological research we refer the reader to the literature.

It should be noted here that the hypothesis of an internal representation of tonal organization is based on an analysis of stimulus-response observations and not typically on an analysis of the sensory aspects of the acoustic signals and the ear. The concept of an internal representation of tonality, often used in the literature, therefore only makes sense within a broader paradigm of cognitive research—one in which mechanisms at lower levels are assumed although not taken into consideration to explain how this representation might come into existence.

Yet there is some support in favor of a hypothesis that cognitive consonance might be due to the internalization of the statistical distribution of tones in the musical environment. Krumhansl (1987) says, "It seems likely that through experience listeners have abstracted and internalized the patterns of tonal distributions, and these are reflected in our empirical studies" (p. 20). Krumhansl (1990) further stresses this point: "This hypothesis is congruent with a wide variety of results showing that humans (as well as other organisms) are highly sensitive to information about frequency of occurrence. Thus, the primary significance of the observed correspondence between statistics of music and psychological data in these cases is to suggest a mechanism through which principles of musical organization are learned" (p. 315).

Models for Tonality

What we are looking for is a model by which aspects of tonal functioning can be explained. What might such a model look like?

Models for explaining tonality have thus far been related to spreading activation models (Bharucha 1987), rule-based models (Bruhn 1988), and supervised learning models (Scarborough et al, this volume). None of these models explains, though, how tonal organization might emerge in the memory of the listener. Both the spreading activation model and the rule-based model involve some direct programming of tonality functions into the artificial memory. This approach is very ad hoc and questionable from an epistemological point of view. There is no learning involved, and so there is no theory about the ontogenesis of tonality functions. (But see Bharucha's chapter in this volume for an alternative unsupervised learning model for the acquisition of tonality.)

The case of supervised learning (with most of the models relying on the back propagation algorithm) is different at first sight because tonality functioning can be obtained after the system learns to associate appropriate input-output pairs. This approach is based on finding the optimal connection strengths in a network model to map inputs to outputs. Yet it is not very clear what this model can tell us about the problem of internal representation of tonality. Neither is it entirely clear why association of tones and chords, rather than detection of invariant features, would be the main determinant for the ontogenesis of tonality functions. Also lacking in this approach is the notion of "cognitive map," which we think is essential for the explanation of cognitive processes.

A further restriction of many of these approaches it that they stick with pitch-class representations rather than data that can be justified by psychoacoustical theory. The world in which these models operate is atomistic and Cartesian. The input representation is typically characterized by a local representation of pitch classes (much in the sense of a symbolic-based representation) and does not promise a very easy elaboration towards the processing of music "as it sounds." Admittedly, input based on acoustic data might be too complicated to deal with in this early stage of research, but one should at least develop models that can in principle be elaborated towards real-world data in future stages.

We have argued recently (Leman, in press) that the problem of the ontogenesis of tonality, a specific example of the general problem of morphogenesis in music, can only be solved by adopting a *subsymbolic* approach. This implies, among other things, that the system should exhibit what we call a "responselike" behavior to stimuli in the environment. This criterion embodies the idea that a system develops tonal semantics only in virtue of the response of the system to the environment. Stated differently, the tones encountered acquire meaning solely because they are relevant for the action of the organism in the environment.

This further involves (a) that tonal functions are built up by a process of self-organization on the basis of the detection of invariant features in the environment (there is no external programmer except the environment), and (b) that the meaning of the system's response can only be known by virtue of the information given in the environment. The first statement is a rather general epistemological point: knowledge is built up by organizational principles inherent in the system and stimulus information provided by the environment. The second statement is a methodological one. The methodology implied is ecological, meaning that the system can be known only by virtue of the environment in which it is embedded. There is no way to understand the system just by looking at its memory. Together these statements propose that after the system has adapted itself to invariant information in the environment, it should be tested in order to discover the map of its self-organized output responses.

Tonality as an Emergent Property of Self-Organization

The model we describe here is based on the assumption that tonality functions might result from a topographic representation of neuronal filters in a distributed memory. This assumption is inspired by recent research in neurobiology, which gives evidence for functional organization of the cortex based on self-organization and feature maps (see for example Palm and Aersten 1986).

Some strong evidence for this kind of memory organization has recently been gathered through experimental research on the dynamic alterability of somatosensory cortical maps. Neurophysiologists such as Merzenich and Jenkins (1983) have hypothesized that the alteration of the details of cortical maps by experience might be *the* principle cortical process: "A self-organizing system is representational. It does not extract information parameter by parameter, performing a computerlike measurement of those parameters. Rather, it creates details of representations from physical continua, and fine-tuning of that creation is a life long process" (p. 165).

Recent work by Suga (1988) provides an abundance of evidence for the existence of cortical computational maps for auditory imaging in the mustached bat. The mustached bat emits complex biosonar signals and listens to echoes for orienting itself and for hunting flying insects. These signals get localized somewhere on an internal map in the cortex, called a computational map (also known as a feature map or cognitive map). The organization of the animal's reaction to its environmental input has been studied in great detail by Suga and coworkers. The map functions as a kind of resonance system in responding to the environmental stimuli. Signals acquire meaning because they are relevant for the action of the organism in the environment. The existence of these maps supports the idea of auditory cognitive maps in other species, including humans. Not much is known about how the bat's computational maps might develop during the early life of the animal, however, so we cannot extrapolate very well to other species in this regard.

The Kohonen Feature Map

The particular geometry and dynamics adopted in our model of the ontogenesis of tonality is based on the Kohonen Feature Map (KFM), a neural network technique based on self-organization (Kohonen 1984). The KFM method, however, is far from being an attempt to model real neural dynamics. As is the case with most neural network models, the network mechanisms adopted are still too general and too abstract to count as a real model of the brain. Still, artificial neural network approaches like the KFM are attractive because they can be more readily related to cortical information processing and empirically-based brain research such as Suga's.

The purpose of the KFM algorithm is to discover a reduced-dimensionality reprersentation of a set of input data. The main reason we (or a processing brain) would want such a reduced representation is because it is much more compact and easier to store and work with than the multidimensional original. The reduced representation should eliminate most of the unnecessary redundancy and noise from the input, while still containing its most relevant aspects. Many structures in animal brains are arranged in the form of such dimensionality-reducing maps.

The KFM algorithm adopted here produces a mapping from an n-dimensional space onto a two-dimensional one, which is represented by a grid of neuronlike elements. For a given n-dimensional input pattern, a certain two-dimensional "bubble" of units in the grid will be activated with one unit in the center of this bubble coming on most strongly. The result of the KFM algorithm is to produce an organization of the neurons in the grid such that similar input patterns (according to some metric) turn on nearby bubbles of activity in the two-dimensional grid. Then, by inspecting the layout of the grid after the network has been trained—that is, seeing what regions are activated by what input patterns—a particular reduced dimensionality topological organization of the input data can be discovered, similar to the spatial organizations found by multidimensional scaling. Finally, this organization can be hypothesized as a possible psychological structure in the minds of experimental subjects and thus human music listeners.

The KFM network can be thought of as comprising two layers of neuron units: the two-dimensional grid layer where the action occurs and an input layer of neurons that relays information from the outside world. Between these two layers are a set of synapses that form full interconnections; that is, every grid neuron has a set of synapses coming into it that connects it to every input neuron. Fig. 4 shows the basic structure of a single grid neuron (input lines, synapses, and output lines are shown), while Fig. 5 shows the complete Kohonen feature map's two-dimensional grid of these neurons, each linked via synaptic connections to the neurons in the input layer. (These connections are shown for only two neurons in the network, but, as just mentioned, in the actual computer model all connections are present.)

Each grid neuron receives a total input computed

Fig. 4. Structure of a single neuron in the two-dimensional grid of the Kohonen Feature Map.

Fig. 5. Structure of the complete Kohonen Feature Map, showing connections from the input neurons to two of the grid neurons.

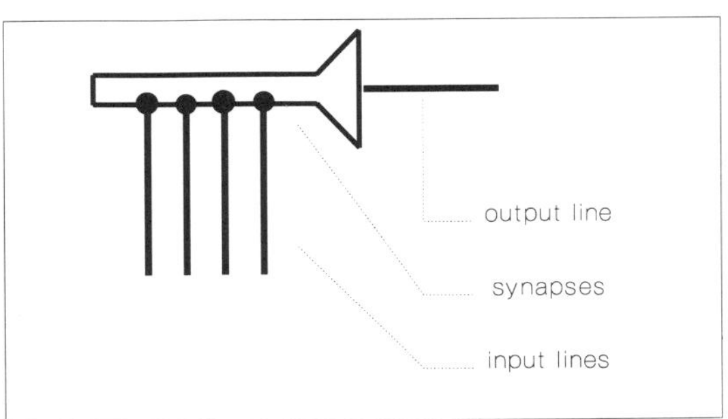

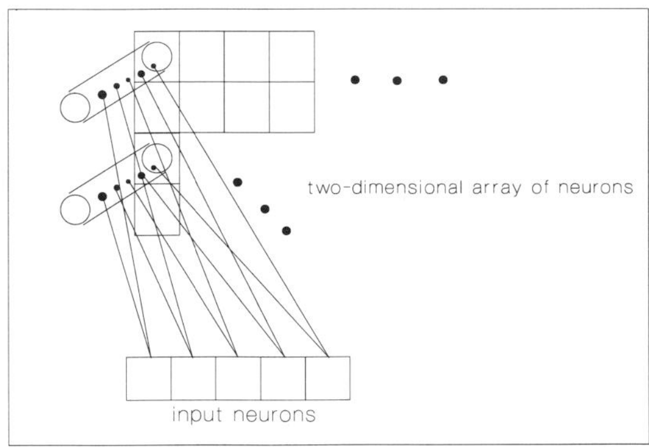

as a weighted sum of the activations of the neurons in the input layer. Each synapse from an input neuron to a grid neuron is modulated by a connection strength called synaptic efficacy; it is these efficacies that serve to weight the inputs to the grid neurons. Often this weighted sum must exceed a threshold or bias before the grid neuron can be activated, but this requirement is not used in our model's version of the KFM. The activation function of the grid neurons used here is just the identity mapping—that is, activation is equal to net input. The net input to grid neuron i is simply:

$$net_i = \sum_j a_j * w_{ji}$$

where a_j is the activation of input neuron j, and w_j is the synaptic efficacy (weight) of the link from input neuron j to grid neuron i. In other words, the net input of each grid neuron is just the inner product of the input vector (the vector of activations of all the input neurons) with the grid neuron's particular synaptic efficacy vector (the weights of the connections leading to that neuron).

The KFM starts with no particular organization among the grid neurons; all synapses start with random weights. But as the map is trained during repeated presentations of the input data set, it begins to self-organize, and topological patterns of certain regions of grid neurons responding to certain sorts of inputs begin to appear. Training consists of making small adjustments to the synaptic strengths over and over again in response to a sort of competition among the grid neurons until the connection strengths perform a stable dimensionality reduction of the input data and yield the appropriate grid organization. The connection strengths can be regarded as the long-term memory of the system which has adapted itself to the environment.

The KFM algorithm proceeds as follows:

1. Initialize the synaptic weights by giving them random values.
2. Choose a *learning rate*, which governs the rate at which the synapse strengths are adjusted, and a *neighborhood radius*, which will be used to specify the size of the "bubble of activity" among the grid neurons in response to a particular input pattern.
3. Select an input pattern at random and use it in the following steps.
4. Present the input pattern to the network and find the grid neuron that becomes most active in response to this input. (This can also be though of as computing the correlation or the Euclidian distance between the input vector and the synaptic efficacy vector of every grid neuron and choosing the grid neuron whose synaptic efficacy vector is most similar to the input vector according to either of these metrics.)
5. For all grid neurons that fall in the neighborhood radius (from step 2) of the neuron selected in step 4, adapt the synapses leading

to those neurons according to the formula

$$w(t+1) = w(t) + a(t) * (v(t) - w(t))$$

where $w(t+1)$ is the synaptic efficacy vector at time $t+1, w(t)$ is the synaptic vector at time t, $a(t)$ is the learning rate at time t, and $v(t)$ is the input vector at time t. Outside the neighborhood area, the synapses are inhibited by a factor of about a tenth of the learning rate. This learning rule will tend to make the "winning" neuron and its neighbors more likely to "win" the competition for this particular input pattern, and those like it, in the future.

6. Decrease the learning rate and neighborhood radius if necessary.
7. Go back to step 3 until the map has finally converged.

Thus the algorithm may be summarized as, for each presentation of an input pattern, finding the best-matching grid neuron and increasing the "match" at this neuron and its topological neighbors. In this way, the bubbles of activity in response to particular input patterns are formed, and nearby bubbles will respond to similar patterns.

An implementation of this KFM algorithm on a distributed computing system of arbitrary size (in particular a Transputer system) is described in Leman and Van Renterghem (1989). This implementation can serve as the basis for "heavy" computations on real data (large input vectors). The model now runs on a Transputer system with 32 processors. This computing power will become necessary in the near future when we will begin using real-world data. The current simulations were run on a Transputer system with four processors. Since the algorithm has a straightforward parallel implementation, the performance gain is quite good. The computer performance measure technique of profile analysis shows a gain factor of about 3.4 when four processors are used instead of one, for networks with 400 neurons, the size used in all the simulations reported here. On a 32-transputer system the performance gain is only 2.5, where the loss in efficiency is due to communication overhead. For networks with more neurons, there is increased performance with greater numbers of transputers.

Data and Representation

We are interested in applying the KFM to musical data, to see if concepts of tonality emerge in the course of self-organizing dimensionality reduction. The representation of input data we use takes into consideration aspects of sensory information processing, as well as cultural characteristics such as the type of data and their statistical distribution. Our ultimate goal is to start from raw acoustic data (music "as it sounds," that is, as it appears as vibrations in the air), but at this stage of our research we adopted a more modest approach over which strict control could be more easily exercised.

Sensory Basis

The sensory basis of the model is founded on Terhardt's psychoacoustical theory for the extraction of tones (Terhardt, Stoll, and Seewann 1982; see also Laden and Keefe, this volume). Although Terhardt's theory is not the only conceivable theory for pitch extraction, it is quite appealing from a musical point of view because of its connection with Rameau's theory of harmony. Rameau (1722/1765), in his theory of music, introduced the concept of the fundamental note as the root of a chord to explain tonal semantics. Terhardt's model provides a psychoacoustical basis for this concept.

Briefly summarized, the theory assumes the existence of *subharmonic templates,* the origin of which may be due to either learning processes or physiological mechanisms (Demany and Semal 1988; van Noorden 1982). These subharmonic templates consist of several subharmonics generated by frequency analysis in the ear in response to the separable sinusoidal components in a complex tone. By comparing these templates to find which subharmonic occurs most frequently in response to the complex tone, a particular single subjective tone becomes activated. This resulting subjective tone is called the residue tone (or virtual tone) and is the tone perceived (the perceived fundamental). This process of subharmonic fusion and comparison occurs at higher levels of the auditory processing system (Zatorre 1988).

Fig. 6. *Localist representations of chords using only those pitches occurring in the chord. C-major triad (a). C-minor triad (b). C-dominant seventh chord (c).*

Cultural Basis

The dataset we used with our model consists of triad and seventh chords built up by combining minor and major third intervals. These are the chords that are most often used in Western tonal music, and so this dataset embodies the cultural basis of this tradition.

The actual representation of chords is very important for the way in which the KFM will perform its classification. Classification can only work provided that the classes one is looking for are reflected in some common invariance in the input data, according to some similarity metric.

We first considered using a simple local representation of chords in which each tone (i.e., pitch class) would be represented by one input neuron, and only those pitches present in the chord would be activated. Examples of this representation are shown for the C-major triad, C-minor triad, and C-dominant seventh chords in Fig. 6. This representation could be used in the KFM with a Hamming distance measure but will not lead to any interesting results because no tonally relevant features can be extracted from it.

We decided on a much more promising representation, which incorporates the sensory considerations just outlined. Examples of this representation, supported by Terhardt's psychoacoustical theory of tone perception, are shown in Fig. 7 for the same chords given above. The distributed vector for each chord is computed by combining the subharmonic templates for each pitch in the chord, as will be described in the following paragraphs. The similarity of pairs of chords encoded in this manner can be measured by simply taking the inner product of the vectors corresponding to their distributed representations. Such a similarity metric results in feature maps that are far more interesting, as the results in the next section will show.

Since the present simulation was an initial attempt to study the principle of tonality ontogenesis, rather than an in-depth exploration, the representation we used was restricted by the use of octave equivalence classes and fixed weights (both described shortly) for determining the influence of individual subharmonic components. We are well

(a)

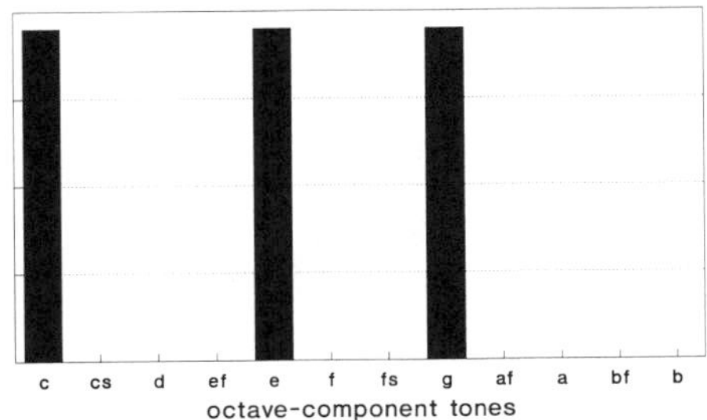

(b)

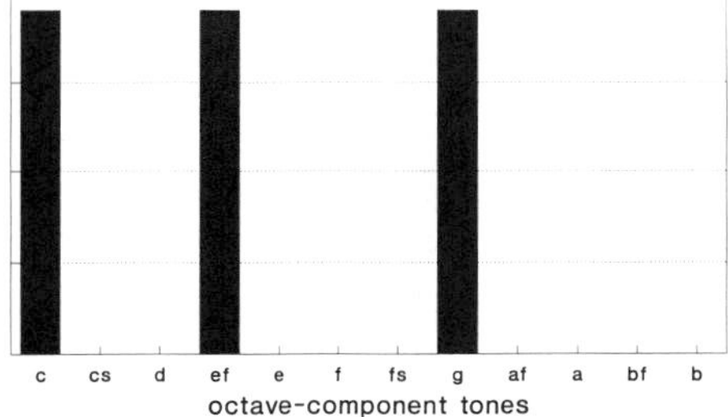

(c)

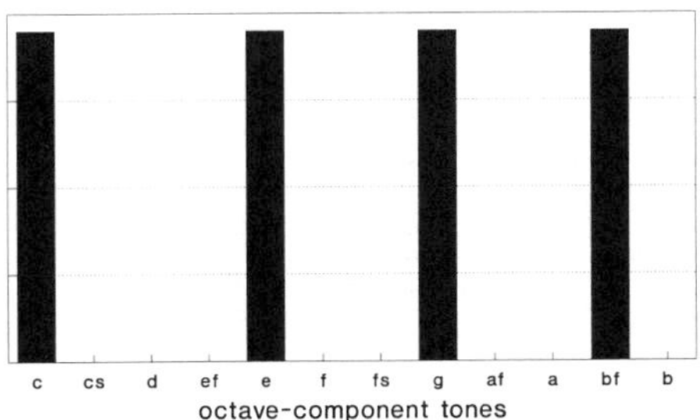

Fig. 7. Distributed representations of chords made by combining Terhardt's subharmonic templates for each pitch occurring in the chord. C-major triad (a). C-minor triad (b). C-dominant seventh chord (c).

(a)

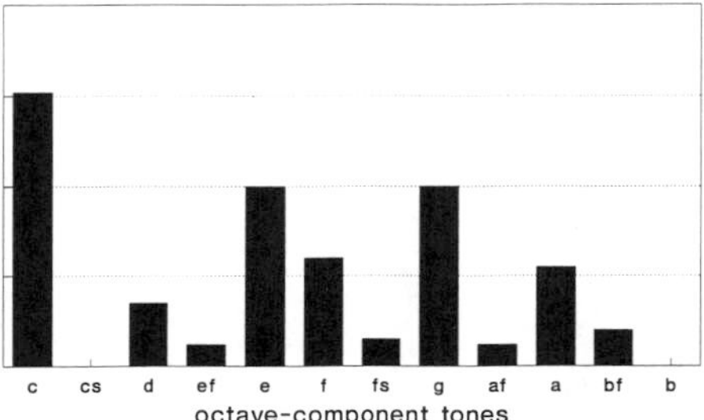

(b)

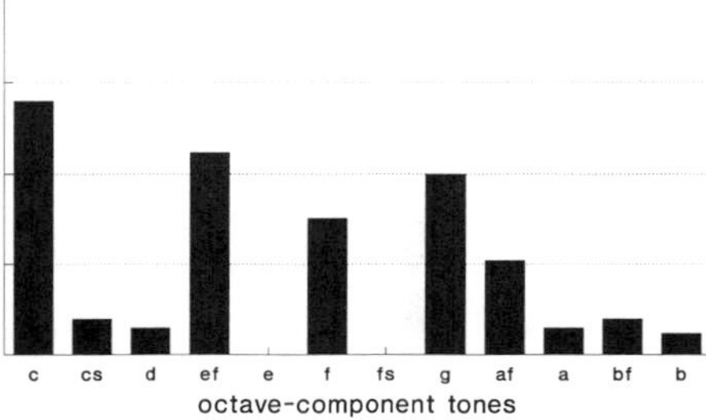

(c)

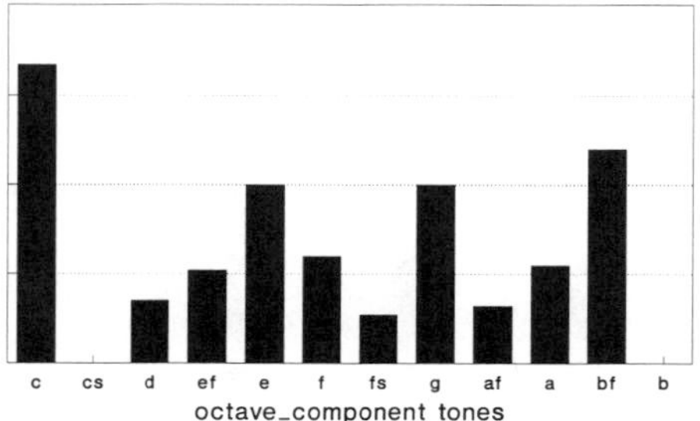

aware that these restrictions impose severe limits on the scope of our model, but we believe that they can be overcome in the very near future.

Rather than specify all the subharmonics in a chord representation by their actual frequency or pitch height, we just use octave-equivalent pitch classes as "bins" that collect the subharmonics. Thus there are only twelve input neurons, each having an activation determined by a weighted sum of all the subharmonics falling into their bin. This is quite a reduction in input size compared with the number of input neurons we would need if we used an extended pitch-height representation.

The weighted-sum activation of each input neuron in this representation essentially corresponds to the virtual or residual pitches computed by subharmonic fusion in Terhardt's theory. Each subharmonic component added into the input neurons is given a fixed weight that is an estimated value for the importance of that pitch class in determining the residual pitch. For example, for a C pitch, the first eight subharmonics are, in descending order: C (related to the original C by an octave below), F, (related to the C by a fifth below), C (octave), A-flat (major third), F (fifth), D (minor seventh), C (octave), and B-flat (major second below C). Since octave components are most strongly present in this subharmonic series, they get the highest fixed weight—1.0—whenever they are added into the input neuron bins. The fifth occurs twice in this series and gets a weight of 0.4, whereas the subharmonic intervals of major third, minor seventh, and major second occur only once each and get weights of 0.12, 0.15, and 0.20 respectively.

The mapping of pitch classes present in the original chord onto the virtual residue pitch classes represented by the input neurons thus can be thought of as a kind of voting system in which each pitch class in the chord assigns votes to the residue pitch classes for which it could be an overtone (i.e., for the residue pitch classes that are its subharmonics). The function that performs this mapping is

$$VPC(i) = \sum_j PC(j) * W(j, i)$$

where *VPC(i)* is the value of support for the *i*th virtual residue pitch class, and thus the value of the

Table 1

local pitch-class representation of C-major triad:

C	C♯	D	E♭	E	F
1.00	0.00	0.00	0.00	1.00	0.00
F♯	**G**	**A♭**	**A**	**B♭**	**B**
0.00	1.00	0.00	0.00	0.00	0.00

corresponding distributed virtual pitch-class representation:

C	C♯	D	E♭	E	F
1.52	0.00	0.35	0.12	1.00	0.60
F♯	**G**	**A♭**	**A**	**B♭**	**B**
0.15	1.00	0.12	0.55	0.20	0.00

ith input neuron; $PC(j)$ indicates the presence or absence of the jth pitch class in the input chord (1.0 if the pitch class is present in the chord, 0.0 if not); and $W(j,i)$ is the voting power of the jth pitch class with respect to the ith virtual pitch class, that is, the fixed weights for the different interval relationships given in the previous paragraph. Since we restrict ourselves to chromatic pitch classes, i and j are from 1 to 12.

Table 1 shows both the pitch classes present in the local representation of a C-major triad (as shown in Fig. 6a and the complete distributed virtual pitch-class representation over the input neurons computed with the previous equation (as shown in Fig. 7a).

First Study

For the first study, we trained a KFM network with input patterns consisting of 115 different chords. These chords have been built up by the combination of minor- and/or major-third intervals. For example, a major triad consists of a major-third interval [M] and a minor-third interval [m]. The combination of intervals corresponding to the complete major triad is notated as [M,m], and one can reconstruct the tones in this chord if a lowest tone is given. For example, given the tone C, we build up the C-major triad by taking the tones C, E, and G, respectively. The short-hand notation for the C-major triad is CM.

Below we give a list of all the chords that have been used in this first study. Inversions and octave spreading were not taken into account because we used octave component pitch-class tones. The percentage between brackets indicates the occurrence of the chord type in music of the classical and romantic period (data based on Bruhn 1988). The first study does not take into account these percentages, but we will return to them in the second study.

- 12 major triads: [M,m] (referred to as CM, C♯M,DM,E♭M, . . .)[43 percent],
- 12 minor triads: [m,M] (CM,C♯m,Dm, . . .) [15 percent],
- 12 diminished triads: [m,m] (Co, . . .) [4 percent],
- 4 augmented triads: [M,M] (C+,C♯+, D+,E♭+) [1 percent],
- 12 major seventh chords: [M,m,M] (CM7, . . .) [1 percent],
- 12 minor seventh chords: [m,M,m] (Cm7, . . .)[1 percent],
- 12 dominant seventh chords: [M,m,m] (Cx7, . . .) [26 percent],
- 12 half diminished seventh chords: [m,m,M] (CO7, . . .) [2 percent],
- 12 augmented seventh chords: [M,M,m] (C+7, . . .) [1 percent],
- 12 minor with major seventh chords: [m,M,M] (Cm−7, . . .) [1 percent], and
- 3 diminished seventh chords: [m,m,m] (Co7, C♯o7, Do7) [7 percent].

(The pattern of augmented triads and the diminished seventh chords is repeated after E♭+ and Do7 respectively, resulting in the reduced number of possible chords for these two classes. That is, the pitches of the next augmented triad, E+, are E, A♭, and C, which are the same as in C+; and the pitches of the next diminished seventh chord, E♭o7 are E♭, F♯, A, and C, the same as in Co7.)

The distributed representation of these chords was obtained by computing the residual pitches as specified in the last section. This dataset was presented at each learning cycle in a random order.

Fig. 8. Patterns of activation (showing response regions) in a 20 by 20 KFM responding to different chords at various points during training. Responses are shown to a C-major triad after 1 training cycle (a); a C-major triad after 10 training cycles (b); a C-major triad after 180 training cycles (c); an F-major triad after 180 training cycles (d); a G-major triad after 180 training cycles (e).

The size of the neural grid used in this experiment was 20 by 20. The learning rate was set to 0.01, with an inhibition factor of 0.002. These values were kept constant during the training session. The radius of the neighborhood was set to 18 and was decreased by 1 after every 10 cycles, so that after 180 cycles we end up with a neighborhood radius of 0.

Figs. 8a, 8b, and 8c show how the network responds to an input of the C-major triad after 1, 10, and 180 cycles respectively. Each point in the figures represents the activation of one neuron at that place in the grid, with the size of the point corresponding to the amount of activation.

After the first cycle of training (Fig. 9a), memory is still totally chaotic. There is no clear center of response to the input. After some training, however, the network responds by activating a cluster, or "bubble," of neurons rather than a single neuron (Fig. 8b). These bubbles emerge because of the adaptation of neuronal activation that falls within the neighborhood of the most highly responding neuron. The region of neurons activated in response to one input pattern is called the *response region* (*RR*). In Fig. 8b this RR is large and diffuse due to the operating neighborhood radius of 18. In Fig. 8c, after 180 cycles, a clearly distinguished bubble has been formed (with the decrease of the radius to 0). Similar bubbles can be seen in Figs. 8d and 8e, which show how the network responds to an input of the F-major and G-major triads, respectively, both after 180 cycles.

If we think of each neuron in the KFM grid as a kind of filter on the inputs, then all the neurons in the response region can be thought of as being tuned more or less roughly to the particular input

Fig. 8

(c)

(d)

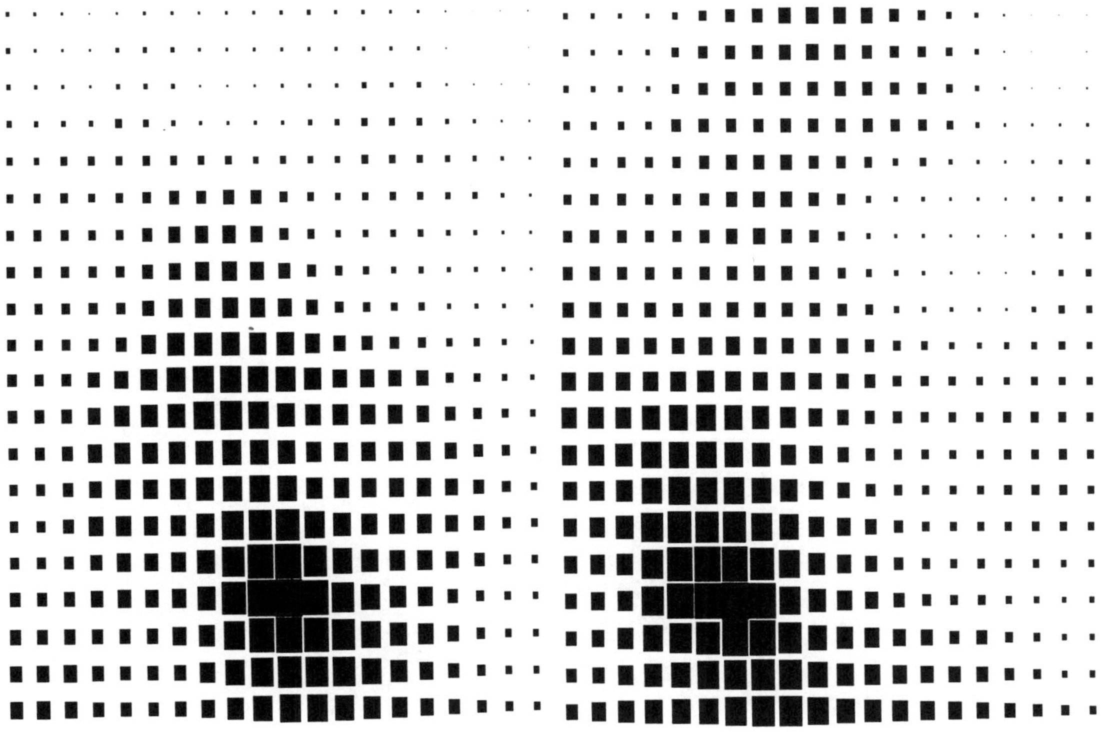

pattern. (Here the tuning can be though of as the match between the input pattern and the neuron's synaptic efficacy vector, as described previously.) The neuron that responds most strongly to a given input, that is tuned most closely to that input, is called the *characteristic neuron* (*CN*) for that input. Both the notion of response region (RR) and the characteristic neuron (CN) are important for the understanding of what is going on during the process of self-organization.

The largest response, and hence the CN, for the C-major triad input shown in Fig. 8a after 1 cycle is located at point (1,6) (with the horizontal x-dimension first, reading from left to right, and then the vertical y-dimension, reading from bottom to top). In Fig. 8b, the CN of the C-major triad input after 10 cycles is located at (3,1), whereas in Fig. 8c, after 180 cycles, the CN is located at (11,4). The CNs of Figs. 8d and 8e, reflecting the responses to the F-major and G-major triads after 180 cycles, are located at (7,4) and (15,5) respectively.

By labeling each characteristic neuron with the particular input(s) it responds most highly to (chords it is most closely tuned to), we can obtain the global patterns of response formed by the KFM algorithm. Figs. 9a, 9b, and 9c provide a global overview of the CN responses of the network after 1, 10, and 180 training cycles respectively.

Interestingly, one can observe the migration of CNs on the map during learning. The response is quite chaotic in the beginning (Fig. 9a) but starts taking form very soon. Fig. 9b is typical for the very early categorization process of the KFM algorithm. Due to the large neighborhood radius (which after

Fig. 8

(e)

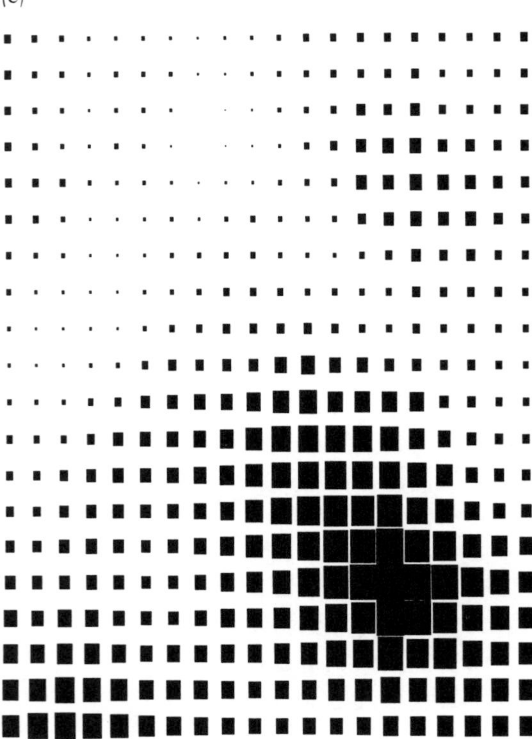

10 training cycles will be 17), the CNs are "pushed" towards the corners, thereby clustering the most similar chords very roughly in four or five categories. It is only when the neighborhood radius is further reduced that these CNs (can) migrate more toward the center. After 180 cycles we obtain the map shown in Fig. 9c.

Fig. 9c shows an organization of CNs in terms of the circle of fifths, at least for some important chord families. But before we invite the reader to look for the circle of fifths in the figure, we should note that the interpretation of the CN-map is *not* straightforward. The KFM organizes the chords according to this principle: similarity means smaller distance. We shall see, however, that the form of the response region may play a decisive role in the factual interpretation of this principle at greater distances over the grid. From our experiences we have learned that the relation of greater distance to lower similarity only holds by itself within a range of two or three neurons.

For the time being, we can look at the global organization of, for example, the major triads on the map shown in Fig. 9c. Starting from the C-major triad at (11,4) and proceeding clockwise, we encounter respectively the F-major triad at (7, 4), the B♭-major triad at (2,5), the E♭-major triad at (1,15), the A♭-major triad at (5,13) and so on. We invite the reader to make links between the major triads around the traditional circle of fifths and see what comes out on the grid (a slightly distorted circle). Dominant chords, minor triads, and minor seventh chords show very similar structures.

The global organization of CNs in terms of circles on the feature map is not an absolute necessity for the explanation of tonal functioning, though. One should be very careful about this. The appearance of global properties, such as the emergent circular structures in this study, depends greatly on the form of the RRs found in the grid. And, indeed, it may happen that the RRs occur as stretched bubbles rather than as circles. This phenomenon can be seen in the RR of the C-major triad in Fig. 8c, which is an oval that fades out towards its center. Fig. 8e shows rather clear "secondary bubbles" above and to the left of the main RR.

Occasionally, it may happen that a response region is clearly split over two regions of the network. In that case the interpretation of the CN-map should take the forms of the RRs into account. An interesting example of this phenomenon is shown in Figs. 10a and 10b. The results in these figures were obtained after 90 training cycles with the data-set used before. All parameters were the same as before, except for the decrease rate of the neighborhood radius. The neighborhood radius was set to 18 at the beginning and decremented every 5 cycles in this case, so that early clustering was reduced. Fig. 10a shows the global organization of the map in terms of CNs after 90 cycles.

Consider the major triads. The global appearance of the circle seen before is broken here between the E-major triad (17,16) and the A-major triad (13,1). Yet there is a connection between these tonally

Fig. 9. Characteristic neuron maps for the dataset of the first study, shown after 1 training cycle (a); 10 training cycles (b); 180 training cycles, showing circular organization of chord groups (c).

(a)

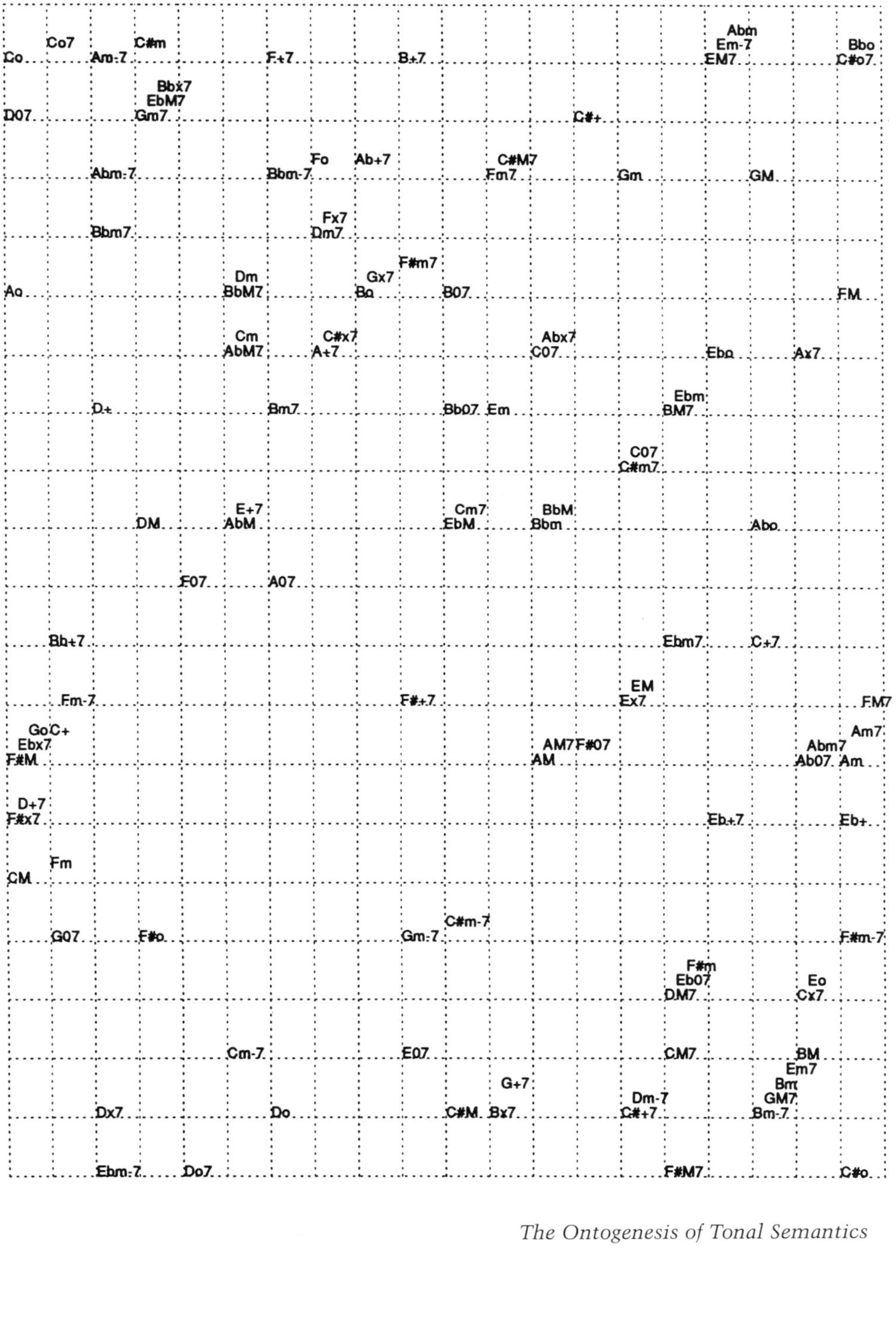

Fig. 9

(b)

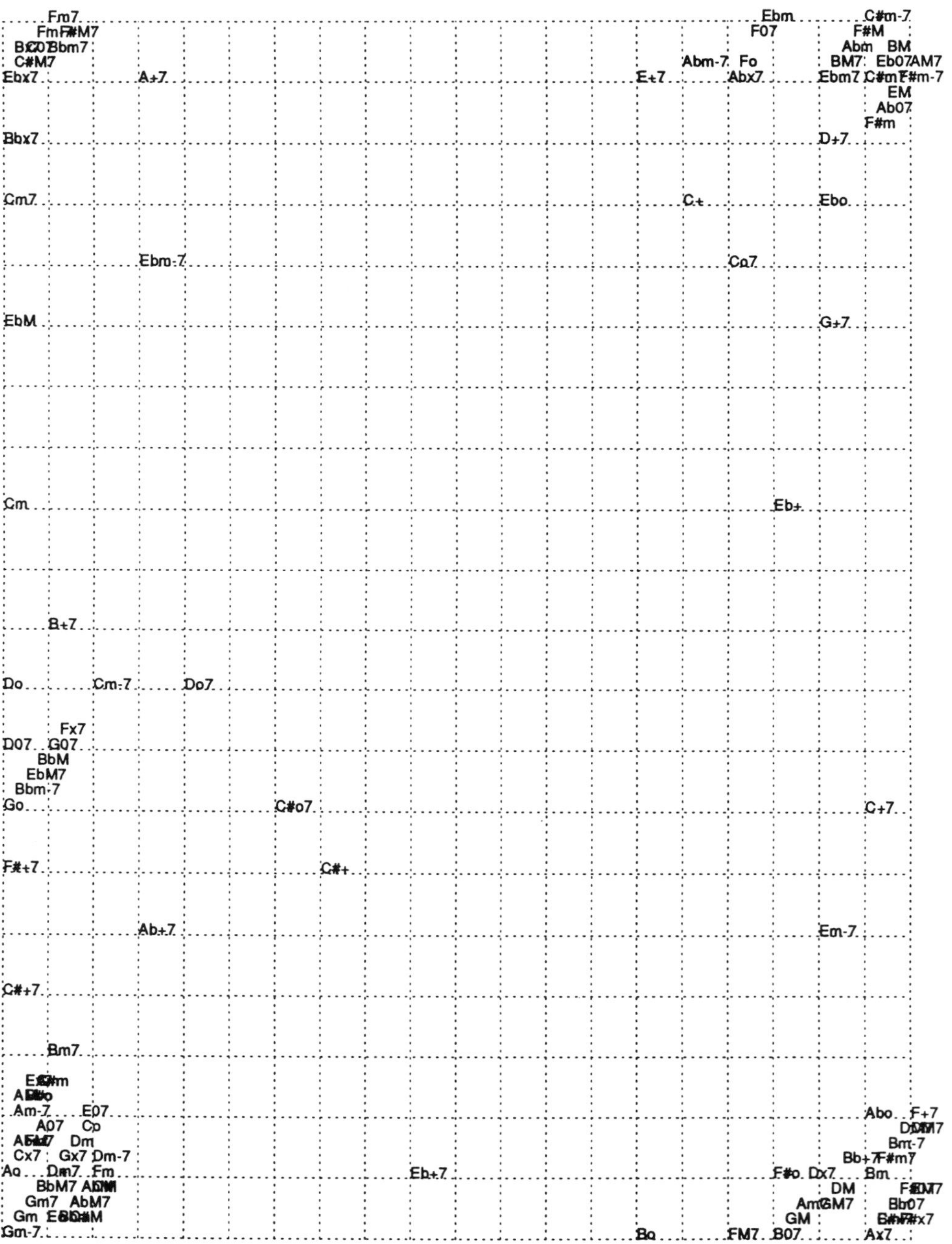

Fm7
Bbm7
C#M7
Ebx7
A+7
Ebm
C#m-7
F07
F#M
Abm
BM
Abm-7
Fo
BM7
Eb07
AM7
E+7
Abx7
Ebm7
F#m-7
EM
Ab07
F#m
Bbx7
D+7
Cm7
C+
Ebo
Ebm-7
Co7
EbM
G+7
Cm
Eb+
B+7
Do
Cm-7
Do7
Fx7
D07
G07
BbM
EbM7
Bbm-7
Go
C#o7
C+7
F#+7
C#+
Ab+7
Em-7
C#+7
Bm7
Am-7
E07
A07
Co
Dm
Cx7
Gx7
Dm-7
Ao
Dm7
Fm
BbM7
Gm7
AbM7
Gm
Gm-7
Eb+7
Abo
F+7
Bm-7
F#m7
Bb+7
Bm
F#o
Dx7
DM
Bb07
GM
Bo
FM7
B07
Ax7

Fig. 9

(c)

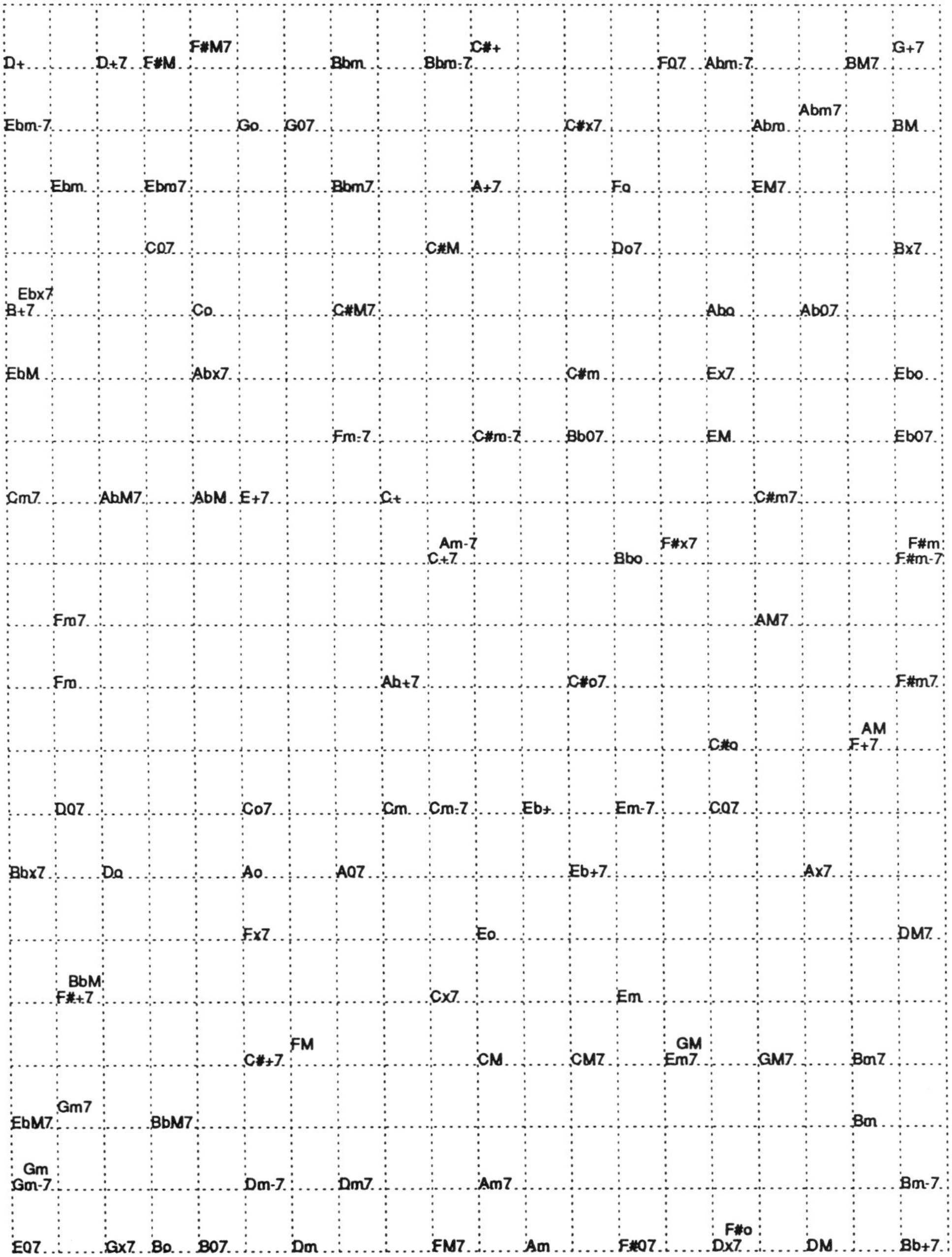

F#M7 C#+ G+7
D+ D+7 F#M Bbm Bbm-7 F07 Abm-7 BM7
Abm7
Ebm-7 Go G07 C#x7 Abm BM
Ebm Ebm7 Bbm7 A+7 Fo EM7
C07 C#M Do7 Bx7
Ebx7
B+7 Co C#M7 Abo Ab07
EbM Abx7 C#m Ex7 Ebo
Fm-7 C#m-7 Bb07 EM Eb07
Cm7 AbM7 AbM E+7 C+ C#m7
Am-7 F#x7 F#m
C+7 Bbo F#m-7
Fm7 AM7
Fm Ab+7 C#o7 F#m7
AM
C#o F+7
D07 Co7 Cm Cm-7 Eb+ Em-7 C07
Bbx7 Do Ao A07 Eb+7 Ax7
Fx7 Eo DM7
BbM
F#+7 Cx7 Em
FM GM
C#+7 CM CM7 Em7 GM7 Bm7
Gm7
EbM7 BbM7 Bm
Gm
Gm-7 Dm-7 Dm7 Am7 Bm-7
F#o
E07 Gx7 Bo B07 Dm FM7 Am F#07 Dx7 DM Bb+7

Fig. 10. Feature map results for the dataset of the first study, but with more rapidly decreased neighborhood radii, after 90 training cycles. Characteristic neuron map (a). Response to an A-major triad, showing split response region (b).

(a)

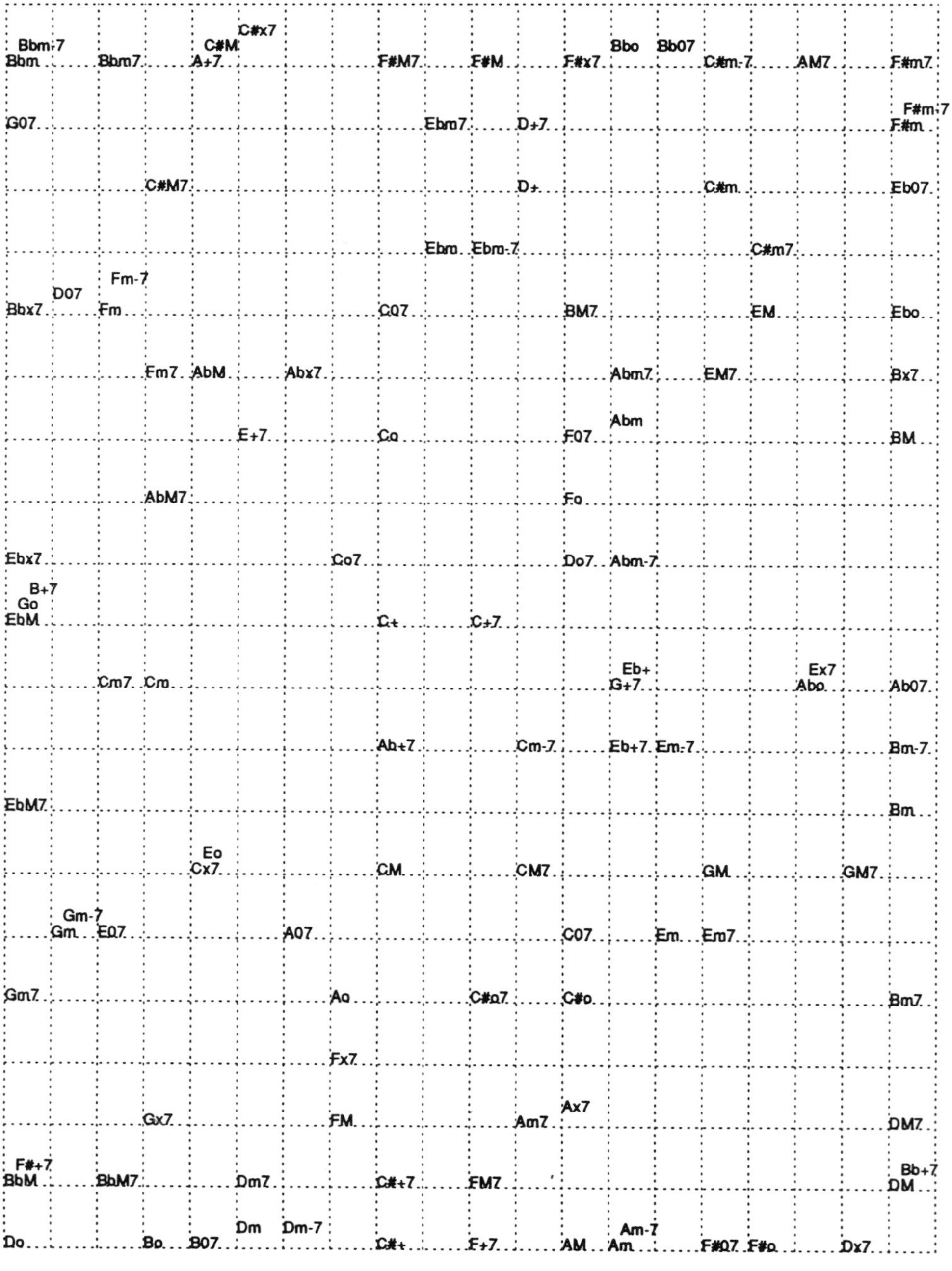

Fig. 10

(b)

related chords (which occur next to each other in the circle of fifths), which can be seen when we consider the RR of the A-major triad, shown in Fig. 10b. The RR of the A-major triad is split over two clearly distinct locations on the grid. The CN of this response region is located in the lower part of the figure, whereas another set of highly responding neurons appears in the upper right corner of the figure. This second portion of the RR lies quite near to the CN for the E-major triad, as we would hope.

On the whole, however, the results shown in Fig. 10a are less stable than those in Fig. 9. We can see this by computing the error between each CN and its corresponding input vector. The optimal solution to the classification problem is obtained when this error is as small as possible, but in the case of the map in Fig. 10a it is still appreciable. For more details and a discussion of this, we refer the reader to the author's doctoral dissertation (Leman, in preparation).

We conclude from this discussion that an inspection of the CN-map alone is often not sufficient to understand the organization of the mapping. The form of the RRs, as well as a consideration of the error between CNs and their input vectors, should also be taken into account in many cases.

We conjecture that in some cases the network might come up with a global mapping of CNs that is very similar to a torus structure, such as the one shown in Fig. 3. This structure can be accounted for by the fact that the RRs of tonal regions at the grid borders are continued at the opposite edge of the grid. Although the organization in terms of a two-dimensional circle has disappeared in this structure, the organization in terms of a circle of fifths is actually still present.

A final remark concerns the statistical distribution of the chords used. In the dataset we used, there are 115 different chords, each of which occurs only once. We did not take into account the statistical distribution of the chords as they would appear in Western music. (This contrasts with the second experiment, described below.) The fact that the neural network came up with some kind of organization anyhow should therefore be explained on the basis of the tonal stability of the input patterns, which is reflected in the error between the CNs and their corresponding input vectors. Tonal stability means that the input patterns can be clearly distinguished from each other. But this implies as well that some chords are more stable (more distinct) than others.

Relevance of the First Study

The chordotopic organization on the basis of the circle of fifths that emerged in a topography of neurons in our first study is closely related to the topology of chords well known in music theory. As mentioned before, there is a large amount of musical psychological data that confirm this kind of structural organization for musical knowledge. One may wonder, however, the extent to which such a feature map might explain tonal functioning, in particular here, the perceptual facilitation of chords.

The present model provides some evidence for explaining chord facilitation on the basis of the response regions within a memory of dispositions (i.e., a memory that causally reacts to stimuli in the environment). One possible explanation of this facilitation could be that the RRs of tonally related chords overlap and interact in some manner, whereas the RRs of chords that are tonally more distant do not overlap and hence do not interact. By "overlap," we mean that the RR of one chord partly covers the RR of another chord. For example, the RR of the C-major triad shown in Fig. 8c partly covers the RR of the F-major triad shown in Fig. 8d. This overlapping will cause an interaction of the activation values of the affected neurons in the time domain. This interaction is based on the interference of activations over time and assumes a gradual fading of the activations soon after the stimulus has disappeared.

The interaction of the activations of neurons in overlapping RRs over time could then explain how a tonal context can be set and how tones get their particular tonal function with respect to this context. For example, imagine what would happen if we provided the sequence of triad chords {C-major, F-major, G-major} as input to our trained map. First a C-major RR would be built up and sustained as long as this chord occurred (Fig. 8c). Then the F-major triad would be heard as input and an F-major RR would respond as usual (Fig. 8d). But meanwhile the activation of the C-major RR will gradually decrease while the F-major RR is being activated. Notice, however, that the neurons in the intersection of both the C-major and F-major RRs would gain new activation because of the F-major RR being turned on.

The same argument holds for the time at which the G-major RR becomes activated (Fig. 8e). The activation of the neurons that fall outside the RR will decrease slightly. But some neurons of the G-major RR also belong to the C-major RR, so again there will be support for the C-major RR. Therefore, after the presentation of the G-major triad, the C-major region would still have a reasonable amount of activation. This could correspond to the tonal context built up by this sequence of chords and could affect the subsequent interpretation of new inputs experienced by the network. (This thought-experiment assumes that the chords are played one after the other, within reasonable time constraints. If there were to be large time gaps between the chords played, then the effect of chord facilitation would be lost.)

This model could be further refined if resonance processes at higher levels of an attentional system are taken into account. The effect would be that a response region could stay activated, even after the end of the stimulus. Up to now, however, this resonance theory has not been implemented in the present model. Models such as ART (Grossberg 1987; see also Gjerdingen, this volume) might be needed to account for the dynamics of attention, short-term memory, and expectation involved in such resonance processes.

Second Study

In a second study, we investigated the effects of the statistical distribution of chords on the feature map's chord classification. We used the same chord types as for the first study, but this time their distribution was taken into account. The distribution was expressed as the percentage of occurrence of each chord type, shown in brackets in the chord list given for the first study. The data were based on Bruhn (1988) who analyzed the occurrence of the different chord types in the music Beethoven, Schubert, and Brahms (in the classical and romantic periods).

The distribution shows high values for the major triads (43 percent), the minor triads (15 percent), and the dominant seventh chords (26 percent). Other chords are much less often used, some of them almost never, such as the augmented seventh chord and the minor with major seventh chord. In the data by Bruhn these get 0.12 percent and 0.00 percent respectively, while both were given 1 percent of occurrence here (giving a slight round-off error).

Fig. 11. Feature map results for the dataset of the second study, with different chord type frequencies, after 90 training cycles. Response to a C-major triad (a). Characteristic neuron map, showing circular organization of chord groups (b).

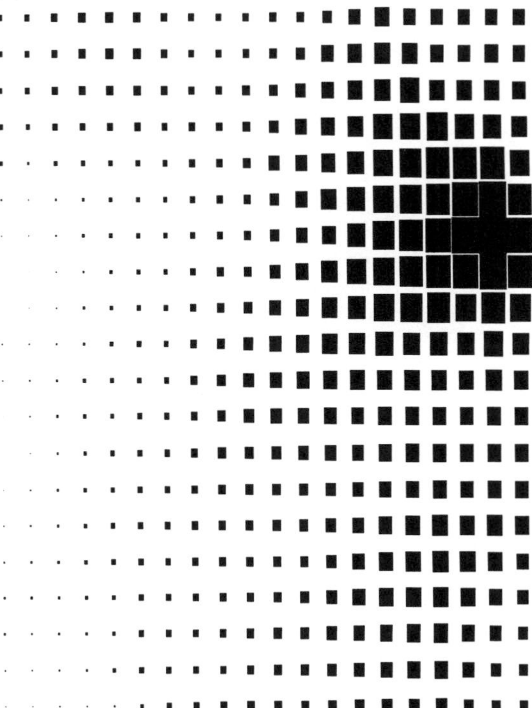

For the present study the percentages can be conceived of as the reflection of the number of times a particular chord type was present in the dataset. For example, the 12 major triads occurred 43 times each in our data set, the 12 minor triads 15 times each, and so on. We ended up with a dataset of 1156 chords (115 different chords, some of them repeated according to the distribution).

The learning rate and inhibition parameters were lower than before because the dataset was bigger. These values were set to 0.001 and 0.0002 respectively. The neighborhood was set to 18 and decremented every five steps. The training finished after 90 cycles.

Fig. 11a shows the resulting RR of the C-major triad in the network trained in this way, the CN of which is located at (19,14). This picture shows the situation after 90 cycles. The form of this RR is concise and similar to the results in the first experiment (Fig. 8c).

Fig. 11b shows the CN-map after 90 cycles. Inspection of this map shows a neat circle organization for major triads, except for the E♭ major triad, which is located more to the center of the grid. Inspection of the error between the CN synaptic vectors and their input vectors reveals small error values for the chords that occur very often (for example, the major triads), although for other chords this error value may be higher. The error reflects the stability of the network's response; thus in general we observe that those chords that have a high frequency of occurrence have a stable response in the network. Of course, one should mention here that these common chords are stable and clearly distinguished from a traditional tonality point of view as well.

Third Study

In a third experiment we used data provided by Parncutt (1989) based on a psychoacoustical theory of pitch perception starting from acoustical data, whereas in the first study we used handmade data. Parncutt used a model of pitch perception based on Terhardt's (1984) theory and computed the "chroma probability profiles of simultaneities of octave-spaced tones." Octave-spaced tones (pitch classes) are the type of tones that we have used throughout this study. Chroma probability is the probability that a particular pitch class is noticed in a musical element or passage of chords (called a *simultaneity*). For the details of how this chroma probability is computed, we refer the reader to Parncutt (1989). It suffices here to say that the output of the computation leads to values for pitch classes that are quite similar to (though slightly different from) the values obtained by our first study based on artificial data (shown in Fig. 7).

The dataset used in this study consisted of 91 different chords, the 115 chords used in the first two studies minus the 12 augmented seventh chords

Fig. 11

(b)

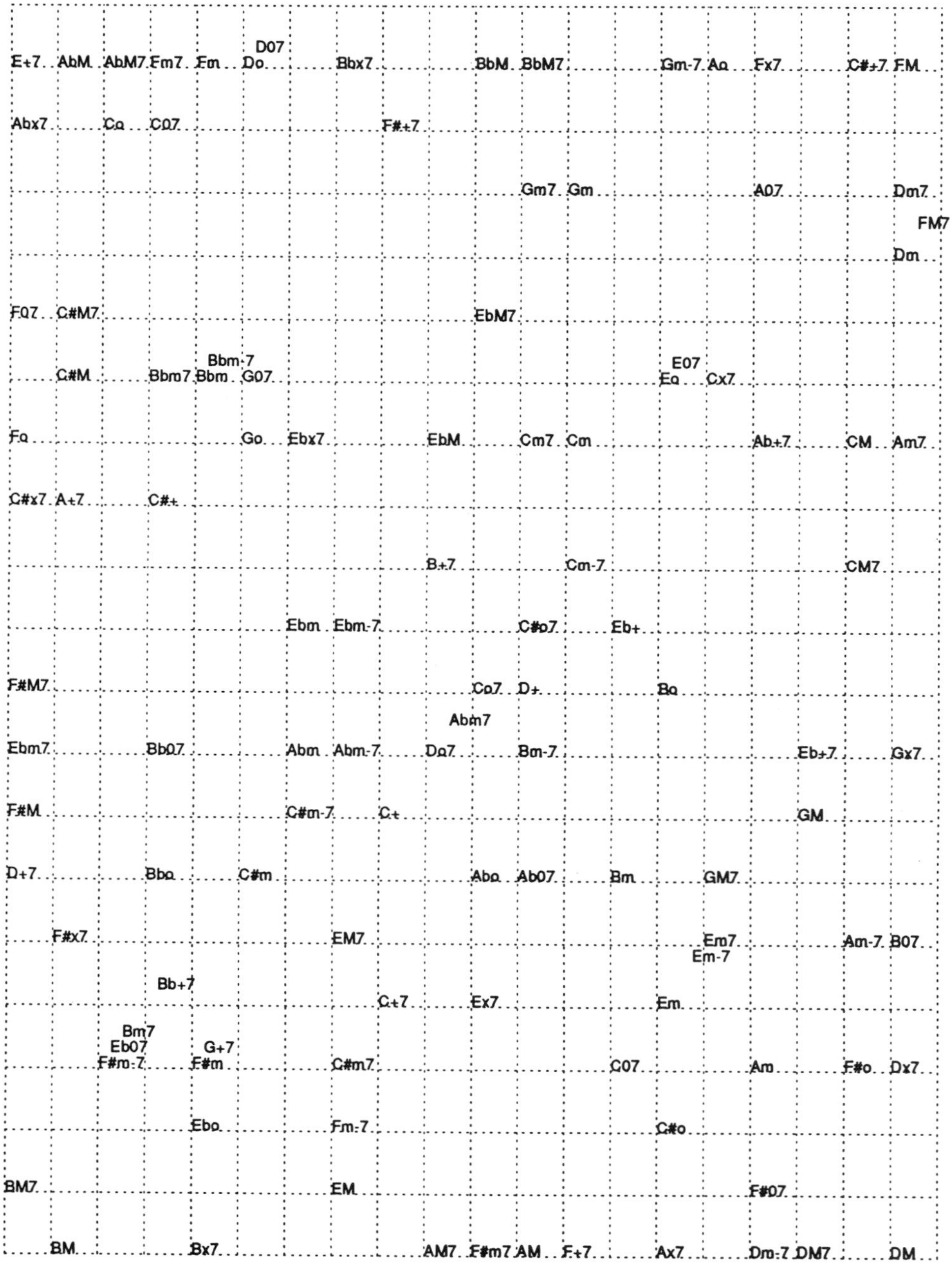

D07
E+7 AbM AbM7 Fm7 Fm Do Bbx7 BbM BbM7 Gm-7 Ao Fx7 C#+7 FM
Abx7 Co C07 F#+7
Gm7 Gm A07 Dm7
FM7
Dm
F07 C#M7 EbM7
Bbm-7 E07
C#M Bbm7 Bbm G07 Eo Cx7
Fo Go Ebx7 EbM Cm7 Cm Ab+7 CM Am7
C#x7 A+7 C#+
B+7 Cm-7 CM7
Ebm Ebm-7 C#o7 Eb+
F#M7 Co7 D+ Bo
Abm7
Ebm7 Bb07 Abm Abm-7 Do7 Bm-7 Eb+7 Gx7
F#M C#m-7 C+ GM
D+7 Bbo C#m Abo Ab07 Bm GM7
F#x7 EM7 Em7 Am-7 B07
Em-7
Bb+7
C+7 Ex7 Em
Bm7
Eb07 G+7
F#m-7 F#m C#m7 C07 Am F#o Dx7
Ebo Fm-7 C#o
BM7 EM F#07
BM Bx7 AM7 F#m7 AM F+7 Ax7 Dm-7 DM7 DM

Fig. 12. Patterns of activation (showing response regions) in a KFM trained with the dataset from the third study, using Parncutt's representation. Responses are shown to a C-major triad after 1 training cycle (a); a C-major triad after 10 training cycles (b); a C-major triad after 180 training cycles (c); an E♭-major triad after 180 training cycles (d).

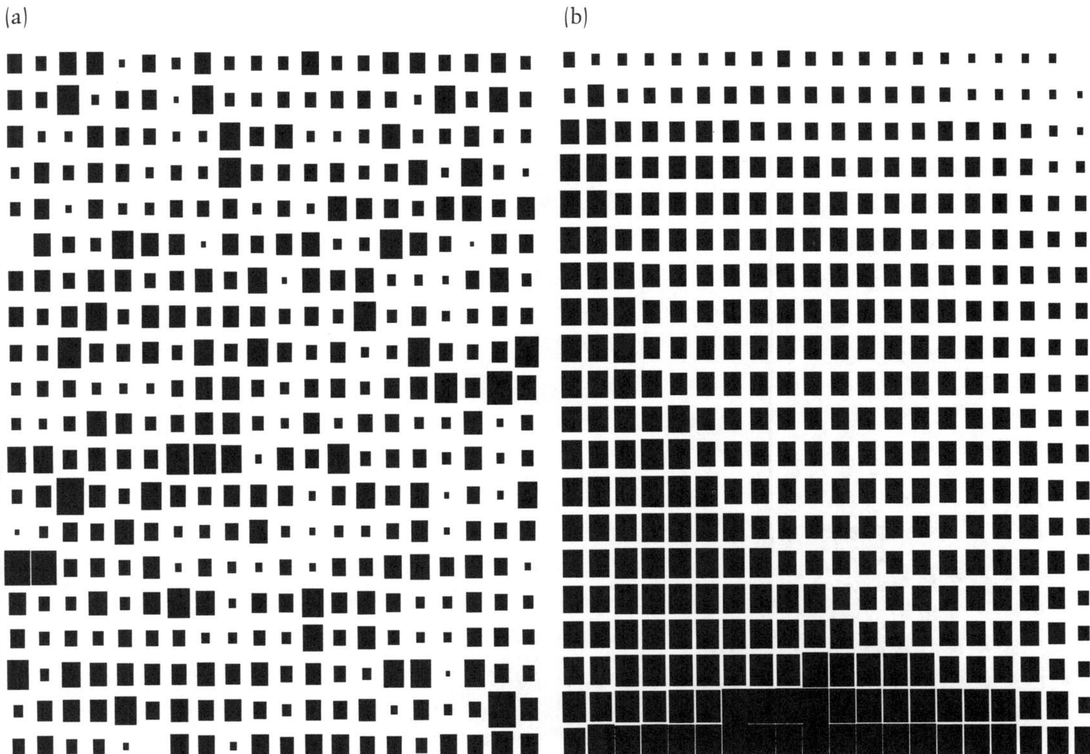

and the 12 minor with major seventh chords. The parameters were exactly the same as in the first study. The results obtained are shown in Figs. 12 and 13. Figs. 12a, 12b, and 12c show the RR of the C-major triad after 1, 10, and 180 cycles respectively. Fig.12d shows the RR of the E♭-major triad after 180 cycles. Figs. 13a, 13b, and 13c show the global map of CNs after 1, 10, and 180 cycles respectively.

Inspection of Fig. 13c shows that the circle of chords we saw previously does not appear as a global structure of this CN-map, even though the error is quite similar to what we obtained before. The irregular form of the global organization in this case should therefore be explained by the irregularities of the RRs, such as the one shown in Fig. 12d.

On the whole we can conclude that the results obtained in the third study are quite similar to those in our first study. Slight differences in the representation of the input may lead to a different global organization of the CN-map. But this could also be a result of the fact that the CN-map does not take into account the relationships between CNs at larger distances, as was mentioned earlier.

Conclusions

The present work is a step toward a straightforward (and perhaps even neurobiologically plausible) subsymbolic approach to the ontogenesis of tonality. The approach is based on the self-organization of chordal functions in neuronal elements. By using a representation of chords based on Terhardt's theory

Fig. 12

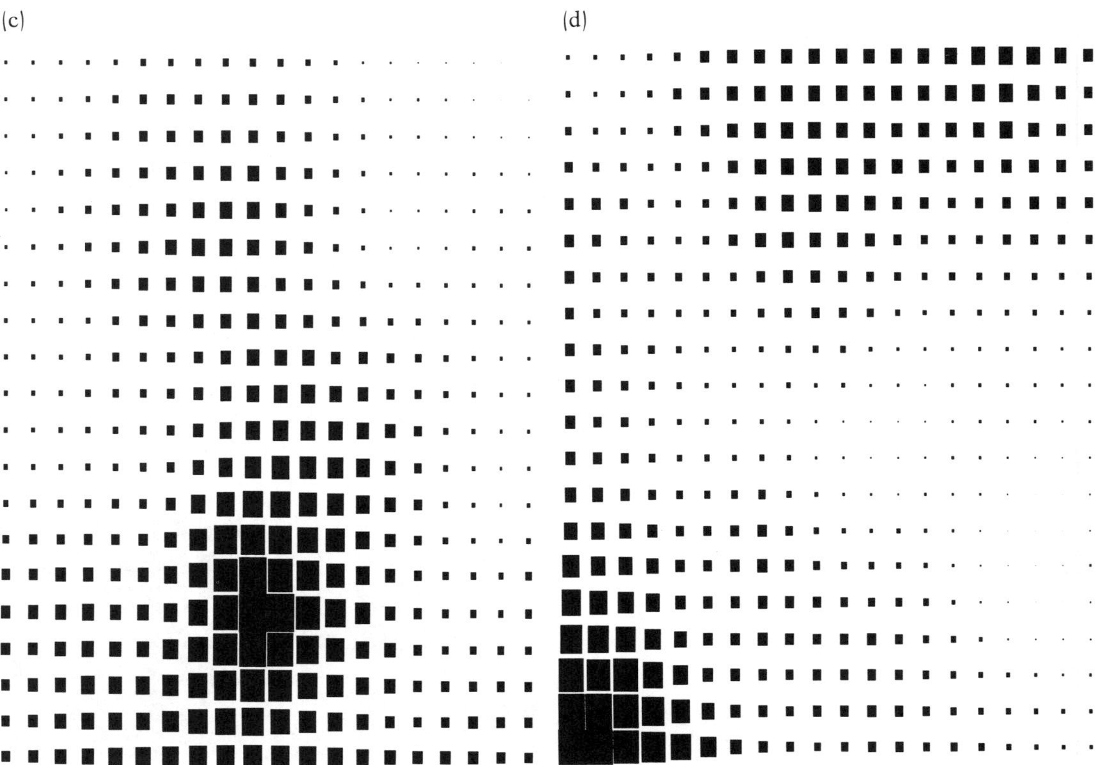

of pitch extraction, we have obtained a classification of chords by the Kohonen Feature Map algorithm. In particular, the artificial memory organizes itself basically in terms of a circle of fifths. Particular forms of response regions, though, must often be taken into account to explain "irregularities" in the global appearance of chordal organization. In addition, we have proposed a mechanism to explain tonal functioning and chordal facilitation, based on the notion of overlapping RRs as a metaphor for the interaction of RRs over time.

The importance of this work is in showing that aspects of tonality can in principle be accounted for by internal representations that develop through self-organization from invariant features in the musical environment. The current model shows that it is possible to adopt an epistemological and methodological approach to the modeling of tonality that is in close agreement with Gestalt psychology and ecological theories of perception.

There is also a predictive aspect to our results. If, disregarding the abstractions inherent in neural network simulations, self-organization does indeed make sense, we think this gives impetus to look for chordal functions at a neuronal level. Experimental research on human cortical functions would be needed to prove the existence of a circle-of-fifths map in the brain. Yet, such a structure might be difficult to find if only CNs—in this case, *actual* neurons—are taken into accoaunt, due to specific forms of feature map response regions, as demonstrated by the studies described here.

A final comment concerns the Krumhansl hypothesis that listeners have abstracted and internal-

Fig. 13. Characteristic neuron maps for the dataset of the third study, shown after 1 training cycle (a); 10 training cycles (b); 180 training cycles (c).

(a)

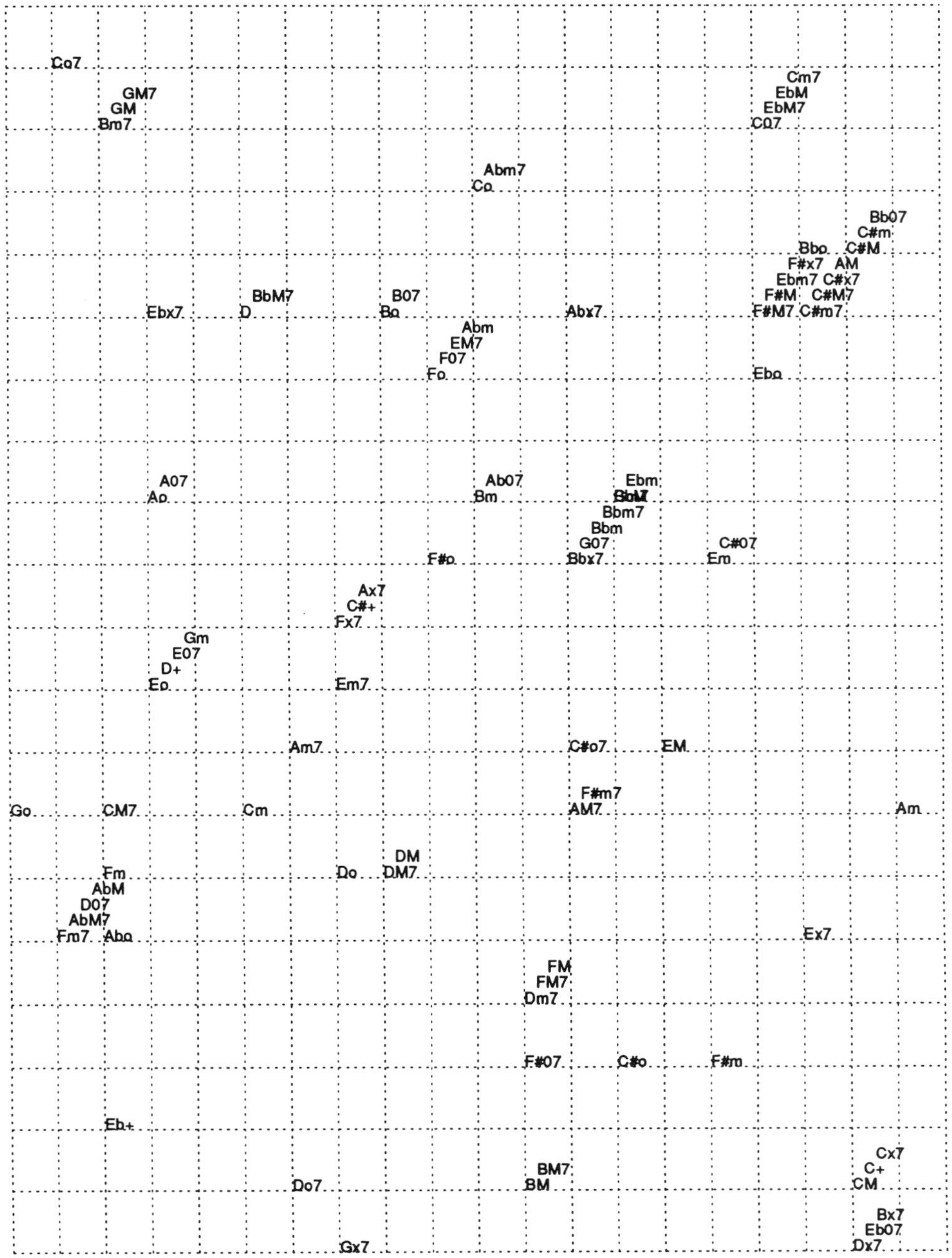

Fig. 13

(b)

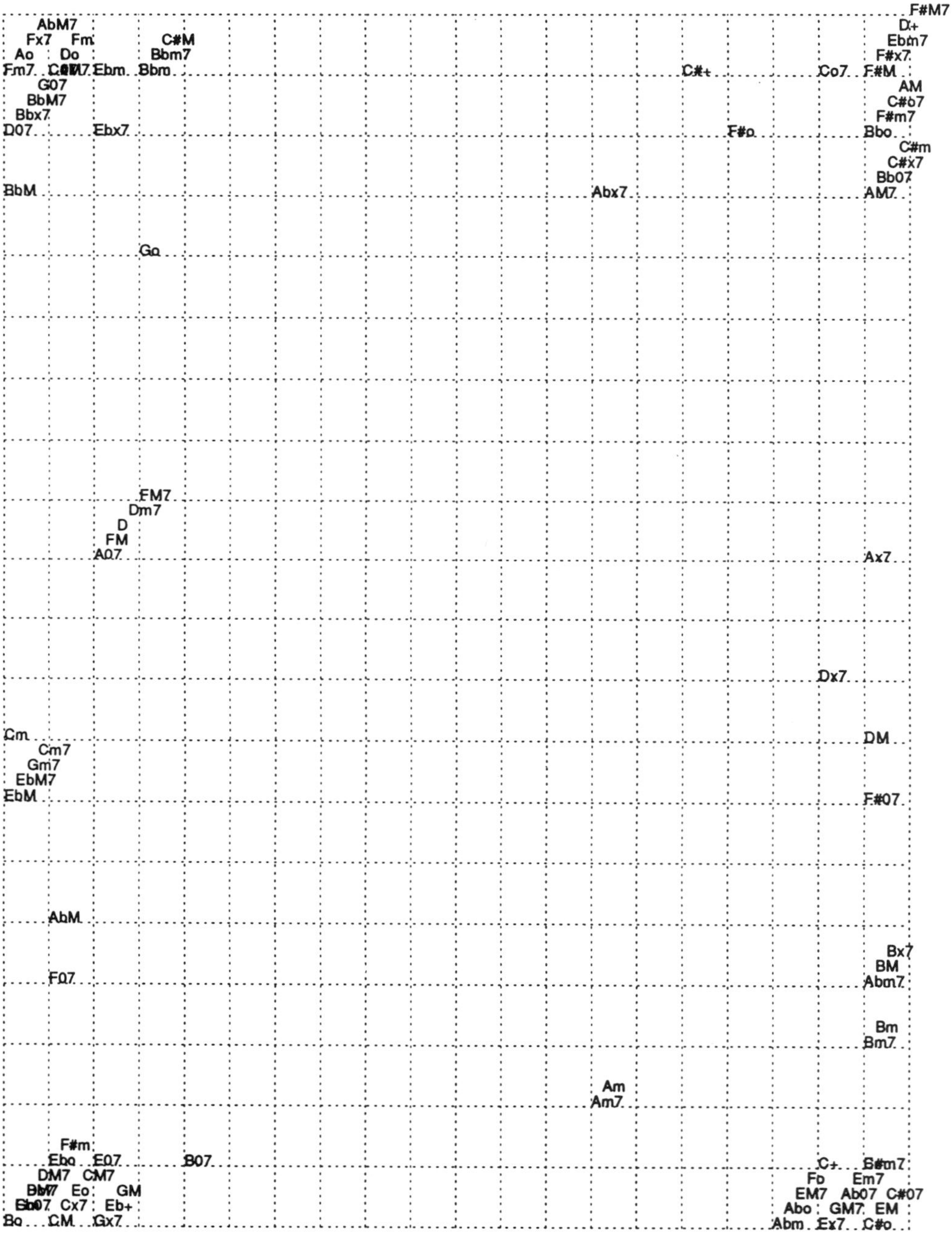

F#M7
D+
Ebm7
F#x7
F#M
AM
C#o7
F#m7
Bbo
C#m
C#x7
Bb07
AM7
AbM7
Fx7
Fm
Ao
Do
Fm7
G07
BbM7
Bbx7
D07
Ebx7
Ebm
C#M
Bbm7
Bbm
C#+
Co7
F#o
BbM
Abx7
Go
FM7
Dm7
D
FM
A07
Ax7
Dx7
Cm
Cm7
Gm7
EbM7
EbM
DM
F#07
AbM
Bx7
BM
Abm7
F07
Bm
Bm7
Am
Am7
F#m
Ebo
E07
B07
DM7
CM7
Eo
GM
Cx7
Eb+
Bo
CM
Gx7
C+
Fo
Em7
EM7
Ab07
C#07
Abo
GM7
EM
Abm
Ex7
C#o

Fig. 13

(c)

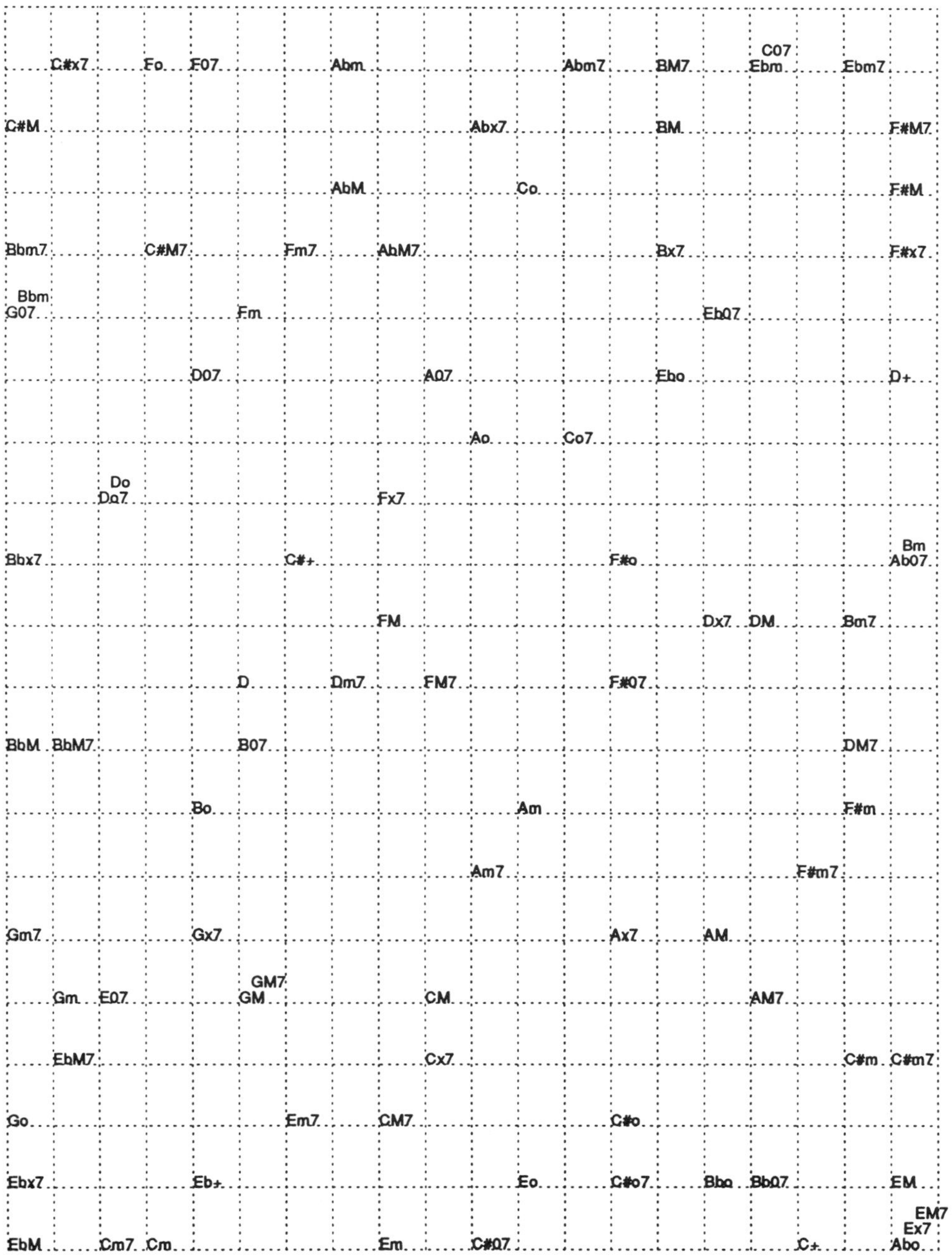

C07
C#x7 Fo F07 Abm Abm7 BM7 Ebm Ebm7
C#M Abx7 BM F#M7
AbM Co F#M
Bbm7 C#M7 Fm7 AbM7 Bx7 F#x7
Bbm
G07 Em Eb07
D07 A07 Ebo D+
Ao Co7
Do
Do7 Fx7
Bm
Bbx7 C#+ F#o Ab07
FM Dx7 DM Bm7
D Dm7 FM7 F#07
BbM BbM7 B07 DM7
Bo Am F#m
Am7 F#m7
Gm7 Gx7 Ax7 AM
GM7
Gm E07 GM CM AM7
EbM7 Cx7 C#m C#m7
Go Em7 CM7 C#o
Ebx7 Eb+ Eo C#o7 Bbo Bb07 EM
EM7
Ex7
EbM Cm7 Cm Em C#07 C+ Abo

ized the patterns of tonal distributions from the music of their culture. Up to now our investigations have not been conclusive on this point, due to the difficulty of specifying exactly what is meant by "tonal distribution." In the present studies we have shown that there is already some tendency toward tonality self-organization even if we start with different chords, not taking into account the distribution of these chords in musical practice. The inclusion of distribution information in our third study did not alter the tonality organization drastically. Thus the question of the effect of distribution of musical stimuli on the development of musical knowledge structures remains an intriguing and open area for further research.

Acknowledgments

I thank H. Sabbe for support in my project. Part of this research has been sponsored by a grant from the Onderzoeksfonds of the University of Ghent and the Belgian National Foundation for Scientific Research (N.F.W.O./F.K.F.O.).

References

Bharucha, J. J. 1987. "Music Cognition and Perceptual Facilitation: A Connectionist Framework." *Music Perception* 5(1):1–30.

Bharucha, J. J. This volume. "Pitch, Harmony, and Neural Nets: A Psychological Perspective."

Bruhn, H. 1988. *Harmonielehre als Grammatik der Musik.* Munich: Psychologie Verlags Union.

Demany, L., and C. Semal. 1988. "Dichotic Fusion of Two Tones One Octave Apart: Evidence for Internal Octave Templates." *Journal of the Acoustical Society of America* 83(2):687–695.

Gjerdingen, R. O. This volume. "Using Connectionist Models to Explore Complex Musical Patterns."

Grossberg, S., ed. 1987. *The Adaptive Brain,* vols. 1–2. Amsterdam: North-Holland.

Helmholtz, H. von. 1863. *Die Lehre von den Tonempfindungen Als Physiologische Grundlage fuer die Theorie der Musick.* Hildesheim: George Olms Verlagsbuchhandlung, unabridged edition, 1968.

Kameoka, A., and M. Kuriyagawa. 1969. "Consonance Theory Part I: Consonance of Dyads." *Journal of the Acoustical Society of America* 45:1451–1459.

Kohonen, T. 1984. *Self-organization and Associative Memory.* Berlin: Springer-Verlag.

Krumhansl, C. L. 1983. "Perceptual Structures for Tonal Music." *Music Perception* 1: 28–62.

Krumhansl, C. L. 1987. "Tonal and Harmonic Hierarchies." In J. Sundberg, ed. *Harmony and Tonality.* Stockholm: The Royal Swedish Academy of Music.

Krumhansl, C. L. 1990. "Tonal Hierarchies and Rare Intervals in Music Cognition." *Music Perception* 7(3): 309–324.

Krumhansl, C., and E. Kessler. 1982. "Tracing the Dynamic Changes in Perceived Tonal Organization in a Spatial Representation of Musical Keys." *Psychological Review* 89:334–368.

Laden, B., and D. H. Keefe. This volume. "The Representation of Pitch in a Neural Net Model of Chord Classification."

Leman, M. 1990. "Emergent Properties of Tonality Functions by Self-organization." *Interface* 19(2–3):85–106.

Leman, M. In press. "Symbolic and Subsymbolic Description of Music." In G. Haus, ed., *Music Processing.*

Leman, M. In preparation. "A Model of Tonal Semantics: Towards a Theory of Musical Cognition." Ph.D. diss., University of Ghent Institute for Psychoacoustics and Electronic Music.

Leman, M., and P. Van Renterghem. 1989. "Transputer Implementation of the Kohonen Feature Map for a Music Recognition Task." *Proceedings of the Second International Transputer Conference: Transputers for Industrial Applications II.* Antwerp: BIRA.

Matthews, M.V., R. Pierce, A. Reeves, and L. A. Roberts. 1988. "Theoretical and Experimental Explorations of the Bohlen-Pierce Scale." *Journal of the Acoustical Society of America* 84:1214–1222.

Merzenich, M., and W. Jenkins. 1983. "Dynamic Maintenance and Alterability of Cortical Maps in Adults: Some Inplications." In R. Klinke and R. Hartmann, eds. *Hearing—Physiological Bases and Psychophysics.* Berlin: Springer-Verlag, pp. 163–168.

Palm, G., and A. Aertsen. 1986. *Brain Theory.* Berlin: Springer-Verlag.

Parncutt, R. 1988. "Revision of Terhardt's Psychoacoustical Model of the Root(s) of a Musical Chord." *Music Perception* 6(1):65–93.

Parncutt, R. 1989. *Harmony: A Psychoacoustical Approach.* Berlin: Springer-Verlag.

Plomp, R. 1976. *Aspects of Tone Sensation.* London: Academic Press.

Rameau, J.-P. 1722. *Traité de l'Harmonie.* Reprinted in facsimile in 1965. New York: Broude Brothers.
Scarborough, D., B. Miller, and J. Jones. This volume. "Connectionist Models for Tonal Analysis."
Suga, N. 1988. "Auditory Neuroethology and Speech Processing: Complex-sound Processing by Combination-sensitive Neurons." In G. M. Edelman, W. Gall, and W. Cowan, eds. *Auditory Function: Neurobiological Bases of Hearing.* New York: John Wiley & Sons.
Terhardt, E. 1984. "The Concept of Musical Consonance: A Link Between Music and Psychoacoustics." *Music Perception* 1(3):276–295.
Terhardt, E., G. Stoll, and M. Seewann. 1982. "Algorithm for Extraction of Pitch and Pitch Salience From Complex Tonal Signals." *Journal of the Acoustical Society of America* 71(3):679–688.
van Noorden, L. 1982. "Two Channel Pitch Perception." In M. Clynes, ed. *Music, Mind, and Brain: The Neuropsychology of Music.* London: Plenum Press.
Wellek, A. 1963. *Musikpsychologie und Musikaesthetick: Grundriss der Systematischen Musikwissenschaft.* Frankfurt am Main: Akademiche Verlagsgesellschaft.
Zatorre, R. J. 1988. "Pitch Perception of Complex Tones and Human Temporal-lobe Function." *Journal of the Acoustical Society of America* 84:566–572.

Jamshed J. Bharucha
Department of Psychology
Dartmouth College
Hanover, New Hampshire 03755 USA
bharucha@eleazar.dartmouth.edu

Peter M. Todd
Department of Psychology
Stanford University
Stanford, California 94305 USA
todd@psych.stanford.edu

Modeling the Perception of Tonal Structure with Neural Nets

What can we say about the perception of music by the silent majority of listeners, those for whom music is written but who neither create music nor can articulate their musical experience? How do they acquire their demonstrably sophisticated intuitions about music patterns typical of their culture? Experiments in the cognitive psychology of music have cast some light on the first question. Recent developments in neural net learning now enable us to explore answers to the second.

In this article, we discuss one aspect of the experience of the nonmusician listener—contextual influences on the perception of pitch. We limit our discussion to tonal implications and expectations and to memory for pitch sequences. We do not presume that this description captures the listener's experience in all its intricacy. We first summarize some psychological research and then explore how neural nets can be employed to model the acquisition of these phenomena through passive exposure.

Two forms of tonal expectancy will be discussed—*schematic* and *veridical*. Schematic expectancies are culture-based expectancies for events that typically follow familiar contexts. Veridical expectancies are instance-based expectations for events that follow in a particular familiar sequence. Schematic and veridical expectancies may conflict, since a specific piece of music may contain atypical events that do not match the more common cultural expectations. This conflict, which was attributed to Wittgenstein by Dowling and Harwood (1985), underlies the tension between what one expects and what one hears, and this tension plays a salient role in the aesthetics of music (Meyer 1956). Schematic expectancies are driven by structures that have abstracted regularities from a large number of specific sequences. Veridical expectancies are driven by encodings of specific sequences. We briefly discuss models of both forms of expectancy and conclude with a model that subsumes both.

Two of the classes of nets that have promise for this research—auto-associative nets and hierarchical self-organizing nets—are only summarized here since their application to music has been described in detail in earlier papers (see Bharucha 1987a; 1987b; Bharucha and Olney 1989). We focus our modeling account on a third class of nets—sequential nets—that learn specific tone sequences (i.e., veridical expectancies) and in doing so exhibit schematic expectancies as an emergent property. The three classes of nets we discuss—auto-associative nets, hierarchical self-organizing nets, and sequential nets—are neither mutually exclusive nor entirely redundant. We present them as fruitful explorations in musical modeling and consider that one of our goals for future research is to discriminate among them computationally and empirically and, if necessary, to search for models that surpass them.

Psychological Aspects of Tonal Expectation

Most people have strong perceptual intuitions about the structure of the music of their culture. These perceptual intuitions are not typically revealed

Computer Music Journal, Vol. 13, No. 4, Winter 1989,

overtly in performance, composition, or even verbalization, since most people without formal musical training lack these skills. Through carefully designed psychological experiments, however, listeners who are unaware of or unable to articulate their musical intuitions can nevertheless be shown to be sensitive to rather subtle deviations from typical musical patterns.

The writings of music theorists have given us a powerful set of hypotheses about the perceptual intuitions of the average listener. Given the extensive training of the music theorists, however, and the theoretical constraints implicit in the language with which their theories are constructed, these hypotheses must be subject to rigorous empirical tests before their applicability to the average, untutored listener is established. Although the results of such experiments may typically confirm the hypotheses of music theorists, they are essential for building our corpus of knowledge about the perceptual intuitions of untutored listeners.

Western listeners show from their responses in psychological experiments that they recognize departures from typical tonal patterns. Furthermore, they have tacit knowledge of the distance relationships between tones, chords, and keys in tonal contexts as would be predicted by the work of music theorists. For example, subjects judge chords to be related to each other in accord with the circle of fifths. These intuitions show up in experimental tasks as disparate as:

Direct subjective measures of relatedness and expectation (Krumhansl and Kessler 1982; Bharucha and Krumhansl 1983; Schmuckler 1988)
Memory confusions (Cuddy, Cohen, and Miller 1979; Krumhansl, Bharucha, and Castellano 1982; Bharucha and Krumhansl 1983)
Response time (Bharucha and Stoeckig 1986; 1987)

Although the pattern of data is often more consistent for musically trained subjects on some of these tasks, there seems to be little difference between musically trained and untrained subjects on reaction time tasks that measure the extent to which a musical context facilitates the perceptual processing of schematically expected events. These tasks reveal systematic patterns of tacit knowledge about the relationship between chords, even in the minds of musically untutored subjects who begin the experiment with profuse apologies about being tone deaf. In these experiments (Bharucha and Stoeckig 1986; 1987; Bharucha 1987b), subjects are instructed to decide whether a target chord is in tune or mistuned. Mistuned chords are constructed by flattening one of the triadic components. When the target chord is preceded by a context (also consisting of a chord), the response time to judge correctly whether the target chord is in tune is monotonically related to the distance of the target from the context along the circle of fifths.

The above result could, in part, be explained by the overlap in harmonic spectra between the context and the target chords. Closely related chords, when played with tones rich with harmonics, have spectral components in common. To test this hypothesis, harmonics shared by context and target were removed, giving closely related targets no acoustic advantage. The target chord was again recognized more quickly following a context to which it was closely related (Bharucha and Stoeckig 1987).

This result establishes definitively that the expectations generated by a tonal context, as measured by the perceptual facilitation of closely related chords, cannot be explained by the harmonic series alone. We are compelled to conclude that the perceived relationships between chords are learned, rather than being somehow inherent in the actual sonic stimuli. Since the perceptual facilitation was found for nonmusicians as well as musicians, the learning must have been passive perceptual learning rather than formal musical training.

Some analogous experiments have been conducted with native listeners of other cultures, though this literature is less conclusive. These experiments have shown, at least for Indian ragas, that native, untutored listeners tend to expect tones that are typical of familiar musical contexts (Castellano, Bharucha, and Krumhansl 1984; Kessler, Hansen, and Shepard 1984; Bharucha 1987b).

Motivation for Neural Net Modeling of Harmonic Expectancies

Neural net models enable us to explore the extent to which these musical intuitions are a consequence of extended passive exposure to the musical regularities of a culture. General purpose learning architectures with units that respond to the presence of musical features can internalize musical regularities by changing the weights of links that connect units. The units themselves can plausibly be shown to develop their specialization to abstract musical features as a result of general principles of self-organization. Examples of these adaptive systems applied to specific musical phenomena are given in the following sections.

One may ask why complicated, often difficult-to-interpret neural net models should be used in the psychology of music when there are many perhaps simpler, symbolic, rule-based models available. Although rule-based models of music have been successful at describing the formal structure of some musical compositions, and have thus provided valuable hypotheses and analytic constraints, they fall short as psychological theories. They fail to account for the acquisition of the rules they postulate, and this ad hoc postulation of rules is not typically limited to a small set of assumptions of which the others are a natural consequence.

Paramount among the psychological constraints on modeling is the constraint that the postulation of cognitive structures must be accompanied by plausible accounts of the innateness or learnability of the structures in question. Few psychological models meet this strict scrutiny, including our own. We suggest, however, that given alternative models or classes of models, the most parsimonious is to be preferred. Neural net models have the capacity to supersede the more traditional rule-based models on parsimony grounds because of their ability to account for the acquisition of intuitions through passive perceptual learning.

Neural net models have the potential to account for perceptual learning of musical structure with only two classes of constraints. First, the net may be constrained by general principles of neural architecture and by constraints specific to the learning algorithms. Second, there must be pitch-tuned input units see (Linsker 1986) however, for an account of how, in vision, even elementary feature detectors can develop from general constraints on the net). The auditory system reveals a tonotopic mapping of pitch, supporting this constraint. It is important to note that no constraints on the specifics of musical structure are required; they emerge as a result of the net's exposure to music. Rule-based systems, in contrast, typically have as many constraints as specific rules of musical structure, with little justification about the origins of those rules.

Schematic Expectancies

Neural net models can be used to demonstrate the passive learning of schematic expectancies in three different musical domains.

Learning Culture-Specific Modes With Auto-associators

The extent to which patterns of schematic expectancy for the tones in musical scales can be captured by an auto-associative net has been explored in earlier work (Bharucha and Olney 1989). Using the delta rule (Rumelhart and McClelland 1986), this net is taught to map from a complete set of scale tones as input to the same scale set as output. It essentially acts as a pattern completion device that suggests, implies, or "fills in" missing tones at its output when presented with a subset of a scale as input.

Such a net exposed to major and harmonic minor scale sets correctly generates patterns of expectancy consistent with the establishment of keys, exhibits the desired ambiguities of key, and can be shown to tacitly embody the structural constraints abstractly summarized by the circle of fifths. Analogously, a net exposed to Indian ragas fills in expected tones when presented with subsets of the raga tones.

An auto-associative net trained on the scales of one culture can be tested with the scales of another, making predictions about tonal implications generated in the minds of listeners hearing an unfamiliar form of music. A net trained on the Western major and minor scales seems to assimilate some Indian ragas to the Western scales, sometimes shifting the tonic (Bharucha and Olney 1989).

Learning Hierarchical Representations Through Self-Organization

Hierarchical relationships, such as between tones, chords, and keys, can be learned passively by algorithms for self-organization (Kohonen 1984; Linsker 1986; Rumelhart and McClelland 1986; Carpenter and Grossberg 1987). Most self-organization mechanisms assume the prior existence of abstract units into which the input units feed. These abstract units initially have no specialization, since the links from the input units are initially random. However, repeated exposure to commonly occurring patterns causes some of these abstract units to tune their responses to these patterns.

One of the more straightforward, self-organization algorithms, called *competitive learning* (Rumelhart and McClelland 1986) accomplishes this as follows. For any given pattern some arbitrary abstract unit will respond more strongly than any other, simply because the weights are initially random. Of the links that feed into this unit, those that contributed to its activation are strengthened and the others are weakened. This unit's response will subsequently be even stronger in the presence of this pattern and weaker in the presence of other, dissimilar patterns. In similar fashion, other abstract units learn to specialize to other patterns. This process can be continued to even more abstract layers, at which units become tuned to patterns that commonly occur in the lower layer.

The overwhelming preponderance of major and minor chords in the popular Western musical environment would drive such a net to form units that respond accordingly. Furthermore, the typical combinations in which these chords are used would drive units at a more abstract layer to register larger organizational units such as keys. The notion that individual neurons specialize to respond to complex auditory patterns has some preliminary empirical support from single-cell recording studies on animals (Weinberger and McKenna 1988).

Once these chord and key units have organized themselves, the net models the implication of tones, chords, and keys given a set of tones. A hierarchical constraint satisfaction net built on this organization has been reported in earlier work (Bharucha 1987a; 1987b). In this net, called MUSACT, activation spreads from tone units to chord and key units and reverberates phasically through the net until a state of equilibrium is achieved. At equilibrium, all constraints inherent in the net have been satisfied.

Given a key-instantiating context, the unit representing the tonic becomes the most highly activated. The other chord units are activated to lesser degrees the further they are from the tonic along the circle of fifths.

Two behaviors of the net illustrate its emergent properties. First, the above activation pattern does not require the tonic chord to be played at all. An F major chord followed by a G major chord will cause the C major chord unit to be the most highly activated. Second, the circle of fifths implicit in the activation pattern cannot be accounted for on the basis of shared tones alone. If a C major context chord is played, the D major chord unit is more highly activated than the A major chord unit, even though the latter shares one tone with the sounded chord (C major) and the former shares none at all. A careful tracking of the net's behavior as activation reverberates and before it converges to an equilibrium state reveals a lower initial activiation of D major over A major, reflecting an initial bottom-up influence of shared tones. As activation has a chance to reverberate back from the key units (a top-down influence), this advantage is lost, and D major overtakes A major. So the circle of fifths is truly an emergent property of the simultaneous satisfaction of elementary associations between tones and clusters of tones. See Bharucha (1987a; 1987b) for details.

Learning With Sequential Nets

Some of the schematic expectancies that are essentially sequential, as in chord progressions, can be modeled with sequential nets. The architecture

Fig. 1. A back-propagation network that develops schematic sequential expectancies from exposure to individual sequences. The input units represent the three major and three minor chords of a key, and the output units represent expectancies for these chords.

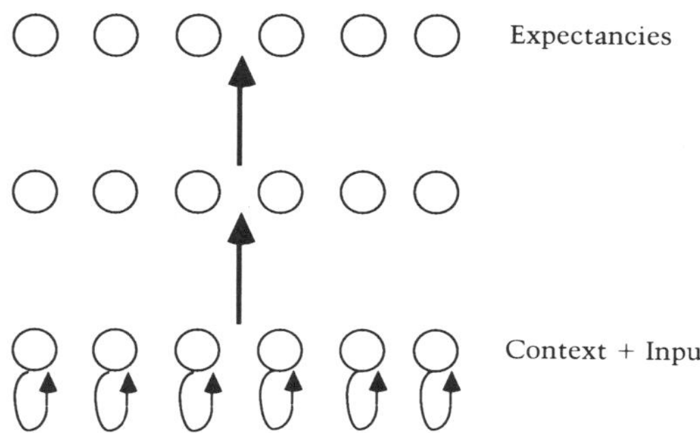

shown in Fig. 1 supports the learning of schematic expectancies from exposure to sequences. It has three layers of units (input, hidden, and output) and links that feed forward only. The input units register the sequence as it is heard, and the activations generated at the output units represent the learned schematic expectancy for the next event.

The input units, labeled "context + input," represent chords, one unit for each of the six most common chord functions—the three major and three minor chords in a given key, i.e., the triads built upon the first six degrees of the major scale. We use a pitch-invariant representation in which all sequences are normalized to a common tonic. Each unit has a self-recurrent connection with an identical fixed weight between 0.0 and 1.0. These recurrent links implement a decaying memory of the sequence presented up to any given point in time. The first chord in a sequence causes the corresponding input unit to be activated, while the other input chord units remain off. When the second chord is presented, its corresponding input unit is activated, while the unit corresponding to the first chord has its original activation multiplied by the weight on the recurrent link. This process of activating new units and decreasing the activation level of previous units in an exponential fashion continues for the entire chord sequence. If a chord is repeated in the sequence, a new surge of activation is added into the decaying activation already present at the corresponding unit. In this way, the "context + input" vector represents a decaying memory of the sequence (the context) plus the current event (the current input from the environment).

We envision the input units being activated by chord units in MUSACT after they have been normalized to a common tonic. This normalization is necessary because the chord sequences cannot be encoded in a pitch-specific format of the kind used in MUSACT, since most people have no absolute identification of pitch in the long term. The sequences must therefore be encoded in a format that is invariant under transposition. In the short term, however, transpositional invariance is biased by absolute pitch information held by MUSACT. Cuddy, Cohen, and Miller (1979) found that after presenting a standard melody, comparison melodies were more likely to be judged the same when they were transposed to a related key than when they were transposed to an unrelated key. The resulting constraints on modeling are thus: absolute pitch information is held in short-term memory without sequential constraints (as in MUSACT), and sequences are held in long-term memory in a pitch-invariant format with sequential constraints. Only the latter aspect of the model will be discussed here.

Each input unit in the net is linked to each hidden unit, and each hidden unit is linked to each output unit. The activation of unit i is a logistic function of the weighted sum of activations received by the unit plus the unit's bias.

Prior to learning, all weights and biases in the net are initialized to small, non-zero real numbers selected at random. For any given sequence, the "context + input" units register the sequence as it is presented to the net. The presentation of each successive event in the sequence causes activation to propagate through the net beginning at the input units, generating expectancies for the next event as output. Initially, these expectancies will be randomly generated by the untrained net.

Learning is accomplished by changing the weights and biases incrementally after each event so as to reduce the disparity between what the net expects—its output—and what actually occurs—the next event in the sequence. Each event in the sequence is thus the target value used to train the expectancies generated by the previous sequence events. The algorithm employed to change the weights and

Fig. 2. The pattern of activation induced by a context converges on the probability distribution of chords given that context. Numbers 1–6 represent the six major and minor chords built upon major scale degrees 1–6.

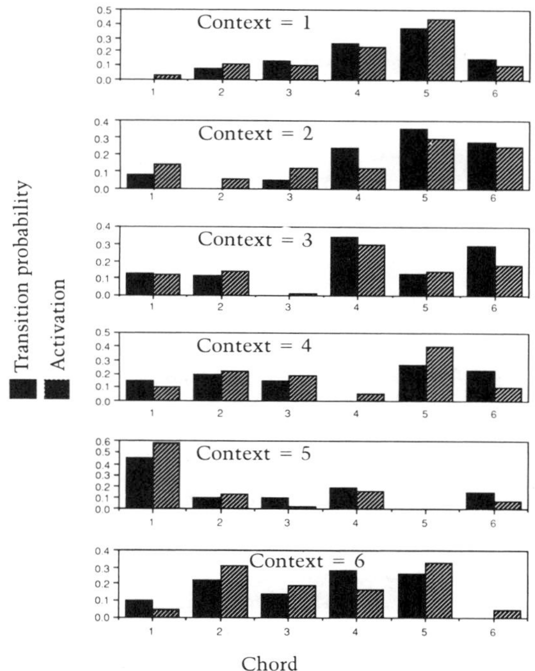

biases is the generalized delta rule (also known as back-propagation) developed by Rumelhart, Hinton, and Williams (1986).

The net was exposed to sequences that embody the transition probabilities of chord functions that are representative of Western music of the common practice era, estimated from Piston (1978). Any other set of sequences could have been used, and we plan to explore other actual and possible styles. After repeated exposure to the sequences, the net learns to expect (i.e., produce as output) the schematic distribution of chords for each successive event in a sequence. This net will not learn individual sequences, but will learn to match the conditional probability distributions of the sequence set to which it is exposed. In other words, each output vector approaches a probability vector representing the schematically expected distribution of chords following the sequence context up to that point.

Figure 2 shows the actual chord probability distribution and the net's output activation following each of six single-chord contexts. The net clearly matches the probability distributions in each case. The numbers 1–6 refer to the major and minor triads built upon the first six tones of the major scale. Note that the net has learned some of the sequential regularities of Western harmony. A tonic context chord generates strong expectations for the dominant and subdominant (top panel), a supertonic context chord generates expectations for the dominant and submediant (second from top), and so on. No rules needed to be encoded in order for these patterns to emerge; they simply reflect the internalization of probability distributions through extended exposure to individual sequences. We would argue that this model is considerably more plausible and parsimonious as an account of perception than are rule-based models.

Probability matching, as observed in the above net, has been shown in a number of psychological experiments. The basic result is that when trying to predict the next event after having witnessed events with a certain probability distribution, prediction patterns tend to align themselves with the probability distribution. This result is notable because it is not the optimal prediction strategy from the point of view of maximizing the expected return, which is to always predict the most likely event and never predict any other.

Probability matching accounts for the aura of schematic expectation that is generated at any given point in a musical sequence, in which no one event is expected to the exclusion of others; some events are highly expected, some are highly unexpected, and others have intermediate expectancies. Graded levels of schematic expectancy provide composers with alternatives that are only subtly different in their typicality and induce in the listener a range of expectancy confirmations and violations.

A prediction that derives from this result is that if subjects are asked to rate how appropriate a chord sounds following a single-chord context, the pattern of ratings would resemble the expectancy vector. Figure 3 shows a strong relationship between the rating judgments on this task, obtained by Bharucha and Krumhansl (1983), and the expectancies gener-

Fig. 3. *Scatter plot showing the relationship between relatedness judgments obtained from subjects and activation generated by the network for a number of different contexts.*

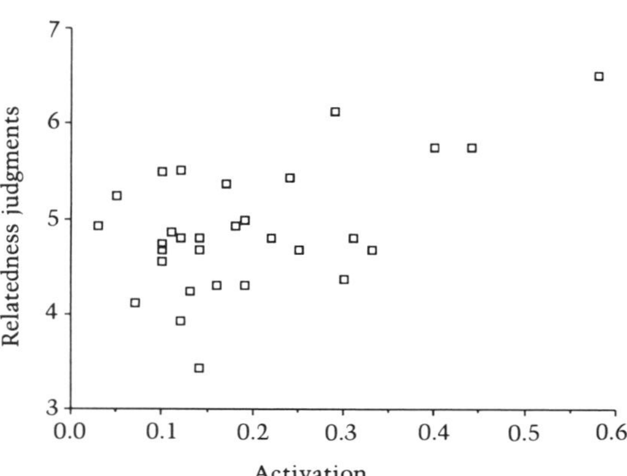

Fig. 4. *A network that learns individual sequences (veridical expectancies) and acquires schematic properties.*

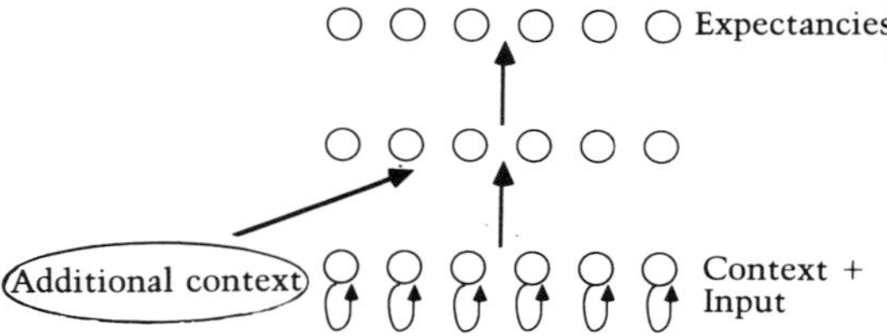

ated by our simulation. The sequential neural net model thus picked up the same sort of schematic expectancies about chord sequences that we find in human listeners.

Veridical Expectancies

The modeling described above focused on the generic cultural expectations and implications embodied in the schematic expectancies of music listeners. But listeners know more than just what musical structures are likely in various contexts in their culture; they know exactly what event is to occur next at particular points in particular pieces of music with which they are familiar.

The sequential schematic expectancy model described above can be modified to learn specific sequences—and thus veridical expectancies—by the addition of input units that serve to distinguish individual sequences in some way. The resulting net structure, with the new group of input units labeled "additional context," is shown in Fig. 4. This architecture is based on the sequential net design proposed by Jordan (1986) and used by Todd (1988) to model melody learning.

The "additional context" units in Fig. 4 individuate sequences by name or other discriminating context. In our simulations, there is one such unit (which we shall call a *name unit*) for each sequence to be learned by the net. Jordan called these units *plan units,* since he was simulating the production rather than the perception of sequences. Two sequences that are identical up to a point and then diverge can be learned by this net because the inputs for the two sequences would have a different name unit turned on for each sequence. This set of units could also be used to encode richer contexts that might include rhythmic, timbral, and other factors that contribute to the recognition of familiar musical sequences.

We exposed a net of the above sort, with six "context + input" units and six output units representing the six diatonic major and minor chords, to 50 sequences of seven successive chords each. Fifty "additional context" name units were needed to distinguish these 50 learned sequences.

After the net had learned these sequences, we studied its ability to learn two new sequences, one with schematically expected transitions and one with schematically unexpected transitions. The two sequences were matched in terms of the number of distinct chords in each. The sequence with schematic transitions started out with a lower summed squared error (on the output units) than the atypical sequence and was learned more quickly. The net thus learned a novel sequence more quickly if it conformed to familiar regularities. This result is in accord with the prevalent intuition that it is difficult to learn sequences of music from other cultures or from unfamiliar historical periods—that is, sequences that violate schematic expectancies.

Fig. 5. Number of cascaded activation steps to reach asymptote for three types of transitions. The more common the transition, the more quickly the expectancies reach asymptote.

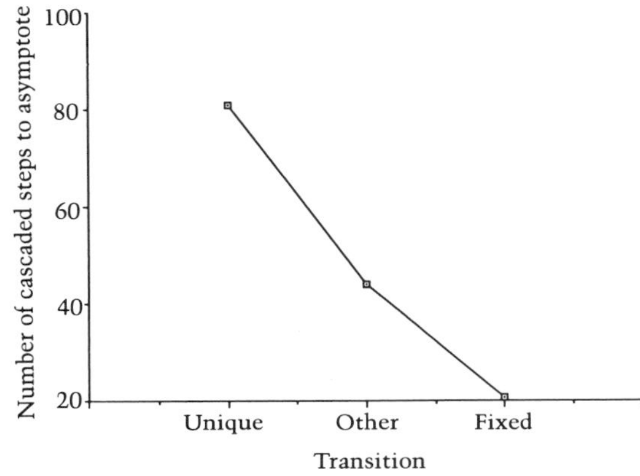

Combining Schematic and Veridical Expectancies in the Same Sequential Net

Even though the sequential net of Fig. 4 was employed to account for veridical expectancies, the above result suggests that this net acquires properties that are often attributed to a cultural schema. The net seems to inadvertently acquire these schematic properties even when the "additional context" units are operative, that is, even when it serves as a memory for individual sequences. More supportive evidence for this passive acquisition of sequential schematic expectancies from veridical sequence learning can be found by exploring the net's behavior when using cascaded activation.

Cascading was first described by McClelland (1979) and McClelland and Rumelhart (1988) and involves restricting the amount of activation that can pass through the net at a given time, thereby enabling one to observe the development of unit activation levels over time. The time-scale involved in cascading is different from the one involved in the generation of sequences by the net; the multistep cascading process occurs *within* each step of the outer sequence. Cascading is typically performed after the net has been trained to produce the proper sequential outputs, and it is then used to watch the activations of units develop from their initial values to the final asymptotic values they end up with as a result of training. For any given input, the input units exert only a fraction of their influence on the hidden units during the initial cascade time steps. The hidden units in turn exert only a fraction of their influence on the output units. Over succeeding time steps, each layer releases a greater fraction of its activation to the next layer, until the units have reached the asymptotic activations on which they were trained.

The cascading algorithm is as follows. The net input, $net_{i,t}$ to a hidden or output unit at time-step t is determined as follows:

$$net_{i,t} = k\sum[w_{ij}a_{jt}] + (1 - k)net_{i,t-1}$$

where the standard net input value, computed by summing up the products of the weights w_{ij} and the current activations a_{jt} of the units connected to unit i, is multiplied by the constant k and added to a fraction of the previous net input.

The constant k is the cascade rate, which determines how fast activations in the net build up to their asymptotic levels.

When cascaded activation is used in a veridical sequence net trained with both schematically expected and unexpected events, the highly expected events reach asymptotic activation much more quickly than unexpected ones. In this way, we can see the effect of learned cultural schemas on the net's performance with particular sequences. In one simulation, we trained the net with sequences that embodied only schematically expected transitions with the exception of one unexpected transition in one sequence. After all the sequences were learned to criterion, including the unexpected transition, the net was tested with the cascading algorithm. Figure 5 shows the number of cascade time-steps it took the activation of the single "on" output unit to reach the trained veridical asymptote (here 0.9), starting from its asymptotic activation at the previous sequence step (usually close to 0.0) for each of three transition-type groups. A unique chord transition X-Y is one in which chord X is followed by chord Y in only one sequence and is therefore highly unexpected. A fixed chord transition X-Y is one in which X is always followed by Y and is therefore highly expected. The third category includes all the other transitions of intermediate expectancy. As can be seen in the figure, unique transitions took longer to reach asymptote than fixed transitions, and the others fell in between.

These results indicate that the net used was embodying cultural schema information in its weights, which yielded fast cascade response times for expected transitions. In contrast, these schematic biases had to be overcome when unexpected transitions were being produced, leading to longer cascade times in the unique and other transition type cases. We can thus conclude that this net learned to embody cultural schematic expectancies, even though it was trained to produce merely specific veridical expectancies (the sequential outputs).

Conclusion

The studies reported here have demonstrated that neural net models embodying simple assumptions can learn musical schemas by passive exposure. These assumptions include the existence of general purpose learning architectures that implement competitive learning and supervised learning, and the existence of tonotopic pitch mapping in the auditory system. With these assumptions, the psychological regularities that have previously been attributed to rules develop in the net's behavior as an automatic consequence of exposure to a structured musical environment. Even though this environment typically only includes examples of veridical expectancies in the form of specific pieces of music, schematic expectancies of the likelihood of various musical events in the culture are also abstracted from this exposure.

Acknowledgments

Portions of this paper are extracted from a paper presented at the first Workshop on Music and AI at AAAI, 1988, and portions were presented at the Psychonomic Society meeting in 1988. Among others, the authors wish to thank the following people for their comments and suggestions at various stages of this research: David Evan Jones, Carol Krumhansl, Fred Lerdahl, Jay McClelland, David Rumelhart, and Kristine Taylor.

References

Bharucha, J. J. 1987a. "MUSACT: A Connectionist Model of Musical Harmony." *Proceedings of the Ninth Annual Meeting of the Cognitive Science Society.* Hillsdale, N.J.: Erlbaum Press.

Bharucha, J. J. 1987b. "Music Cognition and Perceptual Facilitation: A Connectionist Framework." *Music Perception* 5 : 1–30.

Bharucha, J. J., and C. L. Krumhansl. 1983. "The Representation of Harmonic Structure in Music: Hierarchies of Stability as a Function of Context." *Cognition* 13: 63–102.

Bharucha, J. J., and K. L. Olney. 1989. "Tonal Cognition, Artificial Intelligence and Neural Nets." *Contemporary Music Review.* Forthcoming.

Bharucha, J. J., and K. Stoeckig. 1986. "Reaction Time and Musical Expectancy: Priming of Chords." *Journal of Experimental Psychology: Human Perception and Performance* 12 : 1–8.

Bharucha, J. J., and K. Stoeckig. 1987. "Priming of Chords: Spreading Activation or Overlapping Frequency Spectra?" *Perception and Psychophysics* 41 : 519–524.

Carpenter, G. A., and S. Grossberg. 1987. "A Massively Parallel Architecture for a Self-organizing Neural Pattern Recognition Machine." *Computer Vision, Graphics, and Image Processing* 37 : 54–115.

Castellano, M. A., J. J. Bharucha, and C. L. Krumhansl. 1984. "Tonal Hierarchies in the Music of North India." *Journal of Experimental Psychology: General* 113 : 394–412.

Cuddy, L. L., A. J. Cohen, and J. Miller. 1979. "Melody Recognition: The Experimental Application of Musical Rules." *Canadian Journal of Psychology* 33 : 148–157.

Dowling, W. J., and D. L. Harwood. 1985. *Music Cognition.* New York: Academic Press.

Jordan, M. I. 1986. "Attractor Dynamics and Parallelism in a Connectionist Sequential Machine." *Proceedings Eight Annual Conference of the Cognitive Science Society.* Hillsdale, N.J.: Erlbaum Press.

Kessler, E. J., C. Hansen, and R. N. Shepard. 1984. "Tonal Schemata in the Perception of Music in Bali and the West." *Music Perception* 2 : 131–165.

Kohonen, T. 1984. *Self-Organization and Associative Memory.* Berlin: Springer-Verlag.

Krumhansl, C. L., J. J. Bharucha, and M. A. Castellano. 1982. "Key Distance Effects on Perceived Harmonic

Structure in Music." *Perception and Psychophysics* 32:96–108.

Krumhansl, C. L., and E. J. Kessler. 1982. "Tracing the Dynamic Changes in Perceived Tonal Organization in a Spatial Representation of Musical Keys." *Psychological Review* 89:334–368.

Linsker, R. 1986. "From Basic Net Principles to Neural Architecture." *Proceedings of the National Academy of Sciences* 83:7509–7512, 8390–8394, 8779–8783.

McClelland, J. L. 1979. "On the Time-Relations of Mental Processes: An Examination of Systems of Processes in Cascade." *Psychological Review* 86:287–330.

McClelland, J. L., and D. E. Rumelhart. 1988. *Explorations in Parallel Distributed Processing.* Cambridge, Massachusetts: MIT Press.

Meyer, L. 1956. *Emotion and Meaning in Music.* Chicago: University of Chicago Press.

Piston, W. 1978. *Harmony.* 4th ed. New York: Norton.

Rumelhart, D. E., G. E. Hinton, and R. J. Williams. 1986. "Learning Internal Representations by Error Propagation." In D. E. Rumelhart and J. L. McClelland, eds. *Parallel Distributed Processing: Explorations in the Microstructure of Cognition.* Vol. 1. Cambridge, Massachusetts: MIT Press.

Rumelhart, D. E., and J. L. McClelland, eds. 1986. *Parallel Distributed Processing: Explorations in the Microstructure of Cognition.* Vol. 1. Cambridge, Massachusetts: MIT Press.

Schmuckler, M. A. 1988. "Expectation in Music: Additivity of Melodic and Harmonic Processes." Ph.D. diss., Cornell University.

Shepard, R. N. 1989. "Internal Representation of Universal Regularities: A Challenge for Connectionism." In L. Nadel et al., eds. *Neural Connections and Mental Computation.* Cambridge, Massachusetts: MIT Press.

Todd, P. M. 1988. "A Sequential Network Design for Musical Applications." In D. Touretzky, G. Hinton, and T. Sejnowski, eds. *Proceedings of the 1988 Connectionist Models Summer School.* Menlo Park: Morgan Kaufmann.

Weinberger, N. M., and T. M. McKenna. 1988. "Sensitivity of Auditory Cortex to Contour: Toward a Neurophysiology of Music Perception." *Music Perception* 5:355–390.

Robert O. Gjerdingen
Carleton College
Department of Music
Northfield, Minnesota 55057 USA

Using Connectionist Models to Explore Complex Musical Patterns

Introduction

Music teachers often ask their classes to take musical dictation. The teacher commonly plays a short excerpt, perhaps a phrase from a Bach chorale, and then the students attempt to translate the various pitches and durations into the symbols of standard musical notation. Each resulting symbol can be judged true or false, right or wrong. Music teachers also ask their classes to analyze the musical syntax of phrases from Bach chorales. The resulting answers will likely have varying shades of truth or falsity. Students can have legitimate differences of opinion about how to interpret ambiguous musical events or events that have one meaning in prospect and a second in retrospect. And not only students differ in their assessments of complex musical patterns. Acknowledged experts in eighteenth-century music are known to disagree about how, in a given phrase, the chords, rhythms, contours, melodies, textures, timbres, and counterpoint all interact.

Connectionist models offer elegant ways of dealing with multidimensional complexity of the type found in polyphonic, harmonically oriented music. One can, for example, define a musical event as an input pattern of activation that is then transformed by a network of interconnected processing units into an output pattern of activation representing an interpretation of the event. Models that allow for learning often require an explicit teacher prepared to state unambiguously whether, and to what degree, the output pattern is in error (Rumelhart, Hinton, and Williams 1986; Werbos 1988). For relatively low-level musical tasks, like the transcription problem described above, this requirement poses no serious obstacle; but for higher-level tasks, the notion of an explicit teacher becomes problematical. One wonders, for example, if anyone would be comfortable in claiming that one interpretation of a musical phrase is only 69 percent as true as another?

An alternative class of connectionist models comprises the so-called self-organizing networks, networks that learn without explicit teaching inputs (Grossberg 1982; Kohonen 1984). They present an appealing analog of the ordinary listener, someone who without formal training has nevertheless developed a strong sense of how music "works." For many years Stephen Grossberg and his associates have been major contributors to the development of self-organizing networks. In what follows I will explain how Grossberg's *adaptive resonance theory* (ART) (Grossberg 1976; Carpenter and Grossberg 1987) can be used to develop a self-organized, stable category structure for musical patterns of arbitrary complexity, and I will report on a program entitled *L'ART pour l'art* (ART for art's sake), which has been taught some early works of Mozart.

Computer Music Journal, Vol. 13, No. 3, Fall 1989,

An ART Architecture for Analog Input Patterns

Figure 1 shows the basic design of an ART network. Input in the form of a vector of continuous values enters a lower field of processing units (field 1, or F_1). There the vector is normalized and contrast-enhanced before proceeding to the upper field of processing units (field 2, or F_2). The upper field is a shunting, on-center/off-surround, competitive network, the extreme form of which is sometimes called a *winner-take-all* design (Carpenter 1989). For any given F_1 pattern of activation, the multiplicative connections between F_1 and F_2 typically give one local F_2 population of cells slightly higher excitatory input than is given any other population.

Fig. 1. The basic outline of an adaptive resonance theory (ART) network.

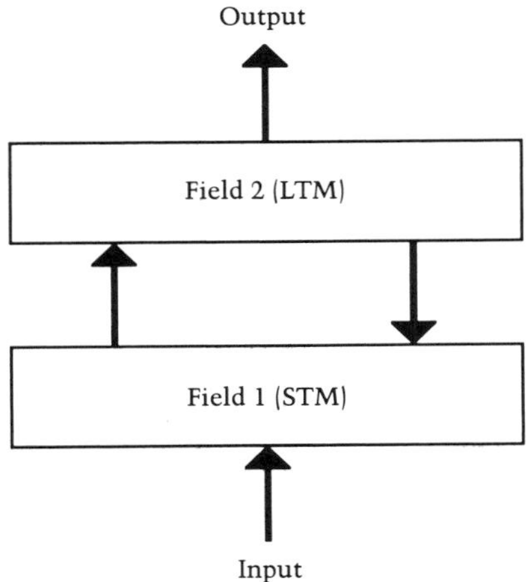

Because of strong lateral inhibition between F_2 populations (off-surround interactions) and recurrent excitation within populations (on-center interactions) this dominant population will be able to suppress all or most of the other populations. The surviving population(s) can be viewed as the network's output, as an interpretation of the original input.

Grossberg's networks are intended to emulate principles of human information processing. In the case of the ART network, F_1 represents a dynamic, short-term memory (STM) and each F_2 population represents a long-term memory (LTM). Short-term memories are simply the activations of cells in F_1. Long-term memories result from adjustments to the strengths of F_1-F_2 connections. These adjustments follow the general form

$$\Delta w_{ij} = Ay_j(x_i - w_{ij}),$$

where w_{ij} is the strength or *weight* of the connection from cell i in F_1 to population j in F_2, y_j is the positive activation of population j in F_2, x_i is the strength of the excitatory signal from cell i in F_1, and A is a constant factor ($A \leq 1$) determining the rate of learning. As the network is exposed to various input patterns, only winning F_2 populations can adjust their connections because only they have a positive term y_j. Thus individual F_2 populations are *adaptive* to specific categories of inputs and can eventually match their vector of w_{ij} to the *critical feature patterns* of a category of input vectors of x_i (Grossberg 1987).

The resonance in ART occurs when learned F_2 memories are read out as top-down feedback to F_1. This feedback mixes with input patterns of activation within the internal structure of F_1, as shown in Fig. 2. F_1 is itself a double feedback circuit whose upper and lower loops share the middle of the three internal levels of F_1. Normalization of activation patterns occurs during the lateral transmission of signals at each level. This is modeled on the automatic gain-control properties of nonspecific inhibitory interneurons (Carpenter and Grossberg 1987). Contrast-enhancement of patterns and the suppression of noise occur during the vertical transmission of signals between levels. These tasks are accomplished by nonlinear signal functions (the $f(x)$ in Fig. 2), generally of the sigmoid or threshold-linear type. It is the resulting normalized, contrast-enhanced blend of input pattern and F_2 feedback that dominates activations in the middle level of F_1.

An ART network quickly settles into an F_1-F_2 feedback resonance, the state during which most learning will occur. What will be learned is not, however, an unmediated input pattern. Rather, the network will learn the above-mentioned mix of the input pattern and an F_2 memory. New variations of patterns are automatically interpreted in the context of previously learned pattern prototypes. In this manner the network shields itself against the capricious miscoding of its memories by anomalous input patterns. The resulting hysteresis-like stability can, however, lead to excessive rigidity. In real pattern domains not every new pattern is a variant of previously established pattern types. Some patterns are absolutely and unpredictably new. The ART architecture overcomes this problem with an "orienting subsystem."

As suggested in Fig. 2, there are comparator cells (c_i) connected to the upper and middle levels of F_1. Because of the action of a nonspecific inhibitory interneuron connected to those same levels as well as to the comparator cells (Carpenter and Grossberg 1987), the length, l, of the comparator-cell vector ($l = (\Sigma c_i^2)^{1/2}$) will vary, assuming a certain range of

Fig. 2. A more detailed view of F_1 showing the orienting subsystem (the comparator cells) and the internal feedback loops where input patterns are mixed with top-down feedback from F_2.

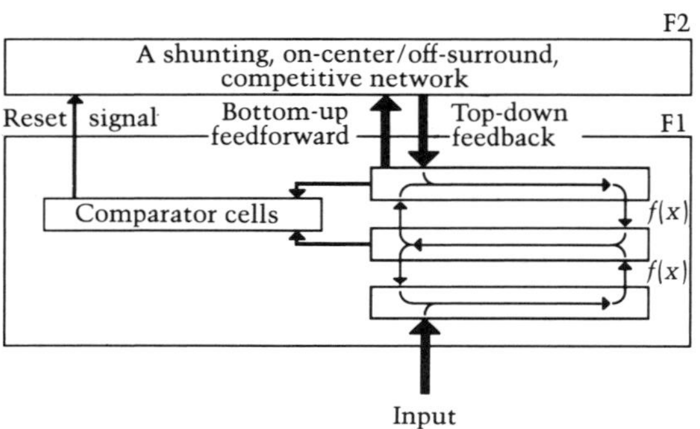

Fig. 3. The conceptual design of L'ART pour l'art. *The lower disk represents F_1, the upper disk F_2.*

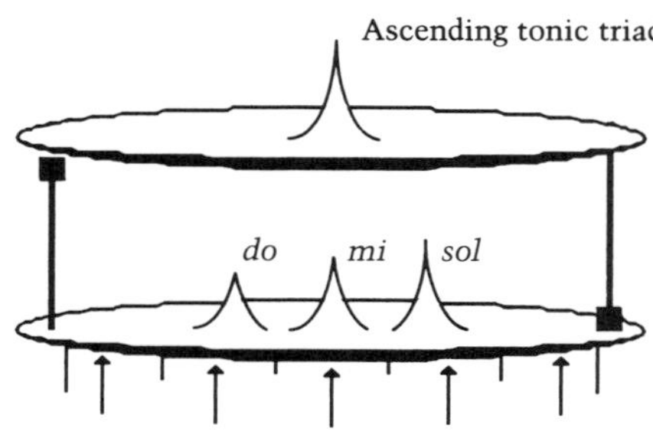

inputs, in proportion to the cosine of the activation vectors of the middle and upper levels of F_1. In simple terms, this means that as a group, the comparator cells are sensitive to the degree of match between F_2 feedback and the mixture of that feedback with the input pattern. When the match is very poor—that is, below a predetermined level—the comparator circuit issues a nonspecific reset signal to F_2. That signal suppresses whichever F_2 population is currently active. Then, depending on various parameters and the exact nature of the input pattern, either another F_2 population with a similar memory will try to meet the comparator criterion or an entirely new population will be selected.

The F_2 design of mutually inhibitory populations is, by itself, capable only of what is called competitive learning. "Competitive learning is an essentially nonassociative, statistical learning scheme" (Rumelhart and Zipser 1985) with some similarities to multidimensional scaling or hierarchical clustering analysis. By itself, a competitive learning model may not be able to achieve a stable coding of arbitrarily changing input patterns (Grossberg 1978). But in an ART network, the F_2 design does not operate in isolation. F_2 and F_1 together form a feedback system wherein patterns of input are processed in the conext of previously learned pattern categories. The resulting multilevel network can develop a temporally stable coding of an arbitrarily complex and changing domain of patterns (Grossberg 1987). Such a domain is typical of musical patterns.

L'ART pour l'art

Figure 3 shows the conceptual form of an ART network for recognizing and categorizing musical patterns. The lower horizontal disk represents F_1, the upper disk F_2. The arrows coming from below F_1 stand for input sent from feature detectors responding to various aspects of the indicated melody. The three peaks in F_1 indicate three cells strongly activated by this input. For the purpose of illustration, let us imagine that these cells correspond directly to the musical concepts *do, mi,* and *sol*—the tones of the tonic triad. Joining the two neural fields are heavy vertical lines that represent an excitatory path from every cell in F_1 to every population in F_2 and vice versa. At the ends of these vertical lines are darkened squares indicating the modifiable strengths of the connections w_{ij} and w_{ji}. The lone peak in F_2 indicates that a single population has had a winning response to this particular F_1 pattern of activation.

The height of each peak in F_1 is drawn proportionally to each cell's presumed level of activation. Normalization of patterns across F_1 requires that when a new cell receives strong input excitation, the activation levels of previously excited cells must be decreased. The increasing height of the peaks from *do* to *mi* to *sol* thus does not express the notion that *sol* causes the intrinsically strongest response. *Sol* is strongest because it was the tone most recently heard. As the three-note melody would have been performed, each new tone in the present would strongly excite an appropriate cell, which in turn would inhibit the cells still responding to tones from the recent past. When *mi* sounds, its cell inhibits the previously excited cell for *do*, and when *sol* sounds, its cell inhibits the cell for *mi* and further inhibits the cell for *do*. This *recency effect*, as it is called in psychology, permits an ART network to maintain a simple record of temporal order. Indeed, these fading traces of recent events form the ART network's short-term memory.

By definition short-term memory is limited. As new cells become strongly active, the weakest cells in F_1—those retaining traces of the earliest events—become completely inhibited and disappear from short-term memory. For the network to retain a memory of a long series of events, a long melody for instance, it must have a way of remembering individual melodic segments. This is where F_2 and possibly higher-level fields $F_3 \cdots F_n$ come into the picture.

If the F_2 population in Fig. 3 fully adapts its F_1-F_2 connections to conform to the F_1 pattern of activation, it will develop a long-term memory of an ascending tonic triad. Should that pattern or a slight variant of it reoccur later, the same F_2 population will again exhibit a strong response. In fact, because of adaptation to the F_1 pattern, later responses will be faster and stronger than earlier ones. Of course the exact F_1 pattern that will be learned by the w_{ij} vector of an F_2 population depends on how, or whether, the F_1 pattern varies. If, for instance, F_1 is always presented with an ascending tonic triad performed as, say, three quarter notes, then that exact pattern will be learned by an F_2 population. If, on the other hand, rapid, rhythmically irregular ascending tonic triads are randomly interspersed with descending or broken triads, then a more general pattern such as simply "tonic triad" may be learned. Much depends on the entire repertory of patterns to which the network is exposed in its "formative years."

In an ART network, not only does bottom-up input flow from F_1 to F_2, but also top-down feedback flows from F_2 to F_1. We might variously describe this feedback as a template, a prototype, an expectation, or a schema based on the particular F_2 population's experiences with a class of F_1 patterns. For example, if F_1 cells register the first two tones of an ascending tonic triad, the "ascending-tonic-triad" population in F_2 will already begin to respond, and as it does, it will send signals to F_1. The top-down feedback to the F_1 cells responding to the first two tones of the triad will merely reinforce those cells' activations. But the feedback to the cell for the third tone of the triad will prime that cell to respond more quickly should the tone actually be heard. The feedback biases the network's perception of its inputs and makes its responses to its environment more categorical than statistical.

Music is full of surprises, and F_2 expectations will not always be born out by developing F_1 patterns of activation. In the triadic example just discussed, should quite an unexpected third tone occur, the network's orienting subsystem will automatically react to the mismatch by suppressing the active F_2 population. This action allows a more appropriate population (or a new population) to become maximally active. I suspect that what Leonard Meyer has called the central thesis of the psychological theory of emotions, namely "that emotion or affect is aroused whenever a tendency to respond is arrested or inhibited" (Meyer 1956), may have its physiological basis in the process of a network resetting itself following a mismatch of bottom-up features and a top-down schema.

L'ART pour l'art is a program I have written to test an ART network's ability to make musically valid categorizations of the type of complex patterns that occur in passages of Mozart. *L'ART pour l'art* processes information about complex sets of musical features into the form of schematic recognition categories. Input patterns are derived from Mozart's scores in the following manner. A musical score is viewed as a discrete series of events, each event being the appearance of a new tone in the melody or a new chord. For each event, a tabulation is made of the presence or absence of the 34 specific, low-level musical features listed in Fig. 4. Each

Fig. 4. A listing of individual inputs to F_1 and a symbolic rendering of an F_1 activation vector described in the text.

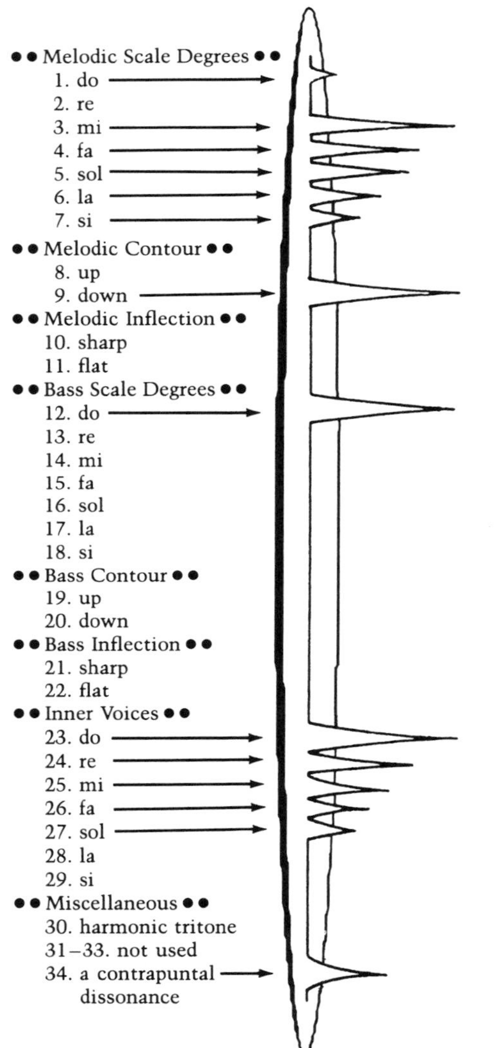

tabulation contributes to an input vector which, in a real-time model, would enter F_1 immediately after the corresponding event sounds in the music. In the computer simulations (which allow for the processing of individual and out-of-order events), each input vector is mathematically preprocessed to imitate the time-dependent interactions of the new vector with previous F_1 activations. The resulting input vector thus represents the new event as well as fading traces of previous events.

Figure 4 shows a typical set of F_1 activations in symbolic form. The four highest peaks above the field represent the new features of some particular musical event. Old features have lower activations and stand for the inhibited traces of earlier events. It may be instructive to correlate the various peaks with the inputs listed below the field. Starting at the left of the field, notice first a cluster of peaks above the inputs for melodic scale degrees. Presumably the network has detected a descending scale of some type, inasmuch as each scale degree from the third up to the leading tone and tonic has a lower level of activation than the previous degree. The higher tones, occurring first in a descending scale, would have been repeatedly inhibited as each new lower tone is sounded. The presumption of a descending scale is strengthened by the next tall peak to the right, a peak directly above the input for a descending melodic contour.

Further to the right, a second solitary peak stands for the tonic in the bass. Perhaps this is a pedal point, since no other bass tones have registered and there are no activations above inputs for changes in the contour of the bass (inputs 19 and 20). The next group of peaks matches input for scale degrees in one or more inner voices and shows the same descending-scale profile as in the melody, although here the descent is from the fifth to the tonic. Finally, the peak on the far right stands for a contrapuntal dissonance—probably not one in the present, since the peak is not very high, but perhaps one in the recent past.

In Fig. 5, we can see that we have in fact decoded the opening of Mozart's minuet *KV1d* (transposed here from F to C), a piece written when he was five years old. The exact moment of the network's response is marked by an asterisk at the end of the second measure. Notice that there is a pedal tonic in the bass and the descending lines in the soprano and alto, just as we surmised from Fig. 4. And the presumed recent contrapuntal dissonance turns out to be the passing tones *d″* and *f″* over the bass *c* on

Fig. 5. L'ART pour l'art *shown responding to the point marked with an asterisk at the end of the second measure of five-year-old Mozart's minuet* KV1d *(transposed here from F to C). The* F_1 *activations are a compressed representation of the activations depicted in Fig. 4.*

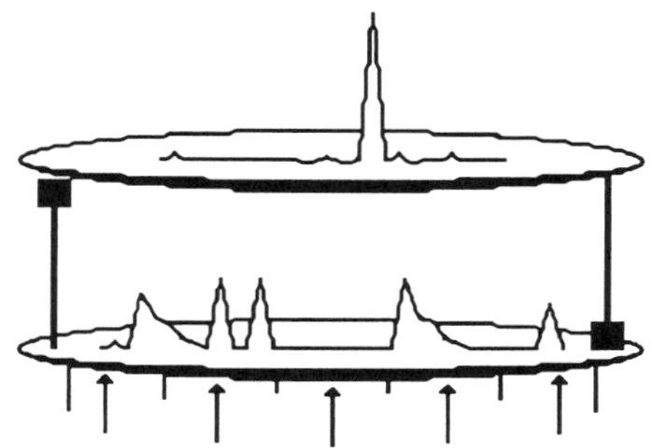

the previous beat. Above the musical score is a computer-generated drawing showing the ART network's response. The lower level (F_1) is the same as in Fig. 4, but with much of the detail compressed. For instance, rather than showing a cluster of separate peaks for melodic scale degrees, the computer drawing shows only the general contour of that cluster. Since short-term memory in an ART network was defined as the vector of active F_1 cells, in this instance F_1 demonstrates STM of about two measures of music or perhaps about three seconds—a time typical for human, short-term musical memory (Dowling and Harwood 1986).

As mentioned earlier, long-term memories in an ART network consist of vectors of w_{ij} modified by individual F_2 populations. The upper level (F_2) of Fig. 4 shows a high peak toward the middle of the field, where one population has learned to respond strongly to the entire F_1 pattern. The population developed a memory of that and similar patterns through modifications made to an originally random vector of w_{ij} over the course of learning trials described below. The resulting vector of w_{ij} records

Fig. 6. A musical rendering of the memory—the learned vector of w_{ij}*—resident in the dominant* F_2 *population of Fig. 5. The size of each symbol indicates the relative strength of the memory trace for that feature. Square noteheads stand for inner voices and* d *stands for a contrapuntal dissonance. Arrows stand for traces of melodic and bass contour.*

what Grossberg has called the critical feature pattern (Grossberg 1987), the relative strengths of the musical features associated with this particular F_1 category of patterns. The critical feature pattern is not, however, simply what was shown in the F_1 activations of Figs. 3 and 4. The population in question responded to all but the first beat of the two measures shown in Fig. 4. So its critical feature pattern is affected by overlapping experiences of five similar events.

The resulting vector of w_{ij} has, as would be expected, a very strong trace of the tonic in the bass and no strong trace of either an ascending or a descending bass contour. On the other hand, there is a very strong trace of a descending contour in the melody. The traces for specific scale degrees in the melody and inner voices have a more complex profile affected by metric factors described below. In Fig. 6, I have tried to translate the entire vector of w_{ij} directly into a type of musical notation so that one can see something of the generic schema that the F_2 population was able to abstract from its experiences with F_1 patterns of activation. The relative size of the symbols in Fig. 6 indicate relative strengths of w_{ij} traces. But the precise weightings of each feature cannot be conveyed in this musical format.

Six of Mozart's earliest compositions were taught to *L'ART pour l'art: KV1a, KV1b, KV1c, KV1d, KV2,* and *KV3.* These pieces are small but nevertheless contain a total of 793 separate musical events. Each learning trial involved teaching all six pieces in varying orders, at slightly different learning rates ($.01 \leq A \leq .05$), and at different tempi (F_1 interactions vary slightly depending on the rate at which new inputs enter). After 12 trials, a stable category structure emerged. That is, the same musical event (occurring at the same tempo) would always activate the same F_2 population.

I arbitrarily allotted *L'ART pour l'art* 25 F_2 populations. The more F_2 populations there are, the more distinctions the network can draw. Conversely, the fewer F_2 populations there are, the more abstract must be each population's memory of an event. For instance, if I had given F_2 only three populations, it might have been forced to interpret every musical event as one of only three categories—tonic, dominant, or subdominant. While this degree of abstraction is of considerable interest within the discipline of music theory, I do not think it typical of the categorizations made by an ordinary listener. Twenty-five populations seemed a large enough set to promise an interesting level of specificity and yet still small enough to be computationally manageable—an ART network does scale up gracefully to very large systems, but any large parallel network simulated on a serial computer requires an enormous number of calculations.

F_2 in *L'ART pour l'art* begins inchoate, then slowly organizes itself, by itself, as it is exposed to F_1 patterns that bear some resemblance to one another. In the early stages of learning, the similarities that the network detects are not always the ones that we would notice first. The contour of the melody and bass, for example, exerted a strong influence on the network's early judgments of similarity, even in cases where, as with dominant and tonic chords, a classical musician might view the patterns as opposites. In truth, it was difficult at times to watch the network making what I considered mistakes. Like a doting parent, I wanted to tell it "No, that's a *deceptive* cadence!" rather than let it work out the problem for itself, which it eventually did. Conversely, sometimes the network would behave so rationally that I would forget how limited its frame of reference was.

As a case in point, we automatically hear Mozart's predominately two-voice pieces as implying harmonic progressions and the corresponding inner voices. The network, by contrast, had no direct way to obtain such information. In fact, *L'ART pour l'art* was not given knowledge of any a priori correlations among its 34 input features. It did not, for instance, know beforehand that the feature "melodic inflection: sharp" had anything to do with melody or that the feature "bass contour: up" had any correlation with the bass line. When one realizes that *L'ART pour l'art* had to establish the possible correlations among any of 34 features in each of 793 events, and that each event was embedded in a short-term memory carrying forward the decaying traces of 4 or 5 previous events, one gains an appreciation of the difficulty of its task.

With early versions of *L'ART pour l'art* I observed that F_2 populations seemed to pay too much attention to passing and neighboring tones. This was not just my own prejudice. By categorizing relatively incidental events as unique entities, the network was preventing itself from recognizing the types of underlying similarity that would allow its understanding to progress to more abstract levels. In thinking about this problem, I realized that my perception and the network's perception differed because I automatically heard the pieces in a metric context. Remembering Leonard Meyer's maxim that "in order for meter to exist, some of the pulses in a series must be accented—marked for consciousness—relative to others" (Cooper and Meyer 1960) I realized that the network needed a way to mark an event for consciousness.

One approach would have been to add new inputs to the lower level, inputs that would signal features such as strong beat, weak beat, downbeat, and so forth. I had in fact once tried this approach with a more primitive type of network. The problem is that such inputs may add little to the network's knowledge. The same chord, melody, or progression may occur in many different metric positions, so the network soon learns to ignore the inputs assigned to meter. Strong beat, for example, is not an invariant feature of dominant triad.

A different and I believe more successful approach is to equate marking an event for consciousness with paying more attention to it. By this rationale, a downbeat is strong because we pay strong attention to it. Instead of adding more inputs to the lower level, one can simulate meter by modulating the F_1 response to input. Input occurring on a downbeat then elicits a larger response than the same input occurring on a weaker beat. I implemented this notion by giving the network five metrically oscillat-

Fig. 7. An early Mozart cadence (transposed here from F to C) shown with the eight F_2 memories that it arouses. Please refer to Fig. 6 for an explanation of the notation. π stands for the trace of a contrapuntal tritone.

ing levels of attention. The network subsequently showed a substantial improvement in the way it handled passing tones and other subsidiary events.

Because nearly all the F_1 patterns learned by each F_2 population contain a trace of the recent musical past, F_2 populations become sensitive to the immediate musical context. This is apparent in those populations that learned the various stages of the standard *galant* cadence shown at the top of Fig. 7. As the cadence unfolds, eight segments of it (shown by the brackets beneath the music) elicit responses in eight of the network's F_2 populations. For each population, I have attempted to translate its vector of w_{ij} into a form of musical notation, as was done earlier in Fig. 6. These eight musical notations—eight F_2 critical feature patterns—are pointed to by arrows from the corresponding segments of the cadence. Clearly each long-term memory takes cognizance of the preceding context. For example, the third memory, which corresponds with the beginning of the cadence's second measure, has traces not only of a IV or ii^6 chord in the present, but also, and more importantly, of the voice-leading progression brought about by a preceding I^6 chord or secondary dominant in the recent past.

Although only a single F_2 population becomes strongly active in response to a particular F_1 pattern, certain weaker F_2 activations can provide a guide to other patterns that share similar musical features. In the upper level of Fig. 4, for instance, there were several subsidiary peaks representing other patterns in which many of the same features also play an important role. In this sense, the relative levels of activation in F_2 indicate relative levels of musical similarity. The ability of a network to gauge multidimensional similarity may assist us in investigations of historical musical styles. We are today, for instance, hard pressed to hear works from the 1760s with the ears of the 1760s. Quite naturally we hear early Mozart with ears accustomed to late Mozart, Beethoven, and so forth. *L'ART pour l'art,* on the other hand, was taught music only from 1761 and early 1762, and so its judgments are limited to patterns found within that narrow period.

In my earlier discussion of the network's categorization of patterns in a stock phrase like the *galant* cadence, I suggested that a group of F_2 populations responded in sequence to the unfolding of the cadence. One can make this sequential excitation of F_2 populations the input to a still higher-level ART network. In Fig. 8, I depict a four-level network, the third and fourth levels of which form an ART network whose input comes from the ART network of the first two levels. The figure shows the network's response to the end of the *galant* cadence just discussed.

The first level depicts the many features associated with the final tonic chord in the cadence. The second level shows a single F_2 population highly activated by this pattern of features. As numbered earlier in Fig. 7, this would be population 8. The third level shows this population, the one in the present, with the highest activation and previous populations in the cadential sequence—populations numbered 7, 6, 5, 4—with progressively lower activations (the peak of population 4, though low and partially obscured, is to the right of population 6). F_3 thus functions as a short-term memory more abstract and spanning more time than that of F_1. It records a temporal series of meaningful musical events. Finally, the fourth level shows a single F_4 population that responds to the entire pattern at F_3 and thus can learn to recognize the entire latter part of the cadence.

Figure 8 presents a hierarchical view of musical

Fig. 8. *A four-level network composed of two ART networks. Output from the lower ART network becomes the input to the upper ART network.*

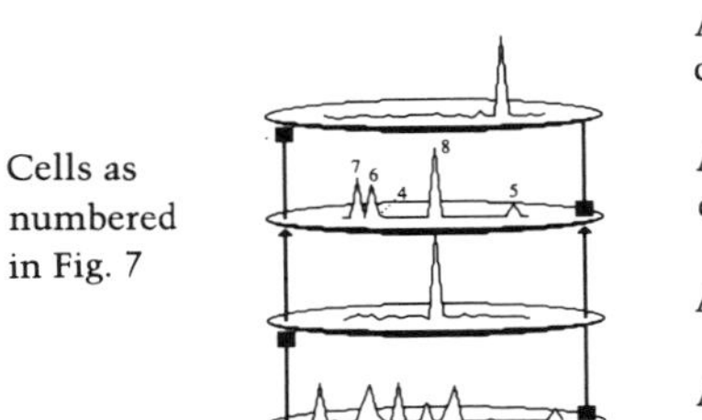

structure. I should point out, however, that the hierarchy implicit in such a network is not a hierarchy of simple pitches. Here bundles of features are recognized as constituting significant musical events; these are then recognized as occurring in schematic sequences, which may themselves be concatenated into still larger musical schemata. Beyond the very lowest levels of such a network, the units of information are not pitches but various musical ideas, concepts, or schemata.

Conclusion

L'ART pour l'art was designed to test the capabilities of a class of self-organizing, neuronlike networks based on Grossberg's adaptive resonance theory (ART). The strong claim has been made by Grossberg and others that an ART network could successfully categorize an arbitrarily large and complex domain of analog patterns. The early works of Mozart, while certainly not as large or complex as the works of Mahler or Richard Strauss, still present a pattern domain of considerable variety and sophistication. The fact that *L'ART pour l'art,* forced to interpret that domain from the perspective of an intentionally spare and insufficient set of input features, was nevertheless able to achieve a musically sound categorization of much of this domain suggests that at least some of the claims for ART architectures may be valid. *L'ART pour l'art* developed memories of critical feature patterns that resemble not simple chords but the harmonic-contrapuntal complexes referred to by musical theorists as voice-leading combinations. The ability of such a small network to derive categorizations comparable to those employed by musical scholars with expert knowledge of this domain indicates that larger ART networks could prove useful tools in the exploration of complex musical patterns and their myriad interactions.

References

Carpenter, G. A. 1989. "Neural Network Models for Pattern Recognition and Associative Memory: A Review." *Neural Networks* 2.

Carpenter, G. A., and S. Grossberg. 1987. "ART 2: Self-organization of Stable Category Recognition Codes for Analog Input Patterns." *Applied Optics* 26:4919–30.

Cooper, G. W., and L. B. Meyer. 1960. *The Rhythmic Structure of Music.* Chicago: University of Chicago Press.

Dowling, W. J., and D. L. Harwood. 1986. *Music Cognition.* Orlando, Florida: Academic Press.

Grossberg, S. 1976. "Adaptive Pattern Classification and Universal Recording, II: Feedback, Expectation, Olfaction, and Illusions." *Biological Cybernetics* 23: 187–202.

Grossberg, S. 1978. "A Theory of Human Memory: Self-organization and Performance of Sensory-Motor Codes, Maps, and Plans." In R. Rosen and F. Snell, eds. *Progress in Theoretical Biology,* vol. 5. New York: Academic Press. Reprinted in Grossberg 1982.

Grossberg, S. 1982. *Studies of Mind and Brain: Neural Principles of Learning, Perception, Development, Cognition, and Motor Control.* Boston: Reidel/Kluwer.

Grossberg, S. 1987. "Competitive Learning: From Interactive Activation to Adaptive Resonance." *Cognitive Science* 11:23–63.

Kohonen, T. 1984. *Self-organization and Associative Memory.* Berlin: Springer-Verlag.

Meyer, L. B. 1956. *Emotion and Meaning in Music.* Chicago: University of Chicago Press.

Rumelhart, D. E., and D. Zipser. 1985. "Feature Discovery by Competitive Learning." *Cognitive Science* 9:75–112. Reprinted in Rumelhart, Hinton, and Williams 1986.

Rumelhart, D. E., G. E. Hinton, and R. J. Williams. 1986. "Learning Internal Representations by Error Propagation." In D. E. Rumelhart, J. L. McClelland, and the PDP Research Group. *Parallel Distributed Processing: Explorations in the Microstructure of Cognition,* 2 vols. Cambridge, Massachusetts: MIT Press.

Werbos, P. J. 1988. "Generalization of Backpropagation with Application to a Recurrent Gas Market Model." *Neural Networks* 1:339–356.

Addendum

The *L'ART pour l'art* model of a self-organizing network for the categorization of complex musical patterns has been further described in two additional articles. The first (Gjerdingen 1989) details a comparison between what may be termed metric and ametric categorizations of early pieces by Mozart. Ametric categorizations are produced when the network receives no explicit information about meter, as in the example of Figs. 4–6. Metric categorizations are produced by a period bias factor that modulates the strength of input signals in synchrony with the musical meter, as in the example of Fig. 7. This modulating bias can be produced by very simple neural circuits with ocillatory outputs that resemble simple musical meters. Such ocillatory circuits are entrained with the perceived periodicities in the music being heard in order to yield the appropriate metrical bias.

The second article (Gjerdingen 1990) provides a fuller account of both the premises of the ART class of self-organizing networks and the results attained by *L'ART pour l'art.* These results, essentially analyses of salient voice-leading patterns in early works by Mozart, vary in quality from one network level to the next. As shown in Fig. 8, *L'ART pour l'art* implies at least five levels of network activity: (1) a level of feature detectors whose binary outputs are indicated by vertical arrows at the bottom of the figure; (2) a level, F_1, that produces dynamic, analog short-term memory representations of recently detected musical features; (3) a level, F_2, that categorizes these short-term memory representations and stores the categorizations as long-term memories preserved in synaptic weights; (4) a level, F_3, that produces a second short-term memory representation, this time of the temporal series of F_2 categorizations; and (5) a level, F_4, that categorizes the various F_3 temporal series.

As analogs of various aspects of human cognition, F_1, F_2, and F_3 functioned quite well, whereas the bottom, implied level of feature detectors and the top level, F_4, did not. F_1 and F_3 are dynamic short-term memory buffers that accurately mimic many of the important characteristics of human short-term memory. And F_2, as an abstracter of Gestalt-like categories, did an excellent job of discerning musically important recurring patterns in Mozart's early works (for example, memory #6 in Fig. 7 captures the V^{4-3} dissonance and resolution that generally precedes a closing tonic chord). These are the sort of tasks for which the then-current ART paradigm, ART 2, was developed. The tasks of the feature-detector and F_4 levels, however, are more specialized and are better performed by alternative self-organizing neural architectures.

Recent research has begun to explore these alternatives. To begin with, the musical feature detectors of the current model operate in a purely binary fashion, indicating the presence or absence of a particular feature. Although this may be appropriate for some musical features, others require detectors that must realistically be assumed to have continuous-valued analog outputs. For example, a feature detector sensitive to ascending melodic contours need have only two output states: "on" = melody moving up, and "off" = melody not moving up. But feature detectors sensitive to musical scale degrees may well require analog outputs in order to reflect the probability of a particular tone representing a particular scale degree. For instance, in the case of modulating from C major to F major, the tone C begins the modulation as an unequivocal scale degree #1 and ends the modulation as an unequivocal scale degree #5. But during the modulation, the tone C is presumably interpreted as a varying mix of these two degrees. Output from a "scale degree #1" detector would decline as output from a "scale degree #5" detector rises.

The self-organization of such variable-output tonal feature detectors implies some form of distributed coding. This is an area of ongoing study within the recently described ART 3 paradigm (Carpenter and Grossberg 1990). An ART 2 network is unsuited for distributed coding because when its orienting subsystem detects an erroneous coding, the resulting reset signal indiscriminately disables all active F_2 nodes. By contrast, in an ART 3 network, the simulation of the action of chemical neurotransmitters allows a reset signal to inhibit F_2 nodes only in proportion to their recent history of activation. Thus, for example, a highly active but erroneous node may be strongly inhibited while other less active nodes are barely affected and remain available to code more accurately the current pattern in short-term memory.

The task of the other problematic level, F_4, is to categorize the temporal sequence of events held in the short-term memory of F_3. But the very qualities that make ART 2 circuits such effective categorizers work to the disadvantage of F_4. With twenty-five nodes in F_3, perhaps five of which are active at any one time, F_4 may encounter over 53,000 distinct temporal sequences. An ART 2 circuit categorizes patterns on the basis of similarity, and two sequences that share the same set of F_3 nodes may, in the context of such a large number of possibilities, seem quite similar even though they have important musical differences. For instance, the sequence of successively activated nodes 4-15-22-7-18 may be lumped together with the sequence 4-22-15-18-7; although their exact orderings are different, they nonetheless possess considerable similarity based on sharing the same set of nodes and having some aspects of ordering in common. Yet if node 18 represents a dominant seventh chord and node 7 a tonic triad, a classically trained musician would likely categorize the two sequences as near opposites. In the style of Mozart it makes a tremendous difference whether the one chord precedes or follows the other.

The humanlike categorization of temporal sequences thus depends on more than the mere search for gross similarities in all sequences of a standard length. Humans are sensitive to sequences of varying lengths, they notice important sequence boundaries, and they are especially sensitive to certain privileged sequences with special syntactical significance. To simulate this type of categorization in a self-organizing network, one must employ a circuit of considerable complexity. For my current studies, I have chosen a circuit called a *masking field* (Cohen and Grossberg 1987), which differs from an ART 2 circuit in four important respects.

First, in a masking-field version of F_4, each F_4 node is no longer connected to all F_3 nodes. Instead it is connected to a random subset of F_3 nodes. The random pattern of interconnection, which demands a large number of F_4 nodes for adequate coverage of F_3, gives the network the basic ability to be sensitive to F_3 sequences of varying length.

Second, the effect produced on an F_4 node by the input from an F_3 cell varies inversely with the number of inputs conncected to that node. If an F_4 node receives input from just a single F_3 cell, that input will have its full effect; if it receives input from two F_3 cells, each of those inputs will have only half its normal effect; and so forth. Thus the total effect of an input signal from a short sequence is as great as that from a long sequence.

Third, the inhibitory interactions between F_4 nodes increase in proportion to the degree of overlap between the nodes' subsets of F_3 cells. Thus there is hardly any inhibition between unrelated sets of inputs and intense mutual inhibition between different temporal orderings of the same set of inputs. In terms of the musical example just discussed, nodes coding the sequences "V^7-I" and "I-V^7" would be maximally inhibitory to each other.

And fourth, the excitatory feedback within each F_4 node varies with the number of F_3 cells that send input to that node. Should all other factors be equal, nodes representing larger F_3 sequences, and implicitly larger contexts, will have an advantage during F_4 competition. A node with a larger subset of F_3 cells can in certain instances thus *mask* the activity of a node with a smaller subset.

In sum, current work on the *L'ART pour l'art* model might be characterized as attempts to sandwich the successful levels F_1, F_2, and F_3 between a masking-field version of F_4 at the top and a more realistic set of feature detectors at the bottom, some of which must employ distributed codes. Two recent pilot studies have shown promising results in these areas. The first used a masking field to categorize subsequences in a long sequence of chords; the second modeled a continuous-valued feature detector that responds to typical melodic figures in Mozart melodies. A discussion of the issues raised by these studies would extend well beyond the scope of this addendum. But it seems fair to say that at least a few more steps can now be taken toward the goal of this work: to develop psychologically defensible models of the self-organization of complex musical knowledge as abstracted from the experience of real music.

References

Carpenter, G. A., and S. Grossberg. 1990. "ART 3: Hierarchical Search Using Chemical Transmitters in Self-Organizing Pattern Recognition Architectures." *Neural Networks* 3:129–152.

Cohen, M. A., and S. Grossberg. 1987. "Masking Fields: A Massively Parallel Neural Architecture for Learning, Recognizing, and Predicting Multiple Groupings of Patterned Data." *Applied Optics* 26:1866–1891.

Gjerdingen, R. O. 1989. "Meter as a Mode of Attending: A Network Simulation of Attentional Rhythmicity in Music." *Intégral* 3:67–92.

Gjerdingen, R. O. 1990. "Categorization of Musical Patterns by Self-Organizing Neuronlike Networks." *Music Perception* 8:339–370.

Peter Desain and Henkjan Honing
Centre for Art, Media, and Technology
Utrecht School of the Arts
Lange Viestraat 2b
NL-3511 BK Utrecht
The Netherlands

Music Department
City University
Northampton Square
London EC1V OHB
United Kingdom

The Quantization of Musical Time: A Connectionist Approach

Introduction

Musical time can be considered to be the product of two time scales: the discrete time intervals of a metrical structure and the continuous time scales of tempo changes and expressive timing (Clarke 1987a). In musical notation both kinds are present, although the notation of continuous time is less developed than that of metric time (often just a word like "rubato" or "accelerando" is notated in the score). In the experimental literature, different ways in which a musician can add continuous timing changes to the metrical score have been identified. There are systematic changes in certain rhythmic forms: for example, shortening triplets (Vos and Handel 1987) and timing differences occurring in voice leading with ensemble playing (Rasch 1979). Deliberate departures from metricality, such as rubato, seem to be used to emphasize musical structure, as exemplified in the phrase-final lengthening principle formalized by Todd (1985). In addition to these effects, which are collectively called *expressive timing*, there are nonvoluntary effects, such as random timing errors caused by the limits in the accuracy of the motor system (Shaffer 1981) and errors in mental time-keeping processes (Vorberg and Hambuch 1978). These effects are generally rather small—in the order of 10–100 msec. To make sense of most musical styles, it is necessary to separate the discrete and continuous components of musical time. We will call this process of separation *quantization*, although the term is generally used to reflect only the extraction of a metrical score from a musical performance.

Computer Music Journal, Vol. 13, No. 3, Fall 1989,

Perception of Musical Time

Human subjects, even without much musical training, can extract, memorize, and reproduce the discrete metrical structure from a performance of a simple piece of music—even when a large continuous timing component is involved. This is surprising, given that the note durations in performance can deviate by up to 50 percent from their metrical values (Povel 1977). Indeed, it seems that the perception of time intervals on a discrete scale is an obligatory, automatic process (Sternberg, Knoll, and Zukofsky 1982; Clarke 1987b). This so-called categorical perception can also be found in speech perception and vision. By contrast, the perception and reproduction of continuous time in musical performance seems to be associated with expert behavior.

Once the discrete and continuous aspects of timing have been separated by a quantization process, each can function as an input to other processes. The induction of an internal clock (Povel and Essens 1985) and the reconstruction of the hierarchical structure of rhythmical patterns (Mont-Reynaud and Goldstein 1985) both rely on the presence of a metrical score, while Todd (1985) has developed a model in which hierarchical structure is recovered from expressive timing alone.

Applications of Quantization

Apart from its importance for cognitive modeling, a good theory of quantization has technical applications. It is one of the bottlenecks in the automatic transcription of performed music, and is also important for compositions with a real-time, interactive component where the computer improvises or interacts with a live performer. Last but not least, a quantization tool would make it possible to study the expressive timing of music for which no score exists, as in improvised music.

Known Methods

Few computational models are available in the literature for separating a metrical score from expressive timing in performed music (Desain and Honing 1988). Available methods produce a considerable number of errors when quantizing the data. The traditional approach is to expand and contract note durations according to a metrical grid that is more or less fixed—the grid being adjustable to incorporate different, low-level subdivisions (e.g., for triplets). Commercial MIDI software uses this method, which often gives rise to a musically absurd output, as shown in Fig. 1. Better results are obtained when the system tracks the tempo variations of the performer (Dannenberg and Mont-Reynaud 1978), though the system still returns an error rate of 30 percent. More sophisticated artificial intelligence (AI) methods use knowledge about meter (Longuet-Higgins 1987) and other aspects of musical structure. A particularly elaborate system originated at the CCRMA center at Stanford University in the automatic transcription project (Chowning et al. 1984). This knowledge-based method uses information about different kinds of accent, local context, and other musical clues to guide the search for an optimal quantized description of the data. It is entirely implemented in a symbolic, rule-based paradigm. This approach can be seen as the antithesis of our approach, in which all knowledge in the system is represented implicitly. We took the connectionist approach because knowledge-based approaches seemed to offer no real solution to manifest inadequacies of the simplistic metrical grid method. As with the majority of traditional AI programs, the sophisticated knowledge these AI methods use is extremely domain dependent (depending on a specific musical style), causing the systems to break down rapidly when applied to data foreign to this style.

Fig. 1. Example of a performed score and its quantization by a commerical MIDI Package using a resolution of 1/64 note.

Connectionist Methods

Connectionism provides the possibility for new kinds of models with characteristics traditional AI models lack, in particular robustness and flexibility (Rumelhart and McClelland 1986). Connectionist models consist of a large number of simple elements, each of which has its own activation level. These cells are inconnected in a complex network, with the connections serving to excite or inhibit other elements. One broad class of these networks, known as *interactive activation and constraint satisfaction networks,* generally converge towards an equilibrium state given some initial state.

An example of the application of these networks to music perception is given by Bharucha (1987) in the context of tonal harmony. These networks have not yet been used for quantization. The quantization model presented in this paper is a connectionist network designed to converge from nonmetrical performance data to a metrical equilibrium state. This convergence is hard wired into the system, and no learning takes place. The model is thought of as a collection of relatively abstract elements, each of which performs a rather complex function compared to standard connectionist models. While it may be possible to express these functions in terms of one of the formalisms for neural networks, this lies beyond the scope of the present article.

Basic Model

Consider a network with two kinds of cells: the *basic cell,* with an initial state equal to an inter-onset interval, and the *interaction cell,* which is connected in a bidirectional manner to two basic cells. Figure 2a shows the topology of a network for quantizing a rhythm of four beats, having its three

Fig. 2. Topology of a basic network (a) and a compound network (b).

Fig. 3. Interactive time intervals in a basic network (a) and a compound network (b).

Fig. 4. Interaction function with a peak at 4 and decay equal to -1.

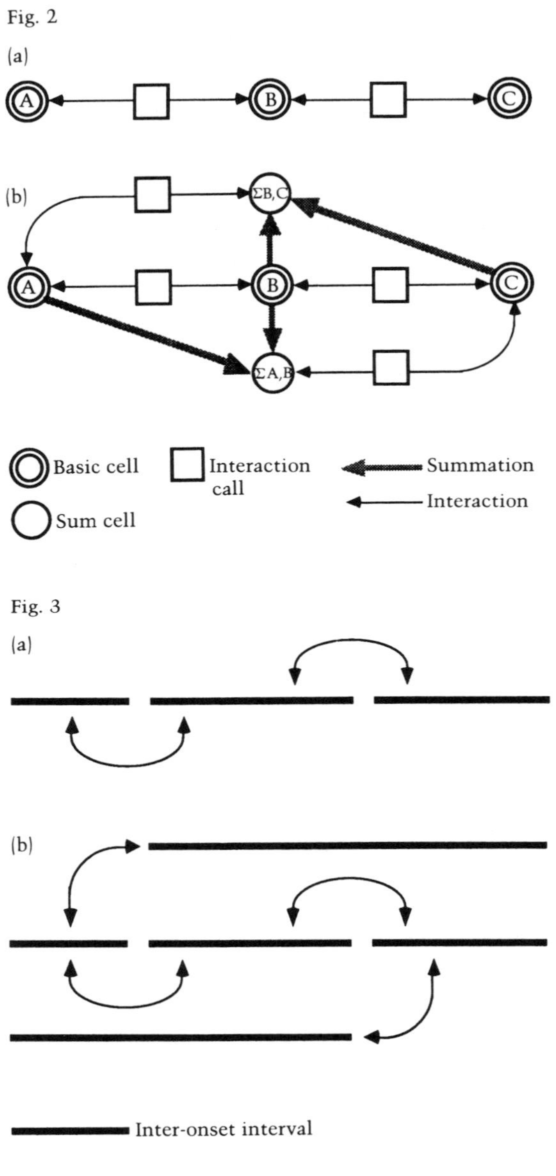

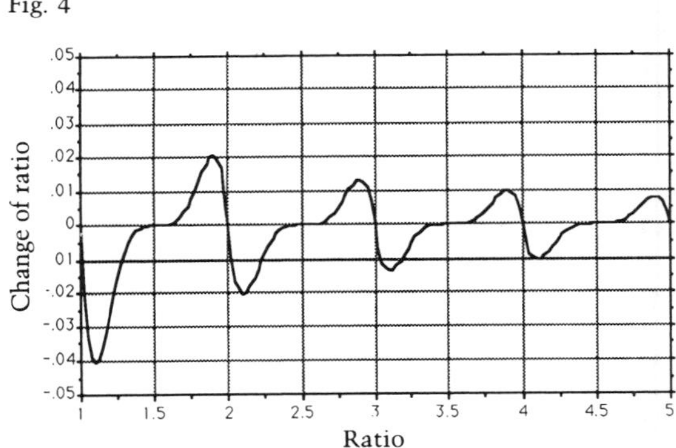

inter-onset intervals set as states of the three basic cells, labeled A, B, and C. There are two interaction cells connected to the basic cells A and B, and B and C, respectively. Each interaction cell steers the two basic cells to which it is connected toward integer multiples of one another, but only if they are already near this state. It applies the interaction function to the quotient of their states (ratios smaller than 1 are inverted). If this ratio were close to an integer (e.g., 1.9 or 2.1), the interaction function would return a *change of ratio* that would steer the two states toward a perfect integer relation (e.g., 2). Figure 3 illustrates the interactions that are relevant in quantizing the four-beat rhythm. One can see that if the ratio is slightly above an integer, it will be adjusted downward, and vice versa as in Fig. 4.

There are constraints to be taken into account for interaction functions. First, the function and its derivative should be zero in the middle region between two integer ratios. In this region it is not clear if the integer ratio above or below is the proper goal, so no attempt is made to change the ratio. Second, the derivative around integer ratios should be negative to steer the ratio towards the integer, but greater than -1 to prevent overshoot that would result in oscillations. Third, the magnitude of the function should decrease with increasing ratios to diminish the influence of larger ratios. A large class of functions meet these constraints. At present we use a polynomial section around each integer ratio.

Fig. 5. State as a function of iteration count for the rhythm 2, 1, 3 in a basic network (a). State as a function of iteration count for the rhythm 1, 2, 3 in a basic network (b).

(a)

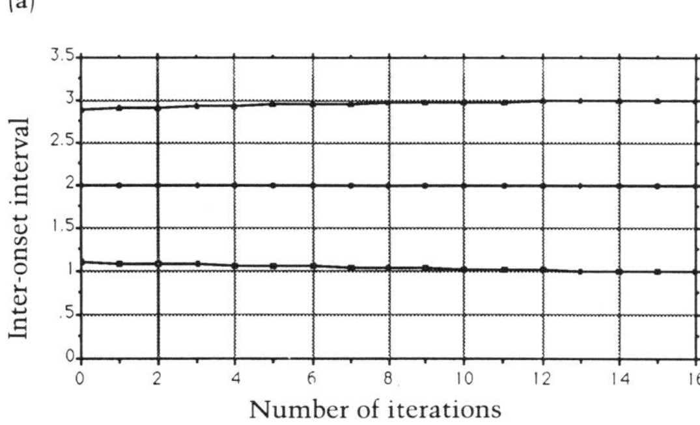

(b)

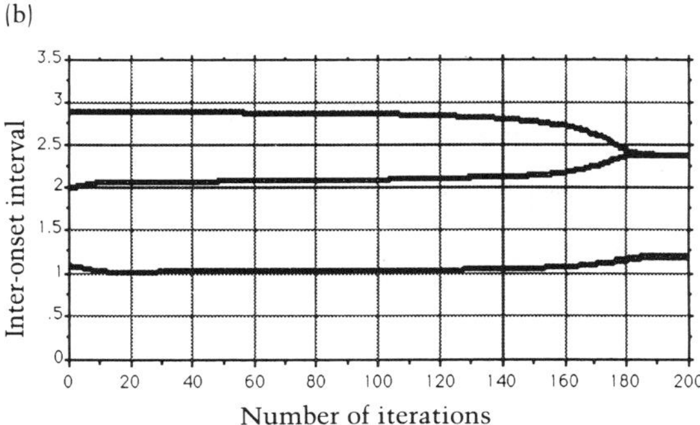

The degree of the polynomial, called the *peak* parameter, is typically between 2 and 12. To realize the decreasing magnitude of the interaction function, each section is scaled with a multiplication factor that is a negative power of the integer ratio. This power is called the *decay parameter*, and is typically between -1 and -3. This interaction function is defined as

$$F(r) = (\text{round}(r) - r) * |2(r - \text{entier}(r) - 0.5)|^p * \text{round}(r)^d,$$

in which the first term gives the ideal change of ratio, the second term signifies the speed of change which is at maximum near an integer ratio (with peak parameter p), and the third term scales the change to be lower at higher ratios (with decay parameter d). It is simple to prove that this interaction function satisfies the constraints mentioned.

From the change of ratio $F(a/b)$, new intervals $a + \Delta$ and $b - \Delta$ are calculated without altering the sum of both intervals.

$$\frac{a+\Delta}{b-\Delta} = \frac{a}{b} + F\left(\frac{a}{b}\right)$$

which implies

$$\Delta = \frac{bF\left(\frac{a}{b}\right)}{1 + \frac{a}{b} + F\left(\frac{a}{b}\right)}$$

In simulating the network, each interaction cell updates the states of the two basic cells to which it is connected. This process is repeated, moving the basic cells slowly towards equilibrium. Equilibrium is assumed when no cell changes more than a certain amount between two iterations. For example, let us take a rhythm with inter-onset intervals of 2, 1.1, and 2.9 csec. As the representation of duration is currently unimportant in the model, they are treated as relative values (tempo has no influence on the quantization). This rhythm is represented in a basic network as three cells with the initial states 2.0 : 1.1 : 2.9. Iterating the procedure outlined above for the interactions between cells labeled A and B, and cells B and C will adjust the durations toward 2 : 1 : 3, where the net reaches an equilibrium. Figure 5a is a graph of the state of each basic cell as a function of the iteration count.

This type of network can of course only quantize very simple rhythms. Consider for instance the rhythm 1.1 : 2.0 : 2.9, which should converge to 1 : 2 : 3. The cell representing 2.9 only interacts with its neighbor 2.0, the resultant ratio 1 : 45 being a long way from an integer. The basic net adjusts these values to 1.2 : 2.4 : 2.4, as seen in Fig. 5b.

What the model fails to take account of is the time interval 3.1, the sum of the first two durations. If this interval were incorporated into the model, it would interact successfully with the third interval (2.9) in such a way that the pair of intervals would gravitate toward the ratio 1. This observation leads to a revised model.

Fig. 6. *State as a function of iteration count for a complex rhythm in a compound network.*

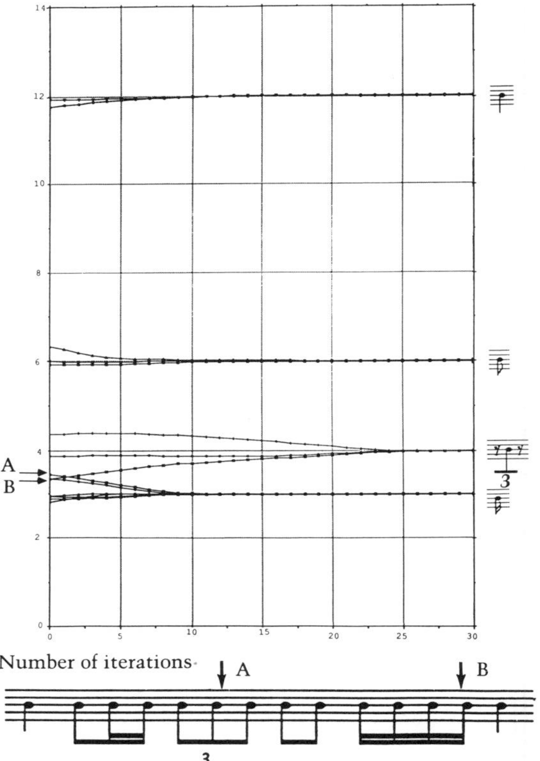

Compound Model

In order to represent the longer time intervals generated by a sequence of notes, *sum cells* are postulated. These cells sum the activation levels of the basic cells to which they are connected. The interaction of a sum cell with its basic cells is bidirectional; if the sum cell changes its value, the basic cells connected to it will all change proportionally. The sum cells are interconnected to cells representing adjacent intervals by the same interaction cells that are used in the basic model. The function of the interaction cells is once again to try to steer the interconnected cells—which may be sum cells, or a mixture of sum cells and basic cells—toward an integer ratio as was shown in Figs. 2b and 3b.

Our earlier example—a duration sequence of 1.1, 2.0, 2.9—is now quantized correctly due to combined effects of interacting sum cells and the interactions between the basic cells. Let us consider a more complex example using the real performance data shown in Fig. 6. In this rhythm the final sixteenth note is played longer than the middle note of the triplet. Nonetheless the local context of the two intervals steers each note towards its correct value as seen in Fig. 6. The compound model produces promising results, even though the network is rather sparse, allowing only adjacent time intervals to interact. A compound network for a rhythm of n intervals consists of n basic cells, $[(n + 1)(n - 2)/2]$ sum cells, and $[n(n^2 - 1)/6]$ interaction cells.

Understanding the Model

In connectionist systems the global behavior emerges from a large number of local interactions. This makes it very difficult to study the behavior of the network at a detailed level. While it may initially seem attractive to use descriptions like "winning cells," "pulling harder," etc., a better understanding of the patterns of change within the network and of the influence of context requires the development of specialized methods. An approach that has proved very useful is what we call the *clamping method.* This entails the clamping, or fixing, of the states of all but one of the cells. The remaining cell is given an activation level in a reasonable range (the independent variable). Then the resulting change that would have taken place—after one iteration—if the cell were free to change its activation level is monitored (the dependent variable). In order to facilitate the interpretation of this measure (the amount of change), the function is negated and integrated to give a curve with local minima at stable points. The state of the experimentally varied cell will tend to move towards a minimum, like a rolling ball on an uneven surface. As such, it can be interpreted as a curve of potential energy. These minima and maxima can now be evaluated and judged in light of the context set up

Fig. 7. Clamping curve for a cell with a left context of 1 (a). Clamping curve for a cell with a left context of 2, 1 (b). Clamping curve for a cell with a left context of 2, 1, 1 (c). Clamping curve for a cell with a left context of 2, 1 with different parameters for the interaction function (d).

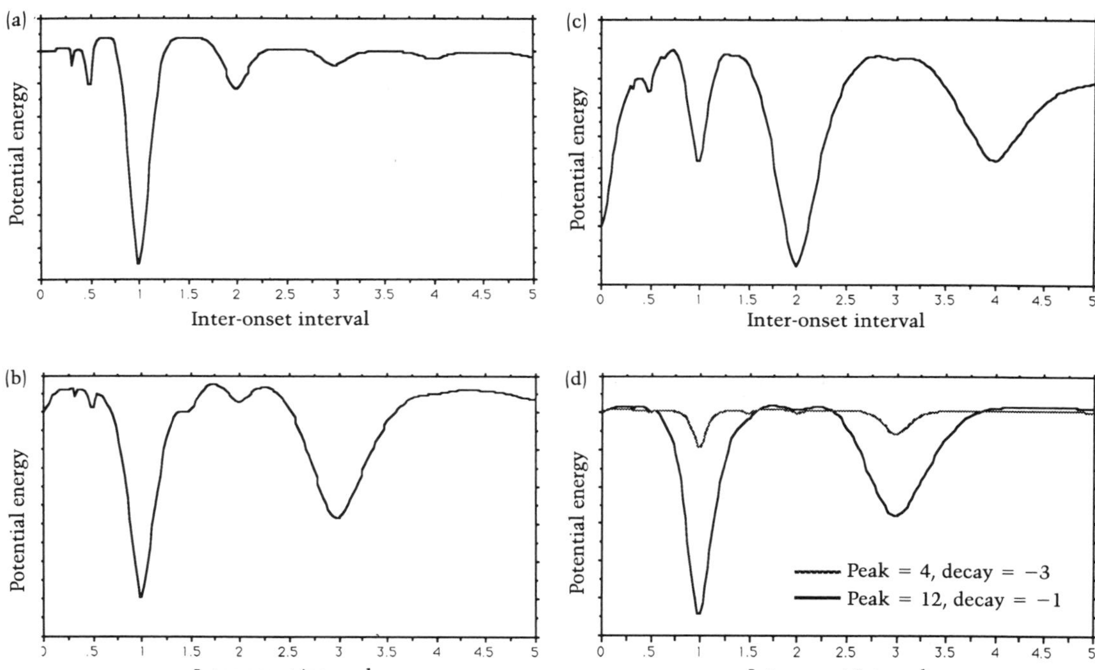

by the surrounding clamped cells. We call the interval between two neighboring local maxima the *catch range.* A value occurring within this range will move towards the minimum between these two maxima, provided the context does not change. The size of the interval where the potential energy stays close to a minimum is called its *flatness value.* It is a measure of the lack of clarity in the context; simple and clear contexts give rise to sharp minima.

Figure 7a shows the potential energy curve of two cells in a basic network; the first has a state of 1; while the other varies between 0–5. The figure shows prominent local minima at 1, 2, 3, 4 and so on, and at the inverse ratios (.5, .33, and so on). These will be the equilibrium states of the second cell. Note the flatter minima at larger ratios.

A graph of the basic interaction (without sum cells) in a 3 cell net with the first two cells clamped to the values 2 and 1 would yield the same curve, since the first cell does not interact with the varying third cell. Introducing sum cells, however, gives a different curve as can be seen in Fig. 7b. A minimum is shown at 3 caused by the interaction of the sum of the first and second basic cells with the last cell (3 : 3 yielding a ratio of 1). The minimum at 3 being strengthened by the interaction of the first cell with the sum of the second two (2 : 4, yielding a ratio of 2). This interaction also results in a weaker minimum at 1.5 (3 : 1.5, a ratio of 2). With a left context of 2 : 1 : 1 the minimum at 3 almost disappears as in Fig. 7c. There is now a strong minimum at 2 because the sum cell—which combines the durations of the second and third cell—is also 2. The sum of the first three cells give rise to the minimum at 4. This clamping method thus gives a clear picture of the mechanisms involved in the complex interactions through a simplification of the process that assumes fixed values in most of the cells. The

Fig. 8. Clamping curves of two notes in the context of an idealized complex rhythm (a). Clamping curves of two notes in the context of a performed complex rhythm (b).

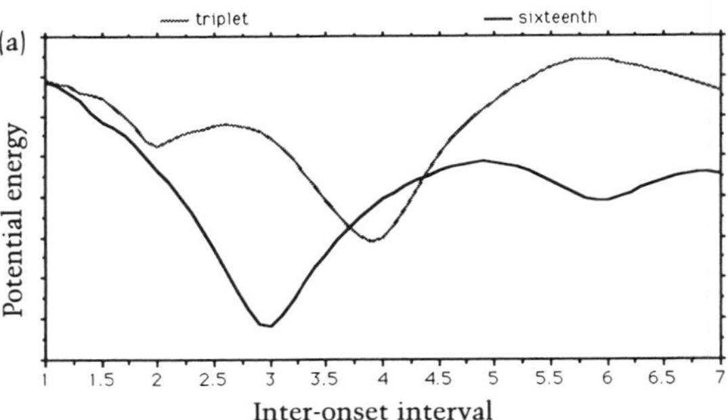

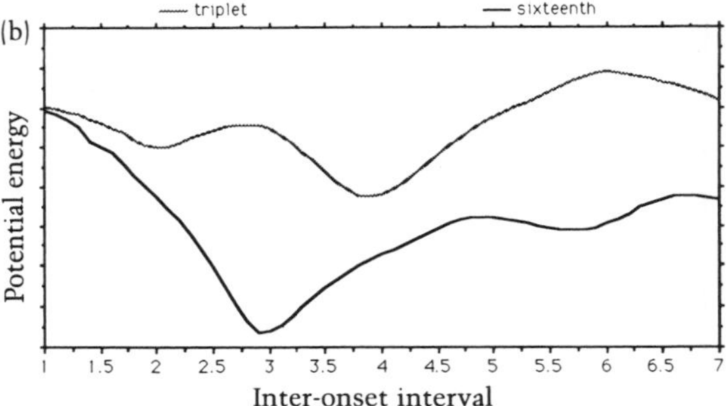

same method can also be used to study the influence of the parameters of the interaction function. In Fig. 7d, which uses the same context as in Fig. 7c, the peak and decay parameters have been changed, showing the effect on the catch range.

If we now return to the more elaborate example shown in Fig. 6, we can study the behavior of the net using the clamping method. Fig. 8a shows the potential energy curves resulting from applying the clamping method to the middle note of the triplet and the final sixteenth note. It shows clearly that the different contexts in which they appear result in different curves and that both will be directed towards the appropriate values. Note the wide catch ranges that allow rather large deviations to be quantized correctly and the smoothness of the curves. This smoothness (the lack of small local minima in the curve) is a result of the large number of interactions (364 and 91 for the triplet and sixteenth notes, respectively), which combine additively to yield each point on the curve. When the clamping experiment is rerun with performance data as context, more complex curves result, with a smaller catch range and a greater flatness, which is shown in Fig. 8b. Nonetheless, the durations still converge towards the correct metrical values.

The position of local maxima in the energy curves constitute the boundaries between the categories into which the data will be quantized. As a result, precise predictions can now be made about the perceptual interpretation of rhythmical sequences with a range of experimentally adjusted durations. It is our intention to compare these predictions with the results of empirical studies.

Implementation

In simulating a connectionist network, the calculated change in the state of one cell can be effectuated immediately (*asynchronous update*), or can be delayed, effectuating the change of all interactions at once (*synchronous update*). For asynchronous updates, a random order of visiting cells is generally preferred. In Table 1, a simplified implementation of the quantization model is given in Common Lisp (Steele 1984), based on synchronous updates. The basic cells are represented as a vector of inter-onset intervals. The sum cells are not represented explicitly, but are recalculated, summing the represented interval of basic cells for each interaction. A macro is provided that implements the iteration over adjacent sum intervals. The described interaction function is the one we used for the Figs. 5 and 6. This simplified version requires the minimum inter-onset interval to be around 1. More elaborate versions run in Common Lisp and in C on stock hardware (Macintosh II and Atari ST series machines).

Further Research

The model we have presented needs high peak values to stabilize accurately. Because this results in smaller catch ranges, we are currently studying the automatic increasing of the peak parameter while

Table 1. Micro version of the connectionist quantizer in CommonLISP

```
;;; MICRO CONNECTIONIST QUANTIZER
;;; 1988 P.Desain and H.Honing

;;; Utilities

(defmacro for ((var &key (from 0) to) &body body)
  "Iterate body with var bound to successive values"
  (let ((to-var (gensym)))
    `(let ((,var ,from)(,to-var ,to))
       (loop ,(when to `(when (> ,var ,to-var) (return)))
             ,@body
             (incf ,var)))))

(defmacro max-index (vector)
  "Return index of last element in a vector"
  `(- (array-dimension ,vector 0) 1))

(defmacro zero-vector! (vector)
  "Set elements of a vector to zero"
  `(for (index :from 0 :to (max-index ,vector))
     (setf (aref ,vector index) 0.0)))

(defmacro incf-vector-scalar! (a b from to)
  "Increment elements in a range of a vector"
  `(for (index :from ,from :to ,to)
     (incf (aref ,a index) ,b)))

(defmacro incf-relative-vector-vector! (a b)
  "Increment elements of a vector proportionally"
  `(for (index :from 0 :to (max-index ,a))
     (incf (aref ,a index) (* (aref ,a index) (aref ,b index)))))

(defun print-vector (times vector &optional (stream t))
  "Print all elements of vector"
  (format stream "~%~3d: " times)
    (for (index :from 0 :to (max-index vector))
    (format stream "~2,1,5$ " (float (aref vector index)))))

;;; control structure for iteration over intervals

(defmacro with-all-intervals (vector (begin end sum) (start
finish) &body body)
  "Iterating over all intervals contained in [start,finish]"
  `(let (,sum)
     (for (,begin :from ,start :to ,finish)
       (setf ,sum 0.0)
       (for (,end :from ,begin :to ,finish)
         (incf ,sum (aref ,vector ,end))
         ,@body))))
```

(cont'd)

```
(defmacro with-intervals (vector (begin end sum) (start
finish) &body body)
  "Iterating over intervals"
  '(let ((,sum 0.0)(,begin ,start))
    (for (,end :from ,start :to ,finish)
      (incf ,sum (aref ,vector ,end))
      ,@body)))

(defmacro with-adjacent-intervals
           (vector (a-begin a-end b-begin b-end a-sum
           b-sum) &body body)
  "Iterating over interval pairs"
  '(let ((max-index (max-index ,vector)))
    (with-all-intervals ,vector (,a-begin ,a-end
,a-sum) (0 (1- max-index))
      (with-intervals ,vector (,b-begin ,b-end ,b-sum)
      ((1+ ,a-end) max-index)
        ,@body))))

;;; Main quantization procedures

(defun quantize! (durations &optional (peak 4)(decay -1))
  "Quantize data in durations vector"
  (let ((changes (make-array (length durations) :initial-
element 0.0)))
    (for (times :from 0)
      (print-vector times durations)
      (update! durations changes peak decay))))

(defun update! (durations changes peak decay)
  "Update all durations synchronously"
  (zero-vector! changes)
  (with-adjacent-intervals durations
    (a-begin a-end b-begin b-end a-sum b-sum)
    (let ((delta (if (> a-sum b-sum)
                     (delta (/ a-sum b-sum) peak decay)
                     (- (delta (/ b-sum a-sum) peak decay)))))
      (incf-vector-scalar! changes (/ delta a-sum) a-begin
      a-end)
      (incf-vector-scalar! changes (- (/ delta b-sum) b-begin
       b-end)))
  (incf-relative-vector-vector! durations changes))

(defun delta (ratio peak decay)
  "Return change of time interval"
  (let ((delta-ratio (interaction ratio peak decay)))
    (/ delta-ratio (+ 1 ratio delta-ratio))))
```

(cont'd)

```
(defun interaction (ratio peak decay)
  "Return change of ratio"
  (let ((position (1- (* 2 (- ratio (floor ratio)))))
        (goal (round ratio)))
    (* (- goal ratio)
       (abs (expt position peak))
       (expt goal decay))))

;;; usage examples
;;; minimum element in data should be larger than 1

;(quantize! (vector 1.1 2.0 2.9))
;(quantize! (vector 11.77 5.92 2.88 3.37 4.36 3.37 3.87
                    6.00 6.34 2.96 2.80 2.96 3.46 11.93))
```

For an updated version of this code, see the following addendum.

the network comes to rest. The dependency of the model on absolute time and absolute tempi is still an open question. The most difficult rhythmic cases for this model are: (1) those that involve additive durations that emerge when rests and tied notes occur in the data and (2) divisive rhythms, such as when a quintuplet is adjacent to a triplet. Our aim is to be able to characterize exactly the limits of the model and to evaluate the computational requirements and the psychological plausibility of the results. A further aim is to develop a robust technical tool for real-time quantization using a process model. Tempo tracking is then an absolute necessity.

Conclusion

We consider the compound model presented here to be promising. In difficult cases the system undergoes a graceful degradation instead of a sudden breakdown: that is, the range in which rhythms are caught and quantized correctly becomes more and more limited. However, it is a paradoxical problem with connectionist models that their adaptability means that even a rough first implementation, with obvious bugs, may exhibit appropriate behavior. In order to increase an understanding of the process involved, it is necessary to develop specialized tools for diagnosis and investigation. The clamping method described here seems to have considerable potential, and we are confident that further tools of a similar sort will develop as connectionist modeling gathers momentum.

Acknowledgments

We would like to thank Dirk-Jan Povel, Steve McAdams, Marco Stroppa, the reviewers of *Computer Music Journal*, and especially Eric Clarke and Klaus de Rijk for their help in this research and their comments on the first version of this paper.

References

Bharucha, J. J. 1987. "Music Cognition and Perceptual Facilitation: A Connectionist Framework." *Music Perception* 5(1): 1–30.

Chowning, J., et al. 1984. "Intelligent Systems for the Analysis of Digitized Acoustical Signals." *CCRMA Report* STAN-M-15.

Clarke, E. 1987a. "Levels of Structure in the Organization of Musical Time." *Contemporary Music Review* 2: 212–238.

Clarke, E. 1987b. "Categorical Rhythm Perception: An Ecological Perspective." In A. Gabrielsson, ed. *Action and Perception in Rhythm and Music.* Stockholm: Royal Swedish Academy of Music. No. 55: 19–33.

Dannenberg, R. B., and B. Mont-Reynaud. 1987. "An On-line Algorithm for Real Time Accompaniment." *Proceedings of the 1987 International Computer Music Conference.* San Francisco, California: Computer Music Association, pp. 241–248.

Desain, P., and H. Honing. 1988. "The Quantization Problem: Traditional and Connectionist Approaches." *Proceedings of the first Artificial Intelligence and Music Workshop.* St. Augustin, West Germany: Gesellschaft für Mathematik und Datenverarbeitung.

Longuet-Higgins, H. C. 1987. *Mental Processes.* Cambridge, Massachusetts: MIT Press.

Mont-Reynaud, B., and M. Goldstein. 1985. "On Finding Rhythmic Patterns in Musical Lines." *Proceedings of the 1985 International Computer Music Conference.* San Francisco, California: Computer Music Association, pp. 391–397.

Povel, D. J. 1977. "Temporal Structure of Performed Music: Some Preliminary Observations." *Acta Psychologica* 41:309–320.

Povel, D. J., and P. Essens. 1985. "Perception of Temporal Patterns." *Music Perception* 2(4):411–440.

Rasch, R. A. 1979. "Synchronization in Performed Ensemble Music." *Acustica* 43(2):121–131.

Rumelhart, D., and J. McClelland, eds. 1986. *Parallel Distributed Processing: Explorations in the Microstructure of Cognition,* vol. 1. Cambridge, Massachusetts: MIT Press.

Shaffer, L. H. 1981. "Performances of Chopin, Bach, Bartok: Studies in Motor Programming." *Cognitive Psychology* 13:326–376.

Steele, G. L. 1984. *Common Lisp: The Language.* Bedford, Massachusetts: Digital Press.

Sternberg, S., R. L. Knoll, and P. Zukofsky. 1982. "Timing by Skilled Musicians." In D. Deutsch, ed. *The Psychology of Music.* New York: Academic Press.

Todd, N. P. 1985. "A Model of Expressive Timing in Tonal Music." *Music Perception* 3(1):33–58.

Vorberg, D. J., and R. Hambuch. 1987. "On the Temporal Control of Rhythmic Performance." In J. Requin, ed. *Attention and Performance* VII.

Vos, P., and S. Handel. 1987. "Playing Triplets: Facts and Preferences." In A. Gabrielsson, ed. *Action and Perception in Rhythm and Music.* Royal Swedish Academy of Music. No. 55:35–47.

Addendum

Peter Desain, Henkjan Honing, and Klaus de Rijk

The design of special tools and methods to study the time-quantization network is of great importance, allowing us to explain and predict behavior for particular data, to examine the influence of the parameters on network performance, etc. The clamping method described earlier is one of these tools. A second method visualizes the state space of the system by only taking rhythms of three inter-onset intervals into account. The three degrees of freedom are mapped to two dimensions by normalizing the total length of the rhythm. Each point (x, y) represents a rhythm of three inter-onset intervals $x : y : 1 - x - y$ in a net of interacting cells. Drawing the rhythm after each interation yields a trajectory toward a stable point in this space: the quantized version of the three intervals.

Plotting the trajectories of different rhythms exhibits the behavior of the network and the stable attractor points in this two dimensional space. They are positioned on straight lines that represent rhythms with an integer ratio of two durations or their sums $(x = y;\ x + y = z$, where z is the third interval length; $2x = y$; etc.). Fig. 9 shows this state space diagram for three intervals adding up to 3/4s with a variety of trajectories traced on it. One can see relatively large areas of attraction around the simple rhythms and relatively small areas around more complex rhythms. These so-called basins of attraction depend on the parameters of the interaction function; when the peak parameter is set to a higher value (see Fig. 9b), more basins of attraction around complex rhythms appear.

Diagrams such as Fig. 9 can form the basis for experiments to test the validity of the connectionist quantizing method as a cognitive model for rhythm perception. For example, we can plot the analogous diagram for human listeners performing a categorical perception experiment on part of the rhythm space and compare it with the output of the quantizer method. The results can be used to adjust the interval-interaction function of the model to more closely match human performance.

A third method amounts to a systematic explora-

Fig. 9. Trajectories in state space of a rhythm of three notes adding up to 3/4. The peak parameter is set to 2 for the upper plot and 6 for the lower.

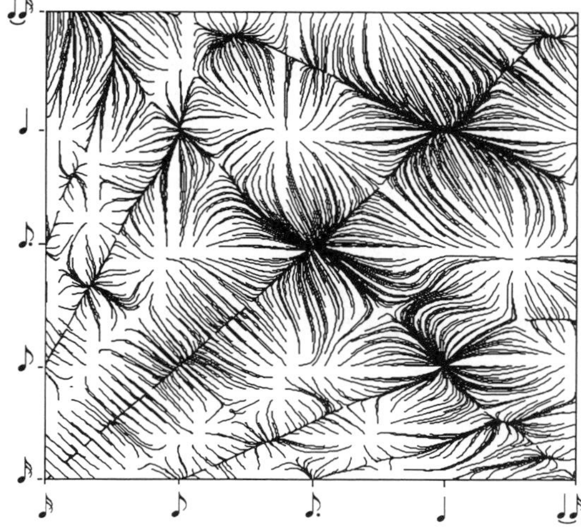

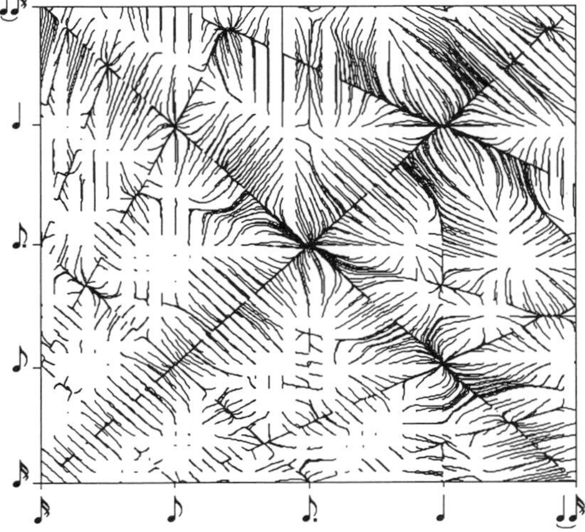

Fig. 10. *Mapping of the parameter space to the number of correct quantizations of a set of 50 rhythms.*

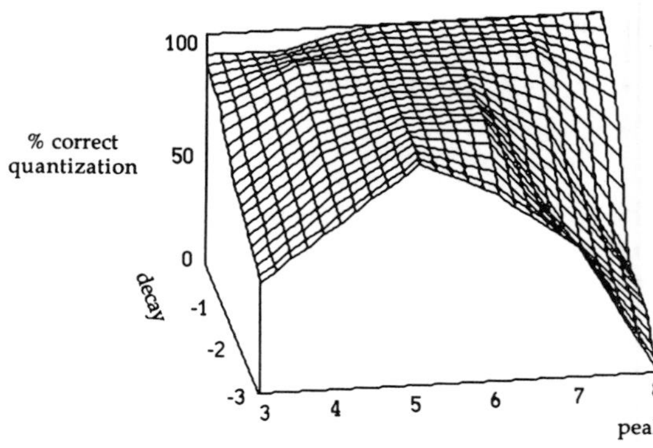

tion of the space of all possible parameter settings. A mapping can be made from this space to the number of correct quantizations of a set of performances. Fig. 10 shows this mapping for a set of about 50 relatively simple rhythms, varying in length from 3 to 14 inter-onset intervals, performed by a musical expert. In this way, we defined implicitly what a "correct" quantization is. The vertical axis shows the percentage of correct quantizations of the system, and the other axes show the parameters' peak and decay. This visualization brings out specific characteristics of the model. First, it shows the model's sensitivity to its parameters. Often connectionist models behave badly in this respect, needing specific parameter settings for different problems. But Fig. 10 shows the system behaves quite well with respect to parameter sensitivity. The surface between a peak value of 4 and 6 and a decay value between 0 and -2 is almost flat. Second, it shows that the two parameters are more or less independent. A decay value between 0 and -1 is most successful, fairly independent of the peak parameter.

Furthermore, families of rhythms with particular characteristics (e.g., rhythms that change meter, syncopated rhythms, rhythms with swing, sloppy performances of rhythms) could be made and tested, yielding insights into the limitations of the model for these specific types of rhythms and the musical and cognitive interpretations of the parameters. We will explore these issues in future research.

Still, the best understanding of such a complex system arises from a mathematical description through which one can search for analytical solutions, prove convergence and stability properties, etc. The present state of progress on a mathematical description is given below, but much remains to be done.

Mathematical Model

Suppose a rhythm is given by a vector x of durations x_i with $1 \leq i \leq N$. At each update, a new duration vector is computed by

$$x^* = x + D(x)$$

where D in this case is a kind of update function. With a certain initial vector x, we can compute a set of vectors, x^*, x^{**}, . . . , hopefully approaching equilibrium—the quantized rhythm. To characterize D, we begin by decomposing it into an update of individual basic cells

$$x_i^* = x_i + D_i(x).$$

An interaction cell connected to cells with values a and b should perform an increment of their ratio given by the interaction function

$$\frac{a^*}{b^*} = \frac{a}{b} + F\left(\frac{a}{b}\right).$$

We convert this change of ratio to a change of time interval $\Delta(a,b)$ under the constraint that the sum of the intervals stays the same:

$$a^* + b^* = a + b$$

$$a^* = a + \Delta(a,b)$$

$$b^* = b - \Delta(a,b).$$

This results in the definition of the change effectuated by an interaction cell:

$$\Delta(a,b) = b\frac{F\left(\frac{a}{b}\right)}{1 + \frac{a}{b} + F\left(\frac{a}{b}\right)}.$$

In a basic net, each basic cell (except the left- and rightmost cell) is connected to two interaction cells (see Fig. 2). Their change is computed by summing the change from each interaction:

$$D_i(x) = \Delta(x_i, x_{i+1}) - \Delta(x_{i-1}, x_i).$$

This describes the complete behavior of the basic network. In the compound network, the value of the sum cells is defined as

$$S_{p,q} = \sum_{j=p}^{q} x_j \qquad 1 \leq p \leq q \leq N.$$

Suppose a sum cell $S_{p,q}$ is changed by an update function $D_{p,q}$ as follows:

$$S^*_{p,q} = S_{p,q} + D_{p,q}(x).$$

A sum cell $S_{p,q}$ is interacting with a number of sum cells on the right $(S_{q+1,\bullet})$ and a number of sum cells on the left $(S_{\bullet,q+1})$, yielding the following definition of $D_{p,q}$:

$$D_{p,q}(x) = \sum_{r=q+1}^{N} \Delta(S_{p,q}, S_{q+1,r}) - \sum_{r=1}^{p-1} \Delta(S_{r,p-1}, S_{p,q}).$$

Here, if $q = N$, the first term vanishes because there are no right neighbors. Likewise, if $p = 1$, the second term vanishes. The change of the sum cells is propagated proportionally to all the basic cells connected to it. In each basic cell the change from all connected sum cells is summed.

$$D_i(x) = \sum_{p=1}^{i} \sum_{q=i}^{N} D_{p,q}(x) \frac{x_i}{S_{p,q}}.$$

Summarizing the above and taking care of leftmost and rightmost intervals, gives

$$D_i(x) = \sum_{p=1}^{i} \sum_{q=i}^{N-1} \sum_{r=q+1}^{N} \Delta\left(\sum_{j=p}^{q} x_j, \sum_{j=q+1}^{r} x_j \right) \frac{x_i}{\sum_{j=p}^{q} x_j}$$

$$- \sum_{p=2}^{i} \sum_{q=i}^{N} \sum_{r=1}^{p-1} \Delta\left(\sum_{j=r}^{p-1} x_j, \sum_{j=p}^{q} x_j \right) \frac{x_i}{\sum_{j=p}^{q} x_j}$$

This describes the behavior of the compound model.

Until now we have assumed $a > b$ in the definition of $\Delta(a, b)$. We can make a modification to eliminate the need for this assumption, as follows:

$$\Delta(a,b) = h(a,b) \frac{F(g(a,b))}{1 + g(a,b) + F(G(a,b))}$$

where $h(a,b)$ and $g(a,b)$ are defined by

$$h(a,b) = \begin{cases} b & \text{if } a > b \\ -a & \text{otherwise} \end{cases}$$

$$g(a,b) = \begin{cases} \dfrac{a}{b} & \text{if } a > b \\ \dfrac{b}{a} & \text{otherwise.} \end{cases}$$

When we implemented these systems, the results were inaccurate or unstable because the change in large sum cells tended to swamp the influence of smaller, local interactions. Therefore we scaled the interaction with the inverse of the interval b. This gave a precedence to local interactions that worked well. Because we still want to refrain for the moment from modeling the dependence of quantization on absolute global tempo, which was introduced implicitly by this change, we normalized this scaling factor with the overall minimum duration. The factor can be incorporated in the definition of $h(a,b)$:

$$h(a,b) = \begin{cases} \min\limits_{1 \leq j \leq N} x_j & \text{if } a > b \\ -\min\limits_{1 \leq j \leq N} x_j & \text{otherwise.} \end{cases}$$

We would still like to characterize the final time-quantized equilibrium state for which

$$D_i(x) = 0.$$

In the simplified network, it can be proven that this condition only holds when all $\Delta(x_i, x_{i+1})$ are zero. This implies that the interaction function F has to be zero for all ratios, which in turn means that all ratios are integers or integers plus 0.5. When the sum cells are introduced, the system is much harder to analyze. All equilibrium points of the simplified system are also equilibrium points of the complete system, but there are many additional

Fig. 11. The process model of the connectionist quantizer.

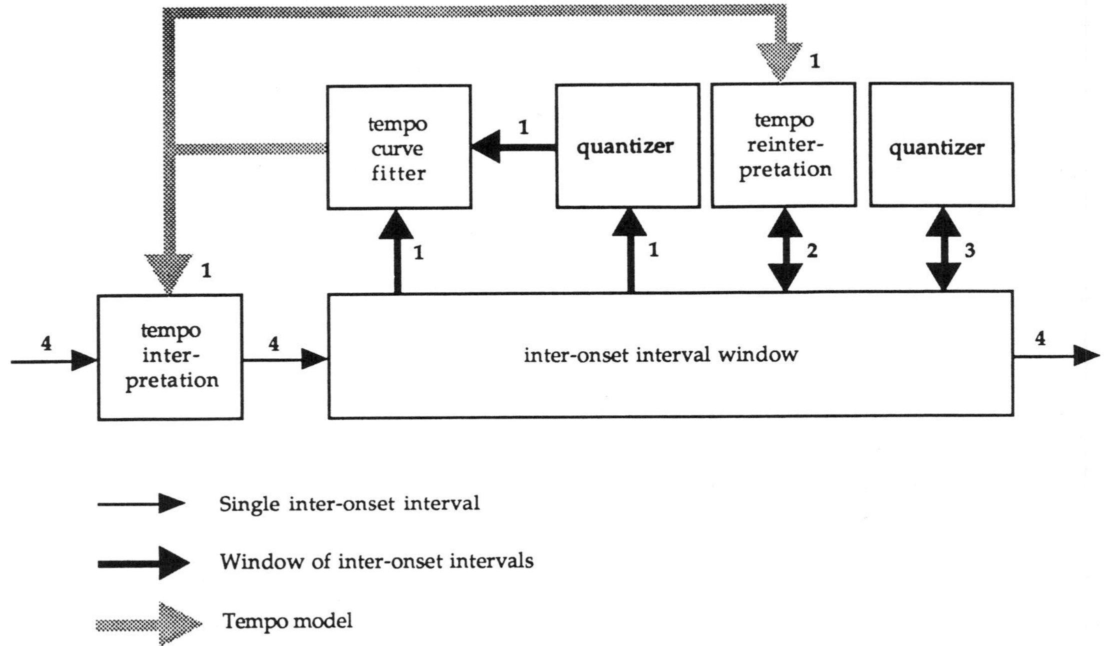

equilibrium points as well. In fact it is not clear yet what exactly are the (stable) equilibrium points of the complete system.

Process Model and Tempo Tracking

A system that takes all of the temporal data available in a piece into consideration is, of course, not feasible when the aim is to develop a robust technical tool for near real-time quantization of longer pieces, nor is such an algorithm plausible as a cognitive model. Luckily, it proved quite simple to design a process version of the quantizer that operates upon a limited window of events. In this system, new inter-onset intervals shift into the window, and metrical durations shift out, being quantized on the way through. With such a model, tempo tracking becomes an absolute necessity since slow global tempo changes spanning a time lapse larger then the window cannot be operated upon nor corrected for.

The architecture we came up with makes use of two main modules, the quantizer and a tempo curve fitter (see Fig. 11). They work in mutual cooperation, communicating via a window of inter-onset intervals. In phase 1 (indicated by the numbered portions of the figure), the quantizer tries to quantize the data in the window. The result is passed, together with the original data, to the tempo curve fitter. This process tries to explain the difference between the quantized and original data as a global tempo change instead of as random fluctuations by fitting a third-order tempo curve to the quantized and original data. With the resulting tempo model, the data window is reinterpreted, and any consistent global change in tempo is removed from the original data in phase 2. The resulting sequence is now simpler for the quantizer module to operate upon. In phase 3 it is given a chance to remove the remaining deviations. Finally, in phase 4, a quantized inter-onset interval is shifted out of the window, and a new interval is shifted in, after being interpreted according to the expected tempo. Then the whole process is repeated on the shifted interval window.

As a result a rhythm can be quantized differently depending on the context established by the preceding data. This of course is the same as we would expect from human listeners. For the implementation of the curve fitter, special care was taken to use appropriate numerical methods, since numerical inaccuracies build up because of the feedback architecture used in the method and can result in oscillations.

Polyphony

The system described so far is unable to deal with inter-onset times that approach zero (as in chords or music with multiple voices). Although it may be possible to use other means to "clean" the data before quantizing it, such as rules for recognizing chord chunks, the general connectionist approach used in the quantizer seems a much better alternative. This is because the context can be taken into account when deciding if for example something is to be considered a chord with some spread, or a regular run of notes, or an arpeggio that has its own metrical structure. By introducing note durations, the system can distinguish between sequential and simultaneous inter-onset intervals (i.e., overlapping intervals indicate polyphony). We are currently experimenting with multiple interlocking networks that can handle polyphony. The preliminary results seem to be promising.

Main Characteristics of the System

In summary, the connectionist quantization system has three main characteristics: (1) It is context sensitive, with precedence of local context, as we demonstrated with the example in Fig. 6 and the results of the clamping method, (2) the system has no explicit musical knowledge. There is no preconceived knowledge of metrical or rhythmical structure used to quantize the performance data other than the notion of "integer ratios." All information is derived from the data itself; and (3) the system exhibits graceful degradation. When the quantizer breaks down in a complex situation, it is often able to maintain musical integrity and consistency at higher levels. The resulting error will only generate a local deformation of the score. Furthermore, this deformation will always be a simplification of the rhythm, not a very complex fragment as produced by some traditional systems (see Fig. 1). On the other hand, when more difficult rhythms are fed into the quantizer, they imply a smaller range of deviations than can be accurately captured by the system. Thus, they will be quantized correctly when performed with a higher accuracy or consistency. Such behavior could be another possible link to human cognitive performance.

Finally, a new version of the connectionist quantizer code using the loop macro is shown in Table 2. This version no longer requires the minimum inter-onset interval to be around one.

Reference

Desain, P., and H. Honing. 1991. "The Quantization Problem: Traditional and Connectionist Approaches." In M. Balaban, K. Ebcioglu, and O. Laske, eds. *Musical Intelligence.* Menlo Park, California: AAAI Press.

Table 2. A new micro version of the connectionist quantizer in Common Lisp with the loop macro

```
;;; MICRO CONNECTIONIST QUANTIZER
;;; (C)1990, Desain & Honing
;;; in Common Lisp (uses loop macro)

;;; utilities

(define-modify-macro multf (factor) *)
(define-modify-macro divf (factor) /)
(define-modify-macro zerof () (lambda(x) 0))

(defun print-state (time intervals)
  "Print elements of interval vector"
  (loop initially (format t "~%~2D: " time)
        for index below (length intervals)
        do (format t "~2,1,5$ " (aref intervals index))))

(defmacro with-adjacent-intervals
    (vector (a-begin a-end a-sum b-begin b-end b-sum) &body body)
  "Setup environment for each interaction of (sum-)intervals"
  `(loop with length = (length ,vector)
         for ,a-begin below (1- length)
         do (loop for ,a-end from ,a-begin below (1- length)
                  sum (aref ,vector ,a-end) into ,a-sum
                  do (loop with ,b-begin = (1+ ,a-end)
                           for ,b-end from ,b-begin below length
                           sum (aref ,vector ,b-end) into ,b-sum
                           do ,@body))))

;;; interaction function

(defun delta (a b minimum peak decay)
  "Return change for two time intervals"
  (let* ((inverted? (<= a b))
         (ratio (if inverted? (/ b a)(/ a b)))
         (delta-ratio (interaction ratio peak decay))
         (proportion (/ delta-ratio (+ 1 ratio delta-ratio))))
    (* minimum (if inverted? (- proportion) proportion))))

(defun interaction (ratio peak decay)
  "Return change of time interval ratio"
  (* (- (round ratio) ratio)
     (expt (abs (* 2 (- ratio (floor ratio) 0.5))) peak)
     (expt (round ratio) decay)))
```

```
;;; quantization procedures

(defun quantize (intervals &key (iterations 20) (peak 5) (decay -1))
  "Quantize data of inter-onset intervals"
  (let* ((length (length intervals))
         (changes (make-array length :initial-element 0.0))
         (minimum (loop for index below length
                        minimize (aref intervals index))))
    (loop for count to iterations
          do (print-state count intervals)
          (update intervals minimum changes peak decay))))

(defun update (intervals minimum changes peak decay)
  "Update all intervals synchronously"
  (with-adjacent-intervals intervals
    (a-begin a-end a-sum b-begin b-end b-sum)
    (let ((delta (delta a-sum b-sum minimum peak decay)))
      (propagate changes a-begin a-end (/ delta a-sum))
      (propagate changes b-begin b-end (- (/ delta b-sum)))))
  (enforce changes intervals))

(defun propagate (changes begin end change)
  "Derive changes of basic-intervals from sum-interval change"
  (loop for index from begin to end
        do (incf (aref changes index) change)))

(defun enforce (changes intervals)
  "Effectuate changes to intervals"
  (loop for index below (length intervals)
        do (multf (aref intervals index)
                  (1+ (aref changes index)))
           (zerof (aref changes index))))

;;; examples

;(quantize (vector 1.1 2.0 2.9))
;(quantize (vector 11.77 5.92 2.88 3.37 4.36 3.37 3.87 6.00 6.34
                   2.96 2.80 2.96 3.46 11.93))
```

III

Applications

Introduction

Connectionist systems are useful for a variety of musical tasks in addition to the modeling of music perception and cognition. In particular, they show promise as a means of algorithmic music composition, as several of the chapters in this part demonstrate. A key feature of this approach is the ability of neural networks and connectionist systems to learn the patterns and features that characterize a set of musical examples and to generalize from these features to compose new pieces. This automatic musical learning gives connectionist composing systems a great advantage over other algorithmic methods that require the explicit formulation and use of a set of compositional rules. Connectionist approaches as parallel constraint-satisfaction techniques are also natural for looking at the problems of musical performance, where many constraints come to bear simultaneously on a performer's choice of movement and position in realizing a musical score. These types of applications may be explored from a psychological viewpoint to gain understanding about the human processes of composition or performance. But they may also be pursued to yield valuable tools in their own right, as sources of top-down information for performance tracking, for instance, or as aids for composers interested in exploring new compositions in a particular style. The use of such tools, particularly in the case of composition, can carry with it certain aesthetic implications and questions, some of which will be addressed by the authors in this part and the next.

By introducing recurrent feedback connections into a feedforward network, a nonlinear dynamic system capable of interesting sequential behavior can be created. Todd uses just such a sequential network to learn sets of simple melodies as sequences of pitches over successive slices of time. Once the network has been successfully trained to reproduce the example melody set, it can create new melodies by extrapolating and interpolating from those it has learned. The new melodies bear featural resemblance to the original examples, yet are stylistically different from melodies produced by other algorithmic composition methods. Todd discusses various ways of representing both pitch and time in such a network and indicates different ways of generating new melodies once training is done. To overcome the problems of limited melody length and lack of global structure, he describes methods of hierarchically stacking similar sequential networks operating at different time scales in his addendum.

Mozer set out to extend Todd's work on connectionist composition but vowed to "do it right this time." Although discussion continues as to his success on this score, his approach and results are impressive. Mozer bolsters the standard recurrent sequential network method with back propagation in time, a learning method that allows longer-range interdependencies between notes in a musical passage to be picked up and used. The usefulness of this technique can immediately be seen in his network's ability to learn interleaved sequences, something that competing transition-probability-based methods cannot do. Mozer's composition network gains further power through the use of a psychologically motivated multidimensional representation of pitch inspired by the work of Shepard, which includes pitch height, pitch chroma, and position on the circle of fifths. The musical potential of this method is indicated in the final examples of melodies composed in the style of Bach. Although lacking somewhat in global structure and coherence, a problem plaguing most of the compositions of connectionist systems, they nonetheless embody the "Bach-like" features of the melodies in the original training set.

Lewis presents a novel approach to connectionist composition quite distinct from sequential melody learning in his chapter. He begins with a feedforward network trained to categorize input musical phrases according to their "aesthetic appeal" as defined by a particular user; the single output unit might have a value of 1.0 for very good input phrases, or 0.2 for rather bad inputs. Then, to produce new phrases, Lewis employs a method he calls creation by refinement, clamping a particular desired value at the output, and propagating error back through the network to change the inputs, rather than the weights (as usually done during network training). By taking advantage of the equivalence of weight change *or* input change to produce a change in network output, Lewis's method adjusts the input phrase until it corresponds to the desired output aesthetic rating. Creation by refinement can also be used to fill in portions of musical passages in a hierarchical fashion, resulting in new compositions that bear appropriate levels of global structure. Lewis further describes enhancements to standard network-training techniques necessary for robust performance of his algorithm.

A still different method of algorithmic composition is described by Kohonen, Laine, Tiits, and Torkkola. Their approach employs a dynamically expanding context (DEC) grammar, which learns context-sensitive rules for the production of new notes in a musical sequence based on the notes that have already appeared. In contrast to other such grammars, though, the DEC method allows the context used in each rule to vary in length according to the specificity required for that rule; for instance, if an A is always followed by a B, then a rule with one context position is all that is required (A→B), but if an A is followed by a B in only certain circumstances, longer contexts will be necessary. Different context lengths allow an important range of generality and specificity for the grammar rules. This method stretches the definition of connectionism by offering another approach to nonheuristic learning, while bearing similarities to the type of pattern learning that recurrent sequential networks perform. The authors also present ways of extending the composition process from melody lines to accompanying parts, something that few other connectionist composition techniques have addressed.

When performing a piece of music on a guitar or other stringed instrument, there are usually multiple choices for how to finger any particular note. Not all of the alternatives are equivalent, however; some will be harder to reach from the previous finger position than others. The choice of an optimal fingering for an entire piece can thus be seen as an attempt to minimize the between-position movements from one note to the next, as Sayegh describes in his chapter. His method for computing such an optimal fingering, called the optimum path paradigm, finds a minimum-cost path through the layered network of possible fingerings for each note. The costs assigned to each link in the network can be set by a predetermined cost function, or can be learned from a corpus of actual performance fingerings by a method similar to Hebbian strengthening of commonly used connections. Sayegh presents the mathematical foundation for this learning rule, and its relation to other more traditional connectionist methods, in his addendum.

Peter M. Todd
Department of Psychology
Stanford University
Stanford, California 94305 USA
todd@psych.stanford.edu

A Connectionist Approach To Algorithmic Composition

With the advent of von Neumann-style computers, widespread exploration of new methods of music composition became possible. For the first time, complex sequences of carefully specified symbolic operations could be performed in a rapid fashion. Composers could develop algorithms embodying the compositional rules they were interested in and then use a computer to carry out these algorithms. In this way, composers could soon tell whether the results of their rules held artistic merit. This approach to algorithmic composition, based on the wedding between von Neumann computing machinery and rule-based software systems, has been prevalent for the past thirty years.

The arrival of a new paradigm for computing has made a different approach to algorithmic composition possible. This new computing paradigm is called *parallel distributed processing* (PDP), also known as *connectionism*. Computation is performed by a collection of several simple processing units connected in a network and acting in cooperation (Rumelhart and McClelland 1986). This is in stark contrast to the single powerful central processor used in the von Neumann architecture. One of the major features of the PDP approach is that it replaces strict rule-following behavior with regularity-learning and generalization (Dolson 1989). This fundamental shift allows the development of new algorithmic composition methods that rely on learning the structure of existing musical examples and generalizing from these learned structures to compose new pieces. These methods contrast greatly with the majority of older schemes that simply follow a previously assembled set of compositional rules, resulting in brittle systems typically unable to appropriately handle unexpected musical situations.

Computer Music Journal, Vol. 13, No. 4, Winter 1989,

To be sure, other algorithmic composition methods in the past have been based on abstracting certain features from musical examples and using these to create new compositions. Techniques such as Markov modeling with transition probability analysis (Jones 1981), Mathews' melody interpolation method (Mathews and Rosler 1968), and Cope's EMI system (Cope 1987) can all be placed in this category. However, the PDP computational paradigm provides a single powerful unifying approach within which to formulate a variety of algorithmic composition methods of this type. These new learning methods combine many of the features of the techniques listed above and add a variety of new capabilities. Perhaps most importantly, though, they yield different and interesting musical results.

This paper presents a particular type of PDP network for music composition applications. Various issues are discussed in designing the network, choosing the music representation used, training the network, and using it for composition. Comparisons are made to previous methods of algorithmic composition, and examples of the network's output are presented. This paper is intended to provide an indication of the power and range of PDP methods for algorithmic composition and to encourage others to begin exploring this new approach. Hence, rather than merely presenting a reduced compositional technique, alternative approaches and tangential ideas are included throughout as points of departure for further efforts.

A Network for Learning Musical Structure

Our new approach to algorithmic composition is first to create a network that can learn certain aspects of musical structure, second to give the network a selection of musical examples from which to learn those structural aspects, and third to let the network use what it has learned to construct new pieces of music. We can satisfy the first step by designing a network that can exactly reproduce a given set of musical examples, because being able to reproduce the examples requires that the network has learned a great deal about their structure.

A network design that meets this music learning goal has been described in a previous paper by this author (Todd 1988). This network has been applied to both the task of algorithmic composition and the psychological modeling of certain aspects of human musical performance, such as tonal expectation (Bharucha and Todd 1989). This design is presented here. As in the original paper, I will restrict the musical domain to the relatively simple class of monophonic melodies. This restriction simplifies the nature of the network by avoiding certain problems associated with the representation of polyphony, which will be indicated later. However, the monophonic domain remains musically realistic and interesting, as the examples will show.

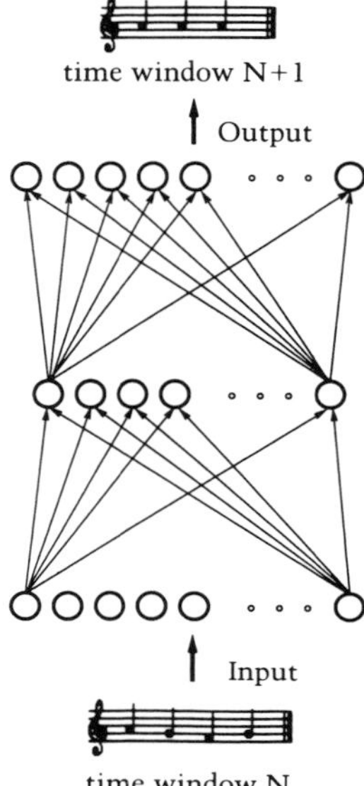

Fig. 1. A network design which can learn to associate time windows (e.g. measures) in a piece of music with the following time windows. Here, one measure as input produces the following measure as output. Circles represent individual units, lines represent directed connections between units, and arrows indicate the flow of activation through the network. Not all units or connections are shown.

Network Design

Since music is fundamentally a temporal process, the first consideration in designing a network to learn melodies is how to represent time. One way time may be represented is by standard musical notation translated into an ordered spatial dimension. Thus, the common staff represents time flowing from left to right, marked off at regular intervals by measure bars. Music could be represented in a similar fashion in a PDP network, with a large chunk of time being processed simultaneously, in parallel, with different locations in time captured by different positions of processing units in the network. In the limiting case, the entire melody could be presented to the network simultaneously; alternatively, and requiring fewer input units, a sliding window of successive time-periods of fixed size could be used. This windowed approach is common in speech applications of various types, as in the NetTalk word-to-speech network (Sejnowski and Rosenberg 1987) and various phoneme recognition systems (Waibel et al. 1987).

In essence, the time-as-spatial-position representation converts the problem of learning music into the problem of learning spatial patterns. For example, learning a melody may consist of learning to associate each measure of the melody with the next one, as illustrated in Fig. 1. Thus when a particular measure is presented as the input to the network, the following measure will be produced as output. Learning to perform such pattern association is something at which PDP networks are quite good. Furthermore, networks are able to generalize to new patterns they have not previously learned, producing reasonable output in those cases as well. Thus, a new measure of music could be given as the input to a trained network, and it would produce as output its best guess at what would be a reasonable following measure. This generalizing behavior is the primary motivation for using PDP networks in a compositional context, since what we are interested in is exactly the generation of reasonable musical patterns in new situations.

While the spatial-position representation of time may be acceptable, it seems more intuitive to treat music as a sequential phenomenon, with notes

Fig. 2. A sequential network design which can learn to produce a sequence of notes, using a memory of the notes already produced. This memory is provided by the feedback connections shown, which channel produced notes back into the network.

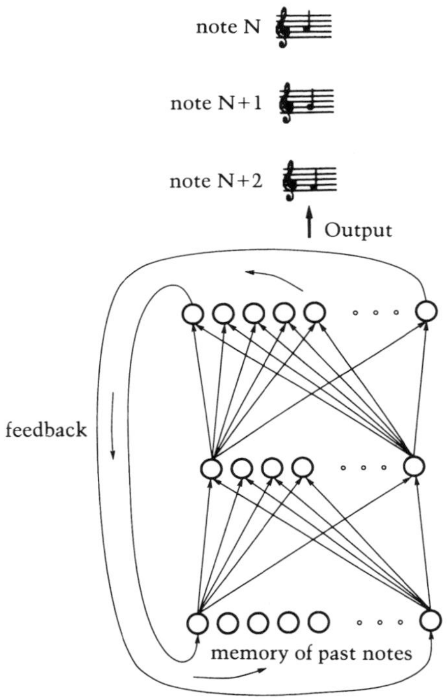

being produced one after another in succession. This view calls for the use of a sequential network, which learns to produce a sequence of single notes rather than a set of notes simultaneously. In this case, time is represented by the relative position of a note in the sequence, rather than the spatial position of a note in a window of units. Where networks utilizing a spatial representation of time learn to associate a successive chunk of time with the previous chunk, sequential networks learn to produce the next note in a sequence based on some memory of past notes in the sequence. Thus, some memory of the past is needed in a sequential network, and this is provided by some sort of feedback connections that cycle current network activity back into the network for later use, as can be seen in Fig. 2.

The learning phases of these two types of networks are very similar—both learn to associate certain output patterns with certain inputs by adjusting the weights on connections in the network. But their operation during production of melodies is quite different. Basically, the windowed-time pattern associator network produces a static output given its input: one window of time in produces one window of time out. The sequential network, on the other hand, cycles repeatedly to yield a sequence of successively produced outputs. Each of these outputs further influences the production of later outputs in the sequence via the network's feedback connections and its generalizing ability. This ongoing dynamic behavior has great implications for the sorts of sequences the network will produce, as will be seen later in this article.

Actually, the windowed-time and sequential-time approaches are not contradictory and may be combined to advantage. A sequential network that produces a sequence of time windows, rather than merely single notes, would learn a different set of associations and so make different generalizations during the composition phase. For the current discussion, though, a standard, single-event output sequential network design of the type first proposed by Jordan (1986a) has been used. A network of this type can learn to reproduce several monophonic melodies, thus capturing the important structural characteristics of a collection of pieces simultaneously. This makes it an ideal candidate for our purposes.

Jordan's sequential network design is essentially a typical, three-layer, feedforward network (Dolson 1989) with some modifications mostly in the first (input) layer, as shown in Fig. 3. One set of units in the first layer, called the *plan units*, indicate which sequence (of several possibilities) is being learned or produced. The units do this by having a fixed set of activations—the *plan*—turned on for the duration of the sequence. In effect the plan tells the network what to do by designating or naming the particular sequence being learned or produced.

The *context units* (also called *state units*) make up the remainder of the first layer. These units are so named because they maintain the memory of the sequence produced so far, which is the current con-

Fig. 3. The sequential network design used for compositional purposes in this paper. The current musical representation requires note-begin (nb) and pitch (D4-C6) units, as shown for both output and context; context units also have self-feedback connections. Each network output indicates the pitch at a certain time slice in the melody.

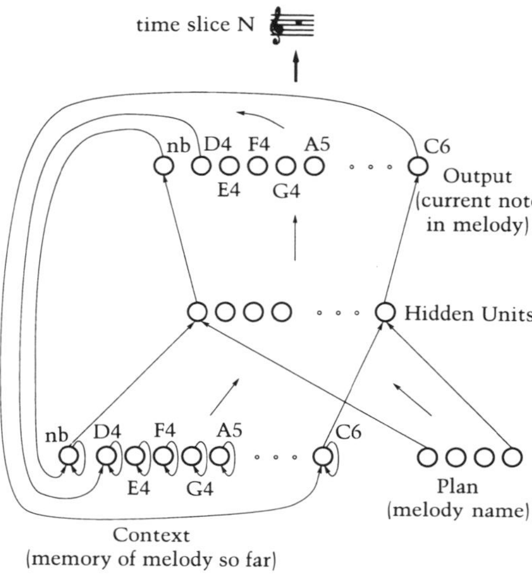

text or state that the network uses to produce the next element in the sequence. Each successive output of the network is entered into this memory by the feedback connections indicated from the output units to the context units.

A memory of more than just the single previous output is kept by having a self-feedback connection on each individual context unit, as shown in Fig. 3. These connections have a strength (weight) of less than 1.0, so that each context unit computes an exponentially decreasing sum of all of its previous inputs, which are the network's outputs. For example, if the self-feedback strength were 0.8, then a unit's memory would decrease proportionally by the amounts 0.8, 0.64, 0.51, 0.41, etc., as long as nothing new were entered into its memory. This connection strength cannot be greater than 1.0 or the activation values of the context units would explode exponentially.

The context units and plan units are all fully interconnected by a set of learned, weighted connections to the next layer of units, the *hidden units.* The hidden units are so named because they are neither at the network's input nor output, and so are in some sense buried inside the network. The hidden units combine the weighted information from the (fixed) plan units and the (evolving) context units, processing it via their logistic activation functions (Dolson 1989). They then pass on this processed information through the final set of weights to the output units. The output units then determine what the network will produce as the next element in the sequence. Each successive output is also finally passed along the feedback connections back to the context units, where they are added into the changing context. This in turn enables the computation of the following element in the sequence, and the cycle repeats.

The actual number of the various types of units used in the network depends on several factors. The number of plan units must be sufficient to specify different plans for all the different sequences to be learned. For example, we might want to use plans that have only one plan unit on at a time (i.e., with an activation of 1.0), while all the rest of the plan units are off (i.e., they have activations of 0.0). The particular plan unit that is on, for example the third or the fifth, specifies the sequence being processed (i.e., sequence number 3 or number 5). This type of plan is known as a *localist* representation, because each unit represents an entire entity (here an entire sequence) locally, by itself. If we wanted to learn *N* sequences for example, we would need *N* plan units to specify all of them in this way. On the other hand, a binary-coded plan representation would be more compact: in this case, we would need only $\log_2 N$ plan units to create *N* different plans. Thus plan 011 would specify sequence number 4 out of 8 possible, starting with 000. This is a *distributed* type of representation, because each entity is represented by a pattern of activation spread over several units at once.

The number of output units in the network depends on the representation of the sequence elements used, so it cannot be specified until this representation is settled. The number of context units depends on the type of memory desired. We will see below that having an equal number of output units and context units is useful. Finally, the number of hidden units depends on what the network must learn and cannot be exactly specified. If there are too few hidden units, the network may lack the computational power to learn all it is intended to. It is a good idea, however, to keep the number of hidden units as small as possible, because this tends to enhance the network's ability to generalize to new situations (new inputs), which is usually important. This happens because the network is forced to squeeze its processing through a narrow channel of few hidden units, so that it must make use of only the most important aspects of the information it is processing. If we have too many hidden units, the network can use them essentially to memorize what it needs to do rather than extracting the important aspects that allow generalization from its training data. But at this point, finding the ideal number of hidden units to use is still a matter of trial and error.

What happens when the sequences to be learned and produced are melodies? In this case, each element of the sequence, and hence each output of the network, is a particular note, with at least some indication of pitch and duration. The plan units now represent the name of the particular melody being processed. Correspondingly, the context units store a representation of the sequence of notes produced so far for this melody. The output units code the current note of the melody. The hidden units have no special interpretation in this case other than to help compute each successive note output of the network.

In the musical sequential networks investigated so far, the relationships of the feedback connections from the output units to the context units have all been one-to-one. That is, for each output unit, there is a single corresponding context unit to which it is connected and which thus maintains an easily interpretable decaying memory of the output unit's recent activity. The weights on all these feedback connections are fixed at 1.0, so that they merely copy the activity of each output unit back to its particular context unit. The self-feedback connections on the context units, which allow the decaying memory of the output copies, have also had fixed weights. These weights, which are the same for all the context units, are usually set between 0.6 and 0.8. Values in this range give a relatively slow memory decay, so that the previous several sequence steps are available to help decide what the next output should be.

The self-feedback weight should not be too large, however, because the built-up memory values would then not change rapidly enough to differentiate the context among successive sequence steps. This differentiation is essential, since only the context changes from one step to the next in the network's input (remembering that the plan units are fixed). Also, the context units typically use a linear activation function, rather than a sigmoidal one. By not using the sigmoidal "squashing" activation function, the context units have increased dynamic range: i.e., their outputs can be anything instead of being restricted to the range from 0.0 to 1.0. This, too, helps to differentiate one context state from another. So the self-feedback weight is chosen to balance the desirability of a long memory trace against the disadvantage of having all the contexts blur together.

All of these feedback connections could be trained during learning rather than remaining fixed, but there are some reasons not to train them. Most importantly, it has not yet proved necessary. The networks investigated so far have learned sufficiently well without these extra degrees of freedom. The training process is also sped up by not including these additional weights that would need to be adjusted during learning. Finally, the fact that these weights are all the same and all unchanging lets us know exactly what the information at the context units will look like. They each compute the same type of decaying memory trace of their corresponding output unit. Knowing this can help us interpret just what the network is doing.

The issue of interpretation is also the main reason why another sequential network structure has not been used for these studies. The design described by Elman (1988) uses feedback connections from the hidden units, rather than the output units, to the context units. Since the hidden units typically compute some complicated, often uninterpretable function of their inputs, the memory kept in the context units will likely also be uninterpretable. This is in contrast to Jordan's design, where, as described earlier, each context unit keeps a memory of its corresponding output unit, which *is* interpretable. [In general, interpretability seems like a good thing, although it is often not necessary. Certainly the Elman type of sequential network could be used for musical purposes; its behavior would simply be less analyzable. The extent to which this matters depends on just how deeply we wish to understand what is going on in the network.]

Melody Representation

Before the structure of the network can be finalized, we must decide upon the representation to use for the melodies to be learned and produced. This representation will determine the number and interpretation of the output units and of the corresponding context units. For the purposes of the current investigation, we will make several simplifying assumptions about the melodic sequences to be used, which affect the representation needed. One of these assumptions is that each monophonic melody is to be represented only as a sequence of notes, each with a certain pitch and duration. All other factors, such as tempo, loudness, and timbre, are ignored. Thus our representation need only capture two types of information: the pitch and duration of each note.

Pitch

To represent the pitch of a given note, two possibilities come to mind. Either the actual value of each pitch can be specified, or the relative transitions (intervals) between successive pitches can be used. In the first case, we would need output units corresponding to each of the possible pitches the network could produce, such as one unit for middle C, one unit for C♯, etc. The context units would then hold memories of these pitches. In the interval case, on the other hand, there would be output units corresponding to pitch changes of various sizes. So one output unit would designate a pitch change of +1 half step, another a change of −3 half steps, etc. To represent the melody A-B-C, then, the output from the actual-pitch network would be {A, B, C}, while the output from the pitch-interval network would be {A, +2, +1} (where the first pitch must be specified so we know from what value the intervals start).

The pitch-interval representation is appealing for several reasons. First, given a fixed number of output units, this representation is not restricted in the pitch range it can cover. The actual-pitch representation is so restricted. For instance, if we only had three output units, we could only represent three actual pitches. But if these output units corresponded to the pitch intervals −1, 0, and +1 half steps, we could cover any range of pitches in a melody by repeatedly going up or down, one half step at a time, at each successive note output. In this case the choice of interval sizes is necessarily limited to the number of output units.

Another advantage of the pitch-interval representation is that melodies are encoded in a more-or-less key-independent fashion. That is, aside from the initial specification of the starting actual pitch value, the network's output contains no indication of the key it is to be performed in (except, perhaps, for indications of key mode, major or minor, based on the intervals used). This key-independent learning is useful for letting the network discover common structure between melodies. If the network is to learn two different melodies in two different keys, then using an actual-pitch representation might obscure patterns of pitch movement present in both. For example, if one melody included the phrase C-G-E-F, and the other included the phrase F♯-C♯-A♯-B, the network would be likely to miss any connection between the two, since they use totally different output units. In a pitch-interval representation, though, these two phrases would be coded identically, allowing the network to see this commonality in the two melodies.

Key independence also allows transposition of an entire melody simply by changing the initial actual pitch (which need not even be produced by the network, but could be specified elsewhere). All of the intervals would remain unchanged, but the different starting pitch would put the rest of the sequence into a different key. In contrast, to transpose a melody in actual-pitch form, every single pitch output would need to be changed—that is, the network would have to be retrained. The ability to transpose the network's output easily may be desirable in some situations.

The ease of transposition that the pitch-interval representation allows is also a major drawback. When an error is made in the production of a sequence of intervals, the rest of the melody will be transposed to a different key, relative to the segment before the error. This type of mistake is glaringly obvious when one hears it—as though someone were singing a melody in one key, and then suddenly switched to another. One error in the interval sequence will thus globally affect the performance of the whole melody. In contrast, mistakes in the output using the actual-pitch representation are purely local. Only the pitch of the individual wrong note will be altered; all the rest of the pitches in the sequence will retain their proper values, so that performance of the melody will be minimally affected.

Since the networks I first looked at were inclined to make errors, I chose the most error-free representation, using actual pitches. The output units thus each represent a single pitch, in a particular octave, as indicated in Fig. 3. Another simplifying assumption about the melodies to be learned now comes into play; all the melodies in the current set of examples have been transposed beforehand into the key of C and have no accidentals. In this way, we only need units representing the pitches in the key of C over the octave range required. By eliminating the need for extra output units for sharps and flats, we have made the network's learning task easier, at the cost of some restriction and preprocessing of the melodies to be learned.

Note also that the output units use a localist representation of the actual pitch. As described above, a localist representation is one in which a single unit denotes an entire entity. In this case, only one unit is on at a time, and each unit itself designates a particular pitch: for example (with three output units), 001 for A, 010 for B, 100 for C. Rests are represented in this scheme by having none of the output pitch units on—000 in this example. This is opposed to a distributed representation—for example, a binary coding scheme such as 100 for A, 110 for C, 111 for D. The localist scheme has the advantage that each pitch representation is equally similar to every other one, in the sense that every pattern overlaps equally with the others (001 and 010 are the same in just one position, as are 001 and 100, and 010 and 100). In the binary-coded case, though, the representation of A is more similar to that of C than of D—100 and 110 are the same in two positions, while 100 and 111 are the same in only one position.

This difference would have an effect while training the network. For example, using the values just given, if a C is produced as output instead of an A, this would be a lesser mistake (since they are more similar) than producing a D for an A. As it learned, the network's knowledge of musical structure would begin to reflect this (probably) erroneous difference. Thus this distributed coding imposes a similarity-measure on the network's outputs that we probably do not want—there is no *a priori* reason to designate A and C as more similar than A and D. The localist pitch representation, which does not impose this differential similarity on the outputs, works better.

In addition, by using a localist pitch representation on the output units, the context units now become individual pitch memories. Since each context unit is connected to a single output unit, it maintains a memory only concerned with that output unit's own pitch. In particular, the context unit's activation level tells how recently and how often or long that pitch has been used in the current melody so far. This memory of pitch use seems like an appropriate thing to make use of in producing the subsequent notes of the melody.

It still seems unfortunate to have to abandon the pitch-interval representation completely. Its advantages could be gained and its drawbacks minimized by incorporating it into a hybrid pitch representation. For instance, intervals could be used for the majority of the network outputs, with the addition of calibrating actual pitches every so often. That is, at the start of every measure (or other suitable period), the actual pitch that the melody should be playing could be included in the network's output. This could be used to recalibrate the melody periodically, so that it remains in the proper key. A hybrid representation of this form could minimize the jarring effect of key changes after errors while retaining the advantages of intervals, such as the

Fig. 4. Network output using extrapolation from a single melody. In each case, both piano-roll-style output and common-practice music notation are shown. Network outputs for the first 34 time-slices are shown, with row 0 (bottom row) corresponding to the note-begin unit, and rows 1–14 corresponding to the pitch units, D4-C6. A black bar indicates the unit is on. Where the network output goes into a fixed loop, this is indicated by repeat bars in the music notation. (a) Melody 1, which the network is originally trained to produce with a plan of 1.0. (b) Extrapolation output using a plan of 0.0. (c) Extrapolation output using a plan of 2.0. (d) Extrapolation output using a plan of 3.0.

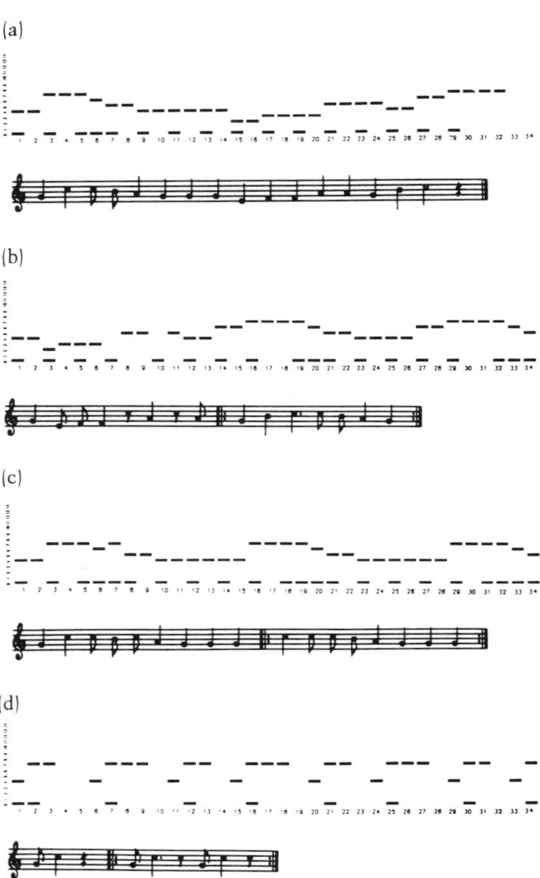

similarity of common pitch movement patterns in different keys.

Duration

The duration of notes in the melodic sequences must also be represented. As with the pitch representation, two clear alternatives present themselves. First, the duration could be specified in a separate pool of output (and context) units, alongside the pitch output units. The units could code for note duration in a localist fashion, with one unit designating a quarter-note, another a dotted eighth-note, etc. Or they could use a distributed representation, with for instance the number of units "on" (activation 1.0) representing the duration of the current note in sixteenth-notes. With the localist representation, the corresponding context units would hold a memory of the lengths of notes played recently in the melody; in the distributed case, the context units would be harder to analyze.

Alternatively, duration can be removed from explicit representation at the output units. Instead, the melody could be divided into equally spaced time slices of some fixed length, and each output in the sequence would correspond to the pitch during one time slice. Duration would then be captured by the number of successive outputs and hence the number of time slices a particular pitch stays on. This is equivalent to thinking of a melody as a function of pitch versus time (as in piano-roll notation), with the network giving the pitch value of this function at equally spaced intervals of time. I am using this time-slice representation for duration at present, in part because it simplifies the network's output—no separate note-duration units are needed. In addition, this representation allows the context units to capture potentially useful pitch-length information, as will be indicated below. The form of this representation can be seen in the example network output in Figs. 4–6.

The specific fixed length of the time slices to use should be the greatest common factor of the durations of all the notes in the melodies to be learned. This ensures that the duration of every note will be represented properly with a whole number of time slices. For example, if our network were only to learn the melody A-B-C with corresponding durations quarter-note, eighth-note, and dotted quarter-note, we would use time slices of eighth-note duration. The sequence the network would learn would then be {A, A, B, C, C, C}.

With this duration representation, the context units now not only capture what pitches were used recently in the melody, but also for how long. This is because the longer a given note's duration is, the more time slices its pitch will appear at the output,

Fig. 5. Network output using interpolation between two melodies. (a) Melody 1, trained with plan 1.0. (b) Interpolation output using a plan of 0.8. (c) Interpolation output using a plan of 0.7. (d) Interpolation output using a plan of 0.5; an additional 34 successive time-slices (68 total) are shown to indicate longer-term behavior. (e) Interpolation output using a plan of 0.2. (f) Melody 2, trained with plan 0.0.

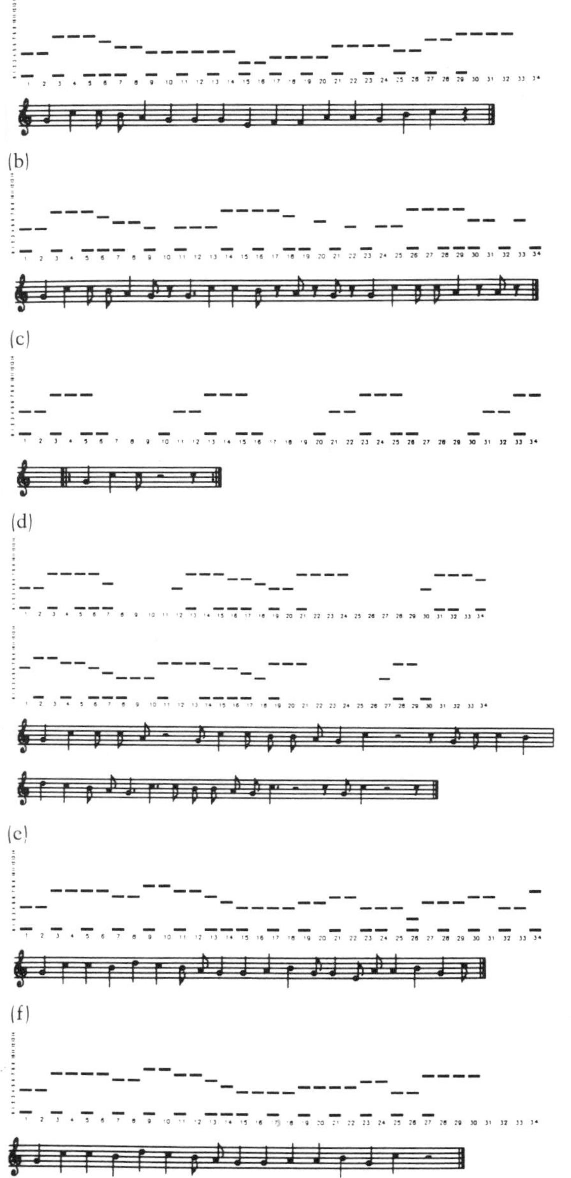

Fig. 6. Network output using altered melody space. (a) Melody 3, trained using plan vector (0.0, 1.0). (b) Melody 4, trained using plan vector (1.0, 1.0). (c) Interpolation output between melodies 1 and 2, incorporating training on 3 and 4, using plan vector (0.5, 0.0). (d) Interpolation output between melodies 1 and 2, trained with 8 hidden units, using a plan of 0.5. (e) Interpolation output between melodies 1 and 2, retrained with 15 hidden units, using a plan of 0.5.

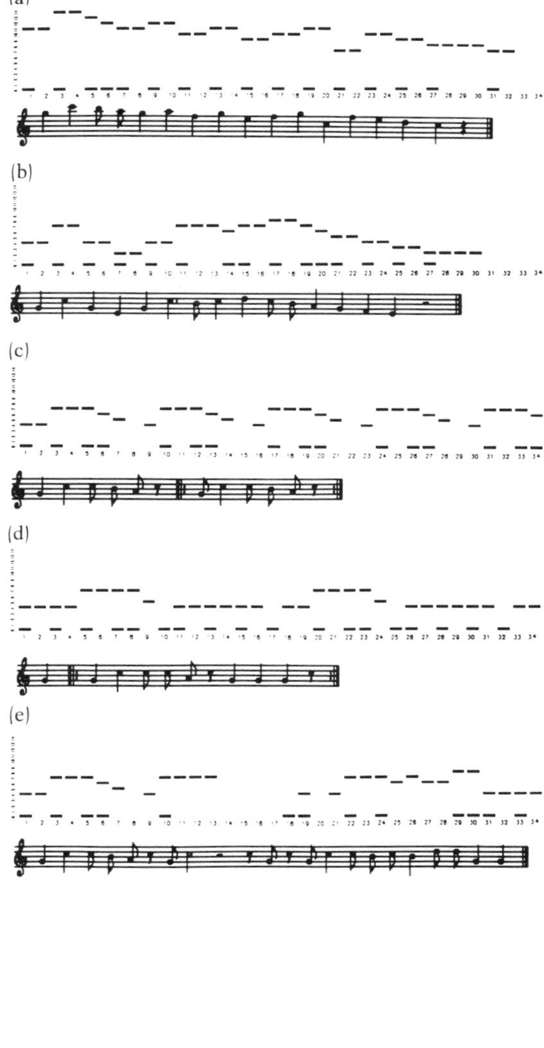

and the greater the corresponding built-up context will be. Returning to the previous example, the context activation for pitch C will be greater than that for pitch B, since C was present for more time slices at the output. This combination of pitch and duration information seems like a useful type of context memory for melody production, which is another reason the current representation was chosen.

An additional piece of information must be included in the network's output when using time slices to represent duration. This is an indication of the time slices on which any notes begin. Without this indication, we would not be able to tell whether the network output {A, A} meant two notes of pitch A, each lasting one time slice, or one note of pitch A that is two time slices in duration. It is essential that our representation allows this distinction to be made, otherwise the network would be unable to deal with melodies with repeated notes of the same pitch.

For this reason, an additional note-begin marking unit is added to the output (and context), as shown in Fig. 3. This unit is on for those time slices in which a new note is begun and off when the time slice merely covers the continuation of a previously started note. The necessary inclusion of this note-begin unit makes the time-slice approach less clean than we might hope, but it still seems more succinct in some ways than having both pitch and duration units in the output. The tradeoff is that the number of output units is reduced when using time slices, but the number of steps in the sequence representation of any particular melody is increased. This is because there will usually be more time slices than notes, and for the duration-unit representation, only complete notes need to be produced at each sequence step.

The presence of the note-begin unit also complicates attempts at representing polyphonic sequences. In principle, it seems as though at each time slice, we should be able to turn on all the output pitch units that are present at the corresponding time in a polyphonic melody. Thus the pitches in chords and harmonic lines could all be represented simultaneously on the output units. The problem, though, is that for each pitch present, we need to be able to independently specify when the corresponding note began. This requires a separate note-begin marker for each pitch possible, which doubles the number of output units, or some other scheme to represent polyphonic onsets. This problem has not yet been solved reasonably, and so again all the examples that follow are monophonic.

Training and Running the Network

Once we have set up a sequential network with the proper number of plan, context, hidden, and output units, chosen a set of melodies for it to learn, and converted these into the appropriate representation, we are ready to train the network to produce these melodies. The steps to accomplish this could proceed as follows. First, the weights in the network would all be initialized to small random values for the beginning untrained state. Second, the particular plan for the first melody in the training set would be clamped onto the plan units (i.e., their activations would be set to the proper values). Next, the activations of the context units would be set to zero, so that we begin the sequence with a clean (empty) context. Then activity would be passed through the network, from the plan and context units (the zero-valued context units having no effect this first time), through the hidden units to the output units. There the final output values produced by the network would be compared to the desired target, namely the first time-slice pitch for the first melody, and the error between the two would be used to adjust the network weights by the method of back-propagation of error (Dolson 1989). Following this, the output values would be passed back along the feedback connections to be added into the current context, and then activity would be passed through the network again and once more compared to the next desired target.

We would repeat this process by cycling the outputs back to the context units, computing the next outputs and errors, and adjusting the weights accordingly for every time slice for the first melody. Then the context units would be set to zero again, the plan for the second melody clamped onto the plan units, and the whole process would be repeated for the new melody. This would continue for all the melodies in the training set until the total summed error produced by the network for this set was below some threshold (i.e., until the network could produce these melodies more or less without mistake).

Note that the outputs of the network change over the course of training. At first, in the untrained state, the outputs produced will be quite different from the desired target values. As the network learns, however, the outputs will get closer and closer to the targets until they are sufficiently close and training can stop. This also means that the context values used by the network will change during training. The contexts computed for a given melody at the beginning of training will be very different from those computed at the end when the melody has been learned, because the contexts are being formed from the changing, fed-back output values. Thus the actual mapping task being learned by the network is not constant: its input values (at the context units) change during training, though its target values remain fixed. In essence the network is shooting at a moving target; as it adjusts its performance and hence its output and context values, what it is trying to learn changes as well. This complicates its learning task.

There is a way around this problem, however. Consider the network after it has successfully learned all the melodies in the training set. In this case, the outputs will all match the targets, and we could feed back the outputs or the targets to the context units with the same effect. This is in fact the actual final mapping we want the network to learn—from the correct outputs (the targets) via the context units to the next output. We may just as well set up this final mapping throughout the entire procedure as the one the network is to learn. This means that, instead of feeding back the output values during training, we should feed back the *target* values and construct the contexts using them. Now the mapping to be learned by the network will not change over the course of training (since the targets remain the same throughout), and the training phase will be much shorter.

One further adjustment can help the training process go more smoothly. Since we are using a localist representation of the monophonic melody pitches, only one output pitch unit will be on at a time, while all the rest are to be zero. In order to accommodate this trend, the network will first learn to turn off all the output units all the time, since this is quite close to the correct behavior and is easily achieved by lowering the biases to the outputs. If we let the network proceed this way initially, it could take a long time to correct this overzealous behavior. Therefore, we would like the impetus to turn the units off (when the target is zero) to be less strong than the impetus to turn them on (when the target is one). This way, the network is less likely to merely turn all the units off. We can accomplish this by using half the normal error whenever the target is zero: that is, in this case use $E = 0.5*(t - o)$, where E is the error at a particular output unit, t is that unit's target value, and o is its actual activation, instead of $E = (t - o)$ as usual (this error is then squared for further computational use). This is the strategy used for the simulations discussed here.

The length of the training process for a particular network and melody set, measured in the number of epochs (cycles through the entire training set), depends on the size of the network, the number of training melodies and their relatedness to each other, and (at least) two network training parameters—the learning rate and the momentum (Dolson 1989). Typically, low learning rates (on the order of 0.05) and high momenta (around 0.8) seem appropriate for the melody learning tasks investigated so far. To give approximate figures on the number of epochs needed in some different training situations, using these parameter values a network with 15 output units and 15 hidden units learned one short melody (34 time steps, as in the examples to come) in 2,000 epochs. To learn two such melodies, 5,500 epochs were required; for four, 8,500 epochs were needed. When fewer hidden units were used in the network—8 instead of 15—it took nearly 50,000 epochs to learn the same two melodies that took 5,500 epochs in the previous case, indicating the increased difficulty of squeezing the needed information into fewer weights. Such training times can translate into many hours of computational time, depending on the hardware used.

In contrast to the slow learning these networks often exhibit, their performance once trained is practically instantaneous. This is because no learning is being computed, and so cycling through a melody once to see how it comes out can go very quickly. During performance, we feed back the actual output values rather than the context values, so that if the network begins to produce different output values (due to our manipulations on it, as will be described shortly), these will affect the stored context and thus the outputs produced in the future. If the target values were fed back during performance, they would always tend to pull the network back toward producing the outputs it was trained to make.

When using the network to produce melodies, one more mechanism should be added to ensure proper behavior. Because we only want one output pitch unit on at a time with the present representation, we should process the final output values to make sure this is so, before the outputs are passed back to the context units or used elsewhere (such as to play the melody on a synthesizer). To accomplish this, we merely choose the output unit with the highest activation above 0.5 and set its new activation to 1.0, while all the others are set to 0.0. If no pitch units have activation above 0.5, this output is interpreted as a rest, and all activations are set to 0.0. By cleaning up the output activations in this way, we guarantee that the context values will accurately reflect just those pitches that were produced in the current sequence. Similarly, the note-begin unit's value is cleaned up, i.e., set to 0.0 or 1.0 depending on which side of 0.5 its original activation lies.

All of the simulations described hereafter were run using SunNet (Miyata 1987), a noncommercial back-propagation learning system implemented in C for use on Sun Microsystems computers. SunNet allows the writing of specialized network training and testing routines using its own internal programming language, giving great flexibility to the possible simulations. Most of the things described here could also be accomplished using *bp*, the back-propagation simulator available in McClelland and Rumelhart's (1988) *Explorations in Parallel Distributed Processing.*

Using the Network for Composition

Once we have trained a sequential network to produce one or more particular melodies, we can begin to use it to compose *new* melodies based on what it has learned. Because the plan vector is the major component of the network controlling which melody is produced, one way to produce new melodies is to give the network new plans. Depending on how many melodies the network was trained on, this will be done in different ways.

Unless otherwise stated, all of the network examples discussed in the following sections used 15 output units—1 note-begin unit and 14 pitch units—corresponding to the pitches in the key of C from D4 to C6, with no accidentals. They also used 15 context units, all with self-feedback connections of strength 0.7, and 15 hidden units. All of the original trained melodies used were 34 time slices in length, padded at the end with rests (as shown in the music notation). Each time slice corresponds to an eighth-note in duration, so that the original melodies are all approximately four measures long. For ease of discussion and interpretation, all the melodies produced by the networks in these examples are presented both in a modified piano-roll notation, with the pitch and the value of the note-begin unit at each time slice indicated individually, and in standard music notation.

Extrapolating from a Single Plan

If our network is trained on only one melody, then we have a single plan from which to extrapolate and choose new plans. For example, a network with a single plan unit was trained to produce melody 1 in Fig. 4a when given a plan of 1.0. Now we can instead give the network a different plan, by setting some other value onto its plan unit. If we let the network proceed with its normal performance, a new melody will be produced by first clearing the context units, then passing activation through the network, cleaning up and collecting the outputs, and cycling them back to the context units to repeat this process for a certain number of time slices.

As the examples in Figs. 4b–d show, a variety of behaviors are possible even in this simple situation. If we first use a plan of 0.0, we get the sequence shown in Fig. 4b, which quickly settles down into a repeating pattern that is 13 eighth-note time slices in length. This pattern, which first extends from time slice 12 to slice 24 and repeats thereafter, is constructed of chunks from various positions in the original melody—the first seven time slices match those at the end of melody 1 from slice 25 to 31, the next six match melody 1 from slice 5 to 10, and the interval from the final G to the beginning G matches the repeated Fs in melody 1 from slice 9 to 12. In essence, chunks of melody 1 that end with the same pitch that another chunk begins with have been spliced together to form the new melody. We will see this sort of behavior throughout the melodies composed by our networks, and the reason is relatively clear—when creating the new melody, the network continues to make the same sorts of transitions it did for the original trained melody (or melodies), occasionally switching to a different point in the original when the contexts (i.e., the pitches most recently played) more closely match that other point. This splicing-at-matching context results in new melodies that are smooth, mostly lacking sudden odd pitch intervals, but still interestingly different from the originals. At first glance, this is similar to behavior we would see in a Markov transition table process trained on this melody, but there are important differences, as will be described below.

The short melodic pattern in Fig. 4b can be seen to repeat indefinitely if we continue to cycle the network beyond the length of the original melody. Such repetition is common to the composed melodies in general. On an intuitive level, this can be explained by the fact that the network has spliced together the beginning and end of the phrase because this matches an interval (the repeated G quarter-notes) from the original melody 1. A more theoretical explanation for this behavior will be provided below.

Similar splicing and repetition can be seen in the sequence in Fig. 4c, produced with a plan of 2.0. In this case, the repeating phrase is also 13 time slices long and matches melody 1 from slice 3 to 14, with the addition of an extra eighth-note C as the second note. The interval from the end of the phrase (G) back to the beginning (C) matches the initial G-C interval in melody 1.

It is unclear where the additional eighth-note C in this melody arises exactly; the fact that there are four time slices worth of C matches the held C at the end of melody 1, but the extra eighth-note (caused by the note-begin unit coming on) is unprecedented. In fact, with most of these network-composed melodies, it is the rhythm (the pattern of note-begins) that is most inexplicable. This is probably because it is hardest for the network to learn when the note-begin unit should be on or off, as compared to which pitch unit should be on; the context is more useful for telling the next pitch than the next note-begin. Thus in the new melodies the pitch will often change without a corresponding note-begin, or a note-begin will be indicated during a rest (for example, see Fig. 4b, time slices 7 and 8). This shows that the network has not fully learned the relationships between pitch-changes or rests and note-begins. Perhaps with more training this relationship would be learned, or perhaps an alternate duration representation scheme, such as those described above, would solve this problem. For now, the melodies produced are interpreted as having note-begins whenever the network generates them and whenever the output changes pitch.

If we increase the plan value still further, to 3.0 for example, we get the interesting rhythmic pattern shown in Fig. 4d. Now we have the G-C interval from the beginning of melody 1 and the C-rest interval from the end of the melody. Because the context decays toward all zeros during the rest, and thus becomes closer to the initial all-zero context state, another G is generated. Interestingly, G-C-rest phrases of two different lengths are produced in this way, in alternation. The reason for this is again unclear; not everything produced by this composition method is predictable, but therein lies much of the usefulness and interest of this approach.

The network is not merely creating a transition-probability matrix and implementing a Markov process. First, unlike a Markov process, the network's behavior is deterministic: given a certain plan, the network will always produce the same sequence as output. Secondly, though the network's next output is dependent on past outputs, like a Markov process, in this case the network uses a memory of its entire past (in the decaying context), rather than just one or two previous steps (that is, the network's state is essentially infinite). Thirdly, and perhaps most importantly, the network can generalize to produce reasonable ouputs for new contexts it has never encountered before. The behavior of a Markov process is undefined for states that are not in its transition matrix. The network, though, will do similar things for similar contexts, even when given a new context. This lets it produce new melodies quite different from those it was originally trained on. Finally, using different plans does not correspond to anything in the Markov process case, except perhaps for switching to whole new transition matrices. Thus we must conclude that the network is doing something else, a topic I will address shortly.

Interpolating Between Multiple Plans

If we train our original network with more than one melody, each having a different plan, then we can generate new melodies by specifying new plans interpolated between the trained ones. As expected, these interpolated melodies share features of the parent melodies between which they are interpolated, more or less in proportion to how similar their plans are to those of the originals.

The melodies in Fig. 5 show this effect. A network with a single plan unit was trained to produce melody 1 with a plan of 1.0 (Fig. 5a), while melody 2 was trained with a plan of 0.0 (Fig. 5f). With a plan of 0.8, the melody shown in Fig. 5b was produced, matching melody 1 primarily up to time slice 14, at which point it makes a transition back to melody 1's beginning; the same thing happens again at slice 26. Little influence of melody 2 can be seen. With a plan of 0.7 (Fig. 5c), though, we get a repeating rhythmic pattern consisting of the G-C transition that begins both melodies 1 and 2, followed by the rest that ends melody 2 after its final G-C transition. A plan of 0.5 (Fig. 5d)—halfway between the two original plans—produces phrases that are complex hybrids of both original melodies. Extra time slices are included in this case to show the behavior of the network beyond the original 34 time slices. Finally, a plan of 0.2 (Fig. 5e) yields a melody starting in a very similar manner to melody 2, but with traces of melody 1, especially the G-E transition at slice 25. Melody 2 does not even contain a E.

Note that even if we change the plan continuously between 0.0 and 1.0, the melodies generated will not change continuously. That is, all plans from 1.0 down to about 0.85 will generate melody 1; all plans from 0.85 down to about 0.73 will generate the melody in Fig. 5b; and so on down to plan 0.0 for melody 2. These discrete bands of different melodies are caused by the effect of the weights from the plan unit (or units when more than one is used) on the hidden units (see Fig. 3). These weights act as biases on the hidden units, causing them to compute different functions of the context values. The context values can be thought of as points in some higher-dimensional space, and the hidden units act as planes to cut this space up into regions for different outputs. Only when these planes have been shifted enough to put some of the context points in different regions will the output melodies be changed. The plans must change quite a bit before they shift the hidden unit planes sufficiently; thus we get bands in which the same melody is generated for different but nearby plans.

In interpolating between two melodies in this way, the network is not simply computing a weighted average of the pitches of the original two melodies, as Mathews did in his graphic score manipulation language GRIN, when he combined *The British Grenadiers* and *When Johnny Comes Marching Home* (Mathews and Rosler 1968). A violation of such averaging can be seen in the case of the E at time slice 26 in the interpolated melody in Fig. 5e, where both original melodies 1 and 2 have a G at this position. Moreover, the network is not computing any strict function of the particular pitches of the original melodies on a time-slice by time-slice basis; proof of this is seen again in the melody in Fig. 5e, which has a G at time slice 25 just before the E at slice 26, even though both melodies 1 and 2 have Fs at both time slices. Thus even though the original melodies are the same at both of these positions, the new melody is different, indicating that something more than just the momentary pitches of the originals is going into its creation (as we would suspect from the previous discussion of spliced transitions).

Interpretations

One way to think about what the network actually is doing is in terms of constructing a complicated, higher-dimensional melody space, with each point in that space corresponding to a melody. The network learns to put one melody at a point identified by the first plan, another melody at a point identified by the second plan, and so on for all the melodies and plans in the training set. When it is given intermediate (or extrapolated) plans, the network then indexes some new point in the melody space between (or beyond) the original melodies. Depending on the structure of the melody space constructed, different new melodies will be produced.

The melody space can be altered in many ways. If we train a network on additional melodies, for instance, the new things it learns will change the space. For example, suppose we train a network with two plan units on melodies 1 and 2 from before and on melodies 3 and 4 as shown in Figs. 6a and 6b, with plans (0.0, 0.0), (1.0, 0.0), (0.0, 1.0), and (1.0, 1.0), respectively. Now if we interpolate between just melodies 1 and 2 as before, by using a plan of (0.5, 0.0), we get the result shown in Fig. 6c. This is quite different from the corresponding interpolated melody in Fig. 5d, when the network was trained only on melodies 1 and 2. Another way to alter the melody space and the resulting composed melodies is to use a different number of hidden units. If we train a network with only 8 hidden units (instead of the 15 used in all other cases) on melodies 1 and 2 with a single plan unit and then use a plan of 0.5 again to interpolate between them, we get the (different) pattern shown in Fig. 6d. Finally, simply retraining the same network design on the same melodies can give different melody spaces each time, due to the random starting point of each training session. Figure 6e shows the interpolation result of using plan 0.5 with the same network and melodies as in Fig. 5, but after going through a different training session. Again the new melody is different from all the others in this discussion.

Now let us go to the opposite extreme of analysis and consider the network's behavior during a single sequence at the time-slice by time-slice level, instead of the whole population of sequences. What the network has learned to do here is to associate particular patterns at the input layer, the context and plan units, with particular patterns at the output units. This pattern association is a type of rule-governed behavior; the network has learned rules of the form "these past pitches mean this pitch is next." Bharucha and Todd (1989) present an example of this behavior in the case of learning chord progressions. These rules emerge from the data the network is trained on. The more often particular sorts of transitions are seen in the training set, the stronger the corresponding pattern-association rule becomes. Furthermore, the nature of the network's computation lets these rules generalize to new situations and new contexts that did not occur in the training set. This generalization occurs based on the similarity of the new situations to prototype situations the network has learned about. This type of generalization is a crucial difference between the network's behavior and that of strict, rule-based compositional systems. Additionally, the rules the network develops are not really symbolic, as they are in most other compositional systems, but rather are stated at a lower descriptive level of vectors of past pitch activity.

Finally, from an intermediate perspective, we can consider the network as it produces an ongoing single sequence. Jordan (1986b) has shown that sequential networks of this type, being nonlinear dynamical systems, can develop attractor limit cycles, that is, repeating sequences that other sequences can fall into. The examples discussed previously showed several instances of this behavior. For instance, the repeating patterns shown in Figs. 4b–d and 5c are limit cycles—once the network begins producing one of these patterns (for the given plan), it will remain locked in this cycle. These limit cycles can be quite short, as in these instances, or quite long, perhaps not emerging until the network has been run for many time slices beyond the length of the original trained melodies. Furthermore, similar sequences are likely to be sucked into these cycles: if we were to alter the initial context, it would only take a few time slices for the sequence to fall back into the original repeating pattern.

Other Methods for Generating New Melodies

The sequential networks presented here are not limited to plan interpolation and extrapolation for creating new melodies. Many other methods are possible. For example, the plan could be changed dynamically throughout the course of the generated melody so that the new sequence might begin close to one of the trained melodies and end close to another. The context could be altered in various ways, either before melody generation to provide a nonzero starting point, or during melody generation to provide more or less sudden shifts to different melodic points. The weights in the network could be changed randomly (or systematically) to alter the overall behavior of the network and probably make it more unpredictable and less likely to mimic the melodies in the training set. Additionally, the network could be treated in a probabilistic, nondeterministic way, by training the output units to have activation levels corresponding to their melodic strength in a particular context, and then actually picking the output to be used in a probabilistic manner based on these levels. In this case, the stronger a pitch fits a particular context, the more likely it is to be picked as the actual output, but other weaker candidates always have a chance of being chosen as well. This probabilistic behavior comes closer to that of a Markov process, but still remains distinct.

Applications and Further Directions

The sequential network described here can be a useful tool for the algorithmic composition of melodic sequences similar, in some ways, to a set of chosen melodies. This method has at least one great advantage over other, rule-based methods of algorithmic composition, which is that explicit rules need not be devised. Rather, the composer need only collect examples of the desired sorts of musical sequences and train the network on them. The training phase, while time-consuming, is automatic, and once done, the network can produce a large variety of melodies based on those it has learned. These new melodies, while incorporating important elements of the training set, remain more or less unpredictable and therefore musically interesting.

As it now stands, the place for this network method of composition is restricted to generating relatively short musical lines, high in local structure but lacking in overall global organization. Still, this can be very useful for generating new phrases based on previously composed examples, for coming up with new rhythmic patterns and interpolating between them, or, if the pitch units are instead interpreted as chord units, for coming up with new chord progressions using elements of old ones. This method can also find use as a means of overcoming composer's block, as suggested by David Cope as one of the applications of his EMI system (Cope 1987).

To extend the network's usefulness to a broader range of musical applications, several problems need to be overcome. First, the network's music representation should be improved to allow polyphony, as well as other musical parameters beyond just pitch and duration. A better way of handling rhythm and timing needs to be developed. Some method for letting the network learn variable-length pattern associations is needed so that it can insert ornamentations or delete passages from sequences. And most importantly, the length of sequences that the network can learn must be increased. This can be improved by the addition of other forms of context, such as a global clock or counter added to the inputs. But the real solution will lie in developing a method for letting the network learn the hierarchical organization of sequences, so that melodies need not be treated as simply one long flat string of notes with no higher-level structure. Approaches such as using the outputs of one slow-moving sequential network as the successive plans of another faster-paced sequence network have been suggested, but the problem remains of learning how to divide the hierarchical structure between the networks involved.

Conclusions

The sequential network methods presented here can be profitable avenues for the exploration of new approaches to algorithmic composition. By training networks on selected melodies and then using the network's inherent, rule-like generalization ability and limit-cycle dynamics, new melodies similar to the original training examples can be generated. The variety of musical patterns that can be created under this one unifying approach indicate its potential for useful application. The possibilities for further work expanding the capabilities of this approach are virtually limitless.

Acknowledgments

This research was supported by a National Science Foundation Graduate Fellowship. Any opinions, findings, conclusions, or recommendations expressed in this publication are those of the author and do not necessarily reflect the views of the National Science Foundation. I wish to thank Dave Rumelhart, Jamshed Bharucha, and Gareth Loy for their encouragement in this research, and Mary Ann Norris for her aid in preparing this paper.

References

Bharucha, J. J., and P. M. Todd. 1989. "Modeling the Perception of Tonal Structure with Neural Nets." *Computer Music Journal* 13(4):44–53.

Cope, D. 1987. "An Expert System for Computer-assisted Composition." *Computer Music Journal* 11(4):30–46.

Dolson, M. 1989. "Machine Tongues XII: Introduction to Neural Nets." *Computer Music Journal* 13(3):00–00.

Elman, J. L. 1988. "Finding Structure in Time." Technical Report 8801. La Jolla: University of California, Center for Research in Language.

Jones, K. 1981. "Compositional Applications of Stochastic Processes." *Computer Music Journal* 5(2):45–61.

Jordan, M. I. 1986a. "Serial Order: A Parallel Distributed Processing Approach." Technical Report ICS-8604. La Jolla: University of California, Institute for Cognitive Science.

Jordan, M. I. 1986b. "Attractor Dynamics and Parallelism in a Connectionist Sequential Machine." *Proceedings of the Eighth Annual Conference of the Cognitive Science Society.* Hillsdale, N.J.: Erlbaum Associates.

Mathews, M. V., and L. Rosler. 1968. "Graphical Language for the Scores of Computer-generated Sounds." *Perspectives of New Music* 6:92–118.

McClelland, J. L., and D. E. Rumelhart. 1988. *Explorations in Parallel Distributed Processing.* Cambridge, Massachusetts: MIT Press.

Miyata, Y. 1987. "SunNet Version 5.2: A Tool for Constructing, Running, and Looking into a PDP Network in a Sun Graphics Window." Technical Report ICS-8708. La Jolla: University of California, Institute for Cognitive Science.

Rumelhart, D. E., and J. L. McClelland, eds. 1986. *Parallel Distibuted Processing: Explorations in the Microstructure of Cognition.* Cambridge, Massachusetts: MIT Press.

Sejnowski, T. J., and C. R. Rosenberg. 1987. "Parallel Networks that Learn to Pronounce English Text." *Complex Systems* 1:145–168.

Todd, P. M. 1988. "A Sequential Network Design for Musical Applications." In D. Touretzky, G. Hinton, and T. Sejnowski, eds. *Proceedings of the 1988 Connectionist Models Summer School.* Menlo Park, California: Morgan Kaufmann.

Waibel, A., et al. 1987. "Phoneme Recognition Using Time-Delay Neural Networks." Technical Report TR-I-0006. ATR Interpreting Telephony Research Laboratories.

Addendum

One of the largest problems with this sequential network approach is the limited length of sequences that can be learned and the corresponding lack of global structure that new compositions exhibit. Hierarchically organized and connected sets of sequential networks hold promise for addressing these difficulties. Several ways of passing control back and forth between the interconnected networks will be described and the remaining issue of learning hierarchical structures will be addressed in this addendum.

The limitation of learnable sequence length faced by the sequential networks used in this chapter is caused by at least two factors. First, these networks learn each sequence in a flat, unstructured way; each note simply follows the previous ones in a long string, with no higher-level organization to aid in recall. Second, repeated sections, which ought to help learning, can actually hinder it, as Jordan (1986a) has pointed out. For instance, if a network with a short context-memory span was trained on the sequence ABCDEEEABCDGG, it might have difficulty learning to produce E-E-E after the first occurrence of the A-B-C-D phrase and G-G after the second occurrence, because the contexts after each occurrence might be too similar to be properly distinguished.

One solution to these problems is first to take the sequence to be learned and divide it up into appropriate chunks (for instance, in the case of the sequence just presented, these could be A-B-C-D, E-E-E, A-B-C-D, and G-G). Next, train a sequential network to produce each of these subsequence chunks with a different plan. Finally, give this network the appropriate sequence of subsequence plans so that it will produce the chunks in the proper order to recreate the entire original pattern. Of course, one way to present this subsequence-generating network with the appropriate sequence of plans is to generate *those* by another sequential network, operating at a slower time scale. Then, by connecting the outputs of that superordinate network to the plan units of the subordinate one, longer sequences may be generated as sets of successive subsequences. These sequences can exhibit greater global structure by virtue of their hierarchical generation. Furthermore, repeated sections now *help* performance, decreasing the number of subsequence chunks that must be learned. A pair of these hierarchically connected sequential networks is show in Fig. 7. For convenience we will call the subordinate subsequence-generating network the *subnet*, and the superordinate subsequence-*plan*-generating network the *supernet*.

These two networks could work together as follows: Each subsequence is assigned an appropriate plan for the subnet to use, as well as a number (for example, 1 for A-B-C-D, 2 for E-E-E, and 3 for G-G). Each supernet output unit corresponds in a localist fashion to one of the subsequences, so that when the *Nth* output unit is turned on, it causes the plan for subsequence *N* to appear on the subnet's plan units. The supernet is trained to produce the necessary sequence of plans, in this case corresponding to 1-2-1-3. To reproduce the entire example sequence, then, the supernet would first output (1,0,0) (turning on just the first output unit, given that there are three), and the subnet would produce the first subsequence, A-B-C-D. Once the subnet was done, the supernet would clear out the subnet's context (to prevent interference between subsequences) and then output the number of the next subsequence to be generated (in this case, (0,1,0) for the second subsequence). The subnet would produce E-E-E. Then the supernet would continue, clearing the subnet context, and outputting first (1,0,0) again, and finally (0,0,1). With this, the entire original sequence would be reproduced.

But one crucial step has been left out of this description: How does the supernet know when to produce the next subsequence plan, and when to sit still and wait for the subnet to finish? There are several ways to achieve this "control passing" between the two networks. Most simply, the supernet could just operate at a fixed rate a few times slower than the subnet. For instance, the supernet could operate at a quarter the speed of the subnet, outputting one subsequence plan for every four outputs of the subnet, and thus structuring the original sequence into subsequences of length four. This approach, though, requires chunking up the original sequence into subsequences all exactly the same

Fig. 7. Two hierarchically connected sequential networks for generating structured sequences. The supernet produces a sequence of plans that control the subsequences produced by the subnet.

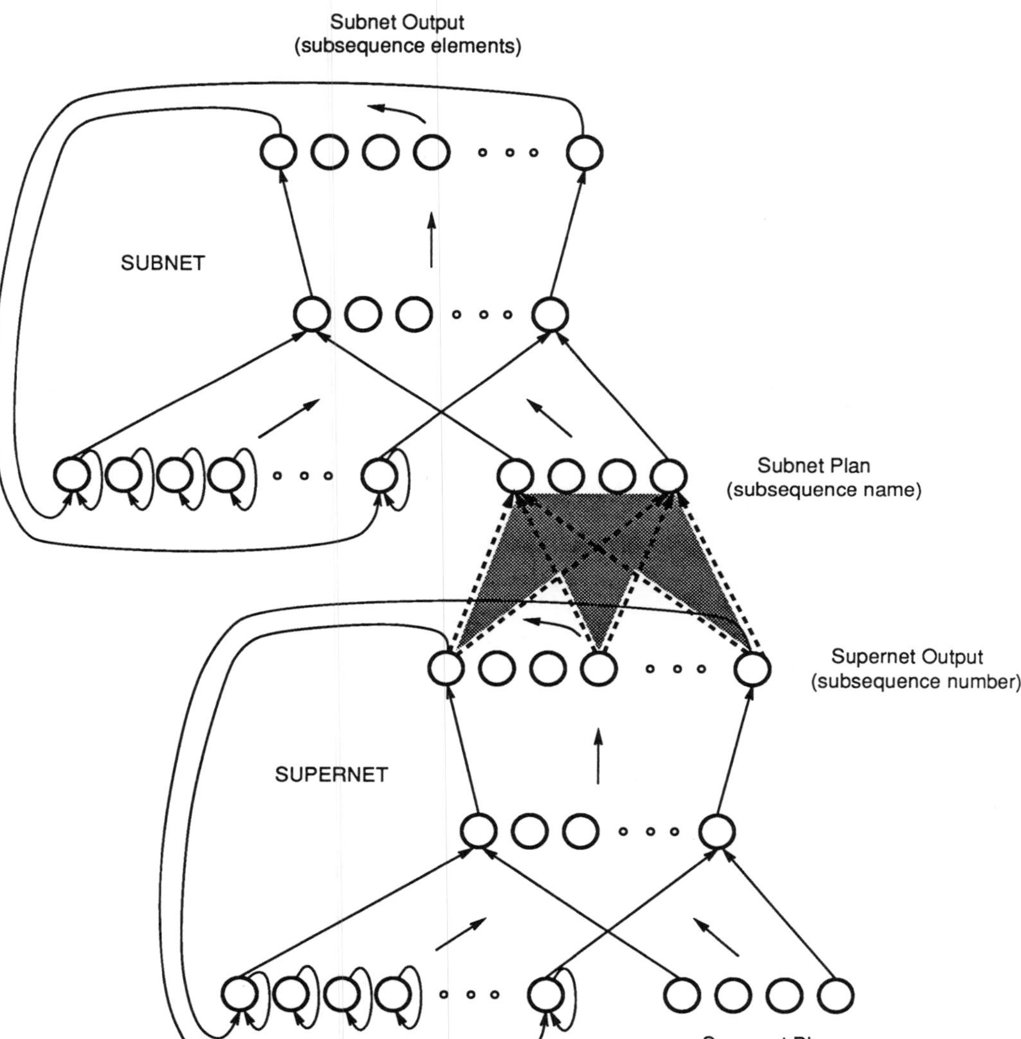

length, which will usually be inappropriate. The example sequence used above, for instance, cannot be sensibly divided up into subsequences of any one particular fixed length.

A second method of passing control from subnet to supernet avoids the problem of fixed-length subsequences. In this case, a new unit is added to the output of the subnet, which indicates that a subsequence is done when it is turned on. The subnet is trained with subsequence patterns having this end-marking unit on in the final output (i.e., simultaneous with the D in the subsequence A-B-C-D). During sequence production, the supernet monitors this unit's activity, and when it sees the unit on, it clicks over one step, clears out the old subnet context, and produces the next subsequence plan. Each subsequence can now be whatever length is appropriate. This method is straightforward and only requires minor alteration of the subsequences to be learned.

It is worth briefly mentioning how the supernet can be made to "click over" in response to the activity of the subsequence-end-marker unit. This unit can be connected to sigma-pi units in the feedback connections of the supernet (see Fig. 8), which gate the flow of activity from the supernet's output units back to its context units. Such a setup allows the supernet actually to be run at the same rate as the subnet. When the end-marker unit is off, no activity will flow back to the supernet context units, so the context values will not change, and hence the supernet output values will not change either. (This setup actually requires the additional complication of having the end-marker unit control the self-feedback values on the context units so that they don't cause a change in context values until the subsequence is done, but this can be accomplished in a similar fashion with sigma-pi units.) Only when the end-marker unit comes on will the sigma-pi units pass activations back to the supernet context units and allow the supernet to produce its next subsequence plan output. Thus units can be updated in the supernet in sync with the subnet; the supernet's outputs just will not change until a subsequence is finished.

Still another method of passing control, attributed to Jordan, is to use a preset plan that is decremented by each subnet output and that clicks the supernet when it reaches zero. This idea has the advantage of not requiring the addition of a subsequence-end marker, but it does require precomputing appropriate plans so that the decrementing will work, as well as additional network connections to implement the decrementing. For instance, if the subsequence A-B-D is to be produced, and there are four output and plan units, then the plan (1,1,0,1) could be used. After the subnet outputs the initial A, represented by output vector (1,0,0,0), negative connections from the output units to the plan units will subtract this vector from the plan, leaving a new plan of (0,1,0,1). Similarly, after the B, or (0,1,0,0), is generated at the output, the plan will be decremented to (0,0,0,1). Finally, after the D, or (0,0,0,1), is generated, the plan will be reduced to all zeros, and the supernet will be nudged into producing the next plan. This approach must be augmented with a way of distinguishing between plans for subsequences that include the same elements in different orders (AB and BA, for example) for it to be useful. But the notion of a changing plan that adjusts to the remaining subsequence elements to be generated is certainly interesting and invites further investigation.

A final technique for signaling the completion of subsequences is to use plans equal to the final context vector for each subsequence. Then, whenever the context becomes the same as the plan, the network has reached the last element in the current subsequence and should start in on the next. This method similarly requires precomputing the plans to be used, but this is easily done, and it avoids the previous drawbacks of fixed subsequence size, altered subsequence structure, and additional network connections. Whether or not the context-based plans are structured to allow easy subsequence learning, though, remains to be seen; it is possible that self-learned plans, which could be used by the first two methods, could greatly improve overall sequence-learning performance in comparison.

The adoption of one of these control-passing methods allows the piggy-backed sequential network system to produce hierarchically organized sequences of relatively great length more or less automatically. (Note, too, that additional super-

Fig. 8. A method of passing control from the subnet back to the supernet. Here when the subnet's subsequence has finished, the end-marking unit comes on and allows the sigma-pi units to gate the supernet's context feedback connections and enable it to produce the next subsequence plan.

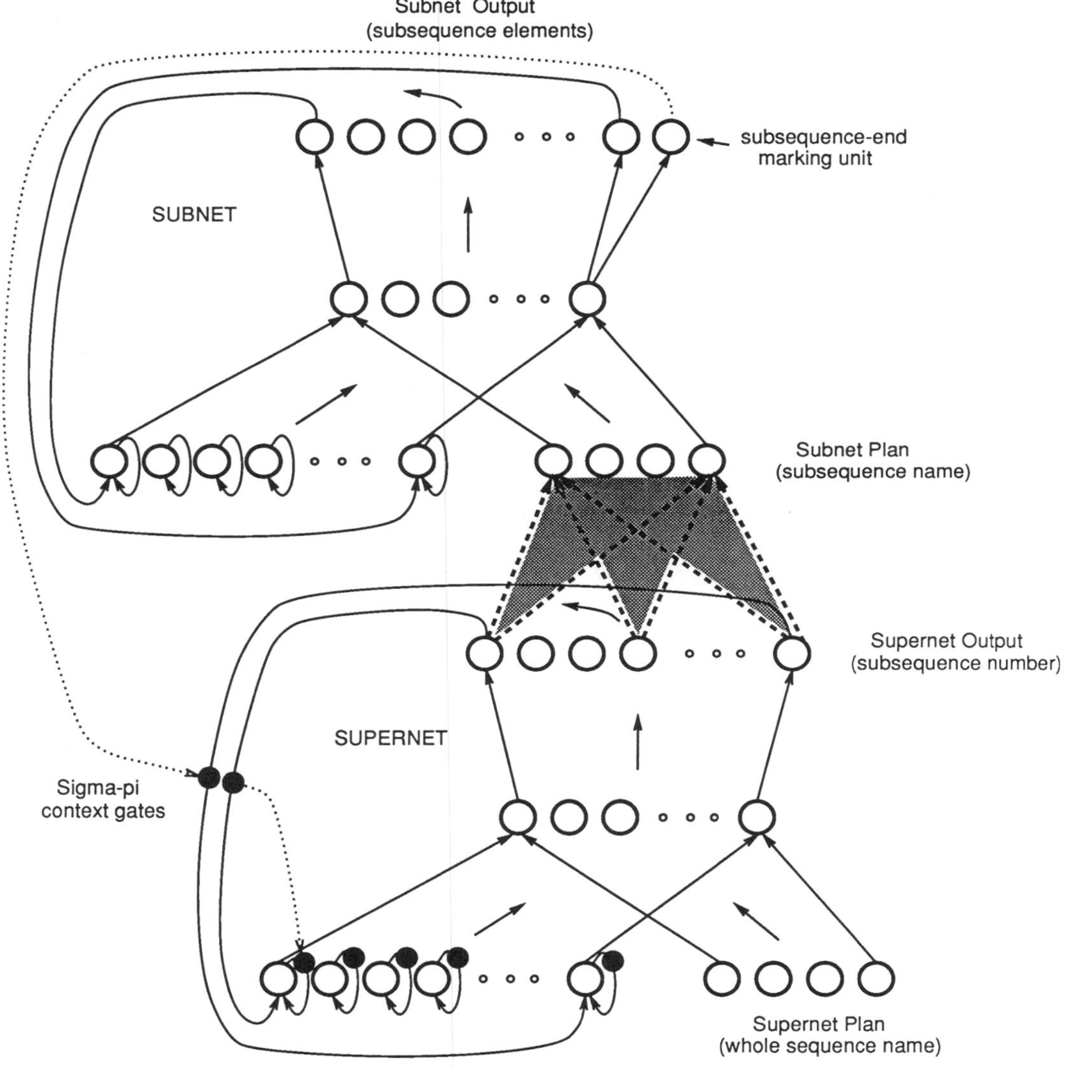

superordinate sequential networks can be added at higher and higher levels to allow increasing length and structural depth in the sequences produced.) The preceding discussion assumes, however, that the original sequence to be learned has already been divided up into appropriate chunks for the subnet to produce. But what we *really* want is this chunking itself to be done automatically, as well. That is, we would like the system to learn the hierarchical structure present in the sequence on its own and use this to divide up the task into appropriate subsequences (and sub-subsequences). This is the hard part. Miyata (1988, 1989) has proposed one method for learning hierarchical action plans in nested sequential networks similar to those described here. His method begins with equal-length subsequences and gradually adjusts these during learning into longer and longer subsequences for more efficient action performance. Although the results he describes in his published works are mostly restricted to rather short action sequences, Miyata has recently begun to apply this method successfully to musical passages of reasonable length.

Several other notions come to mind that could lead to workable methods for learning to cut a sequence into appropriate chunks. The sequence could be cut, and a new plan generated for the next portion, whenever the subnet's prediction error for an individual note in the current subsequence is greater than some threshold. That is, as soon as the current subsequence plan is stretched beyond its ability to produce successive notes accurately—as soon as the subsequence gets too long—one would clear out that plan and swap in a new one. (This is similar to Elman's (1988) analysis of sequence structure in linguistic sequences by looking at prediction error.) Or plan learning could be used in the subnet, but with "sticky" plan units that like to maintain their current values and only snap to new values all at once when the accumulated error back-propagated to them grows great enough. Or the subnet context vectors could be competitively clustered by an additional set of units, with each cluster corresponding to a different subsequence plan; in this case, similar contexts—those nearby in time—would be clustered to the same category, and hence the same plan, but contexts different enough from each other—far enough away in time—would be placed in different clusters, and be associated with different plans. All of these proposals are purposefully sketchy, because they have yet to be tried and may prove to be completely hopeless. But perhaps they contain the germ of an idea that will grow into a useful method for learning hierarchical sequence structure with further investigation.

References

Elman, J. L. 1988. "Finding Structure in Time." Technical Report CRL-8801. La Jolla: University of California at San Diego, Center for Research in Language.

Miyata, Y. 1988. "The Learning and Planning of Actions." Ph.D. diss. University of California at San Diego Psychology Department. Technical Report ICS-8707. La Jolla: University of California at San Diego, Institute for Cognitive Science.

Miyata, Y. 1989. "A PDP Model of Sequence Learning that Exhibits the Power Law." *Proceedings of the Eleventh Annual Conference of the Cognitive Science Society.* Hillsdale, N.J.: Erlbaum Associates, pp. 9–16.

Michael C. Mozer
Department of Computer Science &
Institute of Cognitive Science
University of Colorado
Boulder, CO 80309-0430
mozer@neuron.colorado.edu

Connectionist Music Composition Based on Melodic, Stylistic, and Psychophysical Constraints

In creating music, composers bring to bear a wealth of knowledge of musical conventions. Some of this knowledge is based on the experience of the individual, some is culture specific, and perhaps some is universal. No matter what the source, this knowledge acts to constrain the composition process, specifying, for example, the musical pitches that form a scale, the pitch or chord progressions that are agreeable, and stylistic conventions such as the division of a symphony into movements and the AABB form of a gavotte. If we hope to build automatic music composition systems that can mimic the abilities of a human composer, it will be necessary to incorporate knowledge of musical conventions into the systems. The difficulty is in deriving this knowledge in an explicit form: even human composers are unaware of many of the constraints under which they operate (Loy, this volume).

In this chapter, I describe a connectionist network that composes melodies. The network is called CONCERT, an acronym for CONnectionist Composer of ERudite Tunes. (The "ER" may also be read as ERratic or ERsatz, depending on what the listener thinks of its creations.) Musical knowledge is incorporated into CONCERT via two routes. First, CONCERT is trained on a set of sample melodies from which it extracts rules of note and phrase progressions, which I call *melodic and stylistic constraints.* Second, I have built a representation of pitch into CONCERT that is based on psychological studies of human perception. This representation, and an associated theory of generalization proposed by Shepard (1987), provides CONCERT with a basis for judging the similarity among notes, for selecting a response, and for restricting the set of alternatives that can be considered at any time. I call these constraints imposed by the representation *psychophysical constraints.*

My experiments have been with single-voice melodies, most having 10–20 notes, but I also report on preliminary work with longer pieces having about 150 notes. A complete model of music composition should describe each note by a variety of properties—pitch, duration, phrasing, accent—along with more global properties such as tempo and dynamics. In the experiments reported here, the problem has been stripped to its bare bones, describing a melody simply as a sequence of pitches. Extending the work to notes that vary in duration or other properties is relatively straightforward once the viability of the approach has been established. The burden of the present work has been to demonstrate that CONCERT can discover the appropriate structure in a set of pitch sequences presented to it.[1]

One potential pitfall in the research area of connectionist music composition is the uncritical acceptance of a network's performance. It is absolutely essential that a network be evaluated according to some objective criterion. One cannot judge the enterprise to be a success simply because the network is creating novel output. Even random note sequences played through a synthesizer sound interesting to many observers. Although Todd's (this volume) seminal work on connectionist composition shows great promise, it suffers by the lack of evaluation; consequently, one cannot verify that his network architecture and learning algorithm have the computational power to succeed. In contrast, CONCERT is motivated by well-defined computational goals, which provide the means for evaluating its performance.

Before turning to the details of my approach, I begin by describing a traditional approach to algorithmic music composition using Markov transition tables, the limitations of this approach, and how these limitations may be overcome using connectionist learning techniques.

Transition Table Approaches to Algorithmic Music Composition

One simple but interesting technique in algorithmic music composition is to select notes sequentially according to a *transition table* that specifies the probability of the next note as a function of the current note (Dodge and Jerse 1985; Jones 1981; Lorrain 1980). For example, the transition probabilities depicted in Table 1 constrain the next pitch to be one step up or down the C-major scale from the current pitch. Generating a sequence according to this probability distribution therefore results in a musical random walk. Transition tables may be hand constructed according to certain criteria, as in Table 1, or they may be set up to embody a particular musical style. In the latter case, statistics are collected over a set of examples (hereafter, the *training set*) and the transition table entries are defined to be the transition probabilities in these examples.

The transition table is a statistical description of the training set. In most cases, the transition table will lose information about the training set. To illustrate, consider the two sequences A-B-C and E-F-G. The transition table constructed from these examples will indicate that A goes to B with probability 1, B to C with probability 1, and so forth. Consequently, given the first note of each sequence, the table can be used to recover the complete sequence. However, with two sequences such as B-A-C and D-A-E, the transition table can only say that following an A either an E or a C occurs, each with a 50 percent likelihood. Thus, the table cannot be used to reconstruct the examples unambiguously.

Clearly, in melodies of any complexity, musical structure cannot be fully described by the pairwise statistics. To capture additional structure, the transition table can be generalized from a two-dimensional array to n dimensions. In the n-dimensional

Table 1. Transition probability from current pitch to the next

next	*current pitch*						
pitch	C	D	E	F	G	A	B
C	0	.5	0	0	0	0	.5
D	.5	0	.5	0	0	0	0
E	0	.5	0	.5	0	0	0
F	0	0	.5	0	.5	0	0
G	0	0	0	.5	0	.5	0
A	0	0	0	0	.5	0	.5
B	.5	0	0	0	0	.5	0

table, often referred to as a table of order $n-1$, the probability of the next note is indicated as a function of the previous $n-1$ notes. By increasing the number of previous notes taken into consideration, the table becomes more context sensitive, and therefore serves as a more faithful representation of the training set.[2] Unfortunately, extending the transition table in this manner gives rise to two problems. First, the size of the table explodes exponentially with the amount of context and rapidly becomes unmanageable. With, say, 50 alternative notes and a third-order transition table—modest sizes on both counts—6.25 million entries would be required. Second, a table representing the high-order structure masks the tremendous amount of low-order structure present. To elaborate, consider the sequence AFGBFGCFGDFG♯EFG. One would need to construct a third-order table to represent this sequence faithfully. Such a table would indicate that, for example, the sequence G-B-F is always followed by G. However, there are first-order regularities in the sequence that a third-order table does not make explicit, namely, the fact than an F is almost always followed by a G. The third-order table is thus unable to predict what will follow, say, A-A-F, although a first-order table would sensibly predict G. There is a tradeoff between the ability to faithfully represent the training set, which usually requires a high-order table, and the ability to generalize in novel contexts, which profits from a low-order table. What one would really like is a scheme by which only the *relevant* high-order structure is represented.

Kohonen (1989; Kohonen, Laine, Tiits, and Torkkola, this volume) has proposed exactly such a scheme. The scheme is a symbolic algorithm that, given a training set of examples, produces a collection of rules—a context-sensitive grammar—sufficient for reproducing most or all of the structure inherent in the set. These rules are of the form *context*→*next_note*, where *context* is a string of one or more notes, and *next_note* is the next note implied by the context. Because the context length can vary from one rule to the next, the algorithm allows for varying amounts of generality and specificity in the rules. The algorithm attempts to produce deterministic rules—rules that always apply in the given context. Thus, the algorithm will not discover the regularity F→G in the above sequence because it is not absolute. One could conceivably extend the algorithm to generate simple rules like F→G along with exceptions (e.g., DF→G♯), but the symbolic nature of the algorithm still leaves it poorly equipped to deal with statistical properties of the data. Such an ability is not critical if the algorithm's goal is to construct a set of rules from which the training set can be exactly reconstructed; however, my view is that music composition is an intrinsically random process, and it is therefore inappropriate to model every detail of the training set. Instead, the goal ought to be to capture the most important—statistically regular—structural properties of the training set.

Both the transition table approach and Kohonen's musical grammar suffer from two further drawbacks. First, both algorithms are designed so that a particular note, i, cannot be used to predict note $i+n$ unless all intervening notes, $i+1 \cdots i+n-1$, are also considered. In general, one would expect that the most useful predictor of a note is the immediately preceding note, but cases exist where notes $i \cdots i+k$ are more useful predictors of note $i+n$ than notes $i+k-1 \cdots i+n-1$ (e.g., a melody in which high-pitch and low-pitch phrases alternate, such as the solo violin partitas of J. S. Bach). The second drawback is that a symbolic representation of notes does not facilitate generalization. For instance, invariance under transposition is not directly representable. In addition, other similarities are not encoded, for example, the congruity of octaves.

Connectionist learning algorithms offer the potential of overcoming the various limitations of transition table approaches and Kohonen musical grammars. Connectionist algorithms are able to discover relevant structure and statistical regularities in sequences (e.g., Elman 1990; Mozer 1989). Indeed, connectionist algorithms can be viewed as an extension of the transition table approach, a point also noted by Dolson (this volume). Just as the transition table approach uses a training set to calculate the probability of the next note in a sequence as a function of the previous notes, so does CONCERT. The connectionist approach, however, is far more flexible: the form of the transition function can permit the consideration of varying amounts of context, the consideration of noncontiguous context, and the combination of low-order and high-order regularities.

The connectionist approach also promises better generalization through the use of distributed representations (Hinton, McClelland, and Rumelhart 1986). In a local representation, where each note is represented by a discrete symbol, the sort of statistical contingencies that can be discovered are among notes. In a distributed representation, however, where each note is represented by a set of continuous feature values, the sort of contingencies that can be discovered are among *features*. To the extent that two notes share features, featural regularities discovered for one note may transfer to the other note.

The CONCERT Architecture

CONCERT is a recurrent network architecture of the sort studied by Elman (1990). A melody is presented to it, one note at a time, and its task at each point in time is to predict the next note in the melody. Using a training procedure described below, CONCERT's connection strengths are adjusted so that it can perform this task correctly for a set of training examples. Each example consists of a sequence of notes. The current note in the sequence

Fig. 1. The CONCERT architecture. Rectangles indicate a layer of units, directed lines indicate full connectivity from one layer to another. The selection process is external to CONCERT and is used to choose among the alternatives proposed by the network during composition.

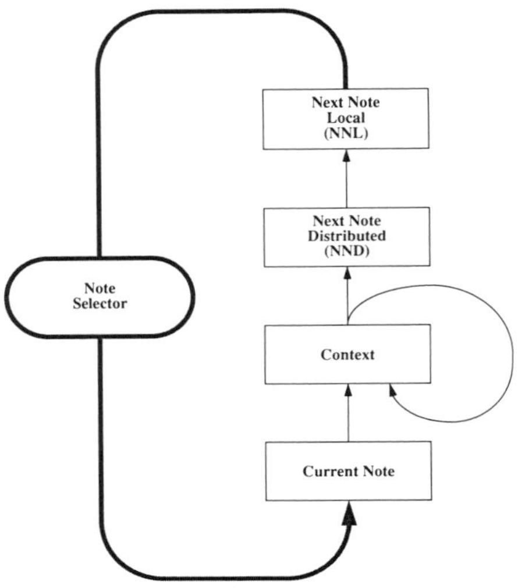

is represented in the input layer of CONCERT, and the prediction of the next note is represented in the output layer. As Fig. 1 indicates, the next note is encoded in two different ways: the next-note-distributed (or *NND*) layer contains CONCERT's internal representation of the note, while the next-note-local (or *NNL*) layer contains one unit for each alternative. The representation of a note in the NND layer, as well as in the input layer, is based on a psychological analysis of human pitch perception (Shepard 1982), which I explain in detail in a following section. For now, it should suffice to say that this representation is distributed, that is, a note is indicated by a *pattern* of activity across the units. Because such patterns of activity can be quite difficult to interpret, the NNL layer provides an alternative, explicit representation of the possibilities.

The context layer can represent relevant aspects of the input history, that is, the temporal context in which a prediction is made. When a new note is presented in the input layer, the activity pattern currently in the context layer is integrated with the new note to form a new context representation. In general terms,

$$\mathbf{c}(n) = f(\mathbf{c}(n-1), \mathbf{x}(n)),$$

where $\mathbf{x}(n)$ is a vector representing the nth note in the input sequence, $\mathbf{c}(n)$ is the context activity pattern following processing of input note n—which I refer to as *step* n—and f is a member of the class of functions that can be implemented by the connectionist hardware. At the start of each sequence the context layer is cleared, that is, $\mathbf{c}(0) = \mathbf{0}$.

CONCERT could readily be wired up to behave as a kth order transition table. In this case, the function f is defined to implement a k element stack in the context layer. This stack would hold on to notes $n-k+1$ through n. The connections from the context layer to the output layer would then have to be set up to realize a lookup table in which each combination of previous notes maps to the appropriate probability distribution over the next note. The architecture is more general than a transition table, however, because f is not limited to implementing a stack, and the mapping from the context layer to the output is not limited to being a simple lookup table. From myriad possibilities, the training procedure attempts to find a set of connections that are adequate for performing the next-note prediction task. This involves determining which aspects of the input sequence are relevant for making future predictions and constructing the function f appropriately. Subsequently, the context layer will retain only *task-relevant* information. This contrasts with Todd's (this volume) work on connectionist composition in which the recurrent context connections are prewired and fixed, which makes the nature of the information Todd's model retains independent of the examples on which it is trained.

Once CONCERT has been trained, it can be run in *composition mode* to create new pieces. This involves first seeding CONCERT with a short sequence of notes, perhaps the initial notes of one of the training examples. From this point on, the output of CONCERT can be fed back to the input, allowing CONCERT to continue generating notes without further external input. Generally, the output of CONCERT does not specify a single note with absolute certainty; instead, the output is a probability distribution over the set of candidates. It is thus necessary to select a particular note in accordance with this distribution. This is the role of the selection process depicted in Fig. 1.

Unit Activation Rules

The activation rule for the context units is

$$c_i(n) = s\left[\sum_j w_{ij}x_j(n) + \sum_j v_{ij}c_j(n-1)\right],$$

where $c_i(n)$ is the activity of context unit i at step n, $x_j(n)$ is the activity of input unit j at step n, w_{ij} is the connection strength from unit j of the input to unit i of the context layer, v_{ij} is the connection strength from unit j to unit i within the context layer, and s is the standard logistic activation function rescaled to the range $(-1, 1)$. Units in the NND layer follow a similar rule:

$$nnd_i(n) = s\left[\sum_j u_{ij}c_j(n)\right],$$

where $nnd_i(n)$ is the activity of NND unit i at step n and u_{ij} is the strength of connection from context unit j to NND unit i.

The transformation from the NND layer to the NNL layer is achieved by first computing the distance between the NND representation, $\mathbf{nnd}(n)$, and the target (distributed) representation of each pitch i, $\boldsymbol{\rho}_i$:

$$d_i = \|\mathbf{nnd}(n) - \boldsymbol{\rho}_i\|,$$

where $\|\cdot\|$ denotes the length of a vector. This distance is an indication of how well the NND representation matches a particular pitch. The activation of the NNL unit corresponding to pitch i, nnl_i, increases as the distance decreases:

$$nnl_i(n) = \frac{e^{-d_i}}{\sum_j e^{-d_j}}.$$

This normalized exponential transform was first proposed by Bridle (1990) and Rumelhart (in preparation). It produces an activity pattern over the NNL units in which each unit has activity in the range (0,1) and the activity of all units sums to 1. Consequently, the NNL activity pattern can be interpreted as a probability distribution—in this case, the probability that the next note has a particular pitch. The distance measure and the exponential function also have a basis in psychological theory (Shepard 1987).

Training Procedure

CONCERT is trained using a variation of the back-propagation algorithm (Rumelhart, Hinton, and Williams 1986). Back propagation is a method for adjusting the connection strengths within CONCERT so that the network can perform the next-note prediction task for a set of training examples. The algorithm requires first defining a measure of the network's performance—of how good a job the network does at predicting each note in each of the training examples. Commonly, a squared difference measure of error is used:

$$E_{lms} = \sum_{p,n,j} (nnl_j(n, p) - \delta(j, t(n, p)))^2,$$

where p is an index over pieces in the training set, n an index over notes within a piece, and j an index over units in the NNL layer; $t(n,p)$ is the target pitch for note n of piece p; and $\delta(a,b) = 1$ if $a = b$ or 0 otherwise. This measure is minimized when the output of the unit corresponding to the correct prediction is 1 and the output of all other units is 0.

Another performance measure is sensible in the context of output units that have a probabilistic interpretation (Bridle 1990; Rumelhart, in preparation). Because each NNL unit's output represents the probabilistic expectation of a pitch, performance depends on predicting the appropriate notes with high probability. This suggests the performance measure

$$L = \prod_{p,n} nnl_{t(n,p)}(n, p),$$

which is the joint probability of making the correct prediction for all notes of all pieces.[3] Equivalently, a new error measure can be defined based on the logarithm of L,

$$E = -\log L = -\sum_{p,n} \log nnl_{t(n,p)}(n, p),$$

because the logarithm is a monotonic function. E is somewhat easier to work with than L.

Back propagation specifies how the weights in the network should be changed to reduce E. This involves computing the gradient of D with respect to the weights in the network: $\partial E/\partial \mathbf{W}$, $\partial E/\partial \mathbf{V}$, and $\partial E/\partial \mathbf{U}$. The first step in this process is computing the gradient with respect to the activity of units in the NND layer and then propagating this gradient back to the weights in layers below. For the error measure E and the NNL-unit activation rule,

$$\frac{\partial E}{\partial \mathbf{nnd}(n, p)} = \left[\frac{\mathbf{nnd}(n, p) - \boldsymbol{\rho}_{t(n,p)}}{d_{t(n,p)}} - \sum_i nnl_i(n, p)\frac{\mathbf{nnd}(n, p) - \boldsymbol{\rho}_i}{d_i}\right].$$

Back propagation still cannot be used to train CONCERT directly, because CONCERT contains recurrent connections, and the algorithm applies only to feedforward networks. Several variations of the algorithm have been proposed for dealing with recurrent networks (Williams and Zipser, in press). I've used the "unfolding in time" procedure of Rumelhart, Hinton, and Williams (1986), which transforms a recurrent network into an equivalent feedforward network. The basic trick involves making a copy of the units in the network for each step in the sequence (Fig. 2). If the sequence has ten notes, there will be ten copies of the input units, $\mathbf{x}(1) \ldots \mathbf{x}(10)$, as for the other pools of units. Thus, $\mathbf{x}(n)$ refers to a particular set of input units, in contrast to the original architecture where $\mathbf{x}(n)$ refers to the input activities at a particular point in time. The weights in each copy of the network are set to be equal to the weights in the original architecture. For example, the weights $\mathbf{W}$ connect $\mathbf{x}(n)$ to $\mathbf{c}(n)$ for each n. Consequently, the dynamics of the unfolded network are identical to those of the original network: $\mathbf{x}(n)$ is integrated with $\mathbf{c}(n-1)$ to form $\mathbf{c}(n)$, and so forth. The difference is that the unfolded network is feedforward; that is, activity in Fig. 2 flows strictly upwards, whereas in Fig. 1 activity flows from the context layer back to itself.

Applying back propagation to the unfolded architecture is therefore straightforward. The error gradient $\partial E/\partial \mathbf{nnd}(n, p)$ is computed at step n. This error is propagated through the copy of the network corresponding to step n, back to the copy corresponding to step $n-1$, and so on. For each copy of the network, this procedure produces a set of suggested weight changes, $\{\Delta\mathbf{W}(i), \Delta\mathbf{V}(i), \Delta\mathbf{U}(i)\}$, where the index i specifies to which step the weight changes correspond. Because there is only one set of underlying weights—the weights in the original network—the weight changes for each step must be summed together to determine the overall change to the underlying weights:

$$\Delta\mathbf{W} = \sum_{i=1}^{n} \Delta\mathbf{W}(i),$$

and similarly for $\Delta\mathbf{V}$ and $\Delta\mathbf{U}$. The actual weight update is performed only after the entire sequence has been presented.

A practical consideration is that in long sequences, the unfolded architecture is deeply layered, and error propagation is computationally expensive. One solution is simply to terminate error propagation after a certain number of steps; however, my simulations were small enough that such a short cut was unnecessary.

Examining the unfolded architecture in Fig. 2, one gains a sense of how CONCERT can discover contingencies far apart in time. Consider, for instance, the input at step 1, $\mathbf{x}(1)$, which is linked to the prediction at step n, $\mathbf{nnl}(n)$, via a series of intermediate layers: $\mathbf{c}(1)$, $\mathbf{c}(2)$, $\cdots$, $\mathbf{c}(n)$, and $\mathbf{nnd}(n)$. The weights along this path are adjusted via back propagation so that input note 1, if it has any predictive utility, will influence CONCERT's output at step n. This is ensured by preserving critical aspects of $\mathbf{x}(1)$ in the context layer until step n. If the propagation of error in the network is limited to a certain number of steps (e.g., Elman 1990), there is no assurance that CONCERT will retain information early in the sequence specifically to make a prediction at a much later step.

Fig. 2. The CONCERT architecture unfolded in time. For each step in the input sequence there is a complete copy of all units in the network. The labels in the boxes indicate the activity vector corresponding to the units: x *for the input (current note),* c *for the context,* nnd *for the NND units, layer, and* nnl *for the NNL units. The number in parentheses indicates the step.*

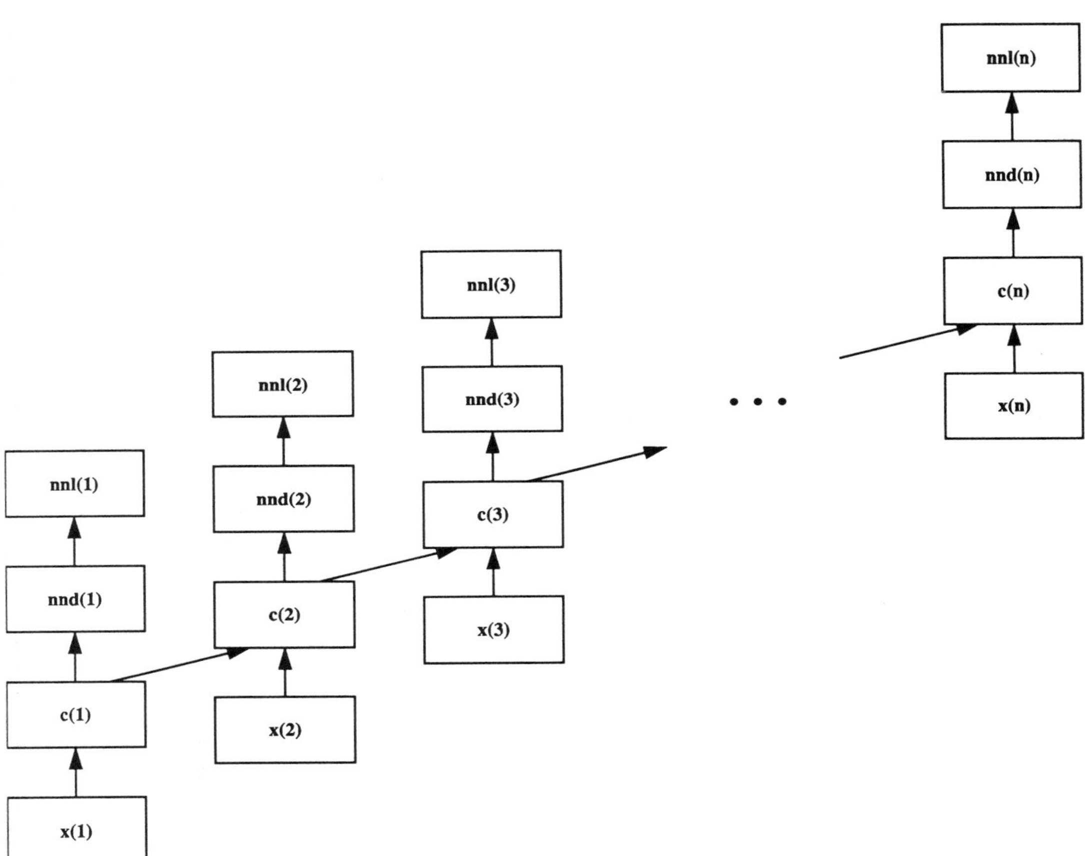

Pitch Representation

Having described CONCERT's architecture and training procedure, I turn to the representation of pitch. To accommodate a variety of music, CONCERT needs the ability to represent a range of about four octaves. Using standard musical notation, these pitches are labeled as follows: C1, D1, . . . , B1, C2, D2, . . . , B2, C3, . . . , C5, where C1 is the lowest pitch and C5 the highest. Sharps and flats are denoted with ♯ and ♭ respectively, e.g., C♯3 and G♭2. Within an octave, there are twelve chromatic steps; the range C1–C5 thus includes 49 pitches.

Perhaps the simplest representation of pitch is to have one unit for each possibility. The pitch C1 would be represented by the activity vector $[100 \cdots]^T$, C♯1 by the vector $[010 \cdots]^T$, and so forth. An alternative would be to represent pitch by a single unit whose activity was proportional to the frequency of the pitch. One might argue that the choice of a pitch representation is not critical because back propagation can, in principle, discover an alternative representation well suited to the task (Hinton 1987). In practice, however, researchers have found that the choice of external representation is a critical determinant of the network's ultimate performance (e.g., Denker et al. 1987; Mozer 1987). Quite simply, the more task-appropriate information that is built into the network, the easier the job the learning algorithm has.

Laden and Keefe (this volume) advocate the approach of including as much information as possible from psychoacoustics into the design of networks for music perception and cognition. They have developed a model of chord classification that categorizes triads as major, minor, or diminished chords. Classification performance is superior with the use of a representation that explicitly encodes harmonics of the fundamental pitches.

In accord with this approach, and because I am asking the network to make predictions about melodies that people have composed or to generate melodies that people perceive as pleasant, a central ingredient of my work has been to furnish CONCERT with a psychologically motivated representation of pitch. By this, I mean that notes that people judge to be similar should have similar representations in the network, indicating that the representation in the head matches the representation in the network. The local representation scheme proposed earlier clearly does not meet this criterion. In the local representation, every pair of pitches is equally similar (using either the distance or angle between vectors as a measure of similarity), yet people perceive pairs of notes such as C1 and C♯1 to be more similar than, say, C1 and A4. Other obvious representations of pitch do not meet the criterion either. For example, a direct encoding of frequency does not capture the similarity that people hear between octaves.

Shepard (1982) has systematically studied the similarity of pitches by asking people to judge the perceived similarity of pairs of pitches. He has proposed a theory of generalization (Shepard 1987) in which the similarity of two items is exponentially related to their distance in an internal or "psychological" representational space.[4] For the internal representation of pitch, Shepard has proposed a five-dimensional space, depicted in Fig. 3. In this space, each pitch specifies a point along the *pitch height* (or *PH*) dimension, an (x,y) coordinate on the *chromatic circle* (or *CC*), and an (x,y) coordinate on the *circle of fifths* (or *CF*). I will refer to this representation as PHCCCF, after its three components. The pitch-height component specifies the logarithm of the frequency of a pitch; this logarithmic transform places tonal halfsteps at equal spacing from one another along the pitch-height axis. In the chromatic circle, neighboring pitches are a tonal halfstep apart. In the circle of fifths, the perfect fifth of a pitch is the next pitch immediately counterclockwise.[5] The proximity of two pitches in the five-dimensional PHCCCF space can be determined simply by computing the Euclidean distance between their representations.

Shepard substantiates the psychological validity of the PHCCCF representation in detail. I will briefly point out some of its benefits. Consider first the PH and CC components. In this three-dimensional subspace, pitches form a helix in which the winding of the helix is due to the chromatic circle and the height is due to the pitch height. As pitches proceed up the chromatic scale, they wind up the helix. Pitches exactly one octave apart are directly above one another on the helix; that is, they have the same locus on the chromatic circle but different values of pitch height. For this reason, octaves have similar representations. Depending on how the PH component is scaled relative to the CC (i.e., how elongated the helix is), pitches such as C1 and C2 may even be closer in the representational space than pitches such as C1 and B1, even though C1 is closer to B1 in frequency.

The circle of fifths endows the representation with other desirable properties. First, the circle localizes the tones in a musical key. Any seven adjacent tones correspond to a particular key. For instance, the tones of the C-major and A-minor diatonic scales—C, D, E, F, G, A, and B—are grouped together on the circle of fifths. The most common pentatonic keys are similarly localized. Second, and perhaps more critical, the circle of fifths can explain the subjective equality of the intervals of the diatonic scale. To elaborate, Shepard points out that people tend to hear the successive steps of the ma-

Fig. 3. Shepard's (1982) pitch representation.

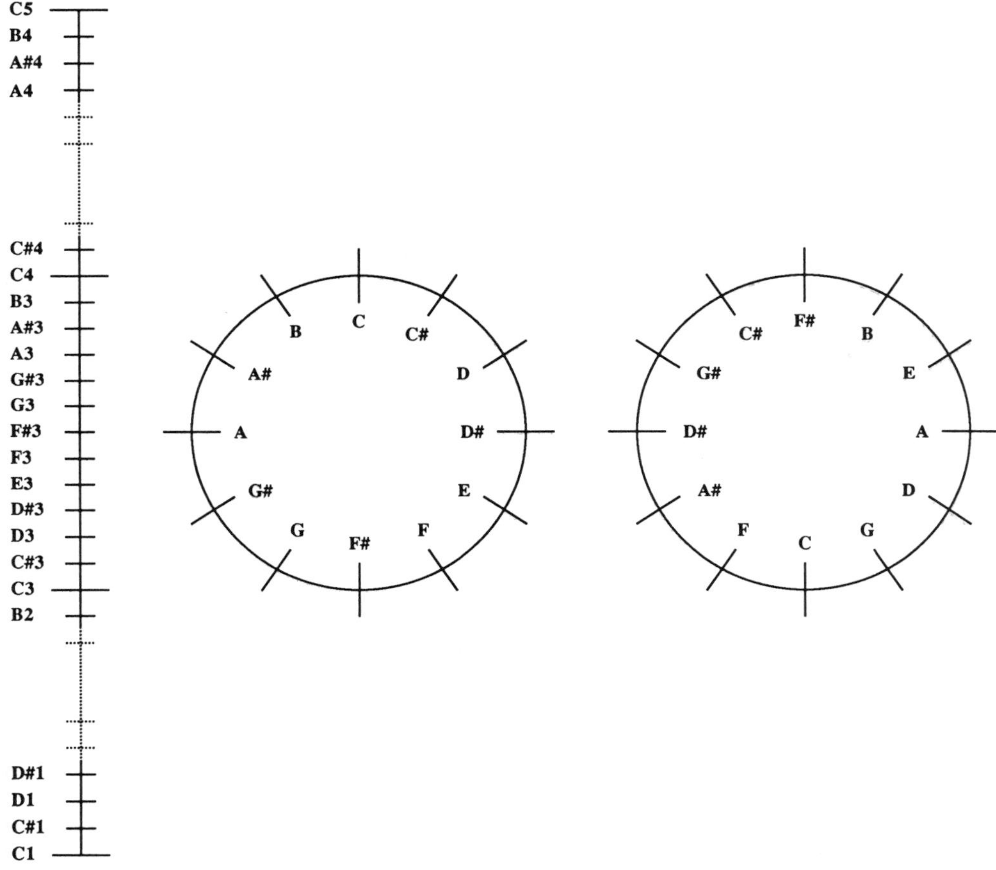

jor scale as equivalent, although with respect to log frequency, some of the intervals are only half as large as others. For example, in C major, the E-F and B-C steps are half tones apart (minor seconds), whereas all others are a whole tone apart (major seconds). The combination of the pitch height and circle of fifths permits a representation in which the distance between all major and minor seconds is the same. This is achieved by using a scale ratio of approximately 3 : 1 for the chromatic circle relative to the circle of fifths.

One desirable property of the overall PHCCCF representation is that distances between pitches are invariant under transposition. Consider any two pitches, say, D2 and G♯4. Transposing the pitches preserves the distance between them in the PHCCCF representation. Thus, the distance from D2 to G♯4 is the same as from E2 to A♯4, from D1 to G♯3, and so forth. See Bharucha (this volume) for a further discussion of the psychological issues involved in the representation of musical pitch.

The relative importance of the PH, CC, and CF components can be varied by adjusting the diameters of the chromatic circle and circle of fifths. For example, if the two circles have the same diameter, then in terms of the CC and CF components, the distance between C and G is the same as the distance between C and B. This is because B is one notch from the C on the chromatic circle and five notches on the circle of fifths, while the G is five notches away on the chromatic circle and one on the circle of fifths. If the diameter of the chromatic circle is increased, however, then C is closer to B than to G (based on the distance in the four-dimensional CC and CF subspace); if the diameter is decreased, C is closer to G than to B. If the diameters of both circles are decreased relative to the pitch-height scale, then pitch frequency becomes the most important determinant of similarity. Shepard argues that the weighting of the various components depends on the particular musical task and the listener's expertise. Based on Shepard's evidence, a reasonable representation for expert musicians is to weigh the CF and CC components equally and to set the diameter of the CC and CF components equal to the distance of one octave in PH. This is the scale shown in Fig. 3.

The final issue to discuss is how the PHCCCF representation translates into an activity vector over a set of connectionist units. A straightforward scheme is to use five units, one for pitch height and two pairs to encode the (x,y) coordinates of the pitch on the two circles. One problem with this scheme is that if the units have the usual sigmoidal activation function, equal spacing of tones in pitch height or on the circles in unit *activity* space is not preserved in unit *net input* space. This means that context units attempting to activate NND units do not reap the full benefit of the representation (e.g., transposition invariance). A second problem with the simple five-unit scheme is that the activity of each encodes a coordinate value directly; there are 7 discrete values for the x- and y-coordinates of the circles, 49 for the pitch height. Consequently, minor perturbations of the activity vector could lead to misinterpretations.

Table 2. Representation of tones on chromatic circle

tone	*representation*					
C	−1	−1	−1	−1	−1	−1
C#	−1	−1	−1	−1	−1	+1
D	−1	−1	−1	−1	+1	+1
D#	−1	−1	−1	+1	+1	+1
E	−1	−1	+1	+1	+1	+1
F	−1	+1	+1	+1	+1	+1
F#	+1	+1	+1	+1	+1	+1
G	+1	+1	+1	+1	+1	−1
G#	+1	+1	+1	+1	−1	−1
A	+1	+1	+1	−1	−1	−1
A#	+1	+1	−1	−1	−1	−1
B	+1	−1	−1	−1	−1	−1

Because of these problems, I have opted for an alternative representation of the CC and CF components. The representation involves six binary-valued units to represent a tone on each circle; the representation for chromatic circle tones is shown in Table 2. This representation preserves the essential distance relationships among tones on the chromatic circle: the distance between two tones is monotonically related to the angle between the tones. Because each unit has to encode only two distinct values, the representation is less sensitive to noise than is one in which each unit encodes a real value.

Unfortunately, I do not believe there is a similar scheme that can be used to encode pitch height in a Boolean space of reasonably low dimensionality that preserves intrinsic distance relationships. Consequently, I have stayed with a single linear unit for pitch height. Its activity is scaled to range from -9.798 for C1 to $+9.798$ for C5. This scaling achieves the desired property that the distance in the CC or CF component between pitches on opposite sides of the circle equals the distance between

Table 3. PHCCCF representation for selected pitches

pitch	PH	CC						CF					
C1	–9.798	+1	+1	+1	–1	–1	–1	–1	–1	–1	+1	+1	+1
F#1	–7.349	–1	–1	–1	+1	+1	+1	+1	+1	+1	–1	–1	–1
G2	–2.041	–1	–1	–1	–1	+1	+1	–1	–1	–1	–1	+1	+1
C3	0	+1	+1	+1	–1	–1	–1	–1	–1	–1	+1	+1	+1
D#3	1.225	+1	+1	+1	+1	+1	+1	+1	+1	+1	+1	+1	+1
E3	1.633	–1	+1	+1	+1	+1	+1	+1	–1	–1	–1	–1	–1
A4	8.573	–1	–1	–1	–1	–1	–1	–1	–1	–1	–1	–1	–1
C5	9.798	+1	+1	+1	–1	–1	–1	–1	–1	–1	+1	+1	+1
rest	0	+1	–1	+1	–1	+1	–1	+1	–1	+1	–1	+1	–1

pitches one octave apart in the PH component.[6]

The PHCCCF representation consists of 13 units altogether. Sample activity patterns for some pitches are shown in Table 3. Rests (silence) are assigned a code, listed in the last row of the table, that distinguishes them from all pitches. The end of a piece is coded by a series of rests.

As with any distributed representation, there are limitations as to how many and which pitches can be represented simultaneously. The issue arises because the NND layer needs to be able to encode a set of alternatives, not just a single pitch. If, say, A1, D2, and E2 are equally likely to be the next note, the NND layer must indicate all three possibilities. To do so, it must produce an activity vector that is nearer to ρ_{A1}, ρ_{D2}, and ρ_{E2} than to other possibilities. The point in PHCCCF space that is simultaneously closest to the three pitches is simply the average vector, $(\rho_{A1} + \rho_{D2} + \rho_{E2})/3$. Table 4 shows the pitches nearest to the average vector. As hoped for, A1, D2, and E2 are the nearest three. This is not always the case, though. Table 5 shows the pitches nearest to the average vector which represents the set {A1, D2, D♯2}. This illustrates the fact that certain clusters of pitches are more compact in the PHCCCF space than others. The PHCCCF representation introduces not only a similarity structure over the pitches but also a limit on the combinations of pitches that can be considered simultaneously. Arbitrary limitations

Table 4. Distance from representation of {A1, D2, E2} to nearest 10 pitches

rank	pitch	distance	rank	pitch	distance
1	D2	2.528	6	C#2	4.422
2	E2	2.779	7	A2	4.422
3	A1	3.399	8	E1	4.441
4	B1	3.859	9	G1	4.497
5	C2	4.130	10	G2	4.497

Table 5. Distance from representation of {A1, D2, D♯2} to nearest 10 pitches

rank	pitch	distance	rank	pitch	distance
1	D2	2.373	6	D#2	3.774
2	C2	3.277	7	A1	3.946
3	E2	3.538	8	F2	4.057
4	C#2	3.654	9	A#1	4.146
5	B1	3.714	10	G1	4.323

are a bad thing in general, but here, the limitations are theoretically motivated.[7]

One serious shortcoming of the PHCCCF representation is that it is based on the similarity between pairs of notes presented in isolation. Listeners of music do not process individual notes in isolation; notes appear in a musical context that suggests a musical key, which in turn contributes to an interpretation of the note. Some psychologically motivated work has considered the effects of context or musical key on pitch representation (Krumhansl 1990; Krumhansl and Kessler 1982; Longuet-Higgins 1976, 1979). I believe that CONCERT could be improved considerably by incorporating the ideas in this work. Fortunately, it does not require discarding the PHCCCF representation altogether, because the PHCCCF representation shares many properties in common with the representations suggested by Krumhansl and Kessler and by Longuet-Higgins.

Simulation Experiments

Extending a C-major Diatonic Scale

To start with a simple experiment, CONCERT was trained on a single sequence consisting of three octaves of a C-major diatonic scale: C1 D1 E1 F1 · · · B3. The target at each step was the next note in the scale: D1 E1 F1 G1 · · · C4. CONCERT is said to have learned the sequence when, at each step, the activity of the NNL unit representing the target at that step is more active than any other NNL unit. In 10 replications of the simulation with different initial random weights, 15 context units, a learning rate of .005, and no momentum, CONCERT learned the sequence in about 30 passes. Following training, CONCERT was tested on four octaves of the scale. CONCERT correctly extended its predictions to the fourth octave, except that in four of the ten replications, the final note, C5, was transposed down an octave. Table 6 shows CONCERT's output for two octaves of the scale. Octave 3 was part of the training sequence, but octave 4 was not. Activities of the three most active output units are shown. Because the output activities can be interpreted as probabilities, one can see that the target is selected with high confidence.

CONCERT was able to learn the training set with as few as two context units, although surprisingly, generalization performance tended to improve as the number of context units was increased. CONCERT was also able to generalize from a two-octave training sequence, but it often transposed notes down an octave.

Learning the Structure of Diatonic Scales

In this simulation, I trained CONCERT on a set of diatonic scales in various keys over a one-octave range, such as D1 E1 F♯1 G1 A1 B1 C♯2 D2. Thirty-seven such scales can be made using pitches in the C1–C5 range. The training set consisted of 28 scales—roughly 75 percent of the corpus—selected at random, and the test set consisted of the remaining 9. In ten replications of the simulation using 20 context units, CONCERT mastered the training set in approximately 55 passes. Generalization performance was tested by presenting the scales in the test set one note at a time and examining CONCERT's prediction. This is not the same as running CONCERT in composition mode because CONCERT's output was not fed back to the input; instead, the input was a predetermined sequence. Of the 63 notes to be predicted in the test set, CONCERT achieved remarkable performance: 98.4 percent correct. The few errors were caused by transposing notes one full octave or one tonal half step.

To compare CONCERT with a transition table approach, I built a second-order transition table from the training set data and measured its performance on the test set. The transition table prediction (the note with highest probability) was correct only 26.6 percent of the time. The transition table is somewhat of a straw man in this environment: a transition table that is based on absolute pitches is simply unable to generalize correctly. Even if the transition table encoded relative pitches, a third-order table would be required to master the environment. Kohonen's musical grammar faces the same difficulties as a transition table.

Table 6. Performance on octaves 3 and 4 of C-major diatonic scale

input pitch	*output unit activities*					
C3	D3	0.961	C3	0.017	E3	0.014
D3	E3	0.972	D3	0.012	F3	0.007
E3	F3	0.982	D#3	0.008	G3	0.006
F3	G3	0.963	F3	0.015	A3	0.010
G3	A3	0.961	G3	0.024	B3	0.012
A3	B3	0.972	A3	0.025	C4	0.002
B3	C4	0.979	A#3	0.010	C#4	0.005
C4	D4	0.939	C4	0.040	E4	0.009
D4	E4	0.968	D4	0.018	F4	0.006
E4	F4	0.971	D#4	0.016	E4	0.005
F4	G4	0.931	F4	0.037	F#4	0.015
G4	A4	0.938	G4	0.044	B4	0.007
A4	B4	0.915	A4	0.080	A#4	0.003
B4	C5	0.946	A#4	0.040	B4	0.011

Learning Random Walk Sequences

In this simulation, I generated ten-element sequences according to a simple rule: The first pitch was selected at random, and then successive pitches were either one step up or down the C-major scale from the previous pitch, the direction chosen at random. The pitch transitions can easily be described by a transition table, as illustrated in Table 1. CONCERT, with 15 context units, was trained for 50 passes through a set of 100 such sequences. If CONCERT has correctly inferred the underlying rule, its predictions should reflect the plausible alternatives at each point in a sequence. To test this, a set of 100 novel random walk sequences was presented. After each note n of a sequence, CONCERT's performance was evaluated by matching the top two predictions—the two pitches with highest activity—against the actual note $n+1$ of the sequence. If note $n+1$ was not one of the top two predictions, the prediction was considered to be erroneous. In ten replications of the simulation, the mean performance was 99.95 percent correct. Thus, CONCERT was clearly able to infer the structure present in the patterns. CONCERT performed equally well, if not better, on random walks in which chromatic steps (up or down a tonal half step) were taken.

Learning Interspersed Random Walk Sequences

The sequences in this simulation were generated by interspersing the elements of two simple random walk sequences of the sort just described. Each interspersed sequence had the following form: a_1, b_1, a_2, b_2, $\cdots$, a_5, b_5, where a_1 and b_1 are randomly selected pitches, a_{i+1} is one step up or down from a_i on the C-major scale, and likewise for b_{i+1} and b_i. Each sequence consisted of ten notes. CONCERT, with 25 context units, was trained on 50 passes through a set of 200 examples and was then tested on an additional 100. In contrast to the simple random walk sequences, it is impossible to predict the second note in the interspersed sequences (b_1) from the first (a_1). Thus, this prediction was ignored for the purpose of evaluating CONCERT's performance. CONCERT achieved a performance of 91.7

Fig. 4. A sample composition produced by CONCERT based on the Bach training set. The first four notes, used to seed CONCERT, are from one of the (transposed) minuets.

Table 7. Bach training examples

piece	*number of notes*
Minuet in G major (no. 1)	126
Minuet in G major (no. 2)	166
Minuet in D minor	70
Minuet in A minor	84
Minuet in C minor	80
March in G major	153
March in D major	122
March in E♭ major	190
Musette in D major	128
Little prelude in C major	121

percent correct. About half the errors were ones in which CONCERT transposed a correct prediction by an octave. Excluding these errors, performance improved to 95.8 percent correct.

To capture the structure in this environment, a transition table approach would need to consider at least the previous two notes. However, such a transition table is not likely to generalize well because, if it is to be assured of predicting a note at step n correctly, it must observe the note at step $n-2$ in the context of every possible note at step $n-1$. I constructed a second-order transition table from CONCERT's training set. Using a testing criterion analogous to that used to evaluate CONCERT, the transition table achieved a performance level on the test set of only 67.1 percent correct. Kohonen's musical grammar would face the same difficulty as the transition table in this environment.

Learning Simple Bach Piano Pieces

As a larger scale test, I trained CONCERT on the treble-clef voice—the melody line—of a set of ten simple piano pieces by J. S. Bach (Table 7). The set of examples is not particularly coherent; it includes a variety of musical styles. The primary thing that the pieces have in common is their composer.

In making the training data, each piece was terminated with an end-of-piece delimiter. This allowed CONCERT to learn not only the notes within a piece but also when the end of the piece was reached. Further, each major piece was transposed to the key of C-major and each minor piece to the key of a-minor. This was done to facilitate learning because the pitch representation does not take into account the notion of musical key; hopefully, a more sophisticated pitch representation would avoid the necessity of this step.

Learning the examples involves predicting a total of 1,240 notes altogether—no small feat. CONCERT was trained with 35 hidden units for 500 passes through the training set. Only one replication of the simulation was conducted due to its heavy computational requirements. During training, the learning rate was gradually lowered from .0005 to .00001. By the completion of training, CONCERT could correctly predict 1176 of the notes, or 93.3 percent. Running CONCERT in composition mode, new pieces can be created. Two examples of its compositions are shown in Figs. 4 and 5. CONCERT specifies the end of a composition by producing an end-of-piece delimiter. The compositions often contain short sequences excerpted from the training examples. This is because CONCERT has learned the training examples so well that in many contexts, it produces a prediction of one note with probability 1. This means that the selection process does not have the opportunity to follow an alternative direction.

The primary deficiency of CONCERT's compositions is that they are lacking in global coherence. A composition might flip back and forth between C-major and a-minor, or it might incorporate aspects of both the marches and the minuets. Because the shorter compositions have less chance of wandering in this manner, they tend to be more agreeable.

Fig. 5. Another composition produced by CONCERT based on the Bach training set. The first four notes are from the Bach musette.

Conclusion

Initial results from CONCERT are encouraging. CONCERT is able to learn musical structures of varying complexity, from simple random walk sequences to Bach pieces containing nearly 200 notes. I presented two examples of structures that CONCERT can learn but that cannot be captured by a simple transition table or by Kohonen's musical grammar. One example involved diatonic scales in various keys, the other involved interspersed random walks.

I have motivated CONCERT's architecture primarily from psychological and computational perspectives but have yet to provide empirical support for this architecture over other possibilities. Is the PHCCCF representation warranted, or would a simpler, perhaps even a local, representation of pitch suffice? Is the NNL layer and the log likelihood performance measure necessary, or could the NNL layer be eliminated and the error be computed directly by comparing the NND activity pattern with the target pitch representation? These questions need to be answered systematically, but informal experiments with alternative architectures and representations have convinced me that CONCERT's performance is remarkably good. These experiments included (1) the use of localist pitch representations, (2) variants in the PHCCCF representation, such as using two units to represent the circles instead of six, and (3) alternative error measures, such as computing the squared difference between the NND and target activity patterns. Each variant yielded significantly poorer results in many of the simulations.

Beyond a more systematic examination of alternative architectures, work on CONCERT is heading in three directions. First, the pitch representation is being expanded to account for the perceptual effects of musical context and musical key. Second, CONCERT is being elaborated to include a representation of note duration as well as pitch. The duration representation, as the PHCCCF representation, is based on characteristics of human perception. Third, CONCERT is being extended to better handle the processing of global structure in music. It is unrealistic to expect that CONCERT, presented with a linear string of notes, could induce not only local relationships among the notes but also more global phrase structure, such as an AABA phrase pattern. To address the issue of global structure, we have designed a network that operates at several different temporal resolutions simultaneously and have begun preliminary simulations (Mozer and Soukup, in preparation).

Acknowledgments

This research was supported by NSF grant IRI-9058450, grant 90-21 from the James S. McDonnell Foundation, and by the Office of Naval Research under Contract N00014-88-K-0559. My thanks to Paul Smolensky, Yoshiro Miyata, Debbie Breen, and Geoffrey Hinton for helpful comments regarding this work, to Peter Todd for his careful reading of the manuscript, and to Hal Eden and Darren Hardy for technical assistance.

Notes

1. Because my work to date considers only the pitch of a note, I used the terms *note* and *pitch* interchangeably.
2. Following Smolensky (1988), I used the phrase *faithful representation* to mean that the represented items can be accurately reconstructed from the representation. A faithful transition table representation of a set of examples would be one that, given the first few notes of any example, could unambiguously determine the remainder of the example.
3. Of course, this interpretation assumes independence of the predictions, which is certainly not true in CONCERT. However, Bridle (1990) provides another justification, somewhat less intuitive, for this performance measure in terms of an information-theoretic criterion.

4. This is one justification for the exponential function in the NNL layer.
5. The perfect fifth is a musically significant interval. The frequency ratio of a note to its perfect fifth is 2:3, just as the frequency ratio of a note to its octave is 1:2.
6. Although a PH scale factor of 9.798 was used for the target NND representation, ρ_i, a PH scale factor of 1.0 was used for the input representation. This was based on empirical studies of what scale factors yielded the best performance. The primary reason that a PH scale factor other than 1.0 on the inputs causes difficulties is that gradient descent in the error surface becomes messier when different units have different activity ranges (Widrow and Stearns 1985).
7. I hope this isn't too reminiscent of the old saying, "It's not a bug; it's a feature."

References

Bharucha, J. J. This volume. "Pitch, Harmony, and Neural Nets: A Psychological Perspective."

Bridle, J. 1990. "Training Stochastic Model Recognition Algorithms as Networks Can Lead to Maximum Mutual Information Estimation of Parameters." In D. S. Touretzky, ed. *Advances in Neural Information Processing Systems 2.* San Mateo, California: Morgan Kaufmann, pp. 211–217.

Denker, J., D. Schwartz, B. Wittner, S. Solla, R. Howard, L. Jackel, and J. Hopfield. 1987. "Automatic Learning, Rule Extraction, and Generalization." *Complex Systems* 1:877–922.

Dodge, C., and T. A. Jerse. 1985. *Computer Music: Synthesis, Composition, and Performance.* New York: Shirmer Books.

Dolson, M. This volume. "Machine Tongues XII: Neural Networks."

Elman, J. L. 1990. "Finding Structure in Time." *Cognitive Science* 14:179–212.

Hinton, G. 1987. "Learning Distributed Representations of Concepts." *Proceedings of the Eighth Annual Conference of the Cognitive Science Society.* Hillsdale, N.J.: Erlbaum Associates, pp. 1–12.

Hinton, G. E., J. L. McClelland, and D. E. Rumelhart. 1986. "Distributed Representations." In D. E. Rumelhart and J. L. McClelland, eds. *Parallel Distributed Processing: Explorations in the Microstructure of Cognition.* Cambridge, Massachusetts: MIT Press, pp. 77–109.

Jones, K. 1981. "Compositional Applications of Stochastic Processes." *Computer Music Journal* 5:45–61.

Kohonen, T. 1989. "A Self-Learning Musical Grammar, or 'Associative Memory of the Second Kind.'" *Proceedings of the 1989 International Joint Conference on Neural Networks.* New York: IEEE, pp. 1–5.

Kohonen, T., P. Laine, K. Tiits, and K. Torkkola. This volume. "A Nonheuristic Automatic Composing Method."

Krumhansl, C. L. 1990. *Cognitive Foundations of Musical Pitch.* New York: Oxford University Press.

Krumhansl, C. L., and E. J. Kessler. 1982. "Tracing the Dynamic Changes in Perceived Tonal Organization in a Spatial Representation of Musical Keys." *Psychological Review* 89:334–368.

Laden, B., and D. H. Keefe. This volume. "The Representation of Pitch in a Neural Net Model of Chord Classification."

Longuet-Higgins, H. C. 1976. "Perception of Melodies." *Nature* 263:646–653.

Longuet-Higgins, H. C. 1979. "The Perception of Music (Review Lecture)." *Proceedings of the Royal Society of London.* London: The Royal Society, 205B:307–332.

Lorrain, D. 1980. "A Panoply of Stochastic 'Canons.'" *Computer Music Journal* 3:48–55.

Loy, D. G. This volume. "Connectionism and Musiconomy."

Mozer, M. C. 1987. "RAMBOT: A Connectionist Expert System That Learns by Example." *Proceedings of the IEEE First Annual International Conference on Neural Networks.* San Diego, California: IEEE Publishing Services, pp. 693–700.

Mozer, M. C. 1989. "A Focused Back-Propagation Algorithm for Temporal Pattern Recognition." *Complex Systems* 3:349–381.

Mozer, M. C. and T. Soukup. 1991. "CONCERT: A Connectionist Composer of Erudite Tunes." In *Advances in Neural Information Processing Systems 3.* San Mateo, California: Morgan Kaufmann.

Rumelhart, D. E. In preparation. "Connectionist Processing and Learning as Statistical Inference." Hillsdale, N.J.: Erlbaum Associates.

Rumelhart, D. E., G. E. Hinton, and R. J. Williams. 1986. "Learning Internal Representations by Error Propagation." In D. E. Rumelhart and J. L. McClelland, eds. *Parallel Distributed Processing: Explorations in the Microstructure of Cognition*, vol. 2. Cambridge, Massachusetts: MIT Press, pp. 318–362.

Shepard, R. N. 1982. "Geometrical Approximations to the Structure of Musical Pitch." *Psychological Review* 89:305–333.

Shepard, R. N. 1987. "Toward a Universal Law of Generalization for Psychological Science." *Science* 237: 1317–1323.

Smolensky, P. 1988. "On the Proper Treatment of Connectionism." *Behavioral and Brain Sciences* 11: 1–74.

Todd, P. M. This volume. "A Connectionist Approach to Algorithmic Composition."

Widrow, B., and S. D. Stearns. *Adaptive Signal Processing.* Englewood Cliffs, N.J.: Prentice-Hall.

Williams, R. J. and D. Zipser. In press. "Gradient-Based Learning Algorithms for Recurrent Connectionist Networks." In Y. Chauvin and D. E. Rumelhart, eds. *Backpropagation: Theory, Architectures, and Applications.* Hillsdale, N.J.: Erlbaum Associates.

J. P. Lewis
Computer Graphics Laboratory
New York Institute of Technology
Old Westbury, NY 11568

Creation by Refinement and the Problem of Algorithmic Music Composition

Introduction

Neural net or connectionist approaches seem well suited for arts applications such as machine composition of music because the structure of art is determined in part by the characteristics and limitations of human perception, rather than by physical law in a more direct form. The problem of generating patterns constrained by this structure is parallel to the perceptual analysis and recognition problems for which connectionist approaches have shown promise (Ballard, Hinton, and Sejnowski 1983).

In contrast, nonconnectionist algorithmic approaches in the computer arts have often met with the difficulty that "laws" of art are characteristically fuzzy and ill-suited for algorithmic description. For example, it is probably safe to say that at present there are no rigorous (meaning, suitable for algorithmic implementation) descriptions of tonal music as a whole, despite centuries of analysis and considerable consensus on fundamental tenets of common practice. Lerdahl and Jackendoff's generative grammar theory (Lerdahl and Jackendoff 1983), one of the most developed current theories of tonal music, is admittedly incomplete (it does not cover nonhierarchical aspects of musical structure, for example). Interestingly, Lerdahl and Jackendoff's theory includes many examples of ambiguity and analysis from multiple points of view—capabilities that are natural in some neural network approaches but that present challenges to rule-based approaches. Some of the issues that arise in developing algorithms for applications such as music composition will be considered in the second section of this chapter.

Creation by Refinement (CBR) is a neural net paradigm developed specifically for "artificial creativity" problems such as the machine composition of music. CBR consists of a learning phase, in which a standard supervised gradient descent learning algorithm trains a network to be a "music critic" (preferentially judging musical examples according to various criteria), followed by a creation phase, in which a haphazard creation is refined by a gradient descent search until it is judged to satisfy the trained criteria. For example, one could in theory train a neural net to recognize compositions by a particular composer and then use CBR to synthesize new compositions in the style of this composer. The CBR paradigm is described more fully in the third section.

It has been questioned whether machines truly can be creative. Although this question is beyond the scope of this chapter, the creative limitations and scope of CBR need to be considered, and these are addressed in the fourth section.

To a considerable extent, the capabilities and limitations of CBR are dependent on capabilities and limitations of the gradient descent network which is used as a critic. As originally presented (Lewis 1988), CBR was of limited practical value for music composition on typical serial computers, due to the computational expense of the back-propagation algorithm (Rumelhart, Hinton, and Williams 1986) used as the critic. CBR awaited the general determination of whether supervised gradient descent learning algorithms such as back propagation were suitable for large problems such as music analysis and composition, via parallel computers or via improvements in the algorithms. Although many questions about the utility of these learning algorithms for large problems are still open, a number of such algorithms with improved properties have appeared recently. In addition, since the original publication of CBR, several variations of this paradigm were introduced that make it more practical on commonly available machines (Lewis 1989). Essentially, these take a "divide-and-conquer" approach, applying CBR to subsections of a larger overall pattern. The final sections of this chapter describe the use of a new adaptive gradient descent algorithm with CBR as well as several divide-and-conquer strategies and show some simple experiments using CBR.

Algorithms for Creation

Many algorithmic methods for the quantitative description and generation of music can be characterized as either probabilistic, such as Markov process approaches (Hiller and Isaacson 1959; Jones 1981), or rule based, such as generative grammars (Lerdahl and Jackendoff 1983; Roads 1979; Lidov and Gabura 1973). The limitations of these methods are complementary: whereas it is expensive to capture global regularity using probabilistic methods, rule-based approaches are poorly suited to describe ambiguity and irregularity and typically must include provisions to weaken the strength or applicability of the rules (as in Lerdahl and Jackendoff 1983).

Probabilistic approaches have a long history in algorithmic music composition, exemplified by early work of Hiller and Xenakis (Hiller and Isaacson 1959; Xenakis 1971). In the general probabilistic approach, musical structure is characterized by the joint nth-order probability distribution functions

$$F(x_1, x_2, \ldots, x_n; t_1, t_2, \ldots, t_n) = P(\mathbf{x}(t_1) = x_1, \mathbf{x}(t_2) = x_2, \ldots, \mathbf{x}(t_n) = x_n),$$

where F specifies the probability that each of the n events x_i occurs at each time t_i, for a suitable encoding of musical events x_t and all applicable t_i and n. For example, third-order distributions ($n=3$) can specify the probabilities of the occurrence of various combinations of three musical events, such as three pitches occuring at particular times. Compositions containing n notes, each specified by pitch, duration, and volume, would be described by a $3 \times n$th-order distribution. If the probability distribution function is used in a descriptive (as opposed to generative) way, then the term *probability* in such a description can be interpreted as the correctness or desirability of particular structures. In simulations the probability distribution function of course describes the probability that particular structures would result from random sampling from that distribution.

In order to generate musical compositions using the general probabilistic approach, we want to generate multivariate random variables representing compositions by sampling from the probability distribution representing a particular style of composition. If the probability distribution is separable (such as a multivariate Gaussian distribution), the sampling is done simply by randomly exploring the inverses of the one-dimensional (marginal) distributions (Kalos and Whitlock 1986). For more general distributions, advanced sampling techniques such as the $M(RT)^2$ algorithm are appropriate (Metropolis et al. 1953).

Unfortunately, the full statistics for a realistic musical composition are an impractical amount of information to identify and use. Therefore, only very restricted subsets of the general probabilistic description have been employed. For example, Markov process approaches limit the description to conditional probabilities for note transitions (Jones 1981). The alternative "fractal" approach limits the description to a particular form of power spectrum, which is equivalent to the second-order moments (i.e., averages of the second-order statistics) (Lewis 1987; Peitgen and Saupe 1988).

Markov processes in particular can capture the local structure of music with accuracy sufficient to mimic various styles of music. The result of discarding higher-order statistics is a lack of large-scale structure, however, and the synthesized composition may appear to wander aimlessly when one considers more than a few measures. Because of the considerable structure in most forms of music, the probability distribution function is not an economical representation—the probability distribution function must represent all possible structures, including those which are not desired, whereas a prescriptive rule need only describe desired structures. For example, a simple algorithmic statement

```
if x1 = a1 then
  x2 := a2
  else
  x2 := random();
```

can be represented as a much less compact probability distribution function that has as its domain all possible values of $x1$ and $x2$. The fact that desirable musical structures can be an extremely small subset of the range of possible structures is indicated by considering the chances of generating a likable composition by picking note values at random.

In contrast, rule-based approaches (Moorer 1972; Lidov and Gabura 1973; Lerdahl and Jackendoff 1983; Roads 1979) naturally represent both large- and small-scale structures, but the rules must be weakened or modified to handle ambiguity and "fuzzy" structure, properties which are characteristic of most forms of music. In fact, music is often best considered not as a single structure but as several simultaneous structures, for example, the common harmonic, melodic, and rhythmic dimensions of music analysis. While unambiguous structural descriptions such as phrase structure grammars translate directly into algorithms, simultaneous ambiguous structure is not easily described using the programming constructs available in most computer languages; artificial intelligence techniques such as demons and backtracking are often required in describing simultaneous musical structure.

The ability of neural network approaches to represent both ambiguity and structure thus appears to be complementary to the respective capabilities of probabilistic and structural approaches. In fact, this is a motivation for the current interest in neural nets in pattern recognition, in preference to the traditional statistical and structural pattern recognition approaches (Ballard, Hinton, and Sejnowski 1983).

Neural Network Approaches to Pattern Creation

Given the proposed advantages of neural network approaches to problems involving capturing the structure of music compositions, how could a neural network be used to *create* new compositions? Existing neural networks address functions such as memory, learning, and classification, but not pattern formation. One possible approach, using a neural net to "interpolate" between compositions, is described by Todd in his chapter (Todd, this volume). We will consider several other approaches to pattern creation by neural nets.

One general approach to pattern creation is suggested by the Doob decomposition of a random process (Doob 1953). The Doob decomposition describes a random process as a deterministic system (a filter) forced by an uncorrelated noise, that is, it splits a correlated random process into a purely deterministic part and an uncorrelated, purely random part. Similarly one can imagine a network which produces a high-entropy output vector from a musical composition given as input, effectively decomposing music into something like common practice (encoded in the weights) and innovation. Then, somehow, the network mapping might be inverted, producing musical compositions from random inputs. Unfortunately there is not a definable inverse of such a network (as there is in the case of a filter representing a stochastic process). Also, there would be no way to train a supervised learning net with the required forward map in the first place: in order for the network to discover a mapping from musical compositions to the high-entropy representation, the network must be presented with training patterns representing this mapping. Such patterns are unavailable since the required mapping is unknown outside of this hypothetical network.

Another approach would be to generate novel patterns by randomly perturbing the weights of a trained network. For example, a network could be trained to associate a small set of labels (input) with a corresponding set of musical compositions (output). If the weights in this network were perturbed, then a new, altered composition would be produced when one of the trained labels was presented.

The difficulty with this approach is that the network weights encode musical structure and constraints, and randomizing the weights will produce novelty at the expense of degrading structure. This is not desirable in applications where structure is considered important. Nor is it necessary—structure is not inconsistent with novelty. There are an infinite number of grammatical sentences (or tonal forms, etc.) despite the constraints of grammar (or tonality, etc.). Perturbing a net may result in unstructured forms without exploring the variety of structured legal forms. Instead, one would like to extract the characteristic structure and constraints from a set of examples, and then generate new forms that reflect this structure while innovating in ways permitted by the learned constraints. This is the approach taken by CBR.

Fig. 1. A simplified schematic of creation by refinement. In the training phase, a standard gradient descent learning net learns a function that maps musical examples presented at its input units to corresponding critique vectors. For each input pattern, the obtained output is compared to the critique (desired output), and if these are sufficiently different, an error signal is fed back into the network to adjust the weights. In the creation phase, the input units are initialized to a random "creation." The creation is repeatedly evaluated using the function learned in training. The difference between this critique of the random creation and a critique representing a desired creation is used as an error signal to refine the creation until it satisfies the critique.

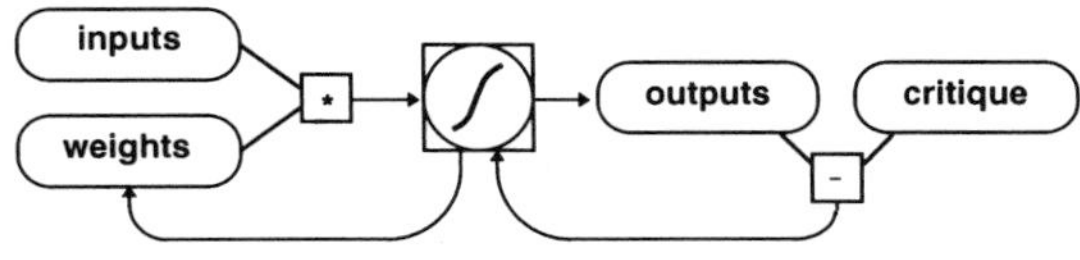

CBR training phase

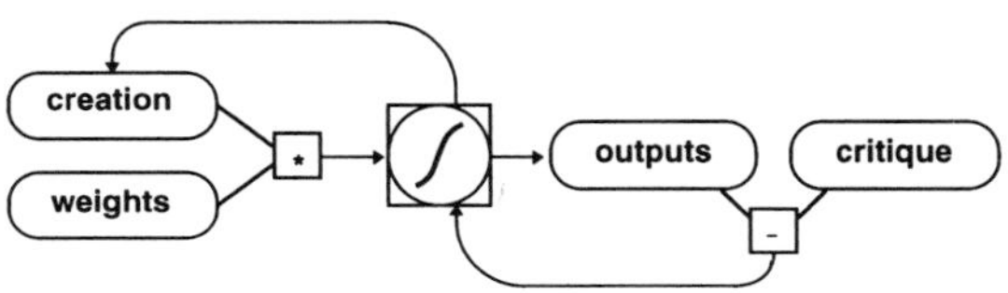

CBR creation phase

Creation by Refinement

The CBR paradigm consists of a learning phase, in which a neural network trained by a supervised gradient descent learning algorithm learns to be a "music critic" (preferentially judging musical examples according to various criteria), followed by a creation phase, in which a haphazard creation given as new input to the network is refined by a gradient descent search until it is judged to satisfy the trained criteria. Since CBR relies on an unspecified gradient descent learning algorithm, it is presented as a paradigm rather than a specific algorithm itself. CBR relies on the ability of this "critic net" to learn an arbitrary mapping, and back propagation and similar algorithms have this ability, at least in theory.

In the learning phase of CBR, a number of musical (and nonmusical) patterns are presented as input to the net, and the trainer's critique of each pattern is presented as the desired (target) output of the net. The differences between the net output and the critique are fed back into the net as a training error E, and the net weights W are adjusted by gradient descent in the direction $-\partial E/\partial W$.

The critique must be numerically expressed but may be many dimensional. A simple example of a training set would be various pitch sequences that are considered musical or nonmusical by the trainer, together with the trainer's corresponding categorization, expressed as a 1 (music), 0 (not music), 0.5 (not very good music), etc. A more complex example might include additional dimensions to describe the style, historical period, composer, or other characteristics of the sequences.

In the creation phase, the inverse of the critical map learned in training is probabilistically explored to generate novel patterns. The network input is relabeled as the "creation" (see Fig. 1).

This creation vector I is set to a random point in the creation space, and the critique (desired output) is set to a value representing a desired type of creation. The creation vector is then refined by a second gradient descent search in the direction $-\partial E/\partial I$, minimizing the difference between the obtained output and the critique vector, and so refining the creation to satisfy the desired criteria. (Note though that in this second gradient descent process, the weights are not changed.) Figure 1 depicts the computational equivalence between the weights on the inputs and input activations—gradient descent optimization can be applied to the creation in the same way it is applied to weights on the inputs.

This procedure is applicable using any supervised gradient descent learning network, since knowledge of the error gradient with respect to the weights entails being able to calculate the error gradient with respect to the inputs: inputs may be considered as weights on "virtual inputs" having a constant value. In the back-propagation algorithm, the error gradient with respect to the creation is available following the complete back-propagation pass. Using the notation of Rumelhart, Hinton, and Williams (1986), this is

$$\frac{\partial E}{\partial i_m} = -\sum_n \delta_n w_{n,m},$$

where E is the total error, i_m is a component of the creation input (i.e., the activation of the mth input unit), $w_{n,m}$ is the weight from input unit m to unit n, δ_n is the back-propagated error component at unit n, and the summation is over all units n receiving input from i_m. The value used to adjust the creation input vector gradually with each iteration of the search will be proportional to this derivative.

Study Case

As an extremely simple example of CBR (suitable for simulation on a napkin), consider a single linear neuron with one input i and one output o that computes $o = wi$, whose training task is to discover the ratio w between inputs i and desired outputs t. The required weight value $w = t/i$ can be found by a gradient descent search minimizing $E = (t - o)^2$, that is, iterated in the direction

$$-\frac{\partial E}{\partial w} = 2(t - o)i.$$

After the neuron is trained, CBR can be applied to produce values consistent with the ratio learned in training: set the input value (now relabeled as the creation input) to a random value, and pick a desired output. The creation input can then be refined by a second gradient descent search, this time iterated in the direction

$$-\frac{\partial E}{\partial i} = 2(t - o)w.$$

This is a roundabout way of arriving at $i = t/w$. Other solutions are not possible in this case because the map learned in training is invertible—CBR is not able to pick different solutions at random because there is only one solution. In realistic applications there are an infinite number of possible solutions. Also, the symmetry found in this simple example between learning and creation searches does not occur in multilayer networks, since the weights in all layers must be searched (that is, trained), but it is only necessary to change the inputs (not the hidden activations) in the backward "search" pass of the creation phase. (But then the hidden and output unit activations are changed as usual during the forward evaluation pass.)

Provisos

We now consider some potential difficulties with the CBR paradigm. To begin with, the learning task has whatever difficulties are associated with the particular learning algorithm (e.g., local minima). Similarly, the network configuration required to learn a particular judgment function may not be known in advance.

The refinement procedure after learning may also arrive at a local minimum, which in this case represents an unsatisfactory creation. This is not a significant difficulty, since the quality of a minimum is known and given by the magnitude of the error. If this error magnitude is not acceptable, the creation phase can be restarted from a different point. Thus CBR as described should be amended to automatically restart when an unsatisfactory creation is obtained. Unlike many optimization techniques where success cannot be guaranteed, CBR with restart is guaranteed to produce a satisfactory solution if allowed to run long enough.

Back propagation and related learning algorithms do not have natural position- and problem-size-invariant learning capabilities. Currently these limitations are approached essentially by increasing the size of the network in proportion to the required number of positions or the problem size. For example, Rumelhart, Hinton, and Williams (1986) achieved position invariance by replicating a trained network in all required positions. These are

Fig. 2. Sketch of the error surface as a function of input for a back-propagation network trained on the exclusive-or problem and expecting a TRUE input relation (i.e., for target output TRUE).

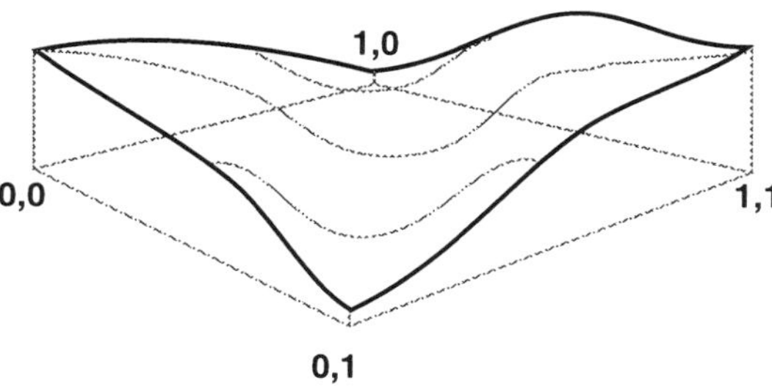

serious limitations, which hopefully will be overcome in future algorithms. The extensions to CBR described later serve as simple attention mechanisms, allowing a fixed-size network a limited degree of position and size invariance.

How would CBR handle a fuzzy common practice dictum such as "the diminished seventh chord is rarely followed by anything but I or V"? The initial random creation may well include violations of such constraints, but would be judged inacceptable. CBR would attempt to refine away these violations. Some may remain, however, especially if they fall at *local* error minima. The musical interpretation of such a case would be that although they are violations, they are justified by surrounding structure—fixing them will make a number of other things worse. With sufficiently few cases, the creation may be judged acceptable.

Number of Creations

In order for there to be more than one creation, the critique function learned in training must be many-to-one. In fact the preimage of a particular critique vector is potentially quite large. In the standard neuron architecture, the output of a unit is a function of the weighted inputs connected to it, that is,

$$o_j = f\left(\sum_k w_{j,k} i_k\right),$$

and in this case the space of equivalent inputs accepted by a particular network unit satisfies

$$\sum_k w_{j,k} i_k = \text{constant}.$$

This space is a hyperplane of dimension $n-1$ for a unit with n inputs. Similarly, holding constant the outputs of all other units with these same inputs reduces the equivalent input space to an intersection of hyperplanes or affine set of typically much lower dimension, but the arbitrarily fixed outputs represent only one point in a hyperplane of inputs accepted by a *subsequent* network layer, increasing the dimensionality again. And if the precision of the units and weights is not infinite but rather tolerates some variation, once again the accepted creation input set is increased.

Completing the Domain

The preimage of a particular critique must also be limited to acceptable creations. This requires that the training set adequately sample the input space; it must include counterexamples as well as examples.

For example, suppose we want to use CBR to generate points at random satisfying the Boolean exclusive-or (XOR) relation. That is, if we set the critique to TRUE, we want CBR to generate either {TRUE, FALSE} or {FALSE, TRUE} at random, and if the critique is FALSE, we want {TRUE, TRUE} or {FALSE, FALSE} to be generated at random. To do this, we would first train a network on the exclusive-or function, probably encoding the Boolean TRUE and FALSE values as unit activation values near 1 and 0 respectively.

In the creation phase, CBR can produce creations anywhere in the preimage of the desired critique. For a back-propagation network with two hidden units trained on the exclusive-or function, the preimage of TRUE (1) satisfies approximately $x+y=1$ (Fig. 2). Consequently, CBR will generate undesired non-Boolean creations such as {0.4, 0.6} as well as the desired Boolean points.

As illustrated in this example, the encoding of the learning problem may well result in a creation space having "illegal" values, such as possible fractional values when Boolean values are encoded in real-valued activations. In these and other cases in which areas of the creation space are not represented in the training data, CBR may generate unexpected and undesirable creations despite successful training.

This problem would be solved if the training set adequately sampled the creation space. For example, the preimages of TRUE and FALSE in the exclusive-or case can be restricted to the desired Boolean points by including additional relations such as $\{0.4, 0.6\} \rightarrow 0.5$ in the training set.

Since in general we may not know how to construct a training set that adequately samples the creation space, the training procedure is amended to allow the CBR creation phase itself to generate the needed samples: when undesirable or nonsensical creations are obtained, they should be added to the training set with a corresponding "undesirable" critique, followed by retraining. This is termed *completing the domain.* In the author's experience completing the domain is often required and can expand the training set considerably.

Impossible Critiques

For most applications the training critiques must be subjectively determined since objective knowledge of the critique function will not be available. It is possible that errors in this determination could lead to a learning task that can only be solved by memorizing the training pairs. In this case exploring the inverse of the learned function will not yield new patterns with the desired structure because generalization is impossible. Refining or expanding the training set may solve this problem if it is recognized.

As an example of this possibility, one could include the date of composition in the critique vector and thus hope to simulate the style of composition in various historical periods (possibly including the future). This would only work if there were truly a functional relationship (other than itemization) including time and some discoverable features of the training compositions. Although historical accounts bias us towards progress-oriented thinking, and progressions of work can sometimes be identified, it would seem that in many cases cultural and other nonmusical influences contribute to stylistic development. In these cases attempts to discover a function relating style to time will fail.

Creation or Imitation?

An obvious application of CBR would be to synthesize new compositions in the style of a celebrated composer, for instance the usually used J. S. Bach. In this case the critique vector would consist of the bit Bach-or-not, possibly together with additional parameters describing mood, etc., and the training set would consist of Bach's compositions, together with other music and nonmusic as required to complete the domain.

Is it really possible that CBR could synthesize new works by the classical masters? We can at least entertain this question: it is known that neural net algorithms such as back propagation can represent an arbitrary function (Stinchcombe and White 1989); the mapping (Bach→1, not-Bach→0) is just one such function given a suitable encoding of the space of music. At present it also seems possible that algorithms such as back propagation can *learn* arbitrary functions, given enough time and examples.

If computing time is the only obstacle, then CBR may live up to this compositional promise—at present, parallel machines having performance figures such as 10^{10} instructions per second are commercially available, and machines with performance greater than some estimates of the human brain's computing power are forecast. The real difficulty, if any, will be in properties of back propagation–like algorithms that are not fully understood at present, such as the relationship between the size and complexity of the problem and the network parameters necessitated.

One familiar indictment of neural networks is that their computational scaling characteristics may be poor—although many "toy" problems have been solved, problems that are N times more complex may require some power (or other fast-growing function) of N times more computation. Thus, by this reasoning, serious problems may not be approachable in the foreseeable future (Minsky and Papert 1988).

This criticism is somewhat misdirected. Although computational scaling is important in computer algorithms applied to large data sets, it would appear that the human mind cannot undertake problems of arbitrary scale. Rather, a large problem is broken into manageable subsets by focusing attention on particular aspects of the problem. The number of these subsets may be quite small, such as Miller's "magic number" seven plus or minus two, which is the number of chunks of familiar information (numbers, city names, etc.) that people can remember easily (Miller 1956). Similarly, neural net algorithms might be adapted to solve large problems by directing the network with an attention mechanism.

A more disturbing class of criticism asserts that supervised learning neural network algorithms have not yet demonstrated interesting properties. One such criticism questions the promise of "computation without programming": although a back propagation–like net may in theory be able to learn an arbitrary function, it may be extremely difficult in practice to find the required net parameters and training data for a particular problem. At present there do not appear to be any theoretical guarantees that finding back propagation–like networks for particular problems is easier than solving these problems by other methods, including exhaustive or random search. Another criticism (Cybenko 1990) notes that from an interpolation/approximation viewpoint, many neural net demonstrations such as NETtalk (Sejnowski and Rosenberg 1986) are very underdetermined, that is, there are many more weights than there are training points. From this point of view, it is not surprising or interesting that these neural networks learn problems successfully. The extent to which networks generalize adequately despite being underdetermined is the interesting and surprising finding.

Finally, although it would be quite impressive if CBR could synthesize new music as if by Bach, it would also be disappointing if CBR were limited to imitating existing styles of music. Suppose CBR were trained with examples of all available styles of tonal music (for example)—would its creations still seem imitative? If in learning the examples the network formed a general notion of tonal music, then CBR could potentially generate any tonal composition. To attribute creativity and deny imitation we would probably require CBR to invent a music that is obviously different from any existing style (although we do not always require this of human composers). From the limited experience in applying CBR to toy problems, we do not know whether the results of such a hypothetical encyclopedic CBR would seem novel or imitative. This question is too speculative to be considered until better examples are available, and even then it will be a matter of philosophy unless there are some criteria for judging if and why a particular idea or form is sufficiently different from its antecedents to be considered novel rather than obvious or inevitable (see also Loy, this volume, for a discussion of the possibility of creativity by neural networks).

Extensions, Applications, and Experiments

CBR as described so far is theoretically interesting but not very practical on typical serial computers due to the computational expense of the back-propagation learning algorithm. To indicate one benchmark, NETtalk (Sejnowski and Rosenberg 1986) is a well-known problem that required a number of hours to learn on a minicomputer. This problem used the back-propagation algorithm with approximately 200 inputs and 10,000 weights. A network of this size can represent only very small musical examples. For example, suppose pitch and duration are encoded using the enumerative (or localist) representation (Sejnowski and Rosenberg 1986), with the pitch and duration values being represented by the input unit with the highest activation in each of several sets of input units enumerating possible note values. Then, if pitch is restricted to one octave (12 possible values) and duration is restricted to whole, half, quarter, and eighth notes, 16 inputs would be required per note, and a net with 200 inputs would represent a musical composition containing only 13 notes.

If it is established that the computational scaling characteristics of back propagation are in fact poor, then even fast parallel machines may not help back propagation to solve large problems in music, given the network size needed for even the small problem in the previous paragraph. But there are at least two ways of dealing with this scaling difficulty. The computational expense of CBR using back propagation can be addressed via improved learning algorithms. And larger problems can also be approached by using some mechanism to divide the problem into manageable portions.

Attentional CBR

In order to partition a large problem into manageable subproblems, we need to provide both an attention mechanism to select subproblems to present to the network and a context mechanism to tie the resulting subpatterns together into a coherent whole. A context mechanism can be provided by context inputs, which during the creation phase are clamped to the values of the surrounding and previously constructed pattern. As an example, to produce elaborations on a short phrase, the training set inputs would consist of sample phrases paired with corresponding embellished phrases (possibly using a suitable null-note representation to allow different phrase lengths), and the critique would (as usual) consist of some critique of the character of the embellishment. In the creation phase, the embellished inputs would be set to random values, but the context inputs would be clamped to the phrase itself.

Of course, attentional strategies do not increase the amount of information stored in a network of a given size. Rather, an attentional strategy trades instances for size—instead of generating a number of small patterns of a particular size, one can generate larger patterns containing information equivalent to various permutations of the collection of small patterns. It is also possible to generate patterns that are large enough to exhaust the information in the network. In this case some substructures will necessarily be repeated, or the structural content of the pattern will be diluted. A certain amount of repetition and dilution of content may be acceptable or desirable from an artistic point of view.

Various compositional approaches are possible depending on the selected attention mechanism. Since all such mechanisms are in some sense informationally equivalent by the storage conservation argument, the particular mechanism should be selected to effect a desired compositional approach, or according to other practical criteria. In *sequential* CBR, prior output (in time) provides the context, and the attention is on the next note or phrase. This is a restricted compositional approach, but one that is suitable for live accompaniment since it depends only on past outputs. In *interactive* CBR, the experimenter selects the subpatterns to present to the network.

The author's experiments have employed *hierarchical* CBR. In this approach, a developing pattern is recursively filled in using a scheme somewhat analogous to a formal grammar rule such as $ABC \rightarrow AxByC$, which expands the string without modifying existing tokens. That is, three tokens (for example, musical notes) labeled A,B,C will be expanded with two additional tokens x,y inserted in the indicated positions. The expanded string $AxByC$ may be rewritten further using a suitable scheme.

This scheme differs from a formal grammar, however, in that the rewrite scheme represents only how the developing pattern is partitioned into subproblems to present to the network; there are no tokens or deterministic rules. Rather, a supervised learning net is trained (as usual) to recognize a particular class of patterns as desirable (grammatical, by our analogy); then portions of a developing creation are clamped (providing context), the pattern is expanded adjacent to the clamped context with random starting values, and these new portions of the pattern are refined to be desirable according to the learned critique (rewriting). The adoption of the hierarchical CBR scheme over other attentional approaches was motivated in part by the fact that tonal music is often analyzed hierarchically (for example, see Lerdahl and Jackendoff 1983); however, hierarchical CBR is hierarchical only in derivation.

As a concrete example of hierarchical CBR, to implement melody generation with the $ABC \rightarrow AxByC$ rewrite scheme, the training set would consist of windows of length five from larger melodies. During the creation phase a three-note window is selected somewhere along the partially constructed melody, and these three notes are clamped to the

A,B,C values. The two remaining notes are initialized to random values and are refined.

It might seem that clamping could be avoided by moving the A,B,C context notes into the critique, that is, the critique function would be

$$x, y \rightarrow Q, A, B, C$$

for a critique vector Q rather than

$$A, x, B, y, C \rightarrow Q.$$

The difficulty with this approach is that it would require the network to learn a multi-valued function—particular x,y values may be usable in several different contexts, and thus associated with several outputs of this type. Thus it is desirable to maintain the original hierarchical approach and extend the neural net simulation software to provide a flag indicating units that need to be clamped during the creation phase.

In a hierarchical CBR scheme used for music composition it is desirable to include an additional context unit that reflects the level of recursion, thus allowing the net to discover and differentiate deep and surface structure if the particular style of music supports this differentiation. This approach would require training patterns categorized according to their "deepness." Deep patterns could be obtained by formal or informal application of structural analysis (Lerdahl and Jackendoff 1983; Westergaard 1975)—for example, we might designate scale degrees 1,2,3, . . . , as the structure underlying the surface sequence 1,2,1,2,3,2,3,4,3, . . .—or possibly by some algorithmic or neural net analysis. The hierarchical CBR experiments described in this chapter do not differentiate deep and surface structure.

Reinforcement CBR

Developing the training set is probably the most difficult aspect of employing CBR (and other supervised learning algorithms). In *reinforcement* CBR some or all of the training set is produced automatically, by completing the domain, rather than being compiled by the experimenter as in the standard supervised learning paradigm. In this scheme, the training phase is interrupted at intervals, and the creation phase is invoked. The resulting creations are evaluated by the experimenter and are added to the training set with a corresponding critique if they are judged to extend the existing training set. After the training set is extended, the net is retrained, followed by the accumulation of new examples, etc., until all sample creations are judged satisfactory by both the experimenter and the network.

Adaptive Learning Algorithm

There have been a large number of proposals for improved gradient descent learning algorithms. Among these are adaptive approaches such as Tenorio and Lee (1989), Mozer and Smolensky (1989), Bailey (1990), Le Cun, Denker, and Solla (1990), and Malakooti and Zhou (1990), all of which add synapses and neurons or delete unneeded synapses or neurons as required, to "grow" (or "shrink") a minimal network suited to a particular problem size.

Adaptive network approaches address a major drawback of neural networks based on back propagation–like algorithms: although networks trained with these algorithms can learn to accomplish tasks without programming, extensive experimentation and considerable patience may be required to discover the network parameters required for a particular problem. A network that has not learned a particular problem may simply require more training, or a larger network may be required. Since training can be very time consuming, the experimenter may be tempted to start with very large networks in the hope of assuring that a long training run will result in the problem being learned. Large (very underdetermined) networks are also problematic, since they can solve the learning task by memorizing aspects of the training patterns rather than by discovering general features. This will result in CBR reproducing the training patterns (or recognizable portions of them) at random, rather than generating new patterns. Adaptive network algorithms can potentially solve these problems by adapting the network architecture to the size of the problem.

The *cascade-correlation* algorithm (Fahlman and

Lebiere 1990) has been employed for several recent CBR experiments. This algorithm begins with a minimal network containing no hidden units and adds a new hidden unit when the existing net appears to approach an asymptote in the error. Each new hidden unit is trained to maximize its correlation with the error across the set of training patterns. In this way, the new neuron attempts to describe some part of the function that is not yet handled by the existing network. After the new neuron is trained, its weights are frozen, and the output layer of the network is retrained until an error asymptote is again reached or until the training is successful. The size of the network is influenced by a patience parameter. This parameter describes when to add a new neuron in terms of a scheme for detecting an asymptote in the error behavior, such as the slope of an error measure with respect to time.

In the author's experience, the cascade-correlation algorithm is an improvement over back propagation but may still fail to learn. One problem centers around detecting when the net has really reached an asymptote: the speed of learning may slow down as the net incorporates information added by a particular neuron. If one is too greedy in specifying the patience parameter, these slowdowns will result in a new neuron being added too soon, and the network will grow without learning anything. Finding a workable patience setting requires patience, and the parameter may need to be varied as the learning progresses and subproblems of varying difficulty are encountered.

CBR employs the cascade-correlation algorithm in a manner directly analogous to the use of back propagation in CBR, with one additional consideration: when the CBR creation phase reveals the need to complete the example domain, an incorrect function has been learned and the existing network should probably be retrained rather than extending the net with new neurons. In the standard cascade-correlation algorithm the neuron weights are fixed after they are first trained, so retraining is not possible. There are several possible solutions to this problem; the solution used by the author is simply to start training a new network whenever patterns are added to the training set.

The cascade-correlation algorithm learns faster than many variations of back propagation, and in addition there is somewhat less risk that the training will fail due to inappropriate network parameters. As in other neural net approaches, however, cascade correlation does not fully realize the ease of use that is promised by the ability of neural networks to perform without programming.

Experiments

CBR has been explored through a number of experiments in music and computer graphics, including generation of melodies and chord sequences, stochastic function and texture synthesis, and the generation of low-resolution imaginary portraits. The experiments were developed in a small Lisp dialect that was extended with vector operations (Lewis 1986). This provided nearly the efficiency of a lower-level language together with interactive programming. The ability to use Lisp as an interpretive scripting language provided considerable flexibility in developing the experiments and eliminated the need to develop custom programs for each experiment. The experiments were conducted on a variety of serial machines with performance ranging up to about six MFLOPS.

The experiments reveal that it is considerably easier to produce useful visual forms than it is to produce interesting musical structures using CBR. This may be explained by the fact that human visual perception of textures is relatively insensitive to statistics higher than the second order (Lewis 1987; Richards 1988), whereas adequate description of the (tonal) music used in these experiments requires much more than the second-order statistics.

Doodle Generation

Figure 3 shows "doodles" generated by a reinforcement CBR experiment. This experiment will be described because it is very easy to perform and yet produces interpretable results. As in many other neural network demonstrations, some of the structure evident in the examples is due to the selection

Fig. 3. "Doodles" generated by reinforcement CBR.

of an appropriate representation space for the learning problem. In this case, the network input units represent the curvature κ of the doodle parameterized by the curve length l (i.e., a vector of curvature values equally spaced along the curve), with 0.5 meaning zero curvature. The curve is then constructed by

$$\theta = \int \kappa dl$$

$$x = \int \cos\theta dl, \quad y = \int \sin\theta dl.$$

The output or critique represents whether the doodle is considered attractive by the experimenter. The network's learning task, then, is to learn the curvature patterns that characterize desirable doodles.

We can make this an easy learning task by providing the vague critique that doodles which are either too straight or too jumbled are undesirable, and everything else is acceptable. In this case, the learning task is simply to generate a small filter over the random creation values, that is, to do a weighted average of several neighboring creation values. If the network is required to discover more specific forms of correlation in curvature, analogies to numerical filtering can guide the selection of network size. The doodles in Fig. 3 are generated using a net whose construction is not based on these considerations, with 150 hidden units in the second layer, 50 more hidden units in a third layer, and a single output unit. A small number of input units, such as 50, is sufficient geometrically to describe these doodles. The training set can be obtained by reinforcement CBR starting from a minimal initial set containing several random vectors and a 0.5 vector (straight line).

Melodies and Chord Sequences

Another simple experiment is the generation of short melodies (Fig. 4). Again in this experiment the problem space was selected to produce a desired structure and thus simplify the network's learning task. In this case, the melodies are produced by hierarchical CBR, starting from an initial form consisting of scale degrees 1, 5, 1 and recursively expanding this using a $AB \rightarrow AxB$ scheme. Thus a 1, 5, 1 skeleton is guaranteed (though it can potentially be obscured by poor elaboration), and a melodic curve to and from the dominant tone is likely.

For this experiment, enumerative encoding is used to represent an abstract seven-note scale within one octave only. This abstract scale can be interpreted as a major, minor, or other scale; Fig. 4 is rendered using a C-major scale. The $AB \rightarrow AxB$ scheme requires an input window of three notes. During the training phase, the input window is situated at random positions on the training melodies. The training set includes melodies generated by a simple algorithmic melody generator. During the creation phase the input units corresponding to A and B are clamped to the values of adjacent, previously constructed notes, and the third note is the random creation. The critique is a single good/bad judgment value. Thus the network has 3×7 inputs and one output. In experiments using the back-propagation algorithm, the author usually starts with networks with two hidden layers with $3N$ and N units, for N inputs.

In a previous paper (Lewis 1989), chord sequences were presented that were generated using a similar hierarchical $AB \rightarrow AxB$ CBR scheme. An **i,v,i** skele-

Fig. 4. Melodies generated using a AB → AxB *hierarchical CBR scheme. Although hierarchical CBR can generate melodies of any length, it is clear in this figure that the* AB → AxB *scheme does not provide adequate context, and the melodies "wander."*

Fig. 5. Sample chord sequences generarted by using hierarchical AB → AxB *CBR. The leading number indicates a common practice (1) versus not-common-practice (0) rating.*

```
(0.200000 I III VII IV III V VII VI V VI VI I)
(0.200000 I II II VII V VII II VII VI III II I)
(0.500000 I IV I II V IV III IV VI II V I)
(0.500000 I V IV V IV V II VII VII III VII I)
(0.800000 I V IV I V V I VI IV V I I)
(0.800000 I I II V VI IV VI VII I I V I)
```

ton was used as a seed sequence. Sample runs are reproduced in Fig. 5. Adjacent chord pairs were picked at random on the growing sequence and provided context for adding an intermediate chord by CBR. The initial training set for this experiment was derived from notions of common practice rather than from actual compositions. The training set was also constructed so as to provide a simple example of a multidimensional critique. Specifically, training patterns were devised to represent an additional critique dimension vaguely reflecting the degree of observance of common-practice chord changes. The usual acceptable/not acceptable critique was effectively split into two parts, one indicating correct enumerative encoding, and the second indicating correct common practice (it is possible that this critique could also be represented by three distinct values of a single nonbinary critique unit). This additional dimension was successfully learned and is reflected in the generated sequences.

A Larger Experiment

We can make the network's learning task easier by selecting a better representation space for pitch. The enumerative (localist) representation of pitch has some advantages (Sejnowski and Rosenberg 1986; Todd 1988), but it also requires the network to learn pitch ordering if the training set includes certain pitch operations such as sequencing. A relative or interval representation (in which a starting pitch is given and subsequent pitches are expressed as intervals up or down from the previous pitch—see Todd, this volume) makes operations in pitch space natural but obscures the individual character of the scale degrees. A general pitch encoding must represent multiple octaves while reflecting the fact that members of a particular pitch class in different octaves are related. These considerations conflict with the limited precision of individual neurons and the desire to restrict the size of a network for efficiency.

For recent experiments focusing on tonal melody composition, the author has selected an ad hoc pitch representation that is essentially relative, enumeratively representing jumps of up to (e.g., in one experiment) +6 and −4 degrees in an abstract seven-note scale, but that is augmented with three units that classify the prior pitch as having a tonic function, a dominant function, or neither.

An initial experiment using this scheme is shown in Fig. 6. Hierarchical CBR was used with a *ABCD→ ABxCD* rewrite scheme. The four-note context in this rule requires a starting melody with a length of at least four. The initial melody is (scale degrees) 1,1,5,1,1, and the outer 1s are deleted after the melody is generated. Additionally, the input pitch representation is extended with one additional unit indicating that a rewrite from a particular context is undesirable, meaning the particular window is well formed and would be degraded by an additional

Fig. 6. Melodies generated using a ABCD → ABxCD *hierarchical CBR scheme.*

tone. As in Fig. 4, the abstract scale is rendered as C major. The training set consists of windows of length five from various melodies, presented to the network as four intervals rather than five pitches. The melodies were selected from a number of folk and classical melodies found in a sight-singing book (Ottman 1967). The training set also contains several examples that were devised to emphasize an upper-neighbor tone elaboration, as shown in the sample training pairs in Fig. 7.

In this experiment and in Fig. 4, preferences for repetition, stepwise motion, and skips of a third or a fifth are apparent. There appear to be preferences for degrees 1 and 5, but this may be largely the result of interpolating the 1, 5, 1 starting melody. In fact, the melodies rarely go outside of the 1-to-5-degree range, although in both experiments the pitch encoding and training sets represent larger pitch ranges (the relative pitch encoding used in Fig. 6 does not limit the melody to an octave).

Figures 4 and 6 are probably too limited to be interesting from other than a theoretical point of view. Although these experiments have not presented computational difficulties and do not appear to be particularly large in comparison to other learning tasks reported in the literature (such as NETtalk), developing the experiments is very time consuming, and several more ambitious experiments have not (yet) succeeded. Experiments involving other dimensions of music such as polyphony and rhythm have still to be tried.

Conclusion

The CBR paradigm provides a fairly satisfactory theoretical approach to the generation of structured novel patterns, in particular for applications such as computer arts where the structure is perceptually evaluated. CBR is conceptually satisfying in that the creation process is not represented by a sequence of rigid rules and in that the criteria learned in training will be fuzzy if the presented patterns so require. CBR can also represent structure more

Fig. 7. Some of the training set corresponding to the critique "good" in the experiment shown in Fig. 6. The counterexamples or "bad" patterns are not represented adequately in music notation since they were obtained by completing the domain and generally violate the enumerative localist encoding constraint.

efficiently than probabilistic approaches, since the network learning algorithm essentially discovers required high-order statistics in the form of fuzzy rules without needing to identify and represent the entire probability distribution function.

Without wishing to add to the mass of philosophical speculation concerning creativity, we note that CBR vaguely resembles subjective impressions of some creative activities in which phases of learning, invention, and refinement are identifiable. The role of chance in artistic creativity has also been widely discussed, and cognitive mechanisms that produce or require random noise in the brain have been proposed (Eccles 1958; Crick and Mitchison 1983; Hopfield, Feinstein, and Palmer 1983).

At the current time CBR must be considered as a hypothetical approach to the problem of tonal music composition. This is an indication of the complexity of this problem, since CBR *is* practical for smaller problems such as the generation of random functions and texture synthesis for computer graphics.

The major difficulty in employing CBR is in learning the critique function, and CBR inherits all of the difficulties of the underlying learning algorithm. The eventual appraisement of CBR will depend on the resolution of issues that affect all applications of supervised gradient descent learning algorithms. These issues include the fact that successful learning cannot generally be guaranteed or predicted. Other problems include efficiency and the lack of position-invariant and problem-size-invariant learning. Improvements in these areas will directly benefit CBR.

References

Bailey, A. 1990. "Automatic Evolution of Neural Net Architectures." *Proceedings of the International Joint Conference on Neural Networks,* vol. 1. Hillsdale, N.J.: Erlbaum Associates, pp. 589–592.

Ballard, D., G. E. Hinton, and T. J. Sejnowski. 1983. "Parallel Visual Computation." *Nature* 306:21–26.

Crick, F., and G. Mitchison. 1983. "The Function of Dream Sleep." *Nature* 304:111–114.

Cybenko, G. 1990. "Complexity Theory of Neural Networks and Classification Problems." In L. B. Almeida and C. J. Wellekens, eds. *Lecture Notes in Computer Science 412: Neural Networks EURASIP Workshop.* New York: Springer-Verlag.

Doob, J. 1953. *Stochastic Processes.* New York: Wiley.

Eccles, J. C. 1958. "The Physiology of Imagination." *Scientific American* 199:135–146.

Fahlman, S., and C. Lebiere. 1990. "The Cascade-Correlation Learning Architecture." Technical Report CMU-CS-90-100. Pittsburgh: Carnegie Mellon University, Department of Computer Science.

Hiller, L., and L. Isaacson. 1959. *Experimental Music.* New York: McGraw-Hill.

Hopfield, J. J., D. I. Feinstein, and R. G. Palmer. 1983. "Unlearning Has a Stabilizing Effect in Collective Memories." *Nature* 304:158–159.

Jones, K. 1981. "Compositional Applications of Stochastic Processes." *Computer Music Journal* 5:45–61.

Kalos, M., and P. Whitlock. 1986. *Monte Carlo Methods.* New York: Wiley.

Le Cun, Y., J. S. Denker, and S. A. Solla. 1990. "Optimal Brain Damage." In D. S. Touretzky, ed. *Advances in Neural Information Processing Systems 2.* San Mateo, California: Morgan Kaufmann, pp. 598–605.

Lerdahl, F., and R. Jackendoff. 1983. *A Generative Theory of Tonal Music.* Cambridge, Massachusetts: MIT Press.

Lewis, J. P. 1986. *Zlisp Manual.* Old Westbury, New York: New York Institute of Technology Computer Graphics Lab.

Lewis, J. P. 1987. "Generalized Stochastic Subdivision." *ACM Transactions on Graphics* 6:167–190.

Lewis, J. P. 1988. "Creation by Refinement: A Creativity Paradigm for Gradient Descent Learning Networks." *Proceedings of the International Conference on Neural Networks,* vol. II. San Diego: IEEE/SOS Printing, pp. 229–233.

Lewis, J. P. 1989. "Algorithms for Music Composition by Neural Nets: Improved CBR Paradigms." *Proceedings of the International Computer Music Conference.* San Francisco: Computer Music Association, pp. 180–183.

Lidov, D., and J. Gabura. 1973. "A Melody Writing Algorithm Using a Formal Language Model." *Computer Studies in the Humanities* 4:138–148.

Loy, D. G. This volume. "Connectionism and Musiconomy."

Malakooti, B., and Y. Zhou. 1990. "An Adaptive Strategy to Design the Structure of Feedforward Neural Nets." *Proceedings of the International Joint Conference on Neural Networks,* vol I. Hillsdale, N.J.: Erlbaum Associates, pp. 432–435.

Metropolis, N., A. W. Rosenbluth, M. N. Rosenbluth, A. H. Teller, and E. Teller. 1953. "Equations of State Calculations by Fast Computing Machines." *Journal of Chemical Physics* 21:1087–1092.

Miller, G. A. 1956. "The Magical Number Seven, Plus or Minus Two: Some Limits on Our Capacity for Processing Information." *Psychological Review* 63:81–97.

Minsky, M., and S. Papert. 1988. *Perceptrons.* Expanded ed. Cambridge, Massachusetts: MIT Press.

Moorer, J. A. 1972. "Music and Computer Composition." *Communications of the ACM* 15:104–113.

Mozer, M. C., and P. Smolensky. 1989. "Skeletonization: A Technique for Trimming the Fat from a Network via Relevance Assessment." In D. S. Touretzky, ed. *Advances in Neural Information Processing Systems 1.* San Mateo, California: Morgan Kaufmann, pp. 107–115.

Ottman, R. 1967. *Music for Sight Singing.* Englewood Cliffs, N.J.: Prentice Hall.

Peitgen, H., and D. Saupe. 1988. *The Science of Fractal Images.* New York: Springer-Verlag.

Richards, W. 1988. *Natural Computation.* Cambridge, Massachusetts: MIT Press.

Roads, C. 1979. "Grammars as Representations for Music." *Computer Music Journal* 3:48–55.

Rumelhart, D. E., G. E. Hinton, and R. Williams. 1986. "Learning Internal Representations by Error Propagation." In D. E. Rumelhart and J. L. McClelland, eds. *Parallel Distributed Processing: Explorations in the Microstructure of Cognition,* vol. 1. Cambridge, Massachusetts: MIT Press.

Sejnowski, T. J., and C. R. Rosenberg. 1986. "NETtalk: A Parallel Network that Learns to Read Aloud." Technical Report EECS-86/01. Baltimore: Johns Hopkins

University, Department of Electrical Engineering and Computer Science.

Stinchcombe, M., and H. White. 1989. "Universal Approximations Using Feedforward Networks with Non-sigmoid Hidden Layer Activation Functions." *Proceedings of the International Joint Conference on Neural Networks,* vol. I. San Diego: SOS Printing, pp. 613–617.

Tenorio, M. F., and W. T. Lee. 1989. "Self Organizing Neural Networks for the Identification Problem." In D. S. Touretzky, ed. *Advances in Neural Information Processing Systems 1.* San Mateo, California: Morgan Kaufmann, pp. 57–64.

Todd, P. M. 1988. "A Sequential Network Design for Musical Applications." In D. S. Touretzky, G. E. Hinton, and T. J. Sejnowski, eds. *Proceedings of the 1988 Connectionist Models Summer School.* San Mateo, California: Morgan Kaufmann, pp. 76–84.

Todd, P. M. This volume. "A Connectionist Approach to Algorithmic Composition."

Westergaard, P. 1975. *An Introduction to Tonal Theory.* New York: Norton.

Xenakis, I. 1971. *Formalized Music.* Bloomington, Indiana: Indiana University Press.

Teuvo Kohonen, Pauli Laine, Kalev Tiits, and Kari Torkkola
Helsinki University of Technology
Laboratory of Computer and Information Science
Rakentajanaukio 2 C,
SF-02150 Espoo, Finland
kari@hutmc.hut.fi

A Nonheuristic Automatic Composing Method

Introduction

In this article we describe an automatic composing method based on a self-learning grammar system that differs in many respects from the standard approaches made in computer music. One of its central characteristics is that it learns its rules from a given set of examples without any heuristic design, and is thereby able to imitate an arbitrary "style." This property is often attributed to neural networks in general, and the method we describe here can be made to fit into this framework. In spite of the rather restricted musicological scope of our method, its ability to generate long, interesting passages with ease serves to justify its discussion in the context of automated music composition.

The basic ideas of this method were developed outside musical research, specifically in speech recognition. As a result, we did not originally consider at all the more ambitious musical objectives such as implementation of higher hierarchical forms or voice leading according to generally accepted musicological rules. Several suggestions have since been made to us, reflecting our own initial thoughts, to combine the present (linear) self-learning grammar with additional grammars that operate at the levels of deep structures to guide the composition process somehow. So far, however, we have not pursued such ideas.

One of the most central arguments against these ideas has been that the present method does not require any musicological expertise or analyses to generate pieces according to any style. Instead, it completely learns its own rules, even if they only represent the surface structure, from the given examples. Thus this method is not restricted merely to classical music, for which plenty of theoretical guidelines are available, but also applies to any other kind of music, even informal or casual styles, for which no musicological theories exist. This unrestricted applicability would be lost immediately if the method were hybridized with a heuristic grammar that forces a deep structure of a fixed musical style into the method's compositional process. Thus, the method we present, though unlikely to capture fully all levels of musical structure, makes up for this deficit by being universally applicable to all styles of music, and requiring no predetermined theoretical knowledge.

The absence of hierarchical structure from the compositions produced by this method may not be a musical disadvantage in every case. There are indeed kinds of music not required to fulfill the standards of an independent artistic creation: background music, improvisations, etc. These may be examples that are intended to affect the minds of people at the preattentive level. Such music does not need to reflect any hierarchical structures. It may be better in these cases just to maintain a feeling of continuity and smoothness over an indefinite span of time. The compositional productions created by the present method belong to this loose category; we do not want to claim that the music produced by it is composed in a finished form but rather "improvised," continuously following the learned, intrinsic rules. We may still use, and learn from devising, an automated method to achieve even this level of compositional skill.

The Present Method in Historical Context

Since the days of Pythagoras, the relationships that apparently exist between music and mathematics have inspired people to suggest theories and carry out experiments to discover analytically definable rules in music. Composing music automatically, guided by random numbers or other random processes, is an old idea, too. The composing machine *Musarithmica mirifica* of Samuel Pepys (1639–

1703) contained decks of cards from which randomly variable melodic turns were drawn. Around 1719, the Prague Cistercian M. Vogt used long, bent nails to describe elementary musical patterns, and by throwing them on the floor, tried to find new melodic forms. Rather pleasant music can also be produced as random combinations of specifically designed standard motives that are made to assemble harmonically, as in the famous dice-throwing compositions of W. A. Mozart. More recently, Markov-chain music is based on the assumption that sequences of notes obey statistical laws. Finally, modern computerized composing has developed from these early attempts through many phases and has given rise to new musicological theories and methods. Composing programs are currently available as standard tools.

The first step in many contemporary attempts to generate music automatically has been the definition of some kind of musical grammar or system of production rules that is then combined with random processes to construct new, continuous melodic and harmonic structures. Determination of these rules is usually based on musical expertise, that is, the exhaustive analysis and understanding of a certain style such as modal or baroque music. Compilation of such a grammar is a tedious heuristic task, as shown by some early implementations (for example, see Baroni and Jacoboni 1978), and acceptable results have only been obtained if the rules have been restricted to the most basic norms of style. In some recent developments (Ebcioglu 1988), the compilation work has been relieved by the use of knowledge databases into which new rules can be added easily, with the aid of logic programming languages. Although these automated development tools facilitate applications of practical significance, the results are still subject to limitations similar to those of the earlier methods. The most severe limitation is the enormous amount of work needed to discover all the characteristic features of a particular style; and then the results are not generalizable to other styles.

A different approach altogether is the self-learning grammar, the rules of which are automatically and systematically constructed on the basis of exemplary material (Kohonen 1985, 1989). It is possible to define very specific rules of appreciable complexity in a context-sensitive grammar by using a wide musical context in each rule. But then to allow a reasonable range of musical variations, a lot of examples will be needed to create a rich grammar of many rules and avoid ending up with a small set of highly restrictive rules. To reach a compromise between these requirements, in the present grammatical method, called dynamically expanding context (DEC), we start with the simplest and most general (context-free) rules and only specify the context more closely when a controversy or conflict in the examples is found. This kind of specification is dynamical, because a rule is replaced by a gradually more specific version only when needed. The amount of context used thus varies from one production rule to another.

The DEC method belongs to the broad category of unsupervised learning algorithms, and no musicological expertise or heuristical analyses are necessary for the construction of the grammar. It is sufficient to collect exemplary material that coherently and consistently expresses a number of the essential regularities characteristic of a particular musical style or its subset and to use this as the input to a program that constructs the grammar. This method is thus applicable to styles whether or not musicological analyses have been made (for example, popular folk music as well as classical, etc.). Another advantage of this method in making new compositions is its ease of use: the composing process proceeds automatically, controlled solely by an appropriately chosen set of parameters. A further interesting aspect of this compositional process is that hybrids of two or more different styles can be made by mixing corresponding examples in teaching.

The DEC grammar was originally developed for the postprocessing of symbol strings in the automatic recognition of speech (Kohonen 1986, Kohonen et al. 1988) where it yielded rather good results. It was then concluded that the optimally specific rules discovered by this method might also be effective in describing the complex patterns of music. The first experiments carried out in 1988 were very encouraging, and so we decided to continue with this line of inquiry. The basic concept for this learning procedure was compact and relatively easy to implement. In particular, ambiguities present in the teaching material were taken into account much more effectively than in the Markovian models, which only combine the ambiguities statistically.

Since 1988 we have produced many hours of finished compositions by this method. As source material we have used both melodic and polyphonic works from several tens of composers, ranging from medieval music to modern jazz. The produced music in general sounds pleasant, even over lengthy periods of listening, and maintains a high degree of melodic coherence. The method automatically defines a great number, say, tens of thousands, of rules that are made directly accessible in a standard relational database through hash coding. Tentative generation of the material for a new piece, even when using personal computers, therefore only takes a few tens of seconds. Given a set of preconstructed grammars, all that is needed for composition is a few parameters that control the random-number generators and an initial key sequence to which the grammar adds new notes.

The method presented here has been introduced and discussed in the context of neural network research mainly because it exhibits many properties characteristic of brain functions and biological learning. For instance, the construction of rules of increasing complexity occurs in an unsupervised, "bottom-up" learning process, and the recall of patterns from memory and their synthesis take place associatively. This work is meant only to demonstrate the degree of competence achievable by a learning system in an idealized, abstract form; it has not yet been implemented in a distributed neural network model.

Restrictions to the Encoding of Source Music

An initial decision in formalizing music concerns the extent to which aspects of performance, such as the dynamics or expressive features in general, and other acoustic qualities of sounds are to be captured in the basic method. Standard musical notation may be seen as an attempt to define or extract the pure, abstract, and invariant qualities and relations of music as contrasted to the physical performance, for which there exist infinitely many possible alternatives. For instance, very often composers do not even specify the instruments to use. The standard score is thus taken as the starting point for transcription into a computerized form. For this transcription, the agogic signs and variations of tempo have not been taken into account; they would have multiplied the alphabet of the grammar and the number of training examples needed. We similarly ignored ornaments, rubatos, quintoles, etc. Furthermore, as it proved difficult for our method to create rules for dynamics, we decided to make the dynamics conform to some standard rhythmic patterns. We used dynamic coding of a very simple style: in the 4/4 time signature, beats 1 and 3 of each measure were just accented more strongly than beats 2 and 4.

In our experiments, we discovered for instance that the music of J. S. Bach is easily rendered by our method and sounds reasonably good. The more complex rhythmic patterns in newer music, such as that of Mozart, caused some problems, though. Initially we had selected the note as the basic symbolic element, specified by its pitch and duration, but it immediately turned out that due to the different lengths of the possible new notes produced by this method, there were plenty of chances for the productions to miss the beats. It was therefore found necessary also to indicate the rhythmic position of the note within the bar or among the beats. Thus the symbolic encoding of each note contains information as the triple: (pitch, length, phase). In the 4/4 time signature, the phase is defined as the rhythmical position within each of the four groups of four semiquavers.

The Self-Learning Grammar

Generally speaking, a grammar may be said to describe regularities in a series of events. A *genera-*

tive grammar may be used to produce a regular sequence of symbols by adding new symbols to a given string on the basis of the grammatical production rules defined. As mentioned earlier, context-sensitive rules are more specific the wider the context they specify; but to construct a sufficiently usable number of such specific rules automatically, plenty of exemplary material would be needed. The amount of context should thus be optimized to reach a compromise between the generality and the specificity of the rules and the number of rules in the grammar.

Since music is produced as a linear, forward-growing string, the context of the last symbol in the string can only be defined backward. Consider the following very simple example where the letters describe a sequence of discrete states, such as notes: ABCDEFG . . . IKFH . . . LEFJ. . . . If we were to try to set up a rule to deduce the next symbol on the basis of one letter, say F (which occurs several times), we would see a threefold conflict: the continuation may be G, H, or J. If we tried to increase the specificity of letter patterns by taking the symbol in front of F for context, we could still see that a twofold conflict prevails: the successor of EF could be G or J. With two symbols in front of F, all the conflicts would be resolved. However, the two-symbol string KF alone would already uniquely define H as its successor (denoted KF→H and meaning the KF is uniquely followed by H, KF implies H, or KF generates the production H). It would then be superfluous to have a longer context for it (IKF→H). Too long a context means too specific and stiff a rule.

The basic idea underlying the dynamically expanding context is that the optimal length of the context, for each symbol (such as F) separately, is determined on the basis of examples and in particular by the conflicts of the above type occurring in them.

To construct the variable-context rules systematically, we first think of a series of hypothetical contexts of gradually increasing length at a particular symbol. For example, around the first occurrence of F in the previous example we define the context level as follows:

Level	*Context*
0	—
1	E
2	DE
3	CDE

up to a certain maximum limit (we had eight levels). Whenever we start recording production rules, we always start at level 0. (The same is true when we apply the rules, say, for the generation of music.) For the first tentative rule from the example string, referring to F, we propose F→G, using level-0 context before the F. But upon scanning further along in the string, we also find F→H, indicating that both of these rules should be invalidated and replaced by EF→G and KF→H, respectively, now using level-1 context. At the third occurrence of F, we again start with F→J, and then because there is a conflict with a previous case (F→G), we continue with EF→J; since the conflict persists (with EF→G), we must make the last rule LEF→J, and also update the previous, still-conflicting rule to DEF→G.

We must not delete the invalidated rules, because they are needed both to check for conflicts and to construct valid new rules. Instead, we provide each rule with a validity indicator, a *conflict bit,* which is initially 0. When a conflict is encountered and a rule is invalidated, its conflict bit is changed to 1.

The constructed rules are best stored in memory as entries in, for example, a relational database. Each entry is a triple, consisting of the left part of the production rule (such as F), the right part of the production rule (such as G), and the conflict bit. The entries are always searched on the basis of the left part.

Although updating all counterparts of the conflicting cases might be done immediately when a conflict is found, it is far simpler if only the last of the conflicting rules is updated and the previous one (at which the conflict occurred) is tentatively only invalidated by changing its conflict bit to 1. If the exemplary data are then scanned iteratively a sufficient number of times (in fact, at maximum half of the number of levels, or four in our case), it is possible to show that all the earlier counterpart rules will be updated, too. To show that this is true for the above example, consider the following construction of rules only around symbol F (although all these operations would be done at the same time for all the other symbols, too). Memory locations in the form of the triple (left part, right part, conflict bit) are indicated at each point of the process under the corresponding heading:

Row in memory	Left part	Right part	Conflict bit

Check first that F was not yet stored in any left-part field. Store the first occurrence of F,F→G, with level-0 context.

1	F	G	0

Next, the second occurrence of F, F→H, is considered; searching the memory entries in the grammar so far on the basis of F alone as the left part of the rules, we find G as the right part of row 1, indicating a conflict with H. The conflict bit of row 1 must now be changed, and the second occurrence of F stored with level-1 context on row 2, after first checking that it was not yet also in memory.

1	F	G	1
2	KF	H	0

Next, the third occurrence of F, F→J, is considered; searching memory on F, G is again found in row 1, and this time the conflict bit is already 1 and so need not be changed. The third occurrence must thus be stored with level-1 context to avoid level-0 conflict, again after first checking that it was not yet stored.

3	EF	J	0

Next, since we have exhausted the input example string, we skip back to the beginning of this string and iterate over the first occurrence of F,F → G. Searching memory on the basis of F, we find it first occurs as the left part of row 1, which has conflict bit 1. Therefore context from the example is expanded to EF, and memory is again searched. There is still a conflict using level-1 context, namely in row 3, with a J as the right part, rather than the G at this position in the example string. To handle this, the conflict bit is set on in row 3, and the first occurrence of F is stored with level-2 context as row 4.

3	EF	J	1
4	DEF	G	0

Consider the second occurrence of F. Searching memory on the basis of F alone, we find row 1 with its conflict bit set to 1. Expanding the context and searching memory on the basis of KF, we see that row 2 matches exactly, and no conflict remains. Now we continue with the third occurrence of F. On the basis of F alone, row 1 with conflict bit 1 is found. On the basis of the expanded EF, conflict bit 1 is still found, in row 3. Now when we expand once more, LEF is not yet in memory so we store it.

5	LEF	J	0

Further iterations do not cause any changes in memory. We see that the valid rules, with different lengths of context, are left on rows 2, 4, and 5, those rows where the conflict bit is 0.

Generation of a New Symbol to Follow a Key Sequence

Let us start with a key (seed) sequence, say CDEF, to which we wish to add symbols based on our learned grammar. When we start at the end of this sequence, a search through the grammar memory on the basis of F finds row 1, where the conflict bit is 1. Thus, this rule is invalid. When we expand the context from the seed sequence from level 0 to

Fig. 1. Representation of the rules stored in the DEC grammar in graph form, showing for each context level the current symbol context in the nodes and the appropriate production on the arcs.

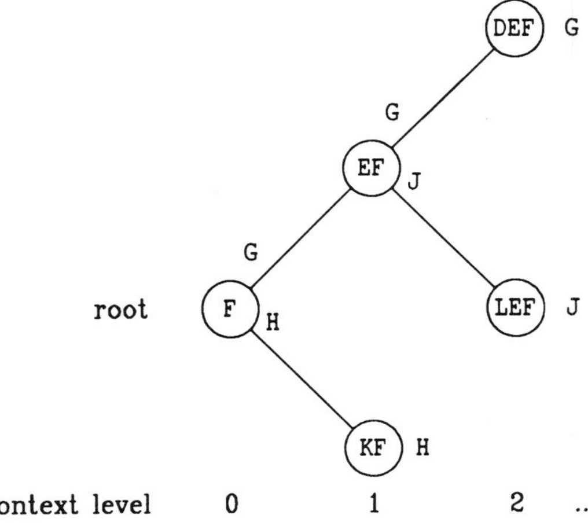

level 1, a grammar search on the basis of EF finds row 3, which still yields the conflict bit 1. The level-2 context search on the basis of DEF, though, finally finds a valid rule in row 4, DEF → G, and the new symbol to add to the seed sequence is thus the production G.

It is no surprise that the new symbol is the same as in one of the original occurrences, from which the memory was formed. If we had preferred a random choice from several alternatives, in order to have more variance in the productions, we might have considered, for example, both context-level-1 and level-2 productions found in the search process (ignoring the value of the conflict bit). Then we would have had two alternatives, J (from row 3) and G (row 4), and we could have randomly selected either one for the new symbol, while still maintaining a certain (varying) degree of continuity (context dependence).

The structure of information stored in memory can be visualized as a graph that interrelates the rules, as shown in Fig. 1. For each particular symbol (such as F above) there exists a tree with its root corresponding to the symbol with context-level 0. If there is a conflict in the examples, at least two arcs then emanate from the root and lead to nodes with context-level 1. The corresponding productions (right sides of rules) can be written on the arcs, as in formal grammars. The leaf nodes in the tree, at which the respective last productions are written, correspond to the total contexts of the valid final rules (with conflict bit 0). For all other nodes the conflict bit is 1, indicating that the corresponding rule has been invalidated.

Generation of new, partly random sequences can now be illustrated in the following way. Assume that the key sequence again is CDEF, and start at the root F, following the arcs until the appropriate leaf (in this case DEF) is found. Along the path from the root to the leaf one encounters several nodes that each lead to alternative productions (possibilities for new symbols). A depth parameter sets the maximum number of nodes backward from the leaves to consider in choosing the next note. Out of this pool of nodes, one of the corresponding productions they indicate is selected at random as the next note to add to the sequence.

Since new combinations of symbols can be generated in these new sequences, they may contain symbol contexts that were not present in the original examples (and thus not in the "rule tree" either). Thus, it may happen that when the tree is searched for the appropriate leaf rule to further extend a sequence being generated, an expanded sequence context that does not occur in the examples (or the tree) may be encountered before the leaves are reached. This also occurs if the maximal defined context level is exceeded during the rule learning (since conflicts at that level were not yet resolved). This, however, does not cause any serious problems in the present application, in which the grammar is only used as an intelligent random-number generator. In these cases, the tree is traced up to the last matching node anyhow, whereafter a new symbol is picked from the last depth-parameter-number of nodes previous to this point, as before.

Figure 2 shows typical context levels in a good-sounding melody. The numbers indicate the levels of context that were used at each consecutive production step, corresponding to one generated note. Two facts are salient: First, the context level has a great variance, which is expected to make a big distinction between DEC-generated and Markov-process music, for example. Second, there are several

Fig. 2. Consecutive context levels used to generate each successive note in the production of a typical good-sounding melody.

```
3 2 2 3 3 1 1 2 2 1 2 3 4 2 2 1 2 3 2 1
1 1 1 2 1 2 1 1 3 2 4 1 2 2 4 5 1 2 5 3
3 4 2 1 2 3 4 4 1 1 3 1 1 2 1 2 2 4 2 2
3 4 1 2 2 2 0 2 1 1 1 1 2 2 1 2 2 1 3 0
2 3 4 0 1 2 1 4 3 3 1 1 2 2 4 2 6 3 4 3
2 2 2 2 3 3 2 2 3 3 2 2 3 3 2 2 2 2 3 2
1 6 2 3 2 2 3 3 2 1 1 1 2 2 1 2 2 1 1 1
2 1 1 1 0 2 0 2 0 1 2 2 2 1 2 2 4 4 3 2
2 3 2 1 6 2 3 2 2 2 2 3 3 2 2 2 2 2 2 1
2 2 4 5 1 2 2 1 2 3 2 1 6 2 3 2 5 5 3 1
2 0 2 0 1 2 2 2 2 3 3 2 2 2 2 1 2 2 4 0
1 2 1 4 2 3 2 2 3 2 1 6 3 3 1 1 2 2 4 4
3 2 2 3 3 2 6 5 3 2 2 3 2 1 1 1 1 2 2 2
```

level-0 productions. These occur because we used parameter values which were supposed to yield greater random variations. Context-level 0 in fact means that only two successive notes at that place have been copied from the original material (which typically contains 2000 or more notes in one grammar). The deeper the context used, the more successive notes have been copied directly from an example melody; therefore level-0 context allows the maximum deviation from the example materials.

Although this composing process contains random elements, the probabilities of the successive notes in a generated sequence do not always match those occurring in the original examples; this is radically different from Markov-chain-generated music. It may rather be said that the DEC grammar selects one good continuation out of a number of possible good continuations for each particular musical context.

Taking Harmonic Successions into Account

It can be seen from the preceding discussion that the context "scope" of the basic grammar is still rather short, using only a few successive notes to generate the next. It does not deal with any higher-level hierarchical structures at all. Even though the correlations of the generated melodic segments, mimicking those correlations found in the examples, give the music produced by this method some feeling of longer continuity, the traditions in Western music prefer more regular and "coherent" chord progressions. A modification of the grammar to that end is easy.

We found experimentally that the last two symbols of the key sequence that the DEC method builds on should always consist of absolute notes (defined by pitch and length). But for the previous symbols in the key sequence, as well as in the grammatical rules describing the productions, one could use the chords implied by the melody notes over the preceding bar, half bar, quarter bar, etc. (Thus, this applies both when the melody notes are those from an example piece of music, during rule construction, and when they are from a new musical sequence being constructed by the DEC method, during composition.)

Since there may be passing notes in the melody that do not belong to the intended chord, identification of a chord over a short succession of notes must be based on approximate pattern recognition techniques. For instance, one may form a histogram of the various pitch classes in the current sequence, also taking into account the lengths of the notes. By comparing such a histogram to those formed corresponding to pure chords, the best match found can be taken as the chord to use. Although this method may not yield a sure identification of chords, in classic-romantic music, for example, a progression of approximate chords will generally still sound pleasant and be reasonably descriptive of the original style.

Polyphonic Productions

Most of our musical productions contain two to four voices, but the grammars that are used for the generation of the accompanying voices are only based on contexts derived from the leading voice; in other words, using key sequences picked up from the first voice, productions for the first, second, etc., voices are generated. Every voice is governed by a separate, although related, grammar. One particular problem caused by this approach concerns the temporal overlapping of notes between the various parts. In order to synchronize the voices, several methods of coping with this problem were tried.

One solution for synchronizing notes would be simply to split long ones. But the tentative, although somewhat arbitrary and restrictive, solution we adopted in our system was first to require that groups of melody notes in the accepted example material coincide with certain checkpoints, such as quarter measures in the 4/4 time signature. Then, during the productions of new melodies, we alleviated the problem of overlapping notes by requiring a new note to start at every checkpoint. (Pauses need not be so constrained, because it is possible to split a pause into two parts of which one can start at a checkpoint.) If in the new production a note failed to start at a checkpoint (because the previous note was too long or short) then we backed up a few notes and started again with different random numbers. In addition, we checked that the groups of notes in the production of the accompanying voices were copies of the exemplary material in the segments between the checkpoints; if not, then once again we backed up and tried a new sequence. We believe that longer copies in the accompanying voices can be tolerated, as long as the melody is new. If these checks result in closer copies, one may again compensate for this by choosing more widely variable random numbers in the generation process. These extra checkups might seem to slow down the production process significantly, but in practice we have been able to use this program rather effectively. Especially if plenty of material is encoded into the memories, such restrictions have not played any significant role.

Some Practical Details of the Method

Example material can be collected from pieces having an arbitrary time signature, but so far we have only produced music in 4/4 time. This time signature creates a strong rhythm that partly compensates for the randomness that is characteristic of this method. The time assignment, in addition to defining the beats, also determines the dynamics in the productions. This is accomplished by placing accents on the quarter notes 1 and 3 in each measure by increasing dynamic (amplitude) values for these notes.

Recall that every note in our system has three values: pitch, length, and beat (or phase). Another way to create an appropriate sense of rhythm in the new productions is thus to have the beat of each note in the production match the rhythmic position of the note in the original material, that is, the phase of the produced note also should be correct. But since this method might then result in copies that are too close to the original melody, we only check the beat value of produced notes at random intervals, and between them allow wrong beat values. Even such intermittent beat checking is able to synchronize the rhythm.

One parameter in the program is therefore needed to define how often on average a note, located in the same beat position as in the original material, is accepted for the production. If the check fails, a backup and new continuation are necessary. During the composing process, it is also possible to reject a sequence and restart the production if it contains exact copies of the example material that are too long. Similarly, it is possible to monitor whether the sequence contains parts that are identical to some other part of the production itself and reject them. Naturally, every additional restriction of this kind slows down the production process, or may even stop it; greater demands on both quality and quantity of the original example material are then posed.

To make the keys or chords of the passages follow a prior plan, artificial modulations can be made to the production. The key sequence, before being used to search the grammar, can be transposed by a specified amount, and a similar but inverse transposition is made on the production found from memory. In this way, a smooth transition from one key to another can be made, via an ambiguous passage that could be perceived in either key. This works as follows, providing there is only one memory in which all material is in the same scale (which we will call the tonic). Assume that you want to continue the current production with a motive that is in the dominant scale. First, transpose the key sequence (the latest notes in the current production) down by a fifth and look for matches in the memory. This is equivalent to using the original key sequence and a memory entirely in the dominant scale. Any matches that you find in the current case are still in the original (tonic) scale, however, and to get the needed transposition into the dominant scale, you finally have to transpose the newly found production upward by a fifth.

Another possibility for specifying keys is to use different grammar databases, corresponding to the different keys, for different parts of the production. For instance, passages in major and minor keys may be collected in different grammars. Still other options are to divide solo and tutti parts in concerto-style music into different grammar partitions. Alternation of styles can be defined manually by using different grammar databases in successive passages. Cadences may also be stored in different grammars. In these ways, the DEC method can be used to structure higher forms, beyond the relatively short scope of melodical forms provided by the grammatical rules. The grammar always automatically sees to it that the transitions between the modulations or other different melodic structures are smooth and continuous.

Finally, transpositions of the whole original material can be added to the grammar; this usually makes chromatic variations in the productions. Inversions and retrograde versions can be used in a similar fashion.

Experiments with the DEC Method

We have applied the DEC self-learning grammar to a wide range of musical styles, from Bach to jazz improvisation. To evaluate the automatically composed music produced in each case and thereby judge this composition method, we had to resort to aesthetic terms such as *good, pleasant, uninteresting,* etc. This may be problematic since these terms are not defined precisely. Our criteria were very subjective and practical: when listening to the new productions, we considered the total experience over the complete piece and compared it with corresponding experience produced by the original pieces that were familiar to us. It must be pointed out that many other programs for automatic composition strive for aesthetic goals different from ours. For instance, the quality of AI music is frequently judged according to the extent to which the generally accepted formal principles of voice leading, harmony, resolutions, etc. are reflected in it. Since we are trying to investigate automatic production of music over a wide range of styles, however, from classical art music to present-day popular music, no single set of aesthetic criteria can be used to evaluate the method's performance, and a human listener is the best judge.

For our very first experiments, we chose a selection of music from the minor polyphonic works of J. S. Bach. Using the works of Bach as test material has been relatively common among the pioneers of computer music. Without doubt one reason for this is that Bach's music is rich in features with respect to melody, harmony, and counterpoint. Moreover it generally sounds good in inversions and retrograde versions, and syncopated, too; and its motives do not always coincide with the bars. This is important, because groups of notes in the productions may appear in rhythmical positions different from the original music. We also anticipated good results because we felt that the music of Bach is more linear and less based on hierarchical structures than the later works of the classical era. Any hierarchical, recursive structures in our source material were only reflected in the productions indirectly; their description was not our primary concern. Also, to make the evaluation of the method's results more straightforward, the test material was chosen from music familiar to a large number of people.

The first results indeed confirmed that the choice of the two- and three-part inventions of J. S. Bach had been appropriate. The test runs produced consistent and pleasant melodic and harmonic patterns. The method was able to operate successfully with a fairly small amount of input data: the first runs were based on only four to six pieces.

Some pianos sonatas of W. A. Mozart were also tried. These works have the advantage that the piano score provides a fairly easy starting point for the input encoding, with only a few simplifications required, such as eliminating ornamentation. With this corpus of music, however, the DEC program first produced unsatisfactory results, probably due to the rhythmic symmetry present in the original material. The generated patterns sounded rather dull rhythmically. It was at this point that we discovered the simple remedy, described earlier, of providing the grammar with information about the position of a note with respect to the beats in a measure. This enhancement was sufficient to distinguish the more subtle roles of the notes in the melodic patterns and to give a fairly steady rhythmic pulse to the productions.

More music was encoded from compositions of Joseph Pranzer and Franz Vincenz Krommer, two contemporaries of Mozart, both of whom mainly wrote simple two-part pieces for clarinet. Their music seemed to produce good results with conditions and parameter settings similar to those used for Mozart. Most of the other classical and romantic music that was used with the method (such as Dvorak and Tchaikovsky) behaved quite similarly.

The method was also applied to some present-day popular music. A grammar was encoded from several dozen Latin-American popular tunes, and the output of the system was played together with simple percussion accompaniment. Even with this added rhythm section, however, the results were not up to our expectations. We suggest that these popular tunes are generally based on symmetric repetitions stronger than in classical music—regularly repeating riffs constitute an important part of popular music. In Latin-American as well as Anglo-American pop and folk music, rhythm plays a much more important role than in most art music. The DEC method, however, is designed to make random variations and so cannot closely match these strong repetitive structures. A good solution for this problem has not yet been invented. It is quite obvious that many changes to the program would be necessary if we wished to produce, for example, good pop music.

Our experiments with popular music were then extended by feeding data from spontaneous live improvisations produced by rock and jazz musicians to the program. The data was read directly from a MIDI keyboard to the computer in our laboratory. This material also presented rhythmic and formal problems similar to the ones experienced with the Latin-American popular music. The output sounded a little more acceptable, although still somewhat arbitrary, not quite conforming to the style of the original examples. After editing, we could produce a few pieces that sounded pleasant.

In short, traditional art music seemed to produce the most pleasant results in the DEC system with almost no editing of the example scores. Some recent experiments have even been conducted with sixteenth-century Italian madrigals, which have also yielded very pleasant results. This has confirmed our belief that linear, polyphonic music is the best source of material for such a mechanical method. In this sort of music, the listener's attention is probably focused more on the melodic continuation and its counterparts than on the structural elements.

An interesting further experiment was recently carried out on a database obtained from a reference book of themes of classical music (Barlow and Morgenstern 1988). This volume includes themes of orchestral music ranging from the middle ages up to the 1950s. The grammar learned from this database thus contained a great number of short fragments from very different sources. To our surprise, the productions from this corpus were experienced as being more coherent and integral than the input material. By this we mean that although the original material only comprised fragmentary passages of different themes totally lacking repetition and structure, the productions generated by the DEC method exhibited repetitions and simple structures. The DEC method may thus be regarded as having found certain simple musical structures from partial inputs representing very different styles. The most striking structures are those motives that link very different passages. Therefore, these motives do not belong to any particular style (except perhaps that of Western art music). They tend to give the productions in which they appear a kind of universal nature, meaning that one cannot say from where each element is originating.

Evaluation of the Test Runs

Our experience with the DEC method has been based on a large number of runs using complete musical pieces to construct grammars and produce new compositions. The resulting demonstrations have shown what kind of music is most suitable as input data and what parameters of the process most centrally determine the musical qualities of the output.

As described in the previous section, our first experiments were carried out with small musical corpuses. The productions were coherent and closely followed the original style. After developments of the program, we then fed larger and larger bodies of music into the same grammar, sometimes up to hundreds of musical works. With a very large and stylistically diverse corpus the user had less control over the process and its end result. Thus the largest possible database does not always lead to the most pleasing music, although the results may be surprising.

In the first experiments, especially with too small a corpus of input data, the production process sometimes led to a cyclic (repeating) sequence that did not exist in the corpus. If this occurs, the last part of the sequence can be deleted and another acceptable continuation tried using different random numbers. Even with a fuller corpus of examples, a produced piece of music about five minutes long usually contains a certain amount of asymmetric, uninteresting repetitions and must be trimmed manually. If a piece is meant for concentrated listening, some higher-level structures, such as transpositions, should be used to heighten the musical interest. This is especially important since the system can generate quite long compositions; in microcomputer implementations of the DEC method we have generated productions with lengths up to around 200 bars. If the method is run in a virtual memory environment, there are no theoretical limits to the length of the productions possible.

Two examples of the DEC method that illustrate the points made in this article are found in the Appendix to this chapter. Example 1 shows a short phrase constructed by the DEC system with an analysis identifying the various motives. Shown in the bottom part of example 1 are the motivic materials used by the DEC system in its construction. Note that the third measure shows a very high degree of motivic combination and reuse, a feature of the DEC system. Example 2 shows a more extended composition in two voices. Here the strengths and weaknesses of the DEC system can be seen. The music is generally pleasing and reasonably correct in its harmonic and melodic usage, but there are wide leaps and odd harmonic progressions in some places.

Discussion

One aspect of the present method to be addressed concerns its utility as a tool for the composer; another relates to its role in composing independent musical pieces.

Most music produced by the DEC method has been made with the goal of creating independent compositions for demonstrations. The generated pieces have usually been accepted without any editing of the final scores; only selection of the instruments used for electronic synthesis has been made manually. In other words, so far we have practically no experience with this method as a tool in a multistep artistic composing process, only as a "black box" producing finished pieces.

In other experiments, we have played instrumental solos over a background produced by the DEC system. This was inspired by the unusual, improvisatory nature of some DEC productions. The method might be developed in this direction to produce coherent backgrounds, which then could be filled in with melodic and improvisational material by a musician. Furthermore, chord sequences and ostinati played over the algorithmically produced backgrounds could result in interesting new musical ideas.

When trying to judge whether our productions may be regarded as independent compositions, we face a difficult aesthetical problem. An emphasis on the originality of a composer has been characteristic of our century. It is even sometimes stipulated that a composer should establish new concepts in each new work. In this sense, the outputs of the DEC system can certainly not be regarded as independent works. On the other hand, borrowing stylistic features and even complete melodies has generally been accepted on a wide scale in Western art music, especially in some earlier periods. Judged from this basis instead, the outputs of the system might be considered as independent compositions.

When the input material is heterogeneous in style, even short output sequences may contain fragments from several compositions and styles. Some experiments with example corpuses consisting of a great number of composers have produced very interesting syntheses. For example, when we combined several pieces from composers such as Haydn, Mozart, Bach, and Brahms, we got productions with many unexpected stylistic changes together with passages where no certain style was dominating. One might say that the ability to synthesize is a central feature of the DEC grammar. In its most successful forms, the present method generates variable but at the same time smooth musical textures, with none of the partial styles dominating over the others.

On the other hand, one should also realize that there are kinds of music that need not possess the qualities of an independent artistic production but may be used instead for example as a background for further musical invention. This form of music could act on people at the preattentive level, and therefore it may be sufficient if it is able to maintain a feeling of musical and emotional continuity. The music produced by the DEC grammar certainly has this property.

Finally, something could be said about the usefulness of our current implementation. The productions of the system should be taken as improvisations, not as complete and structured compositions. Although lack of some higher-level features such as hierarchical construction diminishes the value of our productions as art music, these improvisations are still quite pleasing musical forms. They belong rather in the genre of background entertainment. Creative composers may find ways to use our system beyond what we have done.

References

Barlow, H., and S. Morgenstern. 1988. *Dictionary of Musical Themes.* Rev. ed. London: Faber & Faber.

Baroni, M., and C. Jacoboni. 1978. *A Proposal for a Grammar of Melody.* Montreal: Les Presses de l'Université de Montreal.

Ebcioglu, K. 1988. "An Expert System for Harmonizing Four-part Chorales." *Computer Music Journal* 12(3):43–51.

Kohonen, T. 1985. "Dynamically Expanding Context." Report TKK-F-A592. Helsinki, Finland: Helsinki University of Technology.

Kohonen, T. 1986. "Dynamically Expanding Context." *Proceedings of the Eighth International Conference on Pattern Recognition.* Washington, D.C.: IEEE Computer Society.

Kohonen, T. 1989. "A Self-Learning Musical Grammar, or 'Associative Memory of the Second Kind.'" *Proceedings of the International Joint Conference on Neural Networks.* New York: IEEE, pp. 1–5.

Kohonen, T., K. Torkkola, M. Shozakai, J. Kangas, and O. Ventä. 1988. "Phonetic Typewriter for Finnish and Japanese." *Proceedings of ICASSP, IEEE International Conference on Acoustics, Speech, and Signal Processing.* New York: IEEE.

Appendix

Example 1 is a single-voice production, composed of short segments of variable length; the production is shown at the top, followed by the training examples used in making this production. The context length used by the DEC grammar in production of each note is shown above the notes. The initial key sequence, labelled K, starts off the example. The overlaps between the segments are two or three notes long, corresponding context-levels 2 and 3.

As source material, the upper voices of two-part inventions 1 and 2 by J. S. Bach were used. The key sequence K is shown first; the excerpts from which the other fragments have been taken are shown in sequences a through f.

As a rule we have first transposed all source music to the C-major (or a-minor) key before forming the memory database. Resultingly, sequences K, c, and e are given here in a-minor, though the original key is c-minor.

Our examples are not strictly meant to demonstrate the quality of music achievable by the DEC method. They merely illustrate the operation of the

Example 1.

Example 1. A passage of melody generated by D.E.C. system. Numbers above the notes indicate the context level in D.E.C. grammar for each corresponding rule. The initial key sequence is indicated with the letter 'K'.

Example 1 consists of fragments from the following passages of original music:

K - the initial key sequence: Inventio 2, bar 1 (transposed to a minor key)

a: Inventio 1, bars 1 and 2

b: Inventio 1, bar 8

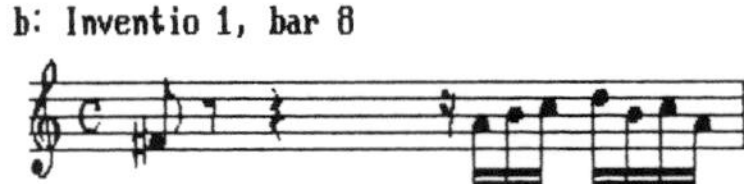

c: Inventio 2, bar 9

d: Inventio 1, bar 8

e: Inventio 2, bars 20 and 21

f: Inventio 1, bar 4

Example 2.

grammar, that is, how the pieces of motives are linked together to produce a smooth passage. When listening to generated music, we find that its quality is rather reflected in the coherence and smoothness of the passages taken over a long time span.

Example 2 presents a longer passage generated by our system. The source material for this production is taken from Joseph Pranzer's "Trois duos concertantes pour deux clarinettes." The tendency of not conforming to a steady rhythmic pulse is observable in this example, resulting in music of a slightly humorous mood.

Samir I. Sayegh
Physics Department
Purdue University
Fort Wayne, Indiana 46805-1499 USA
sayegh@ed.ecn.purdue.edu

Fingering for String Instruments with the Optimum Path Paradigm

Introduction

This paper introduces a new connectionist paradigm, the optimum path paradigm (OPP) and its application to the problem of string instrument fingering. The optimization approach on a Viterbi network is the feedforward phase that maps input to output once the values of the weights are known. The approach taken is a natural one that proceeds from the formulation of the problem, goes through the rule-based and the optimization approaches, and leads to the final learning phase. A discussion of how the optimum path paradigm relates to other connectionist paradigms is also presented. The paper will address the specific problem of fingering for string instruments (Yampolsky 1967; Gilardino 1975), in particular the fingering of homophonic music written for the classical guitar (Gilardino 1975; Sayegh 1987; 1988). The method presented is general, however, and can be used in a variety of musical applications, where the written transcription often carries only partial information about the sound to be rendered—the remaining information depending on context and/or interpretation.

The reason for restricting the study to a particular application is the desire to introduce another level of generality, illustrating different approaches that can be taken. One such approach, the optimization approach, leads naturally to a new connectionist learning paradigm, the optimum path paradigm, whose generality goes beyond musical applications (Sayegh and Manzor-Coats 1988). The *connectionist* aspect of the problem is introduced in a very natural way. In the early phases of the treatment, it is present at the level of constraint propagation (Waltz 1975) or of connectionism (Feldman 1985) and is very closely tied to the nature of the problem. The most interesting aspect is that it then goes one step beyond, culminating in the learning aspect that is absent in similar treatments, although essential for a viable connectionist paradigm.

Computer Music Journal, Vol. 13, No. 3, Fall 1989,

Fingering for String Instruments

A piece written for a string instrument specifies the notes that are to be played, their duration, and a number of other elements relating to rhythm, dynamics, and interpretation. On a string instrument, however, each note can be played in a number of different locations, as shown in Fig. 1, and each location can be accessed by different fingers. The end result is that there are a number of ways of playing one note and a much larger number of ways of playing a sequence of notes. This results in the combined explosion of the a priori possible fingerings of a given piece. In the preceding discussion it has been assumed that notes with the same fundamental frequency but produced on different strings sound exactly the same. If this were true, all fingerings of a given piece would also be equivalent from a musical point of view and would only differ from a mechanical point of view: i.e., some would be easier than others. The problem of fingering would then be that of finding the most convenient fingering among all the possibilities. However, the sounds corresponding to notes with the same fundamental frequency played on different strings are actually different. Although their fundamental pitch is the same, their harmonic content and its decay in time will vary widely from one string to the next (Pujol 1960; Taylor 1978; Carlevaro 1984). As a consequence, "good" fingerings will have to satisfy a number of musical constraints in addition to the physical ones. Formulating and using a system that reflects these constraints constitute the problem of fingering for string instruments.

The representation chosen for guitar fingering is a numerical representation where the lowest note

Fig. 1. *Fingerboard with numerical notation; the rows represent the strings of the guitar and the columns represent fret stops.*

24	25	26	27	28	29	30	31	32	33	34	35	36
19	20	21	22	23	24	25	26	27	28	29	30	31
15	16	17	18	19	20	21	22	23	24	25	26	27
10	11	12	13	14	15	16	17	18	19	20	21	22
05	06	07	08	09	10	11	12	13	14	15	16	17
00	01	02	03	04	05	06	07	08	09	10	11	12

(E) is represented by 0 and each halftone increment corresponds to an increment of 1. More sophisticated representations are possible, but the present one is sufficient for the problem at hand. The result for the guitar fingerboard is represented in Fig. 1. Notice the occurrence of the same note (same number) at different locations on the fingerboard.

The Expert System Approach

In this approach one formulates a set of rules that define what constitutes a good fingering. This can be done at different degrees of sophistication. It is well known, for example, that a Baroque piece is not to be fingered the same way as a twentieth century piece (Gilardino 1975). Similarly, different movements of the same sonata can be fingered according to different general guidelines. Such guidelines can be formulated into a set of rules. The set of rules will still be dependent on individual style, but it is possible to extract general rules that will still apply and constitute the core of the system (Sayegh 1988). The rules are collected through extensive interviews with expert guitarists that spend an appreciable amount of time actually fingering guitar pieces.

The rules can be grouped in two broad classes. The first class of rules relates to ease of execution, while the second class relates to insuring the homogeneity of the sound being produced. The actual rules inspired from these two classes might agree or conflict.

A typical example of a rule relating to the ease of execution is that of remaining in the same position. As long as there are no other rules dictating otherwise, and as long as the notes to be played are accessible in a given position, the position is to be maintained. This rule goes along with those relating to the homogeneity of sound. By remaining in the same position, one has sections of string of approximately the same length that are vibrating, so the relative damping of the higher harmonics of the different notes is similar, thus producing a sound of uniform quality.

After some of the rules have restricted the search space by introducing constraints, the use of constraint propagation will restrict it even further. For example, if a note is to be fingered in a given position, the preliminary search for the next note can be restricted to fingerings in the same position. This process can clearly proceed from both left to right and right to left. It can also be implemented recursively. The system is written in Prolog, which offers many of the needed tools such as depth first search and pattern matching by unification (Balaban and Murray 1985; Bratko 1987). For details concerning implementation, see Sayegh (1988).

The Optimization Approach: Viterbi's Network

The model used in this approach is one in which each transition from one fingering to the next is assigned a weight based on the combined difficulty/uniformity of the transition. With q fingerings per note, the network describing the sequence of m notes will then have q^2 weights on the connections between two consecutive layers and a total of $(m - 1)q^2$ weights and connections. The total number of possible weights that can occur is nq^2, where n is the number of notes that can be played on the instrument. The optimum path is then the path that minimizes or maximizes the sum of the weights on the corresponding connections, depending on whether a good transition is defined in such a way as to have a low or a high weight. In practice, it is easier to think in terms of penalizing a transition that changes string or position. On the other hand, the theoretical treatment is better understood in terms of maximum paths, for reasons which will become clear. The two formulations are equivalent, however, and we will switch back and forth between the two vocabularies whenever convenient.

The problem has now been reduced to that of finding a minimum path on a weighted graph. This problem was independently solved by Dijkstra (1959) and Whiting and Hillier (1960), and the corresponding polynomial time algorithm is called Dijkstra's algorithm. The situation at hand is actually simpler than that for an arbitrary graph since we are dealing with a layered network. A version of Dijkstra's algorithm—better adapted to this particular case and known as Viterbi's algorithm (Viterbi 1967)—has been formulated and initially applied to decoding of convolutional codes and later to a number of other applications including speech recognition and edge detection. Viterbi's algorithm is linear in the number of layers. The basic idea in both Dijkstra's algorithm and Viterbi's version is that if a node on an intermediate layer is part of an overall minimum path, the partial path from the first layer to that node is itself a minimum path, for if it were not, one could then use the better intermediate path to build a better overall path. One can then proceed one layer at a time and compute best paths in parallel, with all nodes of a given layer being updated simultaneously. This particular topology—frequently encountered in brain networks—is called a *laminar network model* (Kohonen 1988).

We apply Viterbi's algorithm to find the best fingering of a given phrase. Following are two crucial observations. First, it is possible to a large extent to capture the essence of good fingering through assignment of the cost of transition from one fingering to the next and then seeking the global minimum path. The individual costs depend on the two fingerings under consideration and are not directly affected by further neighboring fingerings. This assumption is reasonable and is corroborated by experimentation. A number of the rules used by human experts can be reproduced via this assumption. The second observation is that the transition costs from one fingering to another need not be given individually for each pair of possible fingerings. A cost function can be defined analytically based on the general criteria discussed above. A very simple illustrative example that already yields fair performance is a function that penalizes the transition by 1 for a change of position and by 1 for a change of string.

There are several advantages to the optimization approach as described above (Sayegh and Tenorio 1988). One can experiment with different hypotheses for the cost function and compare results with a desired optimum result, successively adjusting the cost function by hand to fit the optimum case. One can thus attempt to capture a certain style of fingering. Finally, a systematic learning approach can be taken based on the observation that the frequency of occurrence of a given connection (transition from one fingering to the next), is inversely proportional to its cost. By observing solution fingerings of an expert human, one can reconstruct the cost function. The learning procedure is discussed in the next section.

Examples

In this first example, a very simple cost function is defined according to the two simplest criteria: penalizing a change of position and penalizing a change of string. The list notation $(N\ S\ F\ P)$ is used, denoting the quadruple: (Note String Finger Position). A transition from a fingering $(N_1\ S_1\ F_1\ P_1)$ to a fingering $(N_2\ S_2\ F_2\ P_2)$ is assigned the weight $z(P_1 - P_2) + z(S_1 - S_2)$, where the N_i stand for notes, S_i for strings, F_i for fingers and P_i for positions, and where $z(0) = 0$ and $z(x) = 1$ for $x \neq 0$. This is a very simple weight function but it already yields significant performance for its simplicity. Consider fingering the four-note sequence G A C E (with note numbers 27, 29, 32, and 36). To make the argument easy to follow, let us assume that notes 27 and 36 have already been assigned a fingering and that for each of the two remaining notes one can choose from two possible fingerings. Figure 2a shows the corresponding network with the assignment of weights for each possible transition from one fingering to the next based on the cost function described above. One can see that there are four different possible paths connecting first to last layer, corresponding to four different fingerings of the four-note sequence. By applying Viterbi's algorithm or simply by comparing all four paths one finds that the fingering of minimum total weight is: ((27 2 4 5)(29 1 1 5)(32 1 4 5)(36 1 4 9)).

It is easy to see that this is indeed the best fingering. It agrees with the one usually used by guitar-

Fig. 2. Possible fingerings on a Viterbi network (a) and standard notation (b).

(a)

SOL LA DO MI (G A C E) (27 29 32 36)

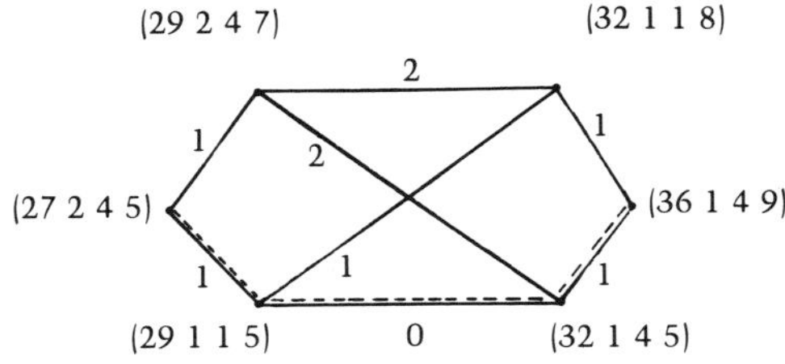

(b)

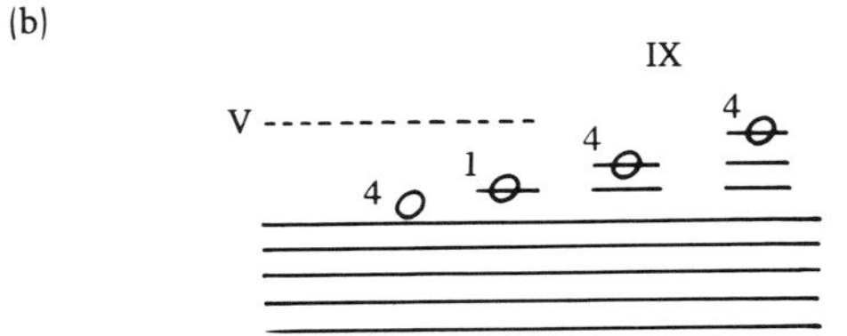

ists and it is easy to understand in the context of the rule-based approach—the hand stayed in position for three notes and when it had to move, it did so through the use of a guide finger as shown in Fig. 2b.

A more sophisticated weighing function (which avoids some of the problems of the previous one such as the excessive number of changes of position) is the function c defined as follows:

$$c(0, |S_2 - S_1|) = 2,$$

$$c(|P_2 - P_1|, 0) = \begin{cases} 3 & \text{if } |P_2 - P_1| = 1, 2 \\ 4 & \text{if } |P_2 - P_1| = 3, 4, \\ 5 & \text{if } |P_2 - P_2| > 4 \end{cases}$$

$$c(|P_2 - P_1|, |S_2 - S_1|) = c(|P_2 - P_1|, 0)c(0, |S_2 - S_1|),$$

where the S_i stand for string numbers and the P_i stand for positions. It is possible to consider functions of increasing complexity. A detailed discussion of the advantages and limitations associated with this approach can be found in Sayegh (1988). It is also possible to define individual weights for each transition. This approach, though not practical if implemented by hand, can be performed automatically. This is done, for example, in the learning phase described in the next section.

Learning through the Optimum Path Paradigm

The learning phase that corresponds to the forward phase described in the previous section consists of estimating the weights of the connections given a set of input/output pairs. The input/output pairs for the fingering problem consist of a collection of musical phrases together with the corresponding fingerings. In a more general context, one needs a set of network configurations and the corresponding optimum paths.

A simple but important observation is that the specification of a solution path is equivalent to the specification of a number of inequalities, stating that the sum of the weights on the connections forming the optimum path is larger than the sum of any combination of weights corresponding to an alternate path. The knowledge of a collection of input/output pairs is therefore equivalent to the knowledge of a large number of inequalities among the entries of the matrix W specifying the transition costs from one fingering to another. The determination of the entries of W or an equivalent set of entries is tantamount to the solution of a large number of inequalities among the matrix elements. This is achieved by introducing a heuristic that relates the frequency of occurrence of a weight as part of the large side of an inequality to its actual value. This heuristic is quite intuitive since the larger a weight is, the more likely it is to occur on the larger side of inequalities involving different weights. Simulations bear out this observation.

When translated back to the network formulation, the heuristic essentially dicates strengthening each connection that occurs on a best path. This is somewhat similar to a form of Hebbian learning (Hebb 1949). Assume, then, that a set of input/output pairs is being generated with the help of a matrix W of actual weights of transitions. The matrix W is assumed to be unknown, however. The task of the optimum path paradigm is to generate W or an equivalent matrix W'.

For an instrument such as the guitar, the size of

Fig. 3. *Weights and optimum path for fingering* acb.

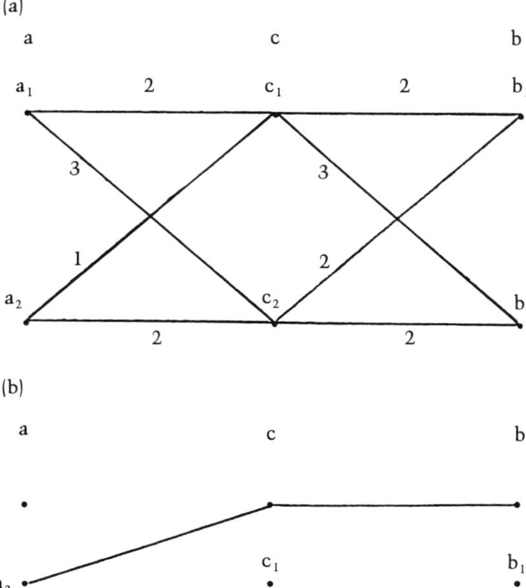

the transition matrix W should be 216×216 to take into account all possible fingerings corresponding to 72 locations for notes extending on 12 frets. Running learning on such examples can only be justified if one is attempting to learn from real data. This would require scanners that are able to read the fingerings alongside the actual notes of each piece. Since such scanners are not yet available, we restrict ourselves to the following example to illustrate the method.

Assume that we have three possible notes to play: *a*, *b*, and *c*. Each note can be played by two different fingerings denoted a_1, a_2 for note *a*, and so forth. We thus have 6 different possible fingerings and 36 possible transitions between the fingerings of 2 notes. The costs of transition, or weights, can be entered in a 6×6 matrix, W.

Through the use of W, one can now plan the optimum fingering for any prescribed sequence of notes. By examining the actual fingerings used and applying the heuristics described above, one can generate a new matrix W' of inferred costs of transition. If the learning is successful, then the use of W' for fingering should result in the same paths as the use of W.

The following example will illustrate the above: the matrix W is given by:

$$W = \begin{matrix} 0 & 1 & 2 & 1 & 2 & 3 \\ 1 & 0 & 1 & 3 & 1 & 2 \\ 2 & 1 & 0 & 1 & 2 & 2 \\ 1 & 3 & 1 & 0 & 3 & 2 \\ 2 & 1 & 2 & 3 & 0 & 1 \\ 3 & 2 & 2 & 2 & 1 & 0 \end{matrix}$$

The upper left 2×2 block of the matrix W corresponds to all possible transitions from *a* to *a*. With two fingerings per note, there are four such transitions, namely,

$$a_1 \rightarrow a_1 = W_{11} = 0,$$

$$a_1 \rightarrow a_2 = W_{12} = 1,$$

$$a_2 \rightarrow a_1 = W_{21} = 1,$$

$$a_2 \rightarrow a_2 = W_{22} = 0.$$

Other blocks are interpreted in the same manner.

Consider now fingering the sequence of three notes *a*, *c*, *b*. Figure 3a shows the network configuration together with the weights on the connections. From the eight possible paths, one chooses the one that corresponds to the smallest sum of weights. The choice is shown in Fig. 3b. Observe that this path determines that the fingering is a_2, c_1, b_1.

Using W, one can generate the optimum path corresponding to the fingering for any sequence of notes. Figure 4 gives the paths for all three-note sequences based on *a*, *b*, *c*. Notice that in a number of cases we have multiple optimum paths. These will necessitate special treatment.

Learning, which consists of building the matrix W', operates as follows. Initialize all entries of W' to 0. Take a sequence such as *a*, *c*, *b*. Compute its optimum path. As indicated in Fig. 4, it is a_2, c_1, b_1. In the matrix W' increment the weights corresponding to the transitions that occurred on an optimum path. In our example this corresponds to the transition $a_2 \rightarrow c_1$, i.e., W'_{25} and the transition $c_1 \rightarrow b_1$, i.e., W'_{53}. The procedure is repeated for all the samples in the training set. Given the small size of the example, all 27 three-note sequences were used for training.

Fig. 4. Optimum paths for three-note sequences as given by W.

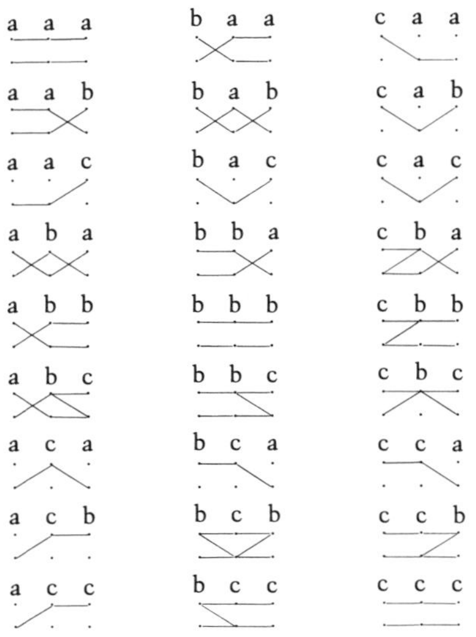

a a a / b a a / c a a
a a b / b a b / c a b
a a c / b a c / c a c
a b a / b b a / c b a
a b b / b b b / c b b
a b c / b b c / c b c
a c a / b c a / c c a
a c b / b c b / c c b
a c c / b c c / c c c

Fig. 5. Optimum paths obtained with W′ *after learning.*

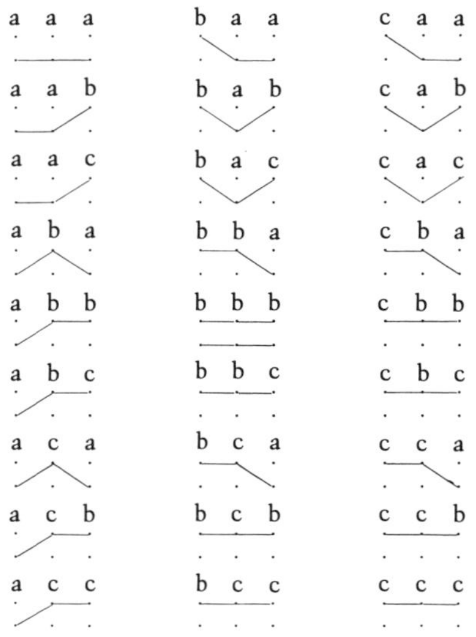

a a a / b a a / c a a
a a b / b a b / c a b
a a c / b a c / c a c
a b a / b b a / c b a
a b b / b b b / c b b
a b c / b b c / c b c
a c a / b c a / c c a
a c b / b c b / c c b
a c c / b c c / c c c

There are a number of different ways of handling ties. They all lead to results that are essentially equivalent, which is an indication that learning is largely immune to noise. The mechanism used in the present example consists of equally dividing the point that is to be assigned to a successful transition among all contributing transitions between the two given notes. For example, consider the sequence *a, a, b*. If it had a unique optimum path, one point would be assigned to the fingering for the $a \to a$ transition and another for the $a \to b$ transition. Having multiple optimum paths, the point for $a \to a$ is now to be shared between the two transitions $a_1 \to a_1$ and $a_2 \to a_2$, both transitions contributing to an optimum path and thus receiving one-half point each. Similarly, $a_1 \to b_2$ and $a_2 \to b_1$ will receive one-half point each.

The procedure presented results in the following W' matrix:

$$W' = \begin{matrix} 2 & 0 & 0 & 5/2 & 0 & 0 \\ 0 & 4 & 7/2 & 0 & 6 & 0 \\ 0 & 7/2 & 3 & 0 & 17/6 & 11/6 \\ 5/2 & 0 & 0 & 3 & 0 & 4/3 \\ 0 & 6 & 17/6 & 0 & 4 & 0 \\ 0 & 0 & 11/6 & 4/3 & 0 & 2 \end{matrix}$$

The fractional values in W' are due to the cumulative effects of multiple optimum paths.

To confirm learning, one now uses W' to generate optimum paths. Since incrementing entries in W' was conceived as a reward, optimum paths must now be interpreted as maximum paths. Figure 5 gives the result of seeking optimum fingerings with W' for all three-note sequences used for training. For all sequences with a unique optimum obtained using W, the learned matrix of weights W' finds the correct fingering. In the case of multiple optimum paths, W' finds at least one of the correct optimum paths. The learning has thus been successful.

Notice that the failure of W' to reproduce multiple paths is due to a large extent to the fact that it operates a refinement of the original W. For example, $a_1 \to a_1$ and $a_2 \to a_2$ have been assigned the same weights in W. This corresponds to the a priori knowledge that the transitions are of equal difficulty, or that taken in isolation the two fingerings are equivalent. However, the fact that $a_2 \to a_2$ has a larger weight than $a_1 \to a_1$ in W' reflects the fact that it has appeared more often combined with other fingerings. This simply means that $a_2 \to a_2$ is globally a better fingering than $a_1 \to a_1$ as reflected in W' and in the removal of most multiple paths.

Most of these difficulties can be removed, of course, by assigning weights that are slightly different from each other to avoid equal sums on paths. The above process of refinement should also be compared to feature selection or learning vector quantization (Kohonen 1988).

Discussion and Conclusion

The formulation of the problem of fingering as an optimization problem resulted in a systematic representation that in turn lead to a very natural and efficient learning paradigm. The formulation using a Viterbi network might be questioned on the grounds that the transition costs are only defined as a function of the next-neighbor fingering and are therefore local in nature. This is not the case, however, and the optimization taking place is truly a global one. This apparent paradox is very similar to what occurs in a number of physical theories that are formulated through the principle of least action. Physical theories in their most straightforward form are formulated as dynamical systems or differential equations. This implies that the next state of the system in the next infinitesimal time interval is dependent on the form of the equation and on the previous state, which seems to suggest a very local behavior. These theories can be reformulated via the least action principle, whereby the evolution of the system can be understood (and computed) by stating that the (global) trajectory taken is the one that minimizes (in fact, leaves stationary) a certain scalar quantity called the action, which can be computed from the differential equation. Perhaps the most celebrated example of a physical theory that can be formulated via a minimum principle is that of propagation of light. This principle was first formulated by Hero of Alexandria. He stated that light propagates in such a way as to minimize the total distance of propagation, thus explaining both propagation in a homogeneous medium as well as reflection. Pierre de Fermat later generalized that what is actually minimized is the time of propagation, thus also accounting for refraction phenomena.

The most interesting aspect of the optimization formulation on a network is that it leads to the learning scheme, which will prove invaluable when means to automatically enter very large numbers of examples become available. The learning has already proved successful on illustrative examples and also in other domains where the collection of a large database is less problematic. Learning phonetic systems is a case worth mentioning, not only because of its success (Sayegh and Manzor-Coats 1988), but also for its great similarity to the fingering problem. In learning to map text to speech, each grapheme could be read as one of several phonemes. The graphemes correspond to the notes and the phonemes to the different fingerings for one note in the guitar case. The problem has usually been treated via a rule-based approach (Hertz 1982; Santos and Nombella 1982), and more recently with a back propagation network (Sejnowski and Rosenberg 1987).

More generally, a number of problems for which inputs and outputs are in alignment are amenable to treatment using the optimum path paradigm. However, the formulation of the optimum path paradigm learning through the system of inequalities approach can sometimes lead to systems of inconsistent inequalities and the breakdown of the optimum path paradigm. This is similar to what happens in pattern recognition (Tou and Gonzalez 1974), including the case of the perceptron (Minsky and Pappert 1969). For example, trying to learn the exclusive-or problem with a perceptron is impossible since the presumed weights have to satisfy a system of inequalities that turn out to be inconsistent. This similarity could be a first step towards a general theory for classifying connectionist learning paradigms.

In the case of the perceptron, the weights are compared to a threshold leading to the required inequalities. In the optimum path paradigm, different sums of the weights are compared yielding inequalities that must be satisfied and solved in order to achieve learning. The perceptron convergence theorem guarantees a solution for the weights if one exists, but it does so as the cost of an adaptive process that requires showing the same training pair a very large number of times with no useful upper bound as to the number of repetitions required during training. The learning situation is similar in back propagation (Werbos 1974; Rumelhart and McClelland 1987; 1988). The optimum path paradigm, on the other hand, need only see each input/output pair once. In this respect it is also closer to Hebbian learning as pointed out earlier, and it learns by a similar mechanism. Indeed, in Hebbian learning, if the same input is introduced repeatedly, the values of the weights tend to grow without bounds, often necessitating the introduction of a forgetting term. In the optimum path paradigm, when the same patterns are showed repeatedly, a scaling factor is introduced to avoid very large values for the weights.

With a similar topology, there is a fundamental difference between most connectionist paradigms, such as back propagation on the one hand and the optimum path paradigm on the other. In the feed-forward phase of back propagation, the output appears on the last layer of the network, while in the optimum path paradigm the output is built by taking a node from each layer in the network including first and intermediate layers.

Despite the wide difference between the optimum path paradigm and back propagation, there are fundamental similarities between them. A theoretical similarity arises from the fact that back propagation performs gradient descent in the space of weights during the *learning phase,* thus searching for the state of minimum energy, in a way similar to actual physical systems. In the optimum path paradigm, during the feed-forward phase, the system looks for the path of minimum total weight or least action, which again is what physical systems do. The success of both paradigms might be rooted in the simple fact that they emulate the ways nature tends to evolve.

A practical similarity is related to the identical topology in the feed-forward phase of back propagation and the optimum path paradigm. A fixed architecture will run both paradigms. Implementing the optimum path paradigm is done at very little extra cost, given the current popularity of back propagation.

Speed, coupled to its efficient learning mechanism, takes the optimum path paradigm a very powerful connectionist tool. Because the feed-forward phase is performed by a fast algorithm, testing as well as the first phase of training are handled at great speed for all realistic sizes of input sets. The learning mechanism, corresponding to the second phase of training, owes its efficiency to the fact that it essentially examines each connection of each output only once, with no need to store it. With such features, the optimum path paradigm becomes very useful, for one finds out very quickly whether it is suited to a particular application or not.

At a certain level it is clear that the optimum path paradigm is suited for capturing the most fundamental aspects of the fingering problem. The concept of minimization underlies a considerable part of the task of fingering and there the optimum path paradigm will succeed. Other more subtle parts of the task might or might not be possible to capture. Testing the optimum path paradigm in that domain requires more efficient means of inputting the data, as well as a formulation of the problem that allows for polyphony.

References

Balaban, M., and M. Murray. 1985. "Machine Tongues X: Prolog." *Computer Music Journal* 9(3):7–12.

Bratko, I. 1987. *Prolog Programming for Artificial Intelligence.* Workingham, England: Addison-Wesley.

Carlevaro, A. 1984. *School of Guitar: Exposition of Instrumental Theory.* New York: Boosey and Hawkes.

Dijkstra, E. W. 1959. "A Note on Two Problems in Connection with Graphs." *Numerische Mathematik* 1:269–271.

Feldman, J. A. 1985. "Connectionist Models and their Applications." *Cognitive Science* 6:205–254.

Gilardino, A. 1975. "Il Problema della dittegiatura nelle Musiche per Chitarra," *Il Fronimo* 10.

Hebb, D. 1949. *Organization of Behavior.* New York: Wiley.

Hertz, S. R. 1982. "From Text To Speech with SRS." *Journal of the Acoustical Society of America* 72(4): 1155–1170.

Kohonen, T. 1988. *Self-Organization and Associative Memory.* Berlin: Springer Verlag.

Minsky, M., and S. Pappert. 1969. *Perceptrons.* Cambridge, Massachusetts: MIT Press.

Pujol, E. 1960. *El Dilema del Sonido en la Guitarra.* Buenos Aires, Argentina: Ricordi Americana.

Rumelhart, D. E., and J. L. McClelland. 1987. *Parallel Distributed Processing.* Cambridge, Massachusetts: MIT Press.

Rumelhart, D. E., and J. L. McClelland. 1988. *Explorations in Parallel Distributed Processing.* Cambridge, Massachusetts: MIT Press.

Santos, J. M., and J. R. Nombella. 1982. "Text-to-Speech-Conversion in Spanish: A Complete Rule-Based Synthesis System." *Proceedings of the IEEE International Conference on ASSP in Paris.* New York: IEEE Press.

Sayegh, S. I. 1987. "Towards an Expert System for Classical Guitar Fingering." Paper submitted to *Computer Music Journal.*

Sayegh, S. I. 1988. "An Artificial Intelligence Approach to String Instrument Fingering." M.S.E.E. Thesis, Purdue University, West Lafayette, Indiana.

Sayegh, S. I., and L. Manzor-Coats. 1988. "Neural Networks as an Alternative to Rule-Based Systems for Learning Spanish Phonetics." *Proceedings of the International Symposium on Artificial Intelligence.* Monterrey, Mexico. Centro de Investigación en Informárica del Instituto Technológico y de Estudios Superiores de Monterrey.

Sayegh, S. I., and M. F. Tenorio. 1988. "Inverse Viterbi Algorithm as Learning Procedure and Application to Optimization in the String Instrument Fingering Problem." *Proceedings of the IEEE International Conference on Neural Networks.* New York: IEEE Press.

Sejnowski, T. J., and C. R. Rosenberg. 1987. "Parallel Networks that Learn to Pronounce English Text." *Complex Systems* 1:145–168.

Taylor, J. 1978. "Tone Production on the Classical Guitar." *Musical New Services.*

Tou, J. T., and R. C. Gonzalez. 1974. *Pattern Recognition Principles.* Reading, Massachusetts: Addison-Wesley.

Viterbi, A. J. 1967. "Error Bounds for Convolutional Codes and an Asymptotically Optimum Decoding Algorithm." *IEEE Transactions on Information Theory* Vol IT-13(2):260–269.

Waltz, D. 1975. "Understanding Line Drawings of Scenes with Shadows." In P. H. Winston, ed. *The Psychology of Computer Vision.* New York: McGraw-Hill.

Werbos, P. 1974. "Beyond Regression: New Tools for Prediction and Analysis in the Behavioral Sciences." Ph.D. diss., Harvard University, Cambridge, Massachusetts.

Whiting, P. D., and J. A. Hillier. 1960. "A Method for Finding the Shortest Path for a Road Network." *Operations Research Quarterly* 11:37–40.

Winograd, T. 1968. "Linguistics and the Computer Analysis of Tonal Harmony." *Computer Music Journal* 12.

Yampolsky, I. M. 1967. *Violin Fingering.* Oxford, England: Oxford University Press.

Addendum

The reason OPP is successful in dealing with the problem of fingering for string instruments is that fingering can be easily thought of as an actual optimization procedure of the sort to which OPP is designed to apply. To use the OPP method, one must only find out the "cost matrix" corresponding to the optimization process. Notice, however, the OPP can still be applied with success even to a number of systems where we do not know a priori whether the underlying dynamics form an optimization process. This reflects the fact that a number of physical systems evolve in the same way according to a least action principle; so do a number of "intelligent" functions such as speech and motor behavior. This similar evolution allows the OPP to be applied in at least an exploratory fashion to a given system, and the speed of OPP training allows one rapidly to test the optimality hypothesis—whether or not a process is amenable to optimization, for example—by this technique. If this hypothesis turns out to be only partly justified, training can then proceed with other, more appropriate connectionist methods that make no assumption about the nature of the system but that are usually, and accordingly, much slower.

Mathematical Justification

The mathematical foundation of OPP is related to a simple observation. Inputs are mapped to outputs through a choice of an optimum path, which is equivalent to the statement of a large number of inequalities among the weights. Since the weights are originally unknowns that are constructed by operating on the training data, the training data is itself equivalent to a large set of inequalities that are to be solved for the unknown weights. The mathematical problem is thus reduced to solving efficiently a very large number of inequalities among those weights. Small inequality systems can be exactly solved by techniques such as the Fourier-Motzkin method (Dantzig 1963), but realistically sized systems require faster, more efficient tools, such as the OPP method.

The learning method described for OPP used a Hebb-like procedure in which transitions that are witnessed in the input training data have their corresponding links or weights in the network strengthened. That is, if a transition from state i to state j occurs in the input training examples, w_{ij} will be increased in the network (where during optimization we will be maximizing the path value by picking transitions with the largest weights). Thus, the more frequently a particular transition occurs in the inputs, the bigger its corresponding weight will be, similar to the Hebbian notion of increasing the connection strength between mutually active neurons. The following argument gives an indication of why it is appropriate to have the weights W in the transition network set according to the frequency with which their corresponding transitions occur in the input.

Consider a system that produces sequences that are three notes long, or equivalently, transition paths consisting of only two transitions, like those shown in Fig. 4. These paths will be the inputs from which OPP will learn. Assume as before that there are also only three different note values possible, and that there are two ways to produce each of these, so that our set of possible note states is $\{a_1, a_2, b_1, b_2, c_1, c_2\}$. Also as before, we want to construct a matrix W of weights corresponding to all the possible transitions between note states, which can be used with the OPP to produce optimum note sequences based on the assumed optimality of the input sequences.

Every time a note sequence, say *b-a-c*, is seen as an input, the particular state transitions used in that sequence, say b_1-a_1 and a_1-c_2, define a set of inequalities indicating that this particular pair of transitions was better than every other corresponding pair. That is, for instance,

$$w(b_1,a_1) + w(a_1,c_2) > w(b_1,a_2) + w(a_2,c_2)$$

and

$$w(b_1,a_1) + w(a_1,c_2) > w(b_1,a_1) + w(a_1,c_1),$$

etc. (In this case since there eight state transition possibilities for each note sequence, and one of those is best, there will be seven inequalities attesting to this fact.) Thus, all of the inputs taken to-

Fig. 6. A uniform distribution of the random variable X (a) leads to a linear dependence between the probability of a weight w being on the larger side of an inequality and the value of w itself (b).

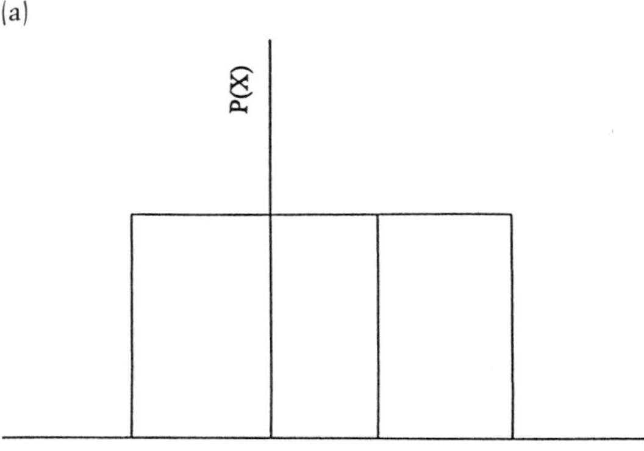

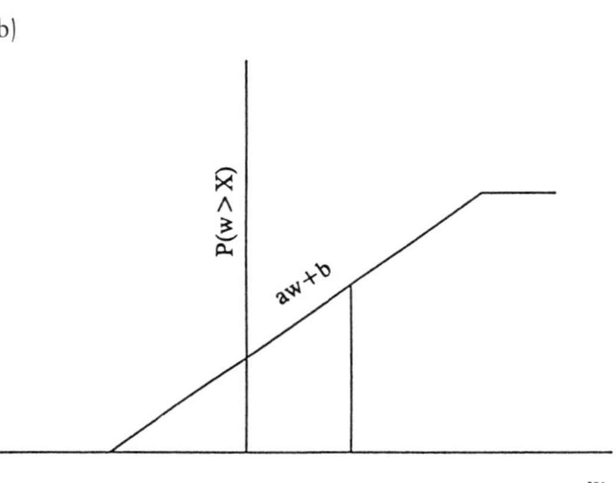

gether define a large set of inequalities in the weights W that we seek; we now need some means of solving this system of inequalities actually to get a set of weights suitable for the OPP.

But notice first that a system of inequalities is invariant under positive scaling (multiplying all unknowns by a positive number) and translation (adding a constant to all unknowns). Therefore, if we can find some set of modified weights W', such that

$$W' = aW + b,$$

where a is a positive (scaling) constant and b is any (translating) constant, then this set W' will also serve to solve the system of inequalities, and our search will be completed.

The next observation we make about systems of inequalities among several unknowns is of a heuristic nature. It is that the larger an unknown in the system, the more often it appears as part of the larger side in the inequalities. Thus, frequency of appearance on the larger side of the inequalities is a good estimate of the size of the unknown weight in question. Since the "larger side" is all that is ever seen in the training inputs—that is, the transitions in the inputs are always those that would appear on the larger side of the inequalities, as demonstrated in the two inequalities in the preceding example—the frequency of transitions found in the inputs is also proportional to the appropriate size of the transition weight. This relationship between weight frequency (both in inequalities and input transition sequences) and actual weight value can be seen as follows.

First, the frequency $f(w)$ of appearance of a weight w on the large side of an inequality is simply some scaled version of the probability

$$P(w + w_j > w_k + w_l)$$

with w_j, w_k, and w_l taking on all allowable values (switching here to a single subscript for ease of discussion).

This can be rewritten as

$$P(w_k + w_l - w_j) = P(w > X),$$

where now we can treat X as a random variable. If X were a uniformly distributed random variable as shown in Fig. 6a, $P(w > X)$ would be simply the area under a rectangle beginning at the first permissible weight value and ending at w.

Thus, $P(w > X)$ would have the form $aw + b$, with $a > 0$ as shown in Fig. 6b. Since this form would apply to all ws in the matrix W, we have the result

$$f(W) = aW + b,$$

so that the frequencies of the weights (transitions) appearing in the inputs are a positively scaled and translated function of the actual weights W, and

Fig. 7. A normal distribution of the random variable X (a) leads to an error function relating the probability of a weight w being on the larger side of an inequality to the value of w itself (b). However, the accessible values of w fall predominantly in the linear portion of the error function.

(a)

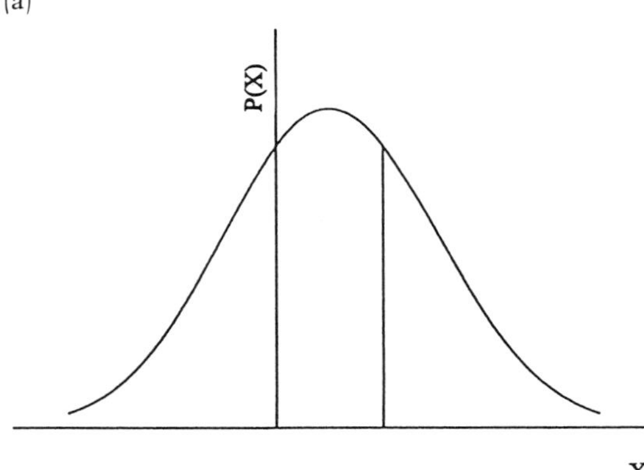

(b)

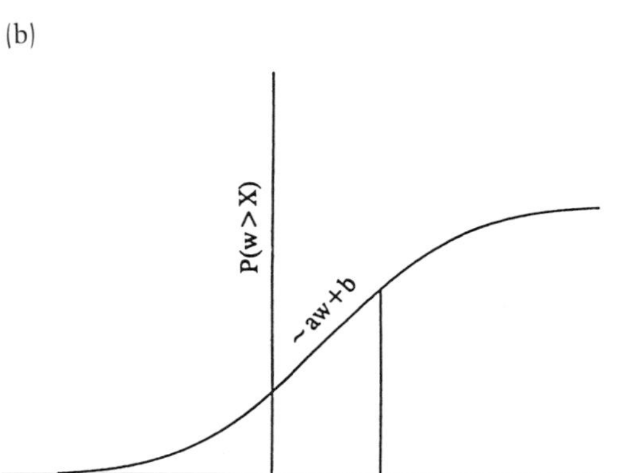

so we can use the frequencies themselves as our weight estimates W'. And since incrementing the weights each time they are seen in the input is essentially equivalent to using their frequencies, the proposed learning method is supported.

But now if we consider systems with longer possible transition sequences and a greater number of possible states to go between, there will be a large number of *w*s in the system. Furthermore, the inequalities will also involve a large number of these *w*s. In this case, the random variable X will no longer be uniformly distributed but will rather tend to a normal (Gaussian) distribution (by the central limit theorem) as a result of summing up many *w*s together (see Fig. 7a).

An argument similar to the preceding one is still possible, however. The area under a given portion of a Gaussian is an error function, so that $P(w > X)$ will have the shape shown in Fig. 7b. And now since the *w*s are restricted to a small region at the center of the range of X (which is the sum of many *w*s), then we can say that the distribution of w, to a good approximation, occurs only in the linear portion of the error function. Thus we still get the relationship $P(w > X) = aw + b$, or again for the whole weight matrix W,

$$f(W) = aW + b.$$

Thus the learning method is supported for large systems of transitions and weights as well.

Relationship to More Traditional Methods

It should be noted that neural network learning methods are often mathematically equivalent in some sense to solving a set of equalities or inequalities as well. For example, the perceptron model itself gives rise to a system of inequalities to be satisfied by network weights and thresholds. Failure of a perceptronlike system to solve a given problem is simply a reflection of the inconsistency of the corresponding system of inequalities. Indeed, any system that uses a hard threshold function is mapping inputs to outputs according to inequalities. In contrast, systems using linear or nonlinear but continuous "squashing" functions map inputs to outputs through a system of *equalities* that are to be solved for the weights (Broomhead and Lowe 1988).

Typically, the training data far exceeds the number of weights, and the solution of the system of equalities or inequalities is to be achieved only in some sense, for example in the sense of minimizing the square of the global error. Such compromising in solving the weight equalities or inequalities can result in a certain form of generalization.

The topology of an OPP network is identical to that of a standard back-propagation (BP) network. In the feed-forward phase of each, all nodes of a given layer compute simultaneously and only need knowledge of the states of units in the previous layer and the values of the weights coming from them. The nature of the operations occurring at the nodes in each type of network does differ, though, with vector product and squashing in the BP case, versus addition and minimization for OPP. A common architecture is possible that would implement these two algorithms, with only the specific operations of nodes being selectable. The number of nodes per layer is a variable in both paradigms, and although the number of layers is in principle variable in OPP, the fact that both paradigms have no more than two active layers at any given time makes a common implementation feasible.

Conclusion

It should be clear from the preceding treatment and remarks that OPP's approach, providing and solving a system of inequalities among the weights of a network, has great generality. Furthermore, the scale- and translation-invariance methods introduced here also have wide applicability. The invariance arguments given to illustrate the validity of the Hebb-like OPP learning method are but an elementary example of this powerful approach; they suggest a further mathematical justification of similar learning rules, although in a context different from that typically encountered in the neural network field.

It is quite surprising that the power of invariance arguments has not been tapped in the connectionist literature, since such tools have been traditionally applied to both algebraic and differential equations for quite some time (Lie and Engel 1890; Bluman and Cole 1974; Sayegh and Jones 1986). And a connectionist network training data corpus can indeed be seen as a set of algebraic equations, with the network's dynamic evolution itself interpreted as obeying a differential system describing activation and weight changes. Such a view is ideally suited to the use of invariance methods as presented here, and so we can expect these methods to shed light on and contribute to the design of future connectionist architectures.

References

Bluman, G. W., and J. D. Cole. 1974. *Similarity Methods for Differential Equations.* Berlin: Springer-Verlag.

Broomhead, D. S., and D. Lowe. 1988. "Multiple Functional Interpolation and Adaptive Networks." *Complex Systems* 2:321–355.

Dantzig, J. B. 1963. *Linear Programming and Extensions.* Princeton, N.J.: Princeton University Press.

Lie, S., and F. Engel. 1890. *Theorie der Transformationgruppen.* Vol. 3. Leipzig: Teubner.

Sayegh, S. I., and G. L. Jones. 1986. "Symmetries of Differential Equations." *Journal of Physics A: Mathematical and General* 19:1793–1800.

IV

Conclusions

Introduction

The proper use of automated methods in aesthetic endeavors is a hotly debated topic at the intersection of the arts and science and technology. In the case of connectionist composition of music, the debate takes on the particular overtones of a struggle between model-based and rule-based composition, as Laske proposes in this part. The very advantage of connectionist systems in letting us avoid the process of specifying compositional rules pushes us instead in the direction of relying on models of previously composed pieces of music. Whether or not this is a drawback is addressed in the following exchange. These letters were prompted by the special issues of the *Computer Music Journal* on neural networks and connectionism (volume 13, number 3 and volume 13, number 4), and appeared two issues later (in volume 14, number 2).

Otto Laske

Letter: Connectionist Composition

Here are some thoughts on Peter M. Todd's paper entitled "A Connectionist Approach to Algorithmic Composition," which appeared in *Computer Music Journal* 13(4):27–43, 1989.

First of all, thank you for printing the article, which shows very clearly that scientific enterprises, at least in music, always have an implicit aesthetics associated with them; connectionism is no exception.

While I thought "the computer" (von Neumann style) had finally freed us composers from existing musics, making it possible to concentrate on possible musics never heard before, the connectionist model of composition—whether it addresses melody, polyphony, or whatever—happily returns us to *model-based composition.* By that term, I mean composition based on remembered musics of the past, in whatever form. This is in contrast to *rule-based composition* (Charles Ames would add constraint-based composition, which I count under rule-based), where no prior model is used—except perhaps a model of a process, but certainly not as a model of precomposed music. I also thought that Iannis Xenakis had freed us from being primarily concerned with surface structures (music as it develops in time) and had learned (relearned) developing deep structures that could be played forward as well as backward. For me this is a criterion for a well-composed piece of music. But in connectionist models, time is felt to be of the essence, so we are happily returned to surface structures—themes and variations! The connectionist model cannot distinguish between deep and surface structure, except if one wants to consider the underlying model (the "existing" music) as a deep structure, which it is only in a relative sense. The fact that one can produce derivatives of musical models that go beyond the model perceptually (i.e., are not recognized as variants of a model), is no proof to the contrary, only a proof of the perceptual limitations of the listeners, but not a proof of the audacity or originality of the model-based composer. Connectionist models of composition seem to come attached with an aesthetics that is more suited to pedagogy and musicology in the orthodox sense than to compositional thinking and composition theory. While it is true that model-based composition abounds even in computer music, nobody will convince me that composing by interpolation and extrapolation is more than a rather primitive notion of composition, showing a lack of notions of composition theory. Clearly, I prefer the freedom of composing with rules regarding deep structure to using models of bygone ages. However, I am open to demonstrations that show that one can do inventive composition using networks without being constrained by models of existing music.

Otto Laske
c/o Newcomp
926 Greendale Ave.
Needham, Massachusetts 02192
USA

Peter M. Todd and D. Gareth Loy

Responses to Laske

Response from Peter M. Todd

Dr. Laske is basically correct in drawing attention to the distinction in underlying concepts between the neural network, learning-based approach to algorithmic composition and the traditional, rule-based approach he prefers. However, his conclusions are disputable. First and foremost, neural networks and connectionist models should be seen not as replacements for rule-based methods, but as additions to them—another technique to be added to the composer's toolbox to further the creative effort. Each technique has its place and its use. A discussion of which method is best should not be taken as anything other than an expression of personal preference.

One of the most useful characteristics of the connectionist approach to composition is that it frees composers from having to come up with rules to describe music that they may not think of in a rule-based manner. Concocting rules to describe one's own (or someone else's) music can be a tedious and constraining endeavor; the connectionist approach allows one instead to compose (or find) examples of music one wants to create and then use a network trained on these examples to help explore the space of pieces that are more or less similar to the original compositions. Thus, the "remembered musics of the past" used in training need not be taken in a pejorative sense, but can mean music created by the composer, whether through-composed or even generated algorithmically by some rule-based method. The neural network can then be used to allow the composer to go beyond these pieces, to explore new aspects of them in a musically reasonable fashion.

To address some of Laske's criticisms of the connectionist approach, it should be noted that networks are not restricted to considering the surface structure of musical works. As I mentioned at the end of my article, a hierarchical network scheme in which the sequential outputs of one network serve as the plans controlling the higher-level output of another network will allow the networks to deal with music at any level desired, however deep. Recent results have also demonstrated the ability of nonhierarchical networks to learn long-term dependencies between their outputs (e.g., relationships between patterns separated by several measures), again allowing deeper structure to emerge. These techniques certainly need to be explored further, but their implications are clear—networks are not limited to flat functions of time at the highest level.

Indeed, through appropriate training, neural networks can approach rule-based behavior arbitrarily closely, again at any depth of structure. By training a network so that certain configurations of the plan produce certain structural characteristics in the output sequence (e.g., if unit 1 is on, the sequence will be rising, while if unit 1 is off, the sequence will be falling; unit 2 controls some aspect of the rhythm; etc.), manipulation of the plan can result in the expected corresponding composite structure in the output. Again, the neural network output will usually not be totally predictable, but this is one of the features of this approach, and once more an indication that it should coexist with rule-based methods that might not have its air of mystery.

As for "the audacity or originality of the model-based composer," judgments about such matters can certainly not be made based on the *method* of composition rather than its *art*. Further, proclaiming the "perceptual limitations of the listeners" as irrelevant for judging either the method *or* the art denigrates the audience and thereby misses the very reason we compose music at all.

Finally, it is ridiculous to speak of "a primitive notion of composition," as if there were an established, universal aesthetic hierarchy of means, let alone ends. The fact that the connectionist approach shows "a lack of notions of composition theory" is one of its virtues, freeing the composer as it does from remembered compositional theories of the past—if not "remembered musics of the past."

Peter M. Todd
Department of Psychology
Stanford University
Stanford, California 94305 USA

Response from D. Gareth Loy

Among the attractions of computer-mediated composition are the two-fold promises: first, that it can increase the efficiency of the composer by assisting with the mechanical aspects of the craft; and second, that it can extend the power of the composer by the rigorous working out of new structuring principles of previously unachievable proportions. In both cases, computers act to free the composer in an important way.

Laske has spoken forcefully in his letter about the freedoms he seeks through computer models of composition. He looks to rule-based compositional techniques for freedom from prior musical agendas, for untrammeled exploration of new compositional vistas opened up by computers, and for freedom from fixation on surface structure. In this way he places himself squarely in the good company of many important composers of our century.

I suggest, however, that freedom, like beauty, is in the eye of the beholder. Just as rule-based sound synthesis seems most compelling where it has no natural model, but quickly becomes unwieldly when one attempts to emulate natural instruments, so rule-based composition seems audacious and original when it emulates no evolved style, but becomes complex to the point of opacity the harder one strives for compositional formalisms that model different styles. One typically finds an explosion of rules in these cases, not unlike the explosion of epicycles that pre-Newtonian astronomers were forced to postulate to describe the elliptic orbits of planets. In composition theory, as in astronomy, one is eventually forced to look for simplifying lines of attack to understand these phenomena. Enter connectionism, which has the potential to free us from this dilemma.

Let us say, for instance, that I possess a compositional aesthetic, be it an historical style, a personal style, or one concocted from chance or whim. If I am seeking to model this style, for either the analysis or synthesis of compositions, and a corpus of examples lies at hand or can be generated in an informal way, then I can increase my powers of observation and prediction about this style in a purely objective fashion through the use of connectionist techniques.

Connectionism offers help in two ways. First, one may forego the necessity of formal specification completely, if desired, and go straight to the production of new materials in a style by training a network on the corpus of examples. Secondly, it is important to note that one can decompose and analyze trained networks to help deduce what the regularities of the style are, thus facilitating its eventual formal specification! Connectionist methods are promising to composition theory because they facilitate the extraction of compositional features from actual composed material (be it music of bygone ages or the output of a million monkeys on music typewriters).

Just because networks have this built-in analytical aspect does not automatically associate them with traditional pedagogy and musicology, though as Laske points out, they should prove to be very useful in those fields as well.

The word *promising* is certainly the operative word when discussing neural network techniques. Like Laske, I also await demonstrations that show that one can do inventive composition using networks. It was my editorial purpose to bring these techniques to the attention of composers so that they may be validated in practice.

D. Gareth Loy
509 Barbara Ave.
Solana Beach, California 92075 USA

Peter M. Todd

Further Research and Directions

The work collected in this volume demonstrates the promise and power of connectionist techniques for a wide variety of musical applications. But efforts to date have only scratched the surface of possible realms in music research where connectionist approaches will prove fruitful. The following paragraphs briefly indicate some of the directions in which investigations could head and some of the recent work which begins to look along those headings. There are a variety of nonmusical connectionist research programs that have something to say to the study of music, and these are also indicated here. The challenges of the musical domain will require further developments of connectionist techniques, as well. And although some vague attempt has been made to lay these topics out in a linear order, this should not obscure the fact that a major source of advances in connectionist research of musical processes will be the complex interactions among systems at the different levels and across the different subdomains mentioned here; top-down, bottom-up, and side-to-side influences among musical processes are likely to offer one of the richest sets of constraints and enhancements in this research, befitting a connectionist modeling endeavor.

Beginning at the high-level end of what we might call the "input side" of music perception and cognition, one of the most important research directions will be the abstraction and analysis of higher-order structure from musical passages. Current connectionist methods are largely limited to relatively local aspects of surface structure. To take into account more global, longer-duration musical structures, perceptual and cognitive grouping mechanisms could be employed. Connectionist techniques for processing syntactic structures in language can also be imported; Pollack has proposed using his recursive auto-associative memory (RAAM), which has been successfully applied to learning well-formed syntactic trees corresponding to sentence structures (Pollack 1989), to analyze similar structures in melodies. Another approach is to use pitch contours occurring at differing time scales, as Mozer has done in further extensions of the work presented in his chapter by using context units with different rates of temporal responsiveness (Mozer 1990).

Hierarchical harmonic analysis will obviously be important to pursue. But equally important is rhythmic analysis and meter and beat perception. Scarborough, Miller, and Jones (1990) have developed a connectionist system of interacting "metronomes," which extract the metric structure of rhythmic patterns. The metronomes are excited by pulses in the input pattern and by other metronomes ticking in sync, and are inhibited by longer-period metronomes ticking out of sync. Over time, active metronomes corresponding to metric structures in the input will emerge most strongly, usually in agreement with human interpretations of the rhythm. D'Autilia and Guerra (1991) present a method of rhythm recognition using stochastic dynamical networks bearing some similarity to this approach. Linster (1988, 1991) uses a more traditional back-propagation network that learns to process rhythms into hierarchical rhythmic structures. When trained on rhythmic patterns from Mozart, her network could accurately generalize to the patterns of other composers with similar styles. Lower-level aspects of rhythm processing, including tempo and duration perception and production, could also connect with network modeling research studying central pattern generators (CPGs), which control repetitive locomotor (and other) movements in animals, as well as with the increasing investigations of oscillatory neural activity.

Models of melody recognition—memory systems that can "name that tune"—are an important and largely untapped network application. Port and Anderson (1989) have developed a recurrent network that processes continuous acoustic signals (rather than pitch-class information) to recognize variously inaccurate performances of short melodies. They have also analyzed complex auditory pattern recognition in terms of a succession of stable states in a dynamic network (Anderson and Port 1990). Further research on such tasks can derive additional benefit from the extensive literature on temporal pattern recognition (both within and beyond the connectionist framework). Models of musical *prediction* are also of interest, as Bharucha and Todd discussed in their chapter. Weigend, Huberman, and Rumelhart (1990) have had great success using feedforward networks to predict the future behavior of time series in domains from sun-spot occurrence to monetary exchange rates; such a technique can be applied to music to investigate what aspects are predictable within a given model and what must be attributed to factors not learnable strictly from the training set (e.g., composer creativity). Other musical learning and memory phenomena, such as recall or recognition confusions, could be naturally captured within the connectionist framework.

An important sphere of human experience that has only recently begun to be addressed by connectionists is emotion. Modeling the emotional effects of melodic and harmonic progressions with connectionist systems could prove challenging and rewarding. Prosodic processing—considering pitch and timbral contours both within and between notes—can also be investigated in terms of its emotional impact. Links to neural network research on speech prosody can be pursued in this regard, as well as the emotional implications of prosody in mother-infant communication.

Connectionist methods are particularly well suited to a variety of applications at the low-level end of music perception. The investigation of timbral dynamics and instrument recognition has direct links to connectionist work on speech processing and voice recognition and research on object-feature abstraction from timbre. Acoustic environment perception, including reverberation, ambience, and source location processing, also has similarities to other signal-processing tasks already employing neural networks, such as sonar signal analysis and categorization.

Shifting over to the "output side" of music production and composition, the low-level end opportunities here include timbre and signal production and modification, as Dolson describes in his addendum. These applications will again have significant ties to connectionist work being done in the speech world.

At a slightly higher level of production, a variety of acoustic characteristics introduced on the path from score to sound could be addressed with connectionist systems. Models of the psychological processes of interpretation leading to particular performance phrasing, dynamics, tempo, timbre, and rhythm would be interesting to explore. Linster (1990) has initiated such an investigation with a network that can perform melodies with the accent structure of any of several learned rhythmic grouping styles. Baggi (1989) has developed a system that simulates a jazz rhythm section by producing appropriate piano, bass, and drum parts to accompany a specified harmonic chord progression. A subnetwork allows the user to adjust the style of a particular performance along dimensions including consonance/dissonance and hot/cool. This system operates independently, though, with no external input from the human performer it may be accompanying; in order to achieve maximal usefulness in such a situation, an accompaniment-generating neural network would have to be able to follow both a score and the real performance. Performance tracking of this type, and the still more difficult task of performance transcription involving multiple instruments, will probably only be possible through a combination of top-down processes, including structural analysis and prediction, and bottom-up processes, including instrument recognition and duration quantization. The possibilities for implementing all of the necessary processes within a unified connectionist framework are intriguing.

An even more ambitious performance-tracking system has been described by Cottrell (1990). His connectionist air guitar network maps EEG inputs from scalp electrodes to control sequences for a standard guitar synthesizer. But difficulties in this mapping have necessitated further enhancements: "In training, the subject listens to Springsteen while 'air guitaring' the lead. The EEG drives the network, resulting in a set of outputs. . . . However, electomyographic noise in the EEG often leads to noise in the output, so it appears necessary to implant arrays of silicon electrodes (developed by Jim

Bower at CalTech) directly into the temporal lobes, eliminating interference from muscle signals. In this case, the network must actually be borne to run." (Cottrell, 1990, p. 413)

In the realm of connectionist composition, methods for producing high-level structure and global organization will have to rely on the development of the sort of analysis techniques mentioned earlier for learning these characteristics from the training set. Composition systems will have to handle musical features beyond the simple pitch and rhythm characteristics addressed so far, including such additional aspects as tempo, dynamics, and instrument choice. Harmonization methods will be useful in moving beyond simple monophonic compositions. In this regard, Lischka (1987, 1991) has begun developing a Boltzmann machine system that relaxes into a harmonization for an input melody (for example from a Bach chorale), based on constraints learned from examples of traditional music education (e.g., choral harmonization). A feedforward network approach that has been applied to the production of chord progressions to accompany Japanese *Enka* songs has also been described (Shibata, Shimazu, and Takashima, 1990).

A method for comparing all of the connectionist composition systems already and yet to be developed will be valuable. A possible and appealing approach is to have a "composition contest," in which each competing system is given the same prespecified training corpus of musical examples—for example, Bach inventions—to learn what it can from. After training, each system would produce a small number of new compositions based on what it has learned. A panel of human judges would then compare these pieces and judge them on the basis of creativity, coherence, and musical structure, and thereby provide reinforcement signals for the development of better composition systems.

There are many further aspects of musical behavior and experience that will be amenable to connectionist approaches. Models of actual neurological processes involved in music perception and cognition will become possible with increasing results from clinical and physiological studies. Developmental models will help paint a picture of the acquisition and growth of musical cognition and ability. Other areas to be explored include birds' processing and production of song and the links to auditory communication in other species, the perception and cognition of different scales and tuning systems and their influences on the organization of other musical concepts, models of how auditory illusions have their effects, and questions in musicological research, including the uses therein of content-addressable databases. There are plenty of challenges to keep us all busy, and plenty of opportunities for cross-disciplinary interactions to yield significant advances in our understanding and appreciation of both music and connectionism.

References

Anderson, S., and R. Port. 1990. "A Network Model of Auditory Pattern Recognition." Research Report 11. Bloomington, Indiana: Indiana University, Cognitive Science Program.

Baggi, D. L. 1989. "NeurSwing: A Connectionist Workbench for the Investigation of Swing in Afro-American Jazz." *Proceedings of the 23rd Asilomar Conference on Signals, Systems, and Computers.* Pacific Grove, California: Maple Press.

Cottrell, G. W. 1990. "The Connectionist Air Guitar: A Dream Come True." *Connection Science* 1:413–414.

D'Autilia, R., and F. Guerra. 1991. "Qualitative Aspects of Signal Processing Through Dynamical Neural Networks." In G. De Poli, A. Piccialli, and C. Roads, eds. *Representations of Musical Signals.* Cambridge, Massachusetts: MIT Press.

Leng, X., G. L. Shaw, and E. L. Wright. 1990. "Coding of Musical Structure and the Trion Model of Cortex." *Music Perception* 8:49–62.

Linster, C. 1988. "Rhythm Analysis With Backpropagation." *Proceedings of Connectionism in Perspective.* Zurich, Switzerland: SGAICO.

Linster, C. 1990. "A Neural Network That Learns to Play in Different Music Styles." *Proceedings of the 1990 International Computer Music Conference.* San Francisco, California: Computer Music Association.

Linster, C. 1991. "Get Rhythm and Use It: Rhythm Representation, Learning, and Application in Neural Networks." In M. Balaban, K. Ebcioglu, and O. Laske, eds. *Musical Intelligence.* Menlo Park, California: AAAI Press.

Lischka, C. 1987. "Connectionist Models of Musical Thinking." *Proceedings of the 1987 International Computer Music Conference.* San Francisco, California: Computer Music Association.

Lischka, C. 1991. "Understanding Music Cognition: A Connectionist View." In G. De Poli, A. Piccialli, and C. Roads, eds. *Representations of Musical Signals.* Cambridge, Massachusetts: MIT Press.

Mozer, M. C. 1990. "Connectionist Music Composition Based on Melodic, Stylistic, and Psychophysical Constraints." Technical Report CU-CS-495-90. Boulder, Colorado: University of Colorado, Department of Computer Science.

Pollack, J. B. 1989. "Recursive Distributed Representations." Technical Report 89-JP-RECURSIVE. Columbus, Ohio: Ohio State University, Laboratory for AI Research. (Also to appear in *Artificial Intelligence.*)

Port, R., and S. Anderson. 1989. "Recognition of Melody Fragments in Continuously Performed Music." *Proceedings of the Eleventh Annual Conference of the Cognitive Science Society.* Hillsdale, N.J.: Erlbaum Associates, pp. 820–827.

Scarborough, D. L., B. O. Miller, and J. A. Jones. 1990. "PDP Models for Meter Perception." *Proceedings of the Twelfth Annual Conference of the Cognitive Science Society.* Hillsdale, N.J.: Erlbaum Associates, pp. 892–899.

Shibata, N., H. Shimazu, and Y. Takashima. 1990. "A Method for Neural Network Based Melody Harmonizing." In M. Caudill, ed. *Proceedings of the International Joint Conference on Neural Networks,* vol. II. Hillsdale, N.J.:Erlbaum Associates, pp. 695–698.

Trubitt, D. R., and P. M. Todd. 1991. "The Computer Musician: Neural Networks and Computer Music." *Electronic Musician* 7(1):20–24.

Weigend, A. S., B. A. Huberman, and D. E. Rumelhart. 1990. "Predicting the Future: A Connectionist Approach." *International Journal of Neural Systems* 1:193–209.

Addresses of Authors

Jamshed J. Bharucha
Department of Psychology
Dartmouth College
Hanover, NH 03755
bharucha@eleazar.dartmouth.edu

Klaus de Rijk
Centre for Knowledge Technology
Lange Viestraat 2B
NL-3511 BK Utrecht
The Netherlands

Peter Desain
Centre for Knowledge Technology
Lange Viestraat 2B
NL-3511 BK Utrecht
The Netherlands

Mark Dolson
Center for Research in Language
University of California, San Diego
La Jolla, CA 92093
dolson@crl.ucsd.edu

Robert O. Gjerdingen
Department of Music
State University of New York at Stony Brook
Stony Brook, NY 11794-5475
rgjerdingen@ccmail.sunysb.edu

Henkjan Honing
Centre for Knowledge Technology
Lange Viestraat 2B
NL-3511 BK Utrecht
The Netherlands
henkjan@hku.uucp

B. Keith Jenkins
Department of Electrical Engineering
University of Southern California
Los Angeles, CA 90089-0272
jenkins@sipi.usc.edu

Jacqueline A. Jones
Department of Computer and Information Science
Brooklyn College of the City University of
New York
Brooklyn, NY 11210
jajbc@cunyvm.bitnet

Douglas H. Keefe
Systematic Musicology Program
School of Music DN-10
University of Washington
Seattle, WA 98195
keefe@u.washington.edu

Teuvo Kohonen
Helsinki University of Technology
Laboratory of Computer and Information Science
Rakentajanaukio 2 C
SF-02150 Espoo
Finland

Bernice Laden
Systematic Musicology Program
School of Music DN-10
University of Washington
Seattle, WA 98195
bladen@u.washington.edu

Pauli Laine
Helsinki University of Technology
Laboratory of Computer and Information Science
Rakentajanaukio 2 C
SF-02150 Espoo
Finland

Otto Laske
c/o Newcomp
926 Greendale Ave.
Needham, MA 02192

Marc Leman
University of Ghent
Institute for Psychoacoustics and Electronic Music
Blandijnberg 2 B-9000 Ghent
Belgium
musico@bgerug51.bitnet

J. P. Lewis
Computer Graphics Laboratory
New York Institute of Technology
Old Westbury, NY 11568

D. Gareth Loy
509 Barbara Ave.
Solana Beach, CA 92075

Benjamin O. Miller
Department of Psychology
Simmons College
300 The Fenway
Boston MA 02151
millerb@babson.bitnet

Michael C. Mozer
Department of Computer Science and Institute of Cognitive Science
University of Colorado
Boulder, CO 80309-0430
mozer@neuron.colorado.edu

Hajime Sano
741 Mar Vista Ave.
Pasadena, CA 91104
sano@vlsi.jpl.nasa.gov

Samir I. Sayegh
Physics Department
Purdue University
Fort Wayne, IN 46805-1499
sayegh@ed.ecn.purdue.edu

Don L. Scarborough
Department of Psychology
Brooklyn College of the City University of New York
Brooklyn, NY 11210
dosbc@cunyvm.bitnet

Kalev Tiits
Helsinki University of Technology
Laboratory of Computer and Information Science
Rakentajanaukio 2 C
SF-02150 Espoo
Finland

Peter M. Todd
Department of Psychology
Stanford University
Stanford, CA 94305
todd@psych.stanford.edu

Kari Torkkola
Helsinki University of Technology
Laboratory of Computer and Information Science
Rakentajanaukio 2 C
SF-02150 Espoo
Finland
kari@hutmc.hut.fi